STUDI E TESTI TARDOANTICHI
PROFANE AND CHRISTIAN CULTURE
IN LATE ANTIQUITY

19

EDITORS IN CHIEF

Franca Ela CONSOLINO
L'Aquila

Carla LO CICERO
Roma

EDITORIAL BOARD

Gianfranco AGOSTI
Roma

Jan DEN BOEFT †
Amsterdam, Utrecht

Isabella GUALANDRI
Milano

Rita LIZZI TESTA
Perugia

Paola MORETTI
Milano

Lieve VAN HOOF
Gent

Vincent ZARINI
Paris

STUDI E TESTI TARDOANTICHI
PROFANE AND CHRISTIAN CULTURE
IN LATE ANTIQUITY

Studies in Theodore Anagnostes

edited by
Rafał Kosiński
Adrian Szopa

BREPOLS

This publication was co-financed by the Pedagogical University of Cracow.

© 2021, Brepols Publishers n.v., Turnhout, Belgium.

All rights reserved.
No part of this publication may be reproduced,
stored in a retrieval system, or transmitted,
in any form or by any means, electronic, mechanical,
photocopying, recording, or otherwise
without the prior permission of the publisher.

Cover picture:
CITTÀ DEL VATICANO, *Biblioteca Apostolica Vaticana*,
Ms.Vat. Lat. 3867, f. 14r, Fifth Century CE
© 2014 Biblioteca Apostolica Vaticana.
Per concessione della Biblioteca Apostolica Vaticana.
Ogni diritto riservato

D/2021/0095/238
ISBN 978-2-503-59257-2
e-ISBN 978-2-503-59258-9
DOI 10.1484/M.STTA-EB.5.121837
ISSN 2565-9030
e-ISSN 2566-0101
Printed in the EU on acid-free paper.

TABLE OF CONTENTS

Rafał KOSIŃSKI & Adrian SZOPA
Introduction   9

THEODORE LECTOR'S WORK
IN THE FRAME OF LATE ANTIQUE HISTORIOGRAPHY

Peter VAN NUFFELEN
True to Their Words. Theodore Lector and his Predecessors   17

Adrian SZOPA
Textual Analysis of the Epitome *of Theodore Anagnostes'* Church
History *– A Few Remarks*   39

Hartmut LEPPIN
Theodoret von Kyrrhos bei Theodor Anagnostes   63

Philippe BLAUDEAU
Victor of Tunnuna as User of the Ecclesiastical History *of*
Theodore Lector: Choices and Objectives   81

Rafał KOSIŃSKI
The Laudatio Barnabae *by Alexander the Monk and its Relation*
to Theodore Lector's Work   101

THE EMPEROR AND POLITICAL AUTHORITIES
IN THEODORE LECTOR'S WORK

Christoph BEGASS
Kaiserwechsel und Kaisererhebungen in der Kirchengeschichte
des Theodoros Anagnostes   133

TABLE OF CONTENTS

Michel KAPLAN
La législation de Zénon et Anastase concernant l'église et les monastères — 161

Dariusz BRODKA
Rebellen und Usurpatoren – Zur Benutzung der Theodor-Lector-Epitome durch Theophanes — 183

THEODORE LECTOR AND HIS EPOCH

Geoffrey GREATREX
Theodore Lector and the Arians of Constantinople — 207

Kamilla TWARDOWSKA
Theodore Lector's Testimonies of Images — 233

Andrzej KOMPA
Social Reality of Constantinople in Theodore Lector — 247

THE AUTHORS — 315

ABBREVIATIONS

ACO	Acta Conciliorum Oecumenicorum
BS	Byzantina Sorbonensia
BSC	Byzantina et Slavica Cracoviensia
CC SG	Corpus Christianorum, Series Graeca
CC SL	Corpus Christianorum, Series Latina
CFHB	Corpus Fontium Historiae Byzantinae
CSEL	Corpus Scriptorum Ecclesiasticorum Latinorum
DOP	Dumbarton Oaks Papers
FM	Fontes Minores
GCS	Die griechischen christlichen Schriftsteller der ersten Jahrhunderte
KFHist	Kleine und fragmentarische Historiker der Spätantike
MS	Millennium-Studien
PG	Patrologia Graeca
PLRE	Prosopography of the Later Roman Empire
PO	Patrologia Orientalis
SC	Sources Chrétiennes
TCH	The Transformation of the Classical Heritage
TTH	Translated Texts for Historians

RAFAŁ KOSIŃSKI & ADRIAN SZOPA

INTRODUCTION

The *Church History* of Theodore Lector is a very important source for reconstructing the history of the Eastern Roman Empire in the second half of the fifth and beginning of the sixth century, especially the time of the reign of emperors Zeno and Anastasius. Unfortunately, only a few fragments of the Church History and the fragmental Epitome from the beginning of the seventh century have been preserved to the present day. Due to this, reconstructing the original text of the work and distinguishing Theodore's content from later amendments and additions is very difficult. Günther Christian Hansen, who prepared a critical edition of the fragments of the *Church History* and its *Epitome*, undertook this effort half a century ago. However, no complex analysis of the published texts is included in his edition.

A few decades later, it seems that the time has come to look critically at some hypotheses in the Hansen edition, time to form new research questions about the sources of Theodore's knowledge, as well as for the transmission of the indirect tradition of his work, especially since scholars have put some questions and remarks to the Hansen edition.[1]

Therefore, a few years ago, the idea of a new edition of the *Church History* of Theodore Lector, with translation (first Polish, and then English) and commentary, came into existence, with the intention of creating a handy tool which scholars could use for their research. The outcome of this is the publication of the work

---

[1] See for instance Flusin 1983, pp. 60–67, Van Dieten 1980 or Pouderon 2015.

Studies in Theodore Anagnostes, ed. by Rafał Kosiński & Adrian Szopa, STTA 19 (Turnhout 2021), pp. 9–13
© BREPOLS ❧ PUBLISHERS   DOI 10.1484/M.STTA-EB.5.127973

of Theodore (and John Diakrinomenos), published in Polish[2] in 2019 and in English[3] in 2021.

When preparing the aforementioned publication, we had to answer many questions which arose during our work and which related to the attribution of certain fragments to Theodore Lector, the transmission of his work and its influence on Byzantine historiography. Due to this, we organized two conferences where we discussed the problems that had emerged during our work, and consulted the results of our research with specialists in late antique historiography. The first conference 'Teodora Lektora Historia Kościoła. Gatunek, tradycja, tekst' ('The Church History of Theodore Lector. Genre, tradition, text') was held for Polish scholars at the Pedagogical University of Cracow from 1 to 3 June 2017. The articles that resulted from this conference were published in a special edition of the journal *Res Gestae. Czasopismo Historyczne*.[4] A year later, the Pedagogical University of Cracow and the Jagiellonian University organized a conference entitled 'The Church History by Theodore Anagnostes' for scholars from around the world from 4 to 5 May 2018. This publication is a result of the mentioned conference.

The material gathered relates to a few issues. The first one concerns the placement of Theodore in the tradition of late antique historiography, and his relation to his famous predecessors, whose

---

[2] Kosiński – Szopa – Twardowska 2019.

[3] Kosiński – Twardowska – Zabrocka – Szopa 2021.

[4] *Res Gestae. Czasopismo Historyczne*, 5 (2017), Kraków. In this volume the following conference papers have been published: Michał Stachura, *Kann die Annahme der weltlichen Kriege in die spätantike Kirchengeschichten als diese Gattung der Geschichtsschreibung an die Mustern der militärisch-politischen Zeitgeschichten annähernd bewertet werden? Der Fall des Kirchenhistorikers Sokrates* (pp. 7–24); Robert Suski, *The Epitome – Passive Copying or a Creative Reinterpretation of the Abridged Text* (pp. 25–34); Stanisław Adamiak, *African Authors in the East in the Times of Justinian: Their Works and Sources* (pp. 35–45); Rafał Kosiński, *The Chronicle by George the Monk and Its Relation to Theodore Lector's Work* (pp. 46–73); Mirosław J. Leszka, *Portrayal of Anastasius I (491–518) in the Church history by Theodore Lector. A Few Remarks* (pp. 74–83); Kamilla Twardowska, *The Church Foundations of Empress Pulcheria in Constantinople According to Theodore Lector's Church History and Other Contemporary Sources* (pp. 84–95); Anna Kotłowska, Łukasz Różycki, *De Historiarum indice Theophylacto Simocattae falso attributo observationes selectae* (96–111); Rafał Kosiński, *Corpus Theodorianum. Preliminary Propositions for a New Arrangement of Theodore Lector's Legacy* (pp. 112–25). All articles with open acces: https://resgestae.up.krakow.pl/issue/view/298 (8 September 2021).

work he had studied extensively when preparing Historia Tripartita, a source that gathered information from Sozomen, Socrates and Theodoret. Did he stay close to what he had read in the sources above, or did he create an autonomous historiographical model, which differed from those works? The articles of Peter Van Nuffelen and Hartmunt Leppin tell us of Theodore's wide historiographical perspective.

Unfortunately, a detailed analysis of Theodore's work is impossible as only a few original fragments have been preserved to the present date. When interpreting his *Church History* we are forced to rely on later works from the seventh century, which were based on the original composition or its *Epitome*. Therefore, what did the transmission of the Theodore's text look like? Did it influence other historiographical works? And if yes, to what extent? Who drew information from it? Was the work widely used, or was its reception limited to the radical Chalcedonians associated with Constantinopolitan monastic centres? Why it did not come back into favour until the period of iconoclastic disputes? Among others, a few authors who based their works on the original version of the *Church History* were Victor of Tunnuna and Alexander the Monk, discussed by Philippe Blaudeau and Rafał Kosiński, while Theophanes the Confessor was the one who used the *Epitome* of the *Church History* of Theodore the most. Does his work bring us closer to the original version of the Epitome, or is it a loose paraphrase that reflects the point of view of Theophanes rather than the epitomator? And finally, did Theophanes know the original version of the History of Theodore, apart from the *Epitome*? Dariusz Brodka's article discusses this question.

This attempt to establish the transmission of the text leads us to the issue of the features of the language of the *History*, as well as to the features of the *Epitome*. The anonymous epitomator of the *History* of Theodore did not assume his highly rhetorical style, and the few preserved fragments do not allow us to make definite judgements about the original version of the *Church History*. Therefore, relying on specific features of the language of the preserved fragments, we are unable to say which authors of the early Byzantine period used the original version of Theodore's work. Adrian Szopa writes about these issues in his article.

In the second part of this monography, selected topics which relate to the transmission of Theodore's work and its cognitive value are presented, emphasizing information which allows us to look in detail at certain aspects of the empire and Church at the end of the fifth and beginning of the sixth century – social, political and religious history and the history of the arts. In most cases they intertwine, creating a veritable mosaic, reflecting the life of the empire, especially that of Constantinople in that period.

The juridical frames in which the Church functioned, monasteries in particular, are in essence *Sitz im Leben*, in which the *History of the Church* was created. Michel Kaplan defines this in his article. Theodore Lector writes from the perspective of a citizen of Constantinople and he pays most attention to the city in his work. He was also an eye-witness to some of the events he describes, in particular those that concern the reign of Anastasius. The information included in the *History* are often his observations and cannot be found in other sources. Andrzej Kompa reconstructs the colourful world of Constantinople at the turn of the century on the basis of Theodore's text, confronting it with other sources. Geoffrey Greatrex analyzes in detail information about a dissident religious group – the Arian community. Hansen's view notwithstanding, Theodore Lector pays a lot of attention not only to religious but also to political events. Christoph Begass concentrates on the value of the information on the political history of the empire, analyzing the imperial enthronements and changes on the imperial throne described by Theodore.

Kamilla Twardowska analyzes the significance of the work of Theodore for our understanding of the history of visual arts of late antiquity. The *Church History* allows us to move the date of the emergence of segmental religious painting to the second half of the fifth century or the beginning of the sixth century. It also allows us to determine the canons in religious art at the beginning of the sixth century, confirming the existence of a belief in the miraculous and healing powers of religious paintings.

We would like to thank all the authors of this monography, hoping that their work will contribute to a better understanding of *Church History* of Theodore Lector and will inspire scholars to pursue further analysis of the work.

Bibliography

Flusin 1983 = Bernard Flusin, *Miracle et histoire dans l'œuvre de Cyrille de Scythopolis*, Paris.

Kosiński – Szopa – Twardowska 2019 = *Historie Kościoła Jana Diakrinomenosa i Teodora Lektora*, ed. by Rafał Kosiński – Adrian Szopa – Kamilla Twardowska, Kraków.

Kosiński – Twardowska – Zabrocka – Szopa 2021 = *Ecclesiastical Histories of John Diakrinomenos and Theodore Lector*, ed. by Rafał Kosiński – Kamilla Twardowska – Aneta Zabrocka – Adrian Szopa, Berlin.

Pouderon 2015 = Bernard Pouderon, 'Théophane, témoin de l'Épitomè d'histoires ecclésiastiques, de Théodore le Lecteur ou de Jean Diacrinoménos?', *Travaux et Mémoires* 19, pp. 279–314.

Van Dieten 1980 = Jan Luis van Dieten, 'Synodicon vetus. Bemerkungen zu einer Neuausgabe', *Annuarium Historiae Conciliorum* 12, pp. 62–108.

THEODORE LECTOR'S WORK
IN THE FRAME OF LATE ANTIQUE
HISTORIOGRAPHY

PETER VAN NUFFELEN

TRUE TO THEIR WORDS. THEODORE LECTOR AND HIS PREDECESSORS

By adding a four book compilation of Socrates, Sozomen and Theodoret to his own *Ecclesiastical history*, Theodore Lector was an innovator in the history of ecclesiastical historiography. As such, he directly inspired the *Historia Tripartita* of Cassiodorus, composed in Constantinople between 544/5 and 551.[1] Innovations, however, rarely appear out of thin air. This chapter offers an inventory of the evidence for earlier ecclesiastical histories that went over terrain already covered by earlier authors, that is, works that we would also call compilations. The evidence is largely fragmentary and as such, the chapter also seeks to complete our knowledge of Greek and Latin ecclesiastical historiography.

As we shall see, Theodore's innovation does not lie so much in the explicit reliance on earlier authors, which was common practice among ancient historians and of which examples can be found among earlier ecclesiastical historians. Rather, it lies in the fidelity to their words and the professed intention to indicate similarities and differences between the three authors. We shall conclude by suggesting that Theodore Lector's *Historia Tripartita* is the result of the impact on historiography of the rise of the so-called *Väterbeweis*: citation of the very words of an authoritative Father of the Church became a necessary argument in theological debate.[2]

---

[1] Van Hoof – Van Nuffelen 2017, pp. 287–88; Van Ginkel 1995, pp. 52–54 argues that John of Ephesus may have used a collation of Socrates, Sozomen, and Theodoret.

[2] Graumann 2002; Dietrich 2018.

Studies in Theodore Anagnostes, ed. by Rafał KOSIŃSKI & Adrian SZOPA, STTA 19 (Turnhout 2021), pp. 17–37
© BREPOLS ❧ PUBLISHERS   DOI 10.1484/M.STTA-EB.5.127974

1. *Eusebius the compiler*

The earliest predecessor of Theodore is Eusebius of Caesarea himself – at least according to Theodore's own interpretation. As all historians, Theodore situates himself in a tradition. In his preface, he aligns his own form of historiography with that of Eusebius, by subtly redefining the latter's project: 'The most admirable Eusebius, called son of Pamphilus, made the effort to collect the learned men who have written about such ecclesiastical matters from the beginnings – I mean not only of writers among the Christians but also among the Jews – and he made a historical narrative until the twentieth year of the Christ-loving and truly ordained by God rule of Constantine the most praiseworthy and blessed'.[3] The formulation picks up exactly the terms used by Theodore to describe his own activity in the preceding lines of the preface.[4] *Sylloge* is a term commonly used for compilations and excerpt collections,[5] and thus Eusebius' ecclesiastical history is redefined as a compilation, just as Theodore's own work. In the preface to his ecclesiastical history, Eusebius had acknowledged using earlier authors (whom he indeed copiously cites), but he made clear enough that these are not historians, that they offered at best fragmentary accounts of their own times, and that he thus was making a coherent historical narrative out of material that was not historical in nature.[6] We do not know if this assessment of Eusebius was shared by other late antique readers and writers, but there can be no doubt that Theodore interpreted the work

---

[3] Theodore Lector, *Historia Tripartita* 1 (ed. Hansen 1995): Εὐσεβίου τοῦ θαυμασιωτάτου τοῦ ἐπίκλην Παμφίλου κεκμηκότος περὶ τὴν συλλογὴν τῶν ἀνέκαθεν τὰς τοιαύτας ἐκκλησιαστικὰς ὑποθέσεις λογίων ἀνδρῶν συγγεγραφότων, οὐ μόνον λέγω τῶν παρὰ Χριστιανοῖς φιλοσοφησάντων, ἀλλὰ καὶ παρ' Ἑβραίοις, καὶ τήνδε τὴν ἱστορικὴν σύνταξιν ποιησαμένου ἄχρι τοῦ εἰκοστοῦ ἔτους τῆς φιλοχρίστου καὶ ὡς ἀληθῶς ὑπὸ θεοῦ χειροτονηθείσης βασιλείας Κωνσταντίνου τοῦ πανευφήμου καὶ μακαριωτάτου, ...

[4] Theodore Lector, *Historia Tripartita* 1 (ed. Hansen 1995): Ἔκ τινος ψήφου ἐπιξενοῦσθαί μοι λαχόντι κατὰ τὸ ὑμέτερον Παφλαγόνων ἔθνος ἐν μητροπόλει τοὔνομα Γάγγρᾳ, ἐν αὐτῇ τε ἀπολαύσαντι τῆς σῆς ἱερᾶς ὁμοῦ καὶ τιμίας μοι κεφαλῆς, ἠναγκαζόμην παρ' αὐτῆς, ἐξαυτῆς τὰς ὑποθέσεις ληψόμενος, συναγαγεῖν τῶν ἐκκλησιαστικῶν ἱστοριῶν τοὺς ἐκθέντας καὶ μίαν τινὰ ἐξ αὐτῶν ἁρμόσασθαι σύνταξιν.

[5] See the following works, with further references: Manafis 2018; Németh 2018; Odorico 2014.

[6] Eusebius of Caesarea, *Ecclesiastical history* 1.1.3–5 (ed. Schwartz – Mommsen 1999).

of the father of ecclesiastical history in this way because it gave his own kind of writing history a grander pedigree. Possibly, though, his judgement was not merely self-serving: an understanding of Eusebius essentially handing on the testimony of earlier church fathers may well have been shaped by the rise of the *Väterbeweis* noticed above.

2. *Sozomen's* Epitome

One of the authors used by Theodore, Sozomen (writing *c.* 445),[7] had intended to cover the history from the beginning of the church (that is, after the Ascension of Christ) until his own day. When realising that he could not find anything to add to his predecessors, he revised his plan and decided to continue Eusebius. But he did compose an epitome of the period that Eusebius had covered: 'At first, I intended to write that history from the beginning. Realising, then, that others had already tried their hand at it until their own times (Clement and Hegesippus, very wise men who followed on the Apostolic succession, and Africanus the historian and Eusebius called son of Pamphilus, a man intimately acquainted with the Sacred Scriptures and the poets and writers of the Greeks), I composed an epitome in two books of all events that have come to us and that happened to the churches after the ascension to the heavens of Christ until the deposition of Licinius. Now, if God permits, I shall set about narrating what happened after these'.[8] Modern scholarship tends to define an epitome as the abbreviation of a single work, but ancient vocabulary was not that precise.[9] We should understand Sozomen as saying that he wrote what we would call a breviary, that is,

---

[7] Van Nuffelen 2004, p. 61.

[8] Sozomen, *Ecclesiastical history* 1.1.12–13 (ed. Bidez – Hansen 1995): ὡρμήθην δὲ τὰ μὲν πρῶτα ἀπ' ἀρχῆς ταύτην συγγράψαι τὴν πραγματείαν. λογισάμενος δὲ ὡς καὶ ἄλλοι ταύτης ἐπειράθησαν μέχρι τῶν κατ' αὐτοὺς χρόνων, Κλήμης τε καὶ Ἡγήσιππος, ἄνδρες σοφώτατοι, τῇ τῶν ἀποστόλων διαδοχῇ παρακολουθήσαντες, καὶ Ἀφρικανὸς ὁ συγγραφεὺς καὶ Εὐσέβιος ὁ ἐπίκλην Παμφίλου, ἀνὴρ τῶν θείων γραφῶν καὶ τῶν παρ' Ἕλλησι ποιητῶν καὶ συγγραφέων πολυμαθέστατος ἵστωρ, ὅσα μὲν τῶν εἰς ἡμᾶς ἐλθόντων ταῖς ἐκκλησίαις συνέβη μετὰ τὴν εἰς οὐρανοὺς ἄνοδον τοῦ Χριστοῦ μέχρι τῆς Λικινίου καθαιρέσεως, ἐπιτεμόμενος ἐπραγματευσάμην ἐν βιβλίοις δύο, νῦν δέ, σὺν θεῷ φάναι, τὰ μετὰ ταῦτα διεξελθεῖν πειράσομαι.

[9] Horster – Reitz 2018.

a brief account of events in a given period, normally relying on literary sources. Indeed, his own statement (ὅσα μὲν τῶν εἰς ἡμᾶς ἐλθόντων ταῖς ἐκκλησίαις συνέβη) indeed defines the scope of his work by the events, and not by the source, as would be the case with what moderns call an epitome (e.g. Jordanes' *Getica* is an epitome of Cassiodorus' *History of the Goths*). Even so, one could wonder to what degree Sozomen's epitome would contain anything that was not in Eusebius, for the authors mentioned are all sources of Eusebius and his statement may betray the fact that he had been unable to find anything else than Eusebius. The epitome is completely lost. One factor in that loss certainly was that Sozomen conceptualised his *Ecclesiastical history* as an independent work, prefacing it with a dedication to Theodosius II and a proemium. This implies that *Epitome* and *Ecclesiastical history* circulated separately.

3. *Sabinus the Arian*

In a Syriac list of authors of ecclesiastical history, catalogued per period they wrote on and found in *Parisinus Syriacus* 9 (thirteenth century), we encounter a certain Sabinus the Arian:

> How many writers wrote ecclesiastical histories from Adam until the Messiah: Africanus, Hegesippus, Josephus and Judah who wrote on the weeks of Daniel.
> From the Messiah until the time of Constantine the Great: Eusebius of Caesarea, Sabinus the Arian and Rufinus of Rome.
> From Constantine the Great until Theodosius the Young: Sozomenus, Socrates and Theodoret.
> From Theodosius the Young until Justinian the Elder: John, priest of Antioch, called Glybo, Theodore Lector of the Church of Constantinople, Zachariah bishop of Melitene, Qura of Batna, John of Asia and Daniel of Tur Abdin. End of these things.[10]

---

[10] Nau 1915, Translation by M. Mazzola:

ܐܝܠܝܢ ܚܪ̈ܒܕ ܐܬܟܬܒ ܐܟܬܒ̈ܐ ܗܣܛܘܪܝܐܣ ܡܢ ܐܕܡ ܥܕܡܐ ܠܡܫܝܚܐ. ܐܦܪܝܩܢܘܣ.
ܘܐܝܓܣܝܦܘܣ. ܘܝܘܣܝܦܘܣ. ܘܝܗܘܕܐ ܗܘ ܕܥܠ ܫܒܘ̈ܥܐ ܕܕܢܝܐܝܠ.
ܘܡܢ ܡܫܝܚܐ ܥܕܡܐ ܠܙܒܢܐ ܕܩܘܣܛܢܛܝܢܘܣ ܪܒܐ. ܐܘܣܒܝܘܣ ܕܩܣܪܝܐ.
ܘܣܒܝܢܘܣ ܐܪܝܢܐ. ܘܪܘܦܝܢܘܣ ܕܪܗܘܡܝ.
ܘܡܢ ܩܘܣܛܢܛܝܢܘܣ ܪܒܐ ܥܕܡܐ ܠܬܐܘܕܘܣܝܘܣ ܙܥܘܪܐ. ܣܘܙܘܡܢܘܣ ܘܣܘܩܪܛܘܣ
ܘܬܐܘܕܘܪܝܛܘܣ.

There are too many names mentioned here to be discussed in detail and I refer to our *Clavis Historicorum Antiquitatis Posterioris* for further information on the authors mentioned here.[11] The intriguing reference to Sabinus the Arian is our interest here. A church historian Sabinus is not attested anywhere else. The only possible identification is Sabinus of Heraclea, who belonged to the Macedonians (a branch of Arianism) and was the author of a collection of synods, which ran from the Council of Nicaea to *c.* 370 and was used by Socrates and Sozomen.[12] Yet his work did not run from Christ until Constantine the Great, contrary to what the list states. If we identify the two Sabini, we must accept that the author of the note (or his source) committed an error, possibly by misinterpreting the citations of Sabinus in Socrates and Sozomen as referring to a full-fledged ecclesiastical history. Such an error is rendered likely by the fact that Rufinus is also misrepresented as the author of a history from Christ until Constantine and not (through his translation and continuation of Eusebius) from Christ until Theodosius I.[13] The alternative, that there was another Sabinus, also an Arian, who wrote a proper ecclesiastical history from Christ to Constantine, is intriguing but less plausible. We have no idea what the narrative would have looked like, but we need not expect it to have been substantially different from what we have in Eusebius, for he too had sympathised with Arius and the Eunomian historian Philostorgius simply continued Eusebius.[14]

---

[11] Van Nuffelen – Van Hoof 2020.

[12] Van Nuffelen 2004, pp. 447–54. On collections of documents as a genre distinct from but related to ecclesiastical history, see Van Nuffelen 2004, pp. 207–09.

[13] In Anonymous of Cyzicus, *Ecclesiastical history* pr. 22 (ed. Hansen 2008) Rufinus is said to have participated in the council of Nicaea. In Greek there therefore seems to have been a tradition of Rufinus having been contemporaneous with Eusebius, which we also find in the list.

[14] Bleckmann – Stein 2015.

4. *Jerome*

Jerome had a tremendous impact on the history of chronography by composing a slightly adapted translation of the chronicle of Eusebius of Caesarea. At one point in his life, he had the intention of also composing an ecclesiastical history: 'In the same way I, who have long been silent (for a certain person who finds my talking punishing has forced me to be quiet), wish to train first in a minor work and to scrape off, as it were, a certain patina from my tongue, so that I can proceed to a wider history. What I set out to write (provided that the Lord gives me life and my detractors stop persecuting me now that I am fleeing and locked away) is an account from the arrival of the Saviour until our age, that is, from the Apostles down to the dregs of the present time, how and through whose agency the Church of Christ was born and came of age, increased through persecutions, was crowned through martyrdom; and how, after she reached the time of the Christian emperors, she became greater in power and riches but lesser in virtues'.[15] Derived from the preface to the *Life of Malchus*, one of Jerome's hagiographies, the passage is preceded by a comparison of the writing of lives of saints to the mock battles fought by the navy in preparation for a real encounter. In other words, history is the real thing, hagiography is just an exercise. The passage suggests that Jerome wanted to compose his own, original history and did not intend to translate Eusebius. Admittedly, the scope of the history starts where Eusebius had started his own history, with the Apostles, and there can be little doubt that the work would have undergone his influence in other ways. By reaching until his own age, however, the work would have been more than a mere translation. At the very least it would have

---

[15] Jerome, *Life of Malchus* 1 (ed. Gray 2015, p. 79, with commentary pp. 106–11): *ita et ego, qui diu tacui – silere quippe me fecit cui meus sermo supplicium est – prius exerceri cupio in paruo opere et ueluti quandam rubiginem linguae abstergere, ut uenire possim ad historiam latiorem. scribere enim disposui – si tamen dominus uitam dederit et si uituperatores mei saltem fugientem me et clausum persequi desierint – ab aduentu Saluatoris usque ad nostram aetatem, id est, ab apostolis usque ad huius temporis faecem, quomodo et per quos christi ecclesia nata sit et adulta, persecutionibus creuerit, martyriis coronata sit et, postquam ad christianos principes uenerit, potentia quidem et diuitiis maior sed uirtutibus minor facta sit.* See also *Chronicle*, pr. p. 7 (ed. Helm 1956).

looked like that of Rufinus of Aquileia, who translated Eusebius' church history and added two books of his own hand.[16]

5. *Gelasius of Caesarea*

Gelasius, the bishop of Caesarea (d. before September 400) is attested to have written an ecclesiastical history, which continued Eusebius and supplemented him.[17] In 1992, P. Nautin advanced the hypothesis that Gelasius wrote a continuation of Eusebius which was simply added to a manuscript of Eusebius, after a prooimion of his own inserted at the end of Eusebius' text. That collection of Eusebius + Gelasius was then excerpted by the compiler of the seventh-century Epitome of Ecclesiastical Histories, our major source for Theodore Lector.[18] This would be the single known example of an ecclesiastical history that consciously continued another one in the same manuscript, discounting the Latin translation and continuation of Eusebius by Rufinus – which as, as a translation, a special case. In fact, Nautin's idea cannot be correct.

Nautin relied on two arguments. First, in the *Epitome of Ecclesiastical Histories*, the excerpts of Eusebius conclude on 'Until here narrates Eusebius' (Ἕως τούτου ἱστορεῖ ὁ Εὐσέβιος). Nautin takes this to be a note drawn from Gelasius, who supposedly had indicated that Eusebius ran until that point, before continuing the narrative himself. This can only seem plausible if one fails to look at the entire lay out of the *Epitome*, as there can be little doubt that it is a marker introduced by the compiler. In fact, the *Epitome* has headings for its major constitutive parts (Euse-

---

[16] In the fifth century a Greek ecclesiastical history circulated under the name of Rufinus, but which, to judge by the extant fragments, included material not in the Latin history of Rufinus. Scholars tend to identify the work with that of Gelasius of Caesarea: Van Nuffelen 2002.

[17] Gelasius of Caesarea F1b (ed. Wallraff – Stutz – Marinides 2018): κατέκρινεν ἐγγράφως Γελάσιον ἐπὶ τὴν ἱστορίαν τῶν μετὰ Εὐσέβιον καὶ ὧν οὐκ ἔγραψεν ὁ Εὐσέβιος ἐλθεῖν. Cf. Photius, *Bibliotheca* 89 (ed. Henry 1959) = Gelasius of Caesarea, *Ecclesiastical history* T5 (ed. Wallraff – Stutz – Marinides 2018): τὰ μετὰ τὴν ἐκκλησιαστικὴν ἱστορίαν Εὐσεβίου τοῦ Παμφίλου. The edition followed is that of Wallraff – Stutz – Marinides 2018.

[18] Nautin 1992. He is followed by Hansen 2008, p. 22, Wallraff – Stutz – Marinides 2018, pp. xxi, li, lxxxi–ii; Stevens 2018, p. 656.

bius, Theodore Lector and John Diacrinomenus).[19] Yet, between the excerpts of Eusebius and those of Theodore, the excerptor intercalated excerpts from Gelasius and Philip of Side and he thus marked clearly that he had ended his excerpts on Eusebius. The note alerts the reader to this fact. Indeed, we should not forget that the title of the collection was Συναγωγὴ ἱστοριῶν διαφόρων ἀπὸ τῆς κατὰ σάρκα γεννήσεως τοῦ Κυρίου καὶ ἑξῆς τὴν ἀρχὴν ἔχουσα ἀπὸ τοῦ πρώτου λόγου τῆς ἐκκλησιαστικῆς ἱστορίας εὐσεβίου τοῦ παμφίλου ('Collection of various histories from the birth in the flesh of our Lord and further, taking its start from the first book of the ecclesiastical history of Eusebius of Pamphilus'). The reader was thus warned that the collection started with Eusebius and that more would follow: hence the compiler added a note when he ended his work on Eusebius. The compiler was a fairly diligent men, for in the excerpts from Eusebius he noted quite often where he had added information to what Eusebius said and where he had taken it from.[20] He does the same in this instance, signalling that he is now adding from Gelasius of Caesarea and, when he finishes using Gelasius, he signals that he adds something from Philip of Side.[21] Then he inserts a heading that signals his return to a major source, Theodore Lector. As shown by P. Manafis, such indications are common in excerpt collections. There is hence no reason to accept that the note 'Until here narrates Eusebius' derives from Gelasius.[22]

Second, Nautin noticed that Photius does not mention the title of the ecclesiastical history, but only that of a proomion,[23]

---

[19] Listed in Manafis 2018, pp. 173–74.

[20] Manafis 2018, pp. 173–74; Stevens 2018.

[21] Hansen 1995, p. 160.

[22] Nautin 1992 is also not very consistent, for he argues that the notice on the sons of Constantine, intercalated between the end note on Eusebius and the first excerpt from Gelasius (printed in Gelasius F1b) is not by Gelasius (neither do Wallraff – Stutz – N. Marinides 2018). Thus he accepts intervention by the compiler at the very spot where he sees an original note of Gelasius. His argument would be more convincing if he could prove that the compiler of the excerpt collection had not intervened at all in the excerpts and had simply selected material from Eusebius + Gelasius. Even in Nautin's reconstruction, there is intervention by a compiler, who he thinks he can distinguish from Gelasius. Stevens 2018 has the same illusion.

[23] Gelasius of Caesarea, *Ecclesiastical history* T5a l. 62–63 (ed. Wallraff – Stutz – Marinides 2018): Ἡ δὲ λοιπὴ βίβλος ἐπιγραφὴν μὲν ἔχει τοιαύτην· Προοίμιον

This indicates nothing more than that the manuscript used by Photius did not carry a title before the preface, and it is hazardous to speculate that it reflects the fact that Gelasius did not give his own work a title and simply added it to a manuscript of Eusebius. The title may have dropped out.

If Nautin's two basic arguments are hardly convincing to start with, his hypothesis generates a series of problems. There is substantial overlap between Eusebius and the fragments attributed to Gelasius. The first fragments that go under the name of Gelasius relate to events of AD 305,[24] that is, material that would belong to book 9 of Eusebius' *Ecclesiastical history*. Indeed, there is overlap with Eusebius until F9.[25] This is not what one would expect if Gelasius continued Eusebius in the same manuscript. Why continue Eusebius' *Ecclesiastical history* in the same manuscript if one rewrites the last third of it? The argument that Gelasius might have revised the last books of Eusebius does not offer an escape route. Indeed, Nautin's based his hypothesis on the structure of the *Epitome of ecclesiastical histories* in which excerpts from Eusebius' *Ecclesiastical history* are followed by a few excerpts from Gelasius. He argued that this reflects exactly the structure of Eusebius + Gelasius. Yet the excerpts from Eusebius come from all ten books,[26] which would mean either that Gelasius copied Eusebius and then started with a long section of repetition anyway or that Gelasius had revised all ten books of Eusebius. The latter option also begs the question of why he then started with a long section of overlap.

Another problem for Nautin's hypothesis is the clear contradiction between Eusebius and Gelasius: Gelasius F3, recording how Diocletian and Maximian were executed on order of the

---

ἐπισκόπου Καισαρείας Παλαιστίνης εἰς τὰ μετὰ τὴν ἐκκλησιαστικὴν ἱστορίαν Εὐσεβίου τοῦ Παμφίλου.

[24] Gelasius of Caesarea, *Ecclesiastical history* F2–3 (ed. Wallraff – Stutz – Marinides 2018).

[25] The statement by Wallraff – Stutz – Marinides 2018, p. li that 'The quotations from Eusebius only reach the reign of Diocletian while the extracts from Gelasius stretch from the time of the persecutions under Diocletian to the revolt of Licinius' is wrong. The last extract from Eusebius is drawn from *Ecclesiastical history* 10.9.6 (ed. Schwartz – Mommsen 1999), the death of Licinius in 325: see Manafis 2018, p. 290.

[26] See Manafis 2018, pp. 275–90.

senate when they tried to regain imperial power, is not only fictitious but flatly contradicts what is in book 8 of Eusebius, as it was excerpted by the epitomator (exc. 103, following the numbering of P. Manafis 2018) noting how Diocletian died of disease and Maximian hung himself. However one construes Gelasius' activity, this is hard to explain. If Gelasius simply continued Eusebius in the sense that his own history constituted a single work with that of Esebius (as Nautin wishes us to believe), it is very curious that such a contradiction would occur: any reader of the manuscript would wonder about the reliability of Gelasius if he reads how the continuation simply contradicts what he had read earlier. If one assumes that Gelasius updated Eusebius by adding material into Eusebius' text, it is impossible that the compiler of the Epitome found Gelasius F3 in his Eusebius + Gelasius. Indeed, if the compiler was able to extract Gelasius F3 from book 8 of Eusebius, this supposes that the compiler would have found there two different versions of the deaths of Diocletian and Maximian next to each other and that he would have been able to identify which version was by Gelasius and which by Eusebius. This would, in turn, entail, that Gelasius marked his additions as such[27] with

---

[27] Stevens 2018, p. 641 argues something on these lines, although it is only on the basis of knowledge of the standard text of Eusebius that one can identify the additions. For Stevens, the additions to Eusebius found in the Eusebius-excerpts of the *Epitome* were identifiable scholia. Yet the fragments from Gelasius cannot be scholia, for F3–9 are too long for being mere scholia. Stevens also argues that the additions to the excerpts of Eusebius in the *Epitome of Ecclesiastical Histories* have a double origin, a scholiast whom he identifies with Gelasius of Caesarea, and the epitomator himself. His thesis is an modification of that of de Boor 1888, who argued that it was unlikely that a seventh-century epitomator would have been able to consult second- to third-century authors like Pierius, Papias, and Africanus, who are cited in the additions. Hence he supposed that two authors had been active: the epitomator and another individual. De Boor proposed as source of the additions Philip of Side, who is cited in Baroccianus 142, one of the manuscripts from which the Epitome is reconstructed. In identifying the scholiast not with Philip but with Gelasius, Stevens builds on Nautin 1992 and the arguments levelled against Nautin can thus also be levelled against Stevens. Attributing the additions to Gelasius is neat but cannot be squared with the rest of the fragments in the *Epitome*. Stevens does not notice, for example, the contradiction between excerpt 103 and Gelasius F3. He assumes that Gelasius added new material to Eusebius as scholia, but why then does the Epitome not cite the Gelasian fragments among the Eusebian material and postpones it doing so until after its end? If Gelasius simply added his material in Eusebius' text, it would appear earlier in the excerpt collection. If Gelasius certainly cannot be the scholiast, I am not convinced that it is possible to distinguish two layers in the additions

his name or clear authorial indications, so that a compiler could separate out Gelasian material from Eusebian material. This is a procedure unheard of, as a comparison with the way Rufinus blends his additions into his translation of Eusebius' ecclesiastical history shows. This option also forces us to accept that not just the compiler of the *Epitome* but all users of F3–9 of Gelasius (the fragments in which there is overlap with Eusebius) were careful enough to extract the additions by Gelasius from the text of Eusebius and cited them as if deriving from an independent text. If such behaviour in a single compiler would be remarkable, the adoption of a similar method by a series of independent authors working across centuries begs belief – especially as we know that the compiler did add material to the excerpts of Eusebius, drawn from many sources.[28] Nautin's hypothesis demands that he would change his habits only for Gelasius and started *extracting* material from Gelasius that he found mixed with Eusebius.[29] The alternative would be that the compiler diligently checked his manuscript of Eusebius + Gelasius against another manuscript of Eusebius so as to identify additions. The latter option is extremely unlikely and effectively contradicts Nautin's hypothesis that the Epitome of Ecclesiastical histories reflects exactly the single manuscript of Eusebius + Gelasius, for then we would have interference with another manuscript of Eusebius.

It should be clear that Nautin's hypothesis does not fit the method of the compiler of the *Epitome* nor the fragments of Gelasius as they are transmitted to us. It should be laid to rest. Thus, Gelasius composed a self-standing ecclesiastical history, which started his work with a summary of earlier events and thus consciously overlapped a bit with Eusebius (as did Socrates, for example). If the excerpts in the Epitome are anything to go by,

---

to the Eusebian excerpts, as done by de Boor and Stevens. There is much authorial intervention in the Eusebian excerpts (see Manafis 2018, pp. 275–90, who has a more complete overview, although he does not yet use a manuscript that Stevens did use (R Bodleian, Auctarium E.4.18). Not all results reached by Stevens convince: § 5 and § 7 both cite Pierius, but according to Stevens one would be by the scholiast and another by the epitomist (p. 645).

[28] This is accepted by scholars who follow Nautin, such as Stevens.

[29] Nautin's hypothesis regarding Gelasius was followed by a similar one regarding Theodore lector (Nautin 1994), which is equally untenable: Delacenserie (2016, pp. 73–74).

he started with the beginning of the life of Constantine.[30] This is irreconcilable with the idea of a continuation of Eusebius in the same manuscript, for in no known instance of a historian expressly continuing a predecessor in the same manuscript,[31] a practice that is well-known among chroniclers,[32] the continuator starts with the overlap we witness here. Given the compiler's careful way of working in the Eusebian fragments, where he lists additional parallels, we may be entitled to think that he did not find much of interest in Gelasius except for political history of the years 305–25 or at least nothing that was worthwhile to add to Theodore Lector.

6. *John of Aegeae (?)*, Ten books of ecclesiastical history *& Anonymous of Cyzicus*, Ecclesiastical history

In *Biblioteca* 41, the patriarch Photius summarises an ecclesiastical history composed by a certain John:

> Read the *Ecclesiastical history* by a certain John. It begins with the reign of Theodosius the Younger, the heresy of Nestorius and his deposition, and goes down to the time of Zeno and the deposition of Peter the heretic, who had usurped the see of Antioch. The style is clear but florid. The author describes in detail the third council held at Ephesus, and also another council held in the same place, I mean the Robber council, which he deifies together with its president Dioscorus and his companions. He also gives a slanderous account of the council of Chalcedon. This justifies the conclusion that the

---

[30] I am assuming that the unnumbered and usually unprinted fragment found in Gelasius of Caesarea, *Ecclesiastical history* F1b l. 2–3 (ed. Wallraff – Stutz – Marinides 2018) (which is not in Hansen, nor in Manafis) is by Gelasius. Note that the fragments as printed by Wallraff – Stutz – Marinides 2018 (an edition that should, however, be used with prudence: Van Nuffelen 2019) deal mostly with Constantine and Nicaea. The confusion of Photius between the Anonymous of Cyzicus (the earliest source for Gelasius of Caesarea) and Gelasius of Caesarea is hence not that remarkable.

[31] It is, of course, different if different authors have been copied in the same manuscript.

[32] Nautin only adduces examples from chronography. He also gives the example of the *Life of Origen* by Pamphilus and Eusebius (Photius, *Bibliotheca* 118, ed. Henry 1959), but this is a different case as both were co-authors of the first five books and Eusebius finished it after Pamphilus' death.

author is John, presbyter of Aegaea, a heretic who wrote especially a book against the council of Chalcedon.[33] The history, according to his statement, is in ten books. I have only read five, containing (as already stated) a record of events from the heresy of Nestorius to the deposition of Peter the heretic.[34]

The manuscript identified the author merely as a certain John and on the grounds of its obvious anti-chalcedonian tendency Photius proposes the plausible but by no means certain identification with the miaphysite presbyter John of Aegeae.[35] The history, as read by Photius, ran from *c.* 428, when Nestorius became bishop of Constantinople and the problems leading to the council of Ephesus (431) started, until *c.* 476, when Peter the Fuller, intermittently bishop of Antioch between *c.* 470 and 488, was deposed by the emperor Zeno (474–91) who had regained power after the usurpation of Basiliscus (475–76).[36] 476 is the only moment when a deposition of Peter the Fuller happened in the reign of Zeno. The five books read by Photius would thus have covered about fifty years. Where do we locate the other five books? They could have followed the account that Photius read. In that case, assuming that the pace of narration was similar and hence that roughly another half a century was covered, John could have been writing in the reign of Justin I (518–27) and Justinian (527–65), during the time of restoration of chalcedonism. The

---

[33] See Photius, *Biblioteca* 55 (ed. Henry 1959).

[34] Photius, *Bibliotheca* 41 (ed. Henry 1959): Ἀνεγνώσθη Ἰωάννου ἐκκλησιαστικὴ ἱστορία. Ἄρχεται ἀπὸ τῆς Θεοδοσίου τοῦ νέου βασιλείας, ἀπ' αὐτῆς που τῆς Νεστορίου βλασφημίας καὶ καθαιρέσεως, καὶ κάτεισι μέχρι Ζήνωνος καὶ τῆς καθαιρέσεως Πέτρου τοῦ αἱρετικοῦ, ὃς τὸν Ἀντιοχικὸν ὑφήρπασε θρόνον. Ἔστι δὲ οὗτος τὴν φράσιν σαφὴς καὶ ἀνθηρός. Διέρχεται δὲ τὴν τρίτην σύνοδον τὴν ἐν Ἐφέσῳ λεπτομερῶς. Ἀλλὰ καὶ τὴν μετὰ ταύτην ἐν αὐτῇ συναγελασθεῖσαν, τὴν ληστρικὴν λέγω· ἣν οὗτος θειάζει, καὶ τὸν ταύτης ἡγεμόνα Διόσκορον καὶ τοὺς σὺν αὐτῷ. Διέξεισι δὲ καὶ τὴν ἐν Καλχηδόνι σύνοδον, διασύρων ταύτην. Ἐξ ὧν ἔστι συμβαλεῖν Ἰωάννην εἶναι τὸν πατέρα τοῦ βιβλίου τὸν πρεσβύτερον τὸν Αἰγεάτην, ὃς καὶ ἰδίως ὡς αἱρετικὸς κατὰ τῆς ἐν Καλχηδόνι συνόδου βιβλίον συνέταξε. Τῆς μέντοιγε ἱστορίας αὐτοῦ δέκα τυγχάνουσι τόμοι, ὡς καὶ αὐτὸς ἐκεῖνος ἐπαγγέλλεται· ὧν ἡμῖν τοὺς πέντε γέγονεν ἀναγνῶναι, περιέχοντας, ὡς ἔφημεν, ἀπὸ τῆς Νεστορίου βλασφημίας μέχρι τῆς τοῦ αἱρετικοῦ Πέτρου καθαιρέσεως. Translation J. H. Freese, adapted.

[35] See further Facundus of Hermiane, *Defense of the Three Chapters* 3.2.20, 5.1.17 (ed. Clément – Vander Plaetse – Fraïsse-Bétoulières 2002–2006). Wright 1872, p. 937 records an attack by John of Aegeae on Theodoret, preserved in Syriac translation.

[36] Kosiński 2010.

other possibility is to locate the five books before the ones read by Photius. In that case, it is likely that John started with Nicaea. This option seems most plausible, given the parallel of the Anonymous of Cyzicus.

The Anonymous of Cyzicus (formerly known as Pseudo-Gelasius of Cyzicus) composed an account of the council of Nicaea because the partisans of Eutyches, having acquired the upper hand under Basiliscus, accused the Chalcedonians of misrepresenting the faith of Nicaea. Indeed, the Encyclical of Basiliscus recognised only Nicaea and Ephesus I and rejected the council of Chalcedon.[37] It became hence important to show that Chalcedon did or did not explicate what was already said in Nicaea. The Anonymous provides an Chalcedonian account of Nicaea to that effect. The work is essentially a compilation of Eusebius, Socrates, Theodoret, Gelasius of Caesarea and Rufinus of Aquileia.[38] If that dependency is not denied, the Anonymous construes an elaborate genealogy of lost sources to enhance the authority of his own work. Indeed, he opens the preface with a reference to an old book, once the property of Dalmatius of Cyzicus, bishop elected *c.* 426–27: 'A very long time ago I had read everything that was said, done and decided in this virtuous and holy synod, when I was still in my father's house. I had found it written in a very ancient book, whose pages contained it all in full detail. They had belonged to the holy and praiseworthy Dalmatius, who was archbishop of the holy and catholic church of the brilliant metropolis of Cyzicus and had come to the then lord of our house, that is, my father in the flesh, who had the position of presbyter in that same holy church'.[39]

---

[37] Evagrius Scholasticus, *Ecclesiastical history* 3.4 (ed. Bidez-Parmentier 1898).

[38] Hansen 2008, pp. 16–43 whose idea of a reliance on Philip of Side is certainly wrong. A thorough study of how the Anonymous composes his narrative is needed.

[39] Anonymous of Cyzicus, *Ecclesiastical history* pr. 2 (ed. Hansen 2008): πάντα τὰ ἐν ἐκείνῃ τῇ ἐναρέτῳ καὶ ἁγίᾳ συνόδῳ λεχθέντα τε καὶ πραχθέντα καὶ διατυπωθέντα πάλαι τε καὶ πρόπαλαι ἀναγνοὺς ἔτι ἐν τῇ πατρῴᾳ οἰκίᾳ διάγων, εὑρηκὼς αὐτὰ ἐν βίβλῳ ἀρχαιοτάτῃ ἐγγεγραμμένα ἐν μεμβράναις ἅπαντα ἀπαραλείπτως ἐχούσαις, γενομέναις μὲν τοῦ θείου καὶ ἀοιδίμου Δαλματίου τοῦ ἀρχιεπισκόπου γενομένου τῆς ἁγίας καὶ καθολικῆς ἐκκλησίας τῆς τῶν Κυζικηνῶν λαμπρᾶς μητροπόλεως, περιελθούσαις δὲ εἰς τὸν τοῦ ποτε ἡμετέρου οἴκου δεσπότην, λέγω δὴ τὸν κατὰ σάρκα πατέρα ἐμόν, τῆς αὐτῆς ἁγιωτάτης ἐκκλησίας πρεσβυτερίου ἠξιωμένον.

The author states that he read the entire book and made many notes from it, for he could not remember everything. The book may have existed,[40] and the Anonymous gives some indications of its content.[41] Yet the reference to an old book reminds one of the pseudo-documentary fictions known from Greek literature,[42] and one suspects here a literary ploy to enhance the claim to authority.

Later he adds that he looked up additional sources to complement his notes, in particular Eusebius and Rufinus. He refers, however, to another, further unknown author: 'John, a certain old and very literate presbyter, in rather old fascicles [did not record] everything'.[43] Again we have no further attestation of this work. It may well be authentic, but it could also be part of a strategy of authentification.[44] Indeed, the Anonymous also turns Rufinus, who wrote about a century after Nicaea, into a participant of the council. At the very least, we may suspect that the information regarding date of the further unknown John given here is not fully reliable.[45]

The strategy of authentification pursued by the Anonymous is thus clear: he obscures the use of later sources, such as Socrates, and suggests that he only used sources that are old and date mostly from close to the council itself. He may be relying on literary fiction; at least, he is willing to turn Rufinus into a participant of the council. Although clearly a compilation, the Anonymous of Cyzicus is in many ways different from Theodore Lector. He focuses on a single, albeit foundational, event and although he regularly references the sources he is using, he obviously composes the narrative in his own words.

---

[40] Cf. CHAP s.v. Anonymous, Account of the council of Nicaea.

[41] Anonymous of Cyzicus, *Ecclesiastical history* pr. 3–7 (ed. Hansen 2008).

[42] Ni Mheallaigh 2008.

[43] Anonymous of Cyzicus, *Ecclesiastical history* pr. 21 (ed. Hansen 2008): Ἰωάννῃ μέν τινι πρεσβυτέρῳ ἀνδρὶ παλαιῷ, ἄγαν γραφικῷ, ἐν τετραδίοις παλαιοῖς λίαν, οὐ μὴν ὅλα.

[44] Honigmann 1953, p. 173 n. 22; Speyer 1971, p. 74.

[45] A more hazardous identification would be with John of Aegeae. It is not uncommon for ecclesiastical historians to use works from authors deemed heretical: Socrates and Sozomen used Sabinus of Heraclea, and Evagrius Scholasticus relied on Zachariah. In line with his practice to suggest that he used sources that date close to the council, he could have turned John of Aegeae in an old presbyter. By the same token, he would have obscured his reliance on a heretical source.

The Anonymous and his strategies of authentification testify to a debate about Nicaea that was current around the reign of Basiliscus. It seems hence likely to take this as the Sitz-im-Leben for John of Aegeae's work too. It would have been driven by theological concerns about continuity with Nicaea in the other two councils, Ephesus and Chalcedon. It is likely to assume (although we cannot know) that John would have used material he found in Socrates, Sozomen and/or Theodoret, and thus that his first five books would have been compilatory in nature. A further indication of this is that these books circulated separately in the age of Photius: readers may not have felt the need to preserve the first part of his work because it did not offer anything original in comparison with the authoritative accounts of the three 'chalcedonian' synoptic historians.

At any rate, theological debate of the 475s seems to have spurred the writing of ecclesiastical histories that resemble in many aspects Theodore Lector, even if the Anonymous of Cyzicus pursued a different method and literary strategy for claiming authority. How John of Aegeae proceeded we cannot tell.

Conclusions

We are used to seeing the independent historical account that starts where one's predecessor left off as the normal way of writing ecclesiastical history. This is indeed how the sequence Esebius-Socrates/Sozomen/Theodoret-Evagrius presents itself to us. But that picture is misleading. We have surveyed the ways ecclesiastical historians of the fourth and fifth century shaped their works when they wished to write on a period that had already been covered by a predecessor. A limited degree of overlap was usual, and can be observed in Socrates, Sozomen and Gelasius of Caesarea in relation to Eusebius of Caesarea. They briefly recapitulated some of the events narrated by their predecessor, so as to set the scene for their own account. If overlap was greater, the historian composed his own, new account, although it could be heavily based on his predecessors, as we have suggested in the case of Sozomen's epitome and the first five books of John of Aegeae.[46]

---

[46] I have left aside Philip of Side, who composed a Christian history from Adam until 426, of epic proportions. This was not an ecclesiastical history

That dependency could be tacitly accepted, as in Sozomen, or obscured, as in the Anonymous of Cyzicus, who turns late sources into eye witnesses of Nicaea and suggests reliance on old and thus authentic reports. What we do not encounter is continuation of a predecessor in the same manuscript, as was wrongly suggested for Gelasius of Caesarea – that is, at least not in the same language. Rufinus of Aquileia added his continuation to his translation of Eusebius and Jerome might have done the same thing had he ever composed his own history. But such a translation and a continuation is obviously a different matter than the continuation of a work in the same language, for there was no pre-existing work to which one could simply add sections or books.

How does Theodore Lector fit into this tradition? On the one hand, he shares with his predecessors the wish to create a new, single account: his express wish is to compose a single narrative out of the three accounts of his predecessors. On the other, his undertaking differs clearly from his predecessors by the much stronger fidelity to the very words of his predecessors. This is linked to another difference: preceding authors who covered anew the terrain already covered by a predecessor (usually Eusebius), defined their scope by the events, by a period, e.g. from the beginning of the church (Sozomen, Jerome, Sabinus) or from Nicaea onwards (John of Aegeae). Theodore's task was not to compose a history from Nicaea until the present day, but to make a single account out of the three of his orthodox predecessors. Their starting point is his. The texts are seen as carriers of authority and the events are seen through them. As a consequence, the way Theodore claims authority is different from what we noticed in the Anonymous of Cyzicus. The latter seeks to show that his sources were eye witnesses of Nicaea and that he used old and venerable texts and reports, suggesting that these are eye witnesses too. Such a strategy stands fully in the tradition of ancient historiography, for which eye witness reports had the highest status. Theodore, by contrast, derives his claim to truth from the authority that Socrates, Sozomen, and Theodoret already have as god-

(there is no church before Christ). At any rate, what we know of the work would not change the conclusions reached here: Van Nuffelen 2004, pp. 209–10; Heyden 2006.

33

beloved and most learned men (θεοφιλεῖς ὁμοῦ καὶ λογιώτατοι ἄνδρες).[47] The re-defining of Eusebius as a compiler picks up the same idea and vocabulary: Eusebius transmits the words of learned men.[48] Attention is shifted away from the events to the texts, which have received authority because they are composed by orthodox and learned men. In this attention to the very words of authoritative writers, we see, I suggest, the impact of the wider cultural shift towards a 'patristic culture', in which the words of figures of authority carried weight. As such, the *Historia tripartita* of Theodore Lector was a work of its times.

Bibliography

Sources

Bidez – Hansen 1995 = Sozomenos, *Kirchengeschichte*, ed. by Joseph Bidez – Günther Christian Hansen, GCS, N.F., 4, Berlin.

Bidez – Parmentier 1898 = *The Ecclesiastical history of Evagrius with the scholia*, London.

Bleckmann – Stein 2015 = Philostorgios, *Kirchengeschichte*, Hrsg. von Bruno Bleckmann – Marcus Stein, KFHist E7. Paderborn.

Clément – Vander Plaetse – Fraïsse-Bétoulières 2002–2006 = Facundus d'Hermiane, *Défense des trois chapitres (à Justinien)*, éd. par Jean Marie Clément – Roel Vander Plaetse, – Anne Fraïsse-Bétoulières, SC 471, 478–79, 499, Paris.

Gray 2015 = Jerome, *Vita Malchi: Introduction, Text, Translation, and Commentary*, ed. by Christa Gray, Oxford.

Hansen 1995 = Theodoros Anagnostes, *Kirchengeschichte*, Hrsg. von Günther Christian Hansen, GCS, N.F., 3, Berlin.

Hansen 2008 = Anonymus von Cyzicus, *Historia ecclesiastica. Kirchengeschichte*, Hrsg. von Günther Christian Hansen, Fontes Christiani 49, Turnhout.

Helm 1956 = *Eusebius: Werke. Volume Seven: Die Chronik des Hieronymus*, Hrsg. von Rudolf Helm, Die griechischen christlichen Schriftsteller der ersten Jahrhunderte 47, Leipzig.

Henry 1959 = Photius, *Bibliothèque, Tome I*, éd. par Rene Henry, Collection des Universités de France, Paris.

---

[47] Theodore Lector, *Historia tripartita* 1 (ed. Hansen 1995).
[48] Theodore Lector, *Historia tripartita* 1 (ed. Hansen 1995): λογίων ἀνδρῶν συγγεγραφότων.

Nau 1915 = 'Une liste de chronographes', ed. by François Nau, *Revue de l'Orient chrétien*, 10, pp. 101–03.

Schwartz – Mommsen 1999 = *Eusebius: Werke. Volume Two, Parts One and Two*, Hrsg. von Eduard Schwartz – Theodor Mommsen, GCS, Leipzig.

Wallraff – Stutz – Marinides 2018 = Gelasius of Caesarea, *Ecclesiastical history. The extant fragments: with an appendix containing the fragments from dogmatic writings*, ed. by Martin Wallraff – Jonathan Stutz – Nicholas Marinides, GCS, N.F., 25, Berlin.

Literature

Delacenserie 2016 = Emerance Delacenserie, *L 'Histoire ecclésiastique' de Socrate de Constantinople: banque de données et autorité historiographiques pour la création d'œuvres originales au VIᵉ s. (Théodore le Lecteur, Cassiodore, la première version arménienne)*, Diss. Ghent University, Ghent.

Dietrich 2018 = Julia Dietrich, 'Augustine and the Crisis of the 380s in Christian Doctrinal Argumentation', *Journal of Early Christian Studies* 26, pp. 547–70.

Graumann 2002 = Thomas Graumann, *Die Kirche der Väter: Väter-theologie und Väterbeweis in den Kirchen des Ostens bis zum Konzil von Ephesus (431)*, Beiträge zur historischen Theologie 118, Tübingen.

Heyden 2006 = Katharina Heyden, 'Die Christliche Geschichte des Philippos von Side, mit einem kommentierten Katalog der Fragmente', in *Julius Africanus und die Christliche Weltchronik*, Hrsg. von Martin Wallraff, Berlin, pp. 209–43.

Honigmann 1953 = Ernst Honigmann, Patristic Studies (Studi e Testi 173), Vatican.

Horster – Reitz 2018 = Marietta Horster – Christiane Reitz, 'Handbooks, Epitomes, and Florilegia', in *A Companion to Late Antique Literature*, ed. by Scott McGill – Edward Watts, New York, pp. 431–50.

Kosiński 2010 = Rafał Kosiński, *The Emperor Zeno: Religion and Politics*, BSC 6, Cracow.

Manafis 2018 = Panagiotis Manafis, *Collections of Historical Excerpts: Accumulation, Selection and Transmission of History in Byzantium*, Diss. Ghent University, Ghent.

Nautin 1992 = Pierre Nautin, 'La continuation de l' "Histoire ecclésiastique" d'Eusèbe par Gélase de Césarée', *Revue des Études Byzantines* 50, pp. 163–83.

Nautin 1994 = Pierre Nautin, 'Théodore Lecteur et sa "réunion de différentes Histoires" de l'Église', *Revue des études byzantines* 52, pp. 213–43.

Németh 2018 = András Németh, *The Excerpta Constantiniana and the Byzantine Appropriation of the Past*, Cambridge.

Ni Mheallaigh 2008 = Karen Ni Mheallaigh, 'Pseudo-Documentarism and the Limits of Ancient Fiction', *American Journal of Philology* 129, pp. 403–31.

Odorico 2014 = Paolo Odorico, 'Du recueil à l'invention du texte: le cas des Parastaseis Syntomoi Chronikai', *Byzantinische Zeitschrift* 107, pp. 755–84.

Speyer 1971 = Wolfgang Speyer, *Die literarische Fälschung im heidnischen und christlichen Altertum: ein Versuch ihrer Deutung*, Handbuch der Altertumswissenschaft, 1. Abt., 2., Munich.

Stevens 2018 = Luke J. Stevens, 'The Origin of the de Boor Fragments Ascribed to Philip of Side', *Journal of Early Christian Studies* 26, pp. 631–57.

Van Ginkel 1995 = Jan Jacob Van Ginkel, *John of Ephesus: A Monophysite Historian in Sixth-Century Byzantium*, Diss. University of Groningen, Groningen.

Van Hoof – Van Nuffelen 2017 = Lieve Van Hoof – Peter Van Nuffelen, 'The Historiography of Crisis: Jordanes, Cassiodorus and Justinian in Mid Sixth-Century Constantinople', *Journal of Roman Studies* 107, pp. 275–300.

Van Nuffelen 2002 = Peter Van Nuffelen, 'Gélase de Césarée, Un compilateur du cinquième siècle', *Byzantinische Zeitschrift* 95, pp. 263–82.

Van Nuffelen 2004 = Peter Van Nuffelen, *Un héritage de paix et de piété: étude sur les histoires ecclésiastiques de Socrate et de Sozomène*, Orientalia Lovaniensia Analecta 142, Leuven.

Van Nuffelen 2019 = Peter Van Nuffelen, 'Review of Gelasius of Caesarea. Ecclesiastical History. The Extant Fragments. With an Appendix Containing the Fragments from Dogmatic Writings. Edited and Translated by Martin Wallraff, Jonathan Stutz and Nicolas Marinides', *Journal of Ecclesiastical History* 70, pp. 148–49.

Van Nuffelen – Van Hoof 2020 = Peter Van Nuffelen – Lieve Van Hoof, eds, *Clavis Historicorum Antiquitatis Posterioris, An Inventory of Late Antique Historiography* (A.D. 300–800), Turnhout.

Wright 1872 = *Catalogue of the Syriac Manuscripts in the British Museum Acquired since the Year 1838*, ed. by William Wright, Part III, London.

Abstract

The chapter offers an inventory of the predecessors of Theodore Lector who composed ecclesiastical histories that overlapped with histories that had been written before. To that end, it edits the fragments of some fragmentary authors. Theodore does not stand out by relying on the accounts of his predecessors but by adopting their very words. It is suggested that this reflects the change in patristic culture whereby citations from acknowledged 'Church Fathers' became crucial for granting authority to statements.

ADRIAN SZOPA

TEXTUAL ANALYSIS OF THE *EPITOME* OF THEODORE ANAGNOSTES' *CHURCH HISTORY* – A FEW REMARKS

When I was going through the process of preparing a translation of the *Epitome* of Theodore Lector's *Church History*, it was not very long before I came to realize that I was confronted with a task apparently both easy and difficult.[1] On the one hand, if we consider the language of the narrative created by the epitomator, in particular as compared with the text of Theodore Lector's original composition, it must be said (objectively) that it is not very difficult in terms of grammar. The scope of the inflectional forms being used and syntactic choices made is definitely limited here. However, it would often turn out that the concise nature of the information content could lead to confusion and even perhaps, on many occasions, to distortions in relation to the original text, which sometimes would have been difficult to avoid in translation. In the present article, I shall take a view of the *Epitome* of Theodore Lector's *Church History* as an independent text and point out certain peculiar characteristics which although they produce more questions than answers should allow us to shed some more light upon the fragmentarily preserved original of Theodore Lector's *Church History*. The crucial point will be to find some insight into the question of how much *Church History* there is in the *Epitome* and to what extent this work can be considered as independent.

There is very little information on the epitomator himself. Apart from some speculative suggestions that could be formulated

[1] Kosiński – Szopa – Twardowska 2019 (polish edition), Kosiński – Twardowska – Zabrocka – Szopa 2021 (english edition).

Studies in Theodore Anagnostes, ed. by Rafał Kosiński & Adrian Szopa, STTA 19 (Turnhout 2021), pp. 39–62
© BREPOLS PUBLISHERS   DOI 10.1484/M.STTA-EB.5.127975

on the basis of his own annotations to the text of the *Epitome*, we have virtually no biographical information on him.[2] Unfortunately, the selection, arrangement, and contents of the works which make up the entire *Epitome* can only tell us a little about the author. His composition can be dated to the years 610–15.[3] In turn, the works from which he had drawn to make his extracts include the church histories by Eusebius of Caesarea, Gelasius of Caesarea, Philip of Side, John Diakrinomenos, and Theodore Lector.[4] The *Epitome* of the latter one can be found preserved in four primary manuscripts: (M) Codex Parisinus suppl. gr. 1156 dating to the 10th–11th centuries, (P) Codex Parisinus gr. 1555

[2] Such grounds for drawing any reasonable conclusions are very uncertain. Of particular value in this regard are apparently the anonymous notes as inserted in the manuscript Codex Parisinus gr. 1555 A following the extracts of John Diakrinomenos' work (fol. 20v–23v) and in the Codex Baroccianus 142 after the *Epitome* of Theodore Lector's *Church History* (240r–v), but only if we assumed that those were composed by the epitomator. Although Bernard Puderon has dedicated a series of articles to these codices (Pouderon 1994, 1997, 1998, 2014), he is only marginally concerned with the figure of the epitomator himself. In one of these articles (Pouderon 1998, p. 183), he attempts to define the religious views held by the author of the notes by referring to him as a Dyophysite with Origenist leanings (*On peut donc le définir comme un diphysite, de tendance origéniste*). Still, he argues that the identification of this particular figure with the epitomator is not very plausible. Considering the complete *Epitome*, Kosiński (Kosiński – Twardowska – Zabrocka – Szopa 2021, p. 231) is correct in pointing out that the epitomator represents the pro-Chalcedon perspective and that he is familiar with the literature of Christian authors, the evidence of which could be found in additions to the text derived from various works of different authors. According to Nautin 1994, pp. 219–25, many of the additions are not the epitomator's own contributions to the text as they were only copied from the original text material. This hypothesis is not very likely, but if we assumed it to be true, it would make our possibilities to arrive at any conclusion on the epitomator even more limited, which just shows how much uncertain the basis for our argumentation really is. We have even less clues on the epitomator's possible origin. Greatrex 2015, p. 139, hypothesizes that he may have come from the East, but there is no irrefutable evidence in support of this view.

[3] Based on Carl de Boor's findings, Opitz 1934, col. 1875 determined the *terminus post quem* for the creation of the *Epitome* to be the year 600, while the *terminus ante quem* – the year 800. Hansen 1995, pp. xxxviii–xxxix narrows this period down to the years 610–15. Treadgold 2007, p. 171 and Blaudeau 2006, p. 536 both follow this particular dating. Kosiński – Twardowska – Zabrocka – Szopa 2021, p. 235) do not call these proposals into question, but they would suggest an earlier dating (years 610–11).

[4] According to the hypothesis proposed by Nautin 1994, pp. 214–15, the epitomator worked on a collection of several Church Histories previously put together by Theodore Lector.

A dating to the 13th–14th centuries, (V) Codex Athos Vatopedi 286 from the 12th century, and (B) Codex Baroccianus 142 from the early 14th century. Correlations among these manuscripts have been a subject of scholarly dispute.[5]

It is very difficult to determine to what extent, in terms of volume and contents,[6] the text of the *Epitome* should overlap with the original *Church History* of Theodore Lector. With the volume taken into consideration, it is assumed that the epitomator would have retained about 10% of the text of the original composition as a result of his work.[7] These opinions are based on the estimates made by G. Ch. Hansen concerning a fragment of the *Epitome* in relation to Theodore Lector's *Historia Tripartita*.[8] Unfortunately, it is much more difficult to venture into conclusions on the original of Theodore's *Church History*. This work survives in a fragmentary form only and even though scholars have discerned traces of the text in a number of extant sources, their arguments for attributing some passages to specific lost works are often highly hypothetical.[9] It seems that what can be considered

---

[5] It is worth comparing the stemmae proposed by Hansen 1995, p. xxxv and Nautin 1994, p. 214. There is rather a general consensus on the assertion that M is a copy of the original complete version of the Epitome. Cf. also Blaudeau 2006, p. 537, Kosiński – Twardowska – Zabrocka – Szopa 2021, p. 234, Manafis 2020, pp. 148–153.

[6] The research indicates very different attitudes of the authors and we certainly cannot treat each epitome as a simple summary of the greater composition. In many cases, they would be quite extensive works, often with considerable degrees of independence in comparison with the original. The authors would not only select details, but they also tended to interpret them sometimes, adding information unknown to the [original] author, and composed the entire work in the original style, which, as Brunt is correct to note (Brunt 1980, p. 478), should rather not allow us to recreate the style of the original. For more on this subject, see e.g. Suski 2017. Hansen asserts that this view is obvious (Hansen 1995, p. xxxix): *Wohl jeder Epitomator, sofern er nicht ganz beschränkt ist, wird sich nicht damit begnügen, das ihm vorliegende Großwerk zu verkürzen, sondern er wird seinerseits etwas Eigenes zugeben suchen.*

[7] Treadgold 2007, p. 171 (although this is, in his own words, a '*rough calculation*'), Pouderon 2014, p. 542: *La proportion entre l'un et l'autre texte est d'aumoins un pour dix.*

[8] Hansen 1995, p. xi and 2–55.

[9] Opitz (1934, cols 1873–75) points to 22 extant fragments of Theodore's *Church History*. In his edition, Hansen 1995, despite his elimination of the passages from the *Parastaseis syntomoi chronikai*, has increased the number of the recognized fragments to 77. To this we should also add the extensive passage entitled Ὑπόθεσις τῆς ἐν Χαλκηδόνι συνόδου, which is allegedly a sort of a summary

as fragments (in the strict sense of this word), i.e., what we can classify as citations or paraphrases based on the original *Church History*, are certainly only 9 passages, of which one survives in two, somewhat different, versions.[10] As material suitable for the purposes of analysis only five of them could be used, namely those fragments which have their counterparts in the *Epitome*: four derived from the work *Contra imaginum calumniatores* by John of Damascus and one excerpt from the acts of the Second Council of Nicaea.[11]

The most extensive fragment is John of Damascus' vividly narrated story of a blasphemy by a man named Olympios, a punishment which would befall him and a miracle taking place on the same occasion.[12] This lengthy 777-word-long passage is reduced in the *Epitome* to a fairly short text of 47 words, which is about 6% of the original.[13] Such a radical (even for an epitome) reduction results in considerable modifications of the content. Let us discuss them in more detail as no other place in the text gives us so much material for comparison. The epitomator reports that the incident took place at the Helenianae Baths (εἰς λουτρὸν Ἐλενιανῶν) and concerns a man named Olympios, who is identified as 'Arian' (Ὀλυμπιός τις Ἀρειανὸς).[14] We do not find the

of the acts of the Council of Chalcedon. For more details, see Hansen 1998, p. 102. For the most recent discussion on this subject, see Kosiński (Kosiński – Twardowska – Zabrocka – Szopa 2021, pp. 136–45), where some of Hansen's attributions are also questioned.

[10] Kosiński – Twardowska – Zabrocka – Szopa 2021, pp. 136–45.

[11] Respectively, Theodore Lector, Fragmenta F1–6a [52a, 51, 22a, 58, 62, 11], and *Fragmentum* 7 [2] and 8 [35] (ed. Kosiński – Twardowska – Zabrocka – Szopa 2021). All references to Theodore Lector and the page numbers refer to the edition by Kosiński – Twardowska – Zabrocka – Szopa 2021. The counterpart of a specific excerpt as per Hansen's edition (Hansen 1995) is given in square brackets.

[12] Johannes Damascenus, *Contra imaginum calumniatores, or.* 3, Florilegium III, 90 (ed. Kotter 1975) and the corresponding Theodorus Lector, *Fragmentum* 1 [52a] (ed. Kosiński – Twardowska – Zabrocka – Szopa 2021). For the corresponding epitome passage, see *Epitome* 115 [465] (ed. Kosiński – Twardowska – Zabrocka – Szopa 2021).

[13] Victor of Tunnuna also cites the same narrative, with a similar proportion of the reduced text which accounts for around 4% of the original (reduction ratio: 777 to 32 words). The greater degree of textual reduction may be due to a change from one language to another.

[14] For the baths of the Helenianae palace, see Janin 1950, p. 130 and Crow – Bardill – Bayliss 2008, pp. 10, 230–31. For Olympios and Euthymios, see the article by G. Greatrex in the present publication.

date of the event as stated in Theodore's original text (Ὑπὸ δὲ ταύτην τὴν ὑπατείαν κατὰ τὸν μῆνα τὸν Δεκέμβριον)[15] and the more detailed characteristics of Olympios, which also included the name of Euthymios, the bishop of the Arian community and the superior of Olympios (Ὀλύμπιος γάρ τις τοὔνομα Εὐθυμίου τοῦ τῆς Ἀρείου θρησκείας ἐξάρχοντος τὸν βαδιστὴν παραχορεύων). Further on, the *Epitome* tells us about the character of Olympios' transgression, which is described as an 'audacious blasphemy' (τολμηρῶς βλασφημήσας). The epitomator is not concerned with the exact nature of this deed or its circumstances (as risqué as they may seem to be). Likewise, the role of Magnos, a presbyter at the Church of the Holy Apostles in Periteichisma, is not mentioned at all.[16] The greatest reduction can be found in the excerpt on the events taking place after the blasphemous act, which also included an account of Olympios' torment and death. Although this is understandable in a way, since this particular excerpt is the least 'factual' of all,[17] what we have here is a perfect example of the difference between the *Church History* and its epitome: a proportion ratio of 191 to 6 (words) speaks for itself.[18] The original *Church History* of Theodore Lector also reports the fact that

[15] Incidentally, this date has been a subject of some controversy. In the classic edition PG XCIV, 1388D, it is given as ἔχοντα αὐτὸν εἰκάδα καὶ πέμπτην ἡμέραν. Nonetheless, εἰκάδα is an emendation of τριακάδα which is the form found in the manuscript. Hansen follows this interpolated lection in his edition (cf. Hansen 1995, p. 131). However, the latest edition of John of Damascus' work disproves this emendation as groundless and keeps τριακάδα. We have assumed this version to be valid in the recent edition of Theodore Lector, which has been justified in ample detail Kosiński – Twardowska – Zabrocka – Szopa 2021, p. 146, n. 172.

[16] We have no information relating to Magnos. For the Church of the Holy Apostles in Periteichisma, see Janin 1969, p. 50.

[17] Of course, if we assume that the epitomator wished to enrich the narrative with the factual information as much as possible, which would seem to be natural, but is not necessarily so. Brunt 1980, p. 487 is right in concluding that *Epitomators in general seem to have aimed not at producing faithful resumés but at recording, sometimes at length, what they thought of most interest, and their principles of selection are at times impenetrable.*

[18] From our viewpoint, this specific passage contains quite a lot of useful information. Theodore writes about the holy spring that supplied water to the baths, Anastasius as a reigning emperor, the Church of Saint Stephen the First Martyr, erected by Aurelian during his consulship, and refers to someone named John, presbyter and ekdikos of that church (as we can see, quite a lot of informative content).

Olympios was a neophyte who converted from Orthodox Christianity to Arianism (as we shall yet see further on). It is worth stressing that there is a certain misrepresentation of facts here on the epitomator's part as he states that some unidentified group of 'the faithful' (οἱ πιστοὶ) would be responsible for the making and hanging of the picture (which portrayed the miracle in question), while Theodore makes it clear that the person behind this action was the emperor Anastasius.

The second part of Theodore's narrative, certainly of particular interest to John, was focused on the picture and the surrounding circumstances. According to the epitomator's account, some Arians (ὑπό τινων Ἀρειανῶν) were to use a bribe (χρήματα λαβὼν) to persuade a certain man named Eutychian, who was in charge of the baths (Εὐτυχιανός τις τῶν διαιταρίων ὁ πρῶτος) to take down the painting. It would lead to his death as a result of some gangrenous disease of the body (αὐτὸς τὸ σῶμα δαπανηθεὶς ἀπώλετο). A much more extended account of the same occurrence which can be found in Theodore Lector does not contribute much in the way of new pieces of information. The miracle itself is depicted here in great detail, with some new threads thrown in, yet the fact that they cannot be found in the *Epitome* is by all means understandable. The only thing that should come as a surprise here is the emperor Anastasius' role in the whole story. The epitomator passes over Theodore's mention that it was the emperor himself who would have the picture reinstalled. It is evident then that the omission of the ruler's role (however positive it may have been even from the perspective of the pro-Chalcedon epitomator) in the both parts of the account is done deliberately.

This case illustrates how differently the emphasis may have been placed. Theodore's more extended narrative is very much reduced into a brief recollection in the *Epitome*. It still can be seen that the epitomator makes a conscious move to interfere in the textual transmission. Not only does he pass over the emperor's role in the whole thing, but he also omits the theological subtleties connected with the Arian heresy. The epitomator makes a mention referring to the Arians, but we can observe here that he is much less preoccupied with the doctrinal nature of the controversy than Theodore, which fits in with a summary character of the *Epitome*.[19] It is possible that, as Greatrex has noted when also analyzing the material in the *Historia Tripartita*, the epitomator actually reflects Theodore's negative attitude towards the followers of Arius' teachings, but he does not offer many details of it.[20] It would appear that by the seventh century the Arian controversy should not have aroused such strong emotions as even a hundred years earlier, and the relatively great number of references to Arians across the *Epitome* may have also been due to the presence of the same subject matter in Theodore.

Aside from the factual content of the *Epitome*, it should be said that on a style level it would be difficult to recognise elements of Theodore Lector's style in the *Epitome*'s transmission. Some lexical elements are the same, while the sentences are definitely very different and it would be hard to find many common features. The epitomator does not attempt to imitate his source in this respect.

The other excerpt from Theodore's work is cited by John of Damascus, but it is unfortunately very short and does not allow us to venture into much deliberation.[21] As a reflection of his

[19] No other dogmatic considerations can be found there, only statements like 'the synod of Chalcedon had determined the true faith' (Theodorus Lector, *Epitome* 38 [373] (ed. Kosiński – Twardowska – Zabrocka – Szopa 2021): ἡ μὲν σύνοδος ἡ ἐν Χαλκηδόνι τὴν ἀληθῆ πίστιν ἐκύρωσε).

[20] For more on this subject, see the article of Geoffrey Greatrex in the present volume. Indeed, it should be admitted that the questions connected with Arians can be found in the *Epitome* surprisingly often. Let us note that the excerpt under consideration is also present in the course of a few other narratives concerning Arians: the passage being discussed here is the third record in a row. Earlier (Theodorus Lector, *Epitome* 113 [462], ed. Kosiński – Twardowska – Zabrocka – Szopa 2021), a reference is made to Theodoric the Amal, who – though an Arian himself – summoned a synod of orthodox bishops, while at *Epitome* 114 [463] (ed. Kosiński – Twardowska – Zabrocka – Szopa 2021), we read that the same ruler had an orthodox deacon at his court, who decided to convert to Arianism, and we get to know the consequences. Some other references to Arian believers can be found at *Epitome* 31 [366]; 90 [431]; 102 [448]; 122 [475] (ed. Kosiński – Twardowska – Zabrocka – Szopa 2021).
Incidentally, let us also mention the transmission in Victor of Tunnuna concerning what happened at the Hellenianae Baths (Kosiński – Twardowska – Zabrocka – Szopa 2021, p. 168 [52b]). This author puts emphasis on some other aspects. He refers to the first miracle only stressing that the blasphemy was against the Holy Trinity and adding several details about the guilty man's death, which would only correspond with John of Damascus' account to a certain extent.

[21] Theodorus Lector, *Fragmentum* 3 [22a] and *Epitome* 85 [425] (ed. Kosiński – Twardowska – Zabrocka – Szopa 2021).

own interests, the author of the florilegium quotes the following passage from Theodore: Εἰς τοσοῦτον γὰρ ἐληλύθει τῆς τόλμης, ὥστε καὶ τὰ τῶν ἐκεῖ γεγονότων μακαρίων ποιμένων ὀνόματα τῶν ἱερῶν διπτύχων ἀνεῖλε καὶ τὰς αὐτῶν εἰκόνας καθεῖλε κατακαύσας τυραννικῶς.[22] In the *Epitome*, whose account is more extended at this place, the counterpart reads as follows: καὶ ἐκ τῶν διπτύχων περιελὼν τὰ ὀνόματα Προτερίου καὶ Τιμοθέου τοῦ Σαλοφακιάλου τὰ τῶν καθηρημένων ἐνέγραψε, Διοσκόρου καὶ τοῦ Αἰλούρου.[23] As can be seen, this particular fragment (taken out of context) would only refer to the fact that 'the names of the shepherds who had died in that time' were removed from the holy diptychs (τὰ τῶν ἐκεῖ γεγονότων μακαρίων ποιμένων ὀνόματα), whereas the *Epitome* provides at this place more factual information drawn out of the broader context of Theodore's narrative and makes it clear who was deposed and who was entered into the holy books. Those details must have certainly been included in the *Church History*, but they were not essential to John's deliberations. On the other hand, the epitomator passes over the question most important to John, namely the removal and burning of the bishops' images. Despite its brevity, this fragment shows very clearly the shifts in emphasis between the original work and the instances of the later use of the same composition.

Another brief quote from Theodore Anagnostes' *Church History*, as found in John of Damascus' work, describes the actions taken by Patriarch Timothy of Constantinople.[24] He would refuse to begin the liturgy before making sure that no image of Macedonius, his predecessor, could be found within the church.[25] The difference in content between Theodore's fragment and the *Epitome* is minimal and could be basically reduced to the fact

---

[22] For he had gone so far in [his] arrogance that he removed from the holy diptychs the names of the shepherds who had died in that time; he further destroyed the images of them and like a despot, had them burned (trans. Kosiński – Twardowska – Zabrocka – Szopa 2021, p. 155).

[23] He then removed the names of Proterios and Timothy Salophakialos from the diptychs and inscribed those of the deposed, Dioskoros and Ailouros (trans. Kosiński – Twardowska – Zabrocka – Szopa 2021, p. 305).

[24] Theodorus Lector, *Fragmentum* 4 [58] and *Epitome* 139 [493] (ed. Kosiński – Twardowska – Zabrocka – Szopa 2021).

[25] On this particular occurrence, see also the article of Kamilla Twardowska in the present volume.

that the epitomator states the name of Timothy, who in John's version of the text is only described as 'this impious man' (Οὗτος ὁ ἀνόσιος). It would not necessarily testify to the epitomator's more favourable attitude towards Timothy, but only to his wish for a concise and precise transmission. All the other alterations are only of a stylistic and lexical nature. Theodore's more complex construction, laden with participles and elaborated conditional structure, is replaced, in the epitomator's version, with three simple sentences (of which two are conditional structures). The epitomator also tends to keep it simple in the lexical field, e.g., the original expression 'the sacred house' (τοὺς σεπτοὺς οἴκους) is replaced with 'church' (ἐκκλησία), while the verb καθαιρέω – with κατασπάω (representing a similar semantic range).

Another passage which would make it possible to confront the epitomator's work with the original is a slightly more complex matter. This narrative concerns the miraculous healing of a painter's withered hand by Gennadius. A relevant fragment from Theodore that we could consider to be close to the original, just like the ones discussed previously, can be found in John of Damascus' work, but it is also incorporated, in a fuller form, in a different manuscript tradition which is more strictly corresponding with the epitomator's text.[26] The fragment as found in the Codex Parisinus gr. 1115 is longer than that of John, while some details (as we shall see) should suggest that the epitomator may have used such a lection of Theodore's original. On the other hand, John of Damascus' florilegium appears to be more in agreement with Theodore in terms of style and it would be difficult to find some definitive resolution here. Eventually, we have three texts that relate the same event, with two being literal citations or paraphrases close to citations, while the third one is the passage from the *Epitome* which draws on the original. If we analyze and compare all these three accounts, some differences can be observed.

According to John's florilegium, a certain painter who painted an image of Christ had both his hands withered (τὼ χεῖρε ἀπέψυκτο). This text also contains the literary form of dual (already

---

[26] Codex Parisinus gr. 1115, 265ᵛ, 7–19 and Theodorus Lector, *Epitome* 47 [382] (ed. Kosiński – Twardowska – Zabrocka – Szopa 2021) respectively.

known since Homer's time, but already obsolete by the time of the period under consideration), which very well corresponds with everything that can be concluded on Theodore's ornate and very much rhetorized style. In the other version, this piece of information is somewhat modified and it is written that only one hand was affected by this condition (τὴν χεῖρα ἐξηράνθη). The epitomator's account is quite evidently based on this version of the text. The sentence begins with the expression that clarifies the context: 'in Gennadius' time' (Ἐπὶ Γενναδίου), after which the whole thing is re-edited and the structure becomes very much simplified. This is interesting in that the verb (the predicate in here) is not changed at all. The original phrase Ζωγράφος τις […] τὴν χεῖρα ἐξηράνθη is replaced with ἡ χεὶρ τοῦ ζωγράφου ἐξηράνθη. This punishment falls on the painter as he dared to paint an image of Christ in imitation of pagan depictions of Zeus. The three accounts are all in agreement at this particular point, but even though the epitomator does not go beyond this statement, the broad accounts refer to some uncertain (ἐλέγετο) opinions according to which some pagan man commissioned such a painting with the covert intention of worshipping Zeus. These two narratives also provide more detailed descriptions of this painted image, which cannot be found in the *Epitome*. It is also noteworthy that John of Damascus' account is cut short here, while the other transmission and the *Epitome* tell the reader of how a painted representation of Christ should look.[27] However, the epitomator approaches his source text here with reserve, adding the phrase 'the historian says' (φησὶ δὲ ὁ ἱστορῶν). Moreover, a considerable factual disparity can be noticed here as well. While the longer account of the Codex Parisinus gr. 1115 speaks of the thick and curly hair (οὖλον καὶ πολύτριχα), the epitomator refers to something completely different (τὸ οὖλον καὶ ὀλιγότριχον). Also, both sources state that Gennadius was responsible for the healing of the painter, though the *Epitome* does not give any details of this event, while it is described in more detail in the other narrative. Due to the existence of the two versions of the original text, this specific fragment is difficult to interpret, but it

---

[27] One of the first opinions on this subject as attested in sources. For more information, see Skrzyniarz 2007.

seems that the epitomator's relation, as it is closest chronologically to the *Church History* and uninvolved in the controversy over the icon worship, should be regarded (in spite of many details missing there) as reliable in a discussion of the value which the two excerpts may have for reconstructing Theodore Lector's original narrative.[28]

The last excerpt which has its counterpart in the *Epitome* can be found in the acts of the Second Council of Nicaea and it seems that it does not contribute much to our discussion. Essentially, both accounts deal with the election of Anatolius to Archbishop of Constantinople, but they are very different as far as details are concerned.[29] It may be due to the epitomator's independence (as I have stressed here several times) as well as to the fact that the particular fragment of Book V of Theodore's *Church History* as included in the council acts is taken completely out of context here. In the *Epitome*, this excerpt is placed within a specific time-frame from the beginning, with the deposition and the subsequent murder of Flavian being mentioned. This detail cannot be found in the relevant surviving fragment of Theodore, which may have come as the result of the fact that the circumstances of this occurrence were originally present in the lost narrative which was antecedent to the extant text. As a matter of fact, however, the precise time context is also given in Theodore's account as well. According to the final preserved sentence of the fragment, it took place 'during the consulate of Protogenes and Asturios' (i.e., in the year 449). Besides, both narratives tell us that Dioskoros elected Anatolius; according to Theodore, he served as *apocrisiarios* in the Church of Alexandria, while the *Epitome* refers to him as the personal *apocrisiarios* to Dioskoros, which is of course one and the same thing. At this point, however, the narratives of the two fragments start to diverge. The epitomator does not mention details such as Eutyches' presence, the common liturgy, and the words spoken by Anatolius – all of them found in Theodore's account. According to the epitomator's relation, Dioskoros was disappointed in his calculations as Anatolius 'had

---

[28] For the dating of the Codex Parisinus gr. 1150 see Alexakis 1996.

[29] Theodorus Lector, *Fragmentum* 7 [2] and *Epitome* 16 [351] (ed. Kosiński – Twardowska – Zabrocka – Szopa 2021).

different views as to the nature of God's providence' (θεὸν δὲ ἔσχε καὶ ἐν τούτῳ τὰ ἐναντία οἰκονομοῦντα). Apparently, behind this sentence, there was a much broader narrative which in Theodore's composition would follow the excerpt mentioned in the council acts, but this is a purely speculative hypothesis and we have no evidence to support it. It was simply beyond the interest of those who prepared an extract from the *Church History* for the purposes of the council and it was not included in the fragment we have cited.

It can be seen in light of the excerpts above that although the amount of text material for analysis is not large, some regularities can be observed.[30] The epitomator's approach to the text is creative as he not only selects the items of information in order to use them in his work, but he also reshapes the content, while the entire composition is presented in a form whose style departs very much from the original. The narration is not only concise, but also stylistically simplified, even though it does not mean that the epitomator makes no attempt to deliver this shortened material in a stylistically embellished manner. Despite the fact that epitomes should be quite naturally characterized by brevity and many simplifications,[31] the author ensures the diversity and richness of the narrative style.[32]

The florid style of Theodore Lector's *Church History* requires the extensive usage of various inflectional forms and the *Epitome* is marked by a similar degree of diversity as well. The richness

---

[30] Should we assume that Hansen's reconstructions are correct, there are at least several other fragments which have their counterparts in the *Epitome* and could be subjected to analysis. The problem is that each corresponding passage of the *Epitome* is reconstructed on the basis of Theophanes' *Chronographia*, and I believe it is dubious to consider them as reflecting the contents of the *Epitome* in full. For a broader coverage of this subject, see the article of Dariusz Brodka in the present volume.

[31] It should be noted that the distinction of genre-specific determinants for the epitome is problematic. In addition, it seems that the epitomator's work (analyzed as a whole) contains elements of both *epitomae auctoris* and *epitomae res tractatae*. Further genre-related research in this particular area is certainly still required.

[32] On the author's literary aspirations, see Hansen 1995, p. xxxix: *Daß unser nicht unbelesener Epitomator auf literarische Ansprüche nicht ganz verzichten mochte, zeigt er übrigens durch den, allerdinge keineswegs regelmäßig angewendeten, akzentuierenden Klauserhythmus, der seinem Produkt ein literarisches Gepräge verleihen soll.* For a similar view, see Blaudeau 2006, p. 537.

of all kinds of inflectional forms can be found in the text. To illustrate this point, it is enough to refer to the forms which are most essential in a language. The verbs are used here in all the modes (the imperative forms can be found as well, which is not something we would expect in a composition like this) and tenses. It remains inexplicable in most cases, of course, where the epitomator followed the original text or where he decided to use some specific form, but this stylistic abundance is definitely noteworthy. There is no doubt that the aorist is the principal tense of the narrative. For 155 fragments of the *Epitome*, this tense is used as many as 141 times in the main clause (or one of the main clauses). The amount of aorist participles is even greater. If the *imperfectum* is used as the predicate of the main clause, it is only in the case of repetitive actions or actions taking place over a certain time, not any one-time events. The *praesens* is used more than a dozen times often following the *genetivus absolutus* syntactic structure,[33] most likely in order to accentuate the rapid sequence of events, but there are also places where we encounter the historical/narrative *praesens*[34] (in this case, the purpose is to achieve a more dynamic pace of narration, which may be stressed, for instance, by a preposition[35]). The present tense can also be found where the epitomator makes direct references to Theodore's statements or indirectly communicated opinions,[36] but also when he speaks of the documents appended.[37] For obvious reasons, the epitomator makes use of the *praesens* when writing about actions which are contemporary to him and continuous.[38] The *perfectum*

---

[33] Theodorus Lector, *Epitome* 6 [341], 7 [342], 8[343], 27 [362], 41 [376], 54 [389], 61 [396], 75 [411], 80 [417], 153 [522] (ed. Kosiński – Twardowska – Zabrocka – Szopa 2021).

[34] Theodorus Lector 2020, *Epitome* 11 [346], 13 [348], 33 [368], 44 [379], 55 [390], 57 [392], 79 [416], 99 [440], 101 [446], 105 [450], 127 [481], 132 [486], 143 [499] (ed. Kosiński – Twardowska – Zabrocka – Szopa 2021).

[35] e.g. εὐθὺς in Theodorus Lector *Epitome* 57 [392] (ed. Kosiński – Twardowska – Zabrocka – Szopa 2021).

[36] Theodorus Lector, *Epitome* 17 [352], 98 [439], 148 [515] (ed. Kosiński – Twardowska – Zabrocka – Szopa 2021).

[37] Theodorus Lector, *Epitome* 151 [520] (ed. Kosiński – Twardowska – Zabrocka – Szopa 2021).

[38] Theodorus Lector, *Epitome* 134 [488], 512 [146], 516 [149] (ed. Kosiński – Twardowska – Zabrocka – Szopa 2021).

is used eight times[39] and the *plusquamperfectum* three times,[40] the use of these tenses is always justified in terms of meaning and structure.

The very sophisticated syntactic structures employed by Theodore Lector becomes very much simplified in the *Epitome*. The epitomator tends to avoid using subordinate clauses, but there is an enormous number of participles on display instead. The *genetivus absolutus* is used very commonly and much more often than in classical Greek, which is not out of the ordinary in that period.[41] In the extant *Epitome*, the conditional sentences can be found seven times.[42] Other notable syntactical structures include the *accusativus cum infinitivo*, of which there are many examples in the text.

Some lexical peculiarities can be found as well, especially as regards certain mannerisms of Theodore/epitomator and some interesting departures from them. For instance, there are diverse names referring to the city of Constantinople. Besides the most common designation 'Constantinople' (ἡ Κωνσταντινούπολις), we have expressions such as 'the Queen' (ἡ βασιλίς), 'imperial city' (ἡ βασιλίς πόλις), or simply 'the city' (ἡ πόλις). We can encounter traces of such phraseology in the very few surviving fragments of Theodore's *Church History*.[43] The name 'Byzantium' is not used even once in the *Epitome*,[44] but there is one instance where the inhabitants of the capital city are called 'Byzantinians'.[45] However, it does not seem that the epitomator avoids using the name

---

[39] Theodorus Lector, *Epitome* 15 [350], 24 [359], 74 [410], 82 [420], 95 [436], 101 [446], 127 [481], 146 [512] (ed. Kosiński – Twardowska – Zabrocka – Szopa 2021).

[40] Theodorus Lector, *Epitome* 52 [387], 73 [409], 127 [481] (ed. Kosiński – Twardowska – Zabrocka – Szopa 2021).

[41] Funk 1961, p. 218 n. 423.

[42] Theodorus Lector, *Epitome* 101 [446], 123 [477], 136 [490], 138 [492], 139 [493], 142 [496] (ed. Kosiński – Twardowska – Zabrocka – Szopa 2021).

[43] Theodorus Lector, *Fragmentum* 1 [52a] (ed. Kosiński – Twardowska – Zabrocka – Szopa 2021).

[44] In the passages which Hansen considers as *Epitome* [452, 470, 511, 519] and reconstructs them on the basis of Theophanes and the *Synodicon Vetus*, the name Byzantium is used several times, which may be an argument against holding them to be literal fragments of the *Epitome*.

[45] Theodorus Lector, *Epitome* 153 [522] (ed. Kosiński – Twardowska – Zabrocka – Szopa 2021): ὑπὸ τῶν Βυζαντίων.

Byzantium deliberately as it can be found in the *Epitome* from the *Church History* by John Diakrinomenos.[46] On this basis, we could come to conclusion that Theodore did not use the name Byzantium in his *Church History*, while the epitomator would simply follow in the footsteps of the original, at least in this regard.

'Diptychs' (τὰ διπτύχα) is another interesting term here. The word is used multiple times throughout the sources in question due to the diptychs' significance in the Church of that period as a beacon of orthodoxy and the Eucharistic communion. In the extant fragments of Theodore's work, they are mentioned twice as τὰ ἱερὰ διπτύχα,[47] while in the *Epitome* they can be found more than a dozen times, not always with τὰ ἱερὰ added to them. A case of particular interest is the place where the diptychs are described once as the 'holy tablets' (αἱ ἱεραὶ δέλτοι).[48] The term ἡ δέλτος itself has no religious connotation (as it refers to a tablet only), but in the plural form, accompanied by the epithet μυστικός or ἱερός, it assumes this particular meaning. It is not certain if this term was used by Theodore himself or introduced by the epitomator with the aim of enriching his narration. If the latter possibility is correct, it would be just another example of the epitomator's efforts to add more diversity to his narrative in spite of its apparent brevity. In any case, it appears that this passage should be given a little more attention and I shall return to this question further on.

Attempts to produce this desired *varietas* can also be seen at those places where the epitomator refers to someone's death. For obvious reasons, such pieces of information have to occur on multiple occasions and the epitomator communicates them in several ways instead of using the same phrases in each particular case. He usually formulates the indicative sentence in the aorist with the use of the verb τελευτάω or ἀποθνήσκω.[49] In other cases,

---

[46] Theodorus Lector, *Epitome* from John Diakrinomenos 3 [527] (ed. Kosiński – Twardowska – Zabrocka – Szopa 2021).

[47] Theodorus Lector, *Fragmentum* 3 [22a] and 5 [62] (ed. Kosiński – Twardowska – Zabrocka – Szopa 2021).

[48] Theodorus Lector, *Epitome* 22 [357] (ed. Kosiński – Twardowska – Zabrocka – Szopa 2021).

[49] Theodorus Lector, *Epitome* 18 [353] (ed. Kosiński – Twardowska – Zabrocka – Szopa 2021): Θεοδόσιος ἐξελθὼν ... ἐτελεύτησε; 32 [367]: Μαρκιανὸς ... ἐτελεύτησεν; 74 [410]: Ἰουλιανὸς ... ἀπέθανεν; 79 [416]: Ὁ Αἴλουρος ... ἀπέθανε.

53

he would use the structure *genetivus absolutus* with the verbs τελευτάω or, rarely, τελειόω.[50] It would be difficult to assume that the need to remain faithful to the original was the reason for such linguistic choices in each specific instance.

At some places, despite his tendency to make the text more varied, the epitomator is very much consistent in staying true to his terminology. This is quite evident in the passages where the narrative deals with elections of new bishops. In the *Epitome*, the bishops are most often ordained, which the epitomator would denote with the verbs χειροτονέω or προχειροτονέω.[51] In an attempt to enrich his narrative, particularly in brief passages, he would only refer to one bishop being succeeded (διαδέχομαι) by another.[52] A more subtle distinction is represented here by the verb προβάλλω, which signifies that a specific candidate was proposed for the office, this eventually always leading up to his ordination in such circumstances.[53] The new bishop could also succeed (ἀντεισάγω) his predecessor.[54] As a matter of fact, it is only twice that the epitomator allows himself to use some other expressions in this specific context and he does it only on the occasion when, in his view, the elevation was unlawful.[55] In the same context, we

---

[50] It is also notable that in the passage which Hansen reconstructs on the basis of Theophanes' account (Theoph. AM 5973 = Hansen 1995, *Epitome* 421, p. 116) there is also a phrase relating to death as well as an example of the *ablativus absolutus* with the verb κοιμάω, which cannot be found in the *Epitome*. This is just another example of the disparity between the places reconstructed from Theophanes and the remaining passages of the *Epitome*.

[51] The verb χειροτονέω can be found at Theodorus Lector, *Epitome* 5 [340], 8 [343], 27 [362], 35 [370], 46 [381], 57 [392], 79 [416], 145 [507] (referring to the election of a hegumen), 154 [523]. The verb προχειροτονέω – to be found at Theodorus Lector, *Epitome* 41 [376], 57 [392], 75 [411], 80 [417], 99 [440], 100 [445] (ed. Kosiński – Twardowska – Zabrocka – Szopa 2021).

[52] Theodorus Lector, *Epitome* 7 [342], 54 [389] (ed. Kosiński – Twardowska – Zabrocka – Szopa 2021).

[53] Theodorus Lector, *Epitome* 16 [351], 44 [379], 138 [492], 154 [523] (ed. Kosiński – Twardowska – Zabrocka – Szopa 2021).

[54] Theodorus Lector, *Epitome* 14 [349], 79 [416] (ed. Kosiński – Twardowska – Zabrocka – Szopa 2021).

[55] Theodorus Lector, *Epitome* 36 [371] (ed. Kosiński – Twardowska – Zabrocka – Szopa 2021) – referring to the unlawful elevation (ἡ ἄθεσμος προαγωγή) of Timothy Aelouros; Theodorus Lector, *Epitome* 57 [392] – Peter the Fuller usurps the bishop's throne for himself (τυραννικῶς ὁ Κναφεὺς τῷθρόνῳ ἐπεπήδησεν). Still, it does not mean that χειροτονέω or προχειροτονέω signified, in the epitomator's

could cite a passage where the issue of a bishop's election is mentioned three times.[56] The epitomator refers there to an unlawful take-over of the bishop's throne by Peter the Fuller (τυραννικῶς ὁ Κναφεὺς τῷ θρόνῳ ἐπεπήδησεν), who would then proceed to ordain a man named John as Bishop of Apamea, although he had already been deposed previously (χειροτονεῖ εὐθὺς ἐπίσκοπον Ἀπαμείας Ἰωάννην τινὰ ἀπὸ καθαιρέσεως), and after Peter the Fuller's banishment, Julian was ordained on the strength of a joint vote in his favour (Ψήφῳ δὲ κοινῇ Ἰουλιανός τις εἰς ἐπίσκοπον προχειρίζεται). Likewise, at the passage 79 [416], the question of a bishop's appointment turns up three times and the epitomator uses a different term for each time.[57] In turn, in a fragment where there is a reference to the appointment of the hegumen of the Stoudite monastery, a form derived from the verb χειροτονέω is used three times.[58]

The epitomator uses the expression ὁ Ῥώμης ἐπίσκοπος with reference to the Bishop of Rome.[59] A slightly different designation can be found at *Epitome* 121 [474], referring to the bishop of 'older' Rome (τὸν τῆς μεγάλης Ῥώμης ἐπίσκοπον), but this appears in the particular context of emphasizing the pontifical dignity and is uttered by Patriarch Macedonius of Constantinople. There is one instance of a departure from the consistent use of this terminology where the bishop is called πάπας.[60] Once again, it seems that no extra communication is intended to be conveyed here, except for some stylistic considerations on account

---

eyes, an election in accordance with the canons or a desired one (from his point of view), which can also be seen in many other situations.

[56] Theodorus Lector, *Epitome* 57 [392] (ed. Kosiński – Twardowska – Zabrocka – Szopa 2021).

[57] Theodorus Lector, *Epitome* 79 [416] (ed. Kosiński – Twardowska – Zabrocka – Szopa 2021).

[58] Theodorus Lector, *Epitome* 145 [507] (ed. Kosiński – Twardowska – Zabrocka – Szopa 2021).

[59] Theodorus Lector, *Epitome* 10 [345], 24 [359], 26 [361], 75 [411], 90 [431], 112 [461], 113 [462] (ed. Kosiński – Twardowska – Zabrocka – Szopa 2021). Incidentally, it is worth reverting to the question of reconstructing the *Epitome* on the basis of Theophanes. At one passage (cf. Hansen 1995, *Epitome* 423, p. 117), as reconstructed on the basis of Theophanes, the title ἐπίσκοπος is omitted and this is something completely out of the ordinary in the *Epitome*.

[60] Theodorus Lector, *Epitome* 24 [359] (ed. Kosiński – Twardowska – Zabrocka – Szopa 2021).

of the fact that several lines further on, at the same place, the phrase Λέων δὲ ὁ ἐπίσκοπος can be found (apparently, the epitomator wished to avoid repeating the same phrasing).

Some diversity can also be seen in referring to the churches as buildings.[61] In most cases, the epitomator makes use of the word ἡ ἐκκλησία, which may signify the institutional Church, a local community, but also the Great Church of Constantinople. At times, when referring to the latter, he adds the adjective μεγάλη.[62] It is definitely less often that a church building is named as ὁ ναός and this designation is mostly used with reference to the churches in Constantinople other than the Great Church.[63] Outside the capital city, this expression is only used with reference to the churches of Saint Euphemia and the Martyress Bassa (both at Chalcedon) and the Basilica Church of Saint Peter in Rome,[64] while the more specific term τό ἀποστολεῖον is used to refer to the Apostoleion of Saint Thomas the Apostle.[65] The epitomator strays from his preferred choice of phrases only twice. At *Epitome* 28 [363], there is a mention of the 'houses of prayer' (ὁ εὐκτήριος οἶκος), but it does not come as much of a surprise since this passage is most probably a later interpolation.[66] A more interesting passage can be found at 22 [357], where none of the above expressions is used to refer to the Church of the Holy Apostles (εἰς τοὺς ἀποστόλους ἐτάφη).[67] Let us add that this is exactly the

---

[61] The exception is made for monasteries, which are referred to as τό μοναστήριον (e.g. Theodorus Lector *Epitome* 12 [347], 73 [409], 134 [488] (ed. Kosiński – Twardowska – Zabrocka – Szopa 2021) or ἡ μονή (e.g., Theodorus Lector, *Epitome* 52 [387], 67 [403], 145 [507] (ed. Kosiński – Twardowska – Zabrocka – Szopa 2021) at all times.

[62] Theodorus Lector, *Epitome* 41 [376], 129 [483] (ed. Kosiński – Twardowska – Zabrocka – Szopa 2021).

[63] Theodorus Lector, *Epitome* 49 [384], 99 [440], 129 [483], 140 [494] (ed. Kosiński – Twardowska – Zabrocka – Szopa 2021).

[64] Respectively, Theodorus Lector, *Epitome* 25 [360] (ed. Kosiński – Twardowska – Zabrocka – Szopa 2021): ἐν τῷ ναῷ Εὐφημίας τῆς μάρτυρος; 55 [390]: τοῦ ἐν Χαλκηδόνι ναοῦ Βάσσης τῆς μάρτυρος; 90 [431]: ἐν τῷ ἀποστολικῷ τοῦ κορυφαίου ναῷ. For the Church of Saint Euphemia, see Janin 1969, pp. 120–24. On the church dedicated to the martyress Bassa, see Janin 1975, pp. 33–34.

[65] Theodorus Lector *Epitome* 59 [394] (ed. Kosiński – Twardowska – Zabrocka – Szopa 2021).

[66] Mango 1998, pp. 61–75, Twardowska 2017, p. 92.

[67] For the Church of the Holy Apostles in Constantinople, see Kazdhan 1991, p. 940.

same passage where the sole instance of the word 'tablet', as referring to the holy diptychs, is attested. These two departures in the narration which is otherwise quite consistent in employing a certain lexical repertoire and in such a laconic record may raise some questions as to its place in the *Epitome*.

Theodore himself makes appearance in the epitomator's narration at least about a dozen or more times. As a general rule, such references are without his name and only limited to phrases like 'as he says' (φησι, ὡς λέγει, λέγει δὲ οὗτος).[68] Sometimes, he is also called 'historian' (ὁ ἱστορῶν).[69] The author's name can be found at just one place in the text.[70] It appears that the epitomator would make references to Theodore in two types of situations. The first one would cover all those instances where he approached the opinions found in the original composition with some reserve. At times, e.g. where the Patriarch of Thessalonica is mentioned, the manner of statement is so assertive that we are able to discern the epitomator's considerable reserve towards the details found there.[71] The other sort of situation can be noticed at the places where Theodore inserted original documents in his work, to which the narrative would refer, and the epitomator decides to communicate it to his readers. In that case, he uses the verb 'attach' (ἐντάττω) in various forms, mostly in the *perfectum*.[72] In three instances, the epitomator refers to other

---

[68] Theodorus Lector, *Epitome* 7 [342], 18 [353], 94 [435] (ed. Kosiński – Twardowska – Zabrocka – Szopa 2021).

[69] Theodorus Lector, *Epitome* 17 [352], 47 [382], 148 [515].

[70] Theodorus Lector, *Epitome* 38 [373] (ed. Kosiński – Twardowska – Zabrocka – Szopa 2021): Ἔστί δὲ τῶν ἀντιγραφέντων γνῶναι τὴν δύναμιν τῶν ταῖς ἐπιστολαῖς ἐντυγχάνοντῶν, ὧν ἔταξεν ὁ Θεόδωρος. Let us note that the grammar structure of this sentence is quite tortuous and it is difficult to propose any definitive and incontrovertible translation. Hansen (1995: 105, 18–19) has suggested the following emendation: τῷ ταῖς ἐπιστολαῖς ἐντυγχάνοντι ἃς. It is difficult to answer the question if the text is corrupt here and this peculiar one-time-only presence of Theodore's name is an interpolation.

[71] Theodorus Lector, *Epitome* 152 [521] (ed. Kosiński – Twardowska – Zabrocka – Szopa 2021).: ἱστέον δὲ ὅτι πατριάρχην ὀνομάζει τὸν Θεσσαλονίκης ἐπίσκοπον ὁ ἱστορῶν, οὐκ οἶδα διατί. Another instance where the epitomator's own view is expressed more directly can be found at *Epitome* 98 [439], where it reads: ἐξ οὗ τοὺς Πέρσας τὰ Νεστορίου οἴμαι φρονεῖν.

[72] Theodorus Lector, *Epitome* 4 [339], 11 [346], 15 [350], 24 [359], 38 [373], 83 [422], 86 [426], 90 [431], 151 [520] (ed. Kosiński – Twardowska – Zabrocka – Szopa 2021).

sources as well.[73] In such cases, however, it is hard to determine if this is indeed the proof of the epitomator's erudition or a record drawn indirectly from the *Church History*.[74] We also encounter such places in the narration where the epitomator shows his reserve towards the details as preserved, referring to their uncertain source of origin. On such occasions, he makes use of several clichéd idiomatic structures which can be rendered, overall, as 'as they say' (ὡς λόγος, ὡς λέγουσιν, ὥς φασιν).

The above aspects of the narration and the comments made on the occasion of discussing those issues make up only a small contribution to our discussion of the *Epitome* as based on Theodore Lector's *Church History* alone. Many other questions may inspire our curiosity and further reflection. Unfortunately, in a majority of cases, we are confronted with questions, but we have practically no possibility of finding satisfactory answers. For example, we could ask the question why Chrysaphios, who turns up three times in the *Epitome*,[75] is described as Χρυσάφιοντὸν Τζουμᾶν only at the third instance. It could be reasonably expected that this should have been clarified at the first opportunity. The narrative of Basiliskos' usurpation is just as surprising. Exactly why is it that Theodore/epitomator puts so much emphasis on the fact that decisions taken by the usurper were issued in the form of edict(s)?[76] Perhaps a more thorough study would help us to find an answer to this question (and there are more questions like this).

---

[73] Theodorus Lector *Epitome* 39 [374] (ed. Kosiński – Twardowska – Zabrocka – Szopa 2021), referring to the *Historia Religiosa* by Theodoret of Cyrrhus; 45 [380], relating to some text by Timothy Aelouros against Pope Leo's *Tome*; *Epitome* 143 [499], where he refers to John Diakrinomenos.

[74] As can be seen in the extant fragments of Theodore, the author would not prefer to identify his sources, which should lead us to a conclusion that such mentions come from the epitomator. The problem is that the amount of material for analysis is strikingly insufficient to warrant such a conclusion; see also Nautin 1994, p. 226. Cf. Kosiński – Twardowska – Zabrocka – Szopa 2021, p. 232, where – should we assume that the text in question is based on Theodore's *Church History* – we can have some information on the sources.

[75] Theodorus Lector, *Epitome* 11 [346], 15 [350], 18 [353] (ed. Kosiński – Twardowska – Zabrocka – Szopa 2021).

[76] Theodorus Lector, *Epitome* 67 [403], 69 [405], 71[407] (ed. Kosiński – Twardowska – Zabrocka – Szopa 2021).

The work on the new edition of Theodore Lector's *Church History* has allowed me to see the complexity of this composition and how significant and at the same time underrated source material it really is. The *Epitome* of the *Church History*, which constitutes a very important (if not the most important) surviving carrier of the original text, is none the less a distinct literary work and it was created with this particular idea in the author's mind. The examples shown above make it very clear that the scope of independence the epitomator wished to achieve was surprisingly broad.[77] He made a point of not becoming just a transparent carrier of someone else's narration. On the contrary, he wished his composition to be regarded as a literary work in its own right, a work in tune with the genre-specific demand of his period. Despite a summary character of his work, he worked toward creating his own style which was much less rhetorized than that of the *Church History*, but not without some aspirations to achieve a certain artistic effect.[78] For all these reasons, drawing conclusions on the original of Theodore Lector's *Church History* on the basis of the *Epitome* is burdened with a great deal of risk. It is also evident that as carriers of the tradition of Theodore Lector's work the passages in the *Epitome* have certain features which are absent in other texts, even those on the basis of which some attempts at their reconstruction could be made (Theophanes' *Chronographia* comes to mind in the first place). This is certainly a strong argument in favour of our conviction that the new edition of Theodore Lector's *Church History* is a well justified effort.

---

[77] Which concerns the part of his composition referring to Theodore Lector's *Church History*. To evaluate the epitomator's conception in full, we should look through the entire *Epitome*, which I intend to do in some other study.

[78] I have decided to pass over some of the epitomator's efforts such as inserting citations in the narration (Theodorus Lector, *Epitome* 10 [345], 48 [383], 56 [391], 114 [463], 131 [485], 132 [486], 142 [496], 145 [507], 148[515]) and the use of titles (127 [481]) (ed. Kosiński – Twardowska – Zabrocka – Szopa 2021). The linguistic richness of the narration can be seen at some other places in the text as well, where it cannot be represented on a systematic basis, e.g., how to render interesting word-plays like at 129 [483] (ed. Kosiński – Twardowska – Zabrocka – Szopa 2021): ἀντέκραζον κράζουσιν καὶ ὑβρίζοντας ὕβριζον. Most likely, this phrase was copied from the original text, but there is of course no way to pass any definitive judgement here.

Bibliography

Sources

Hansen 1995 = Theodoros Anagnostes, *Kirchengeschichte*, ed. Günther Christian Hansen, zweite, durchgesehene Auflage, Berlin.

Hansen 1998 = *Ein kurzer Bericht über das Konzil von Chalkedon*, ed. Günther Christian Hansen, FM, vol. X, ed. by Ludwig Burgmann, Frankfurt: 101–39.

Kosiński – Szopa – Twardowska 2019 = *Historie Kościoła Jana Diakrinomenosa i Teodora Lektora*, przekład, wstęp i komentarz Rafał Kosiński – Adrian Szopa – Kamilla Twardowska, Kraków.

Kosiński – Twardowska – Zabrocka – Szopa 2021 = *The Church Histories of Theodore Lector and John Diakrinomenos*, ed. by Rafał Kosiński – Kamilla Twardowska – Aneta Zabrocka – Adrian Szopa, Berlin.

Kotter 1975 = Iohannes Damascenus, *Die Schriften des Johannes von Damaskos*, herausgegeben vom Byzantinischen Institut der Abtei Scheyern, vol. III, Contra imaginum calumniatores orationes tres, besorgt von Bonifatius Kotter, Berlin – New York.

Lamberz 2008 = *Concilium universale Nicaenum secundum* (787), ed. Erich Lamberz, ACO II 2, III 1, Berolini – Novi Eboraci.

Literature

Alexakis 1996 = Alexander Alexakis, *Codex Parisinus Graecus 1115 and Its Archetype*, Dumbarton Oaks.

Blaudeau 2006 = Philippe Blaudeau, *Alexandrie et Constantinople (451–91). De l'histoire à la géo-ecclésiologie*, Roma.

Brunt 1980 = Peter Brunt, 'On Historical Fragments and Epitomes', *The Classical Quarterly*, Vol. 30, No. 2, pp. 477–94.

de Boor 1884 = Carolus de Boor, 'Zu Theodorus Lector', *Zeitschrift für Kirchengeschichte* 6, pp. 573–77.

de Boor 1884a = Carolus de Boor, 'Zur Kenntnis der Handschriften der griechischen Kirchenhistoriker. Codex Baroccianus 142', *Zeitschrift für Kirchengeschichte* 6, pp. 478–93.

de Boor 1888 = Carolus de Boor, *Neue Fragmente des Papias, Hegesippus und Pierius in bisher unbekannten Excerpten aus der Kirchengeschichte des Philippus Sidetes*, Leipzig.

Crow – Bardill – Bayliss 2008 = James Crow, Jonathan Bardill, Richard Bayliss, *The Water Supply of Byzantine Constantinople*, London.

Funk 1961 = *A Greek Grammar Of The New Testament And Other Early Christian Literature by F. Blass and A. Debrunner*, translated and revised by Robert W. Funk, Chicago – London.

Greatrex 2015 = Geoffrey Greatrex, 'Théodore le Lecteur et son épitomateur anonyme du VIIe s.', in *L'historiographie tardo-antique et la transmission des savoirs*, ed. by Philippe Blaudeau and Peter van Nuffelen, Berlin – Boston, pp. 121–42.

Janin 1964 = Raymond Janin, *Constantinople byzantine, développement urbain et répertoire topographique*, deuxième édition, Paris.

Janin 1969 = Raymond Janin, La géographie ecclésiastique de l'Empire Byzantin, première partie, Le siège de Constantinople et le patriarcat oecuménique, tome III, Les églises et les monastères, deuxième éditon, Paris.

Janin 1975 = Raymond Janin, *La géographie ecclésiastique de l'Empire Byzantin, première partie, Le siège de Constantinople et le patriarcat oecuménique*, t. II: Les églises et les monastères des grands centres byzantins (Bithynie, Hellespont, Latros, Galèsios, Trébizonde, Athènes, Thessalonique), Paris.

Manafis 2020 = Panagiotis Manafis, *(Re)writing History in Byzantium. A Critical Study of Collections of Historical Excerpts*, Abingdon-on-Thames – New York.

Mango 1998 = Cyril Mango, 'The Origins of the Blachernae Shrine at Constantinople', in *Acta XIII Congressus Internationalis Archaeologicae Christianae: Split-Poreč (25.9–1.10.1994)*, ed. by Nenad Cambi – Emilio Marin, t. II, Vatican City, pp. 61–76.

Nautin 1994 = Pierre Nautin, 'Théodore Lecteur et sa "Réunion de différentes histoire" de l'Église', *Revue des Études Byzantines* 52, pp. 213–43.

Opitz 1934 = Hans-Georg Opitz, *Theodoros 48*, in *Realencyclopädie der Classischen Altertumswissenschaft X*, col. 1869–81.

Pouderon 1994 = Bernard Pouderon, 'Le témoignage du Codex Baroccianus 142 sur Athénagore et les origines du Didaskaleion d'Alexandrie', in *Science et vie intellectuelle à Alexandrie (Ier–IIIe siècle après J.-C.)*, ed. by Argoud G. Tours, pp. 163–224.

Pouderon 1997 = Bernard Pouderon, 'Les fragments anonymes du Baroc. Gr. 142 et les notices consacrées à Jean Diacrinoménos, Basile de Cilicie et l'anonyme d'Héraclée', *Revue des Études Byzantines* 55, pp. 169–92.

Pouderon 1998 = Bernard Pouderon, 'Le codex Parisinus graecus 1555 A et sa recension de l'Épitomé byzantin: d'histoires ecclésiastiques', *Revue des Études Byzantines* 56, pp. 169–91.

Pouderon 2014 = Bernard Pouderon, 'Pour une évaluation de l'Épitomè anonyme d'histoires ecclésiastiques: confrontaton des trois historiens sources, de la Tripartite de Théodore le Lecteur et de celle de Cassiodore', *Travaux et Mémoires* 18, pp. 527–45.

Skrzyniarz 2007 = Sławomir Skrzyniarz, 'Theodore Anagnostes, Account of a Blasphemous Painter', in 'Continuity and change. Studies in late antique historiography', *Electrum*, vol. 13, ed. by Michał Stachura – Dariusz Brodka, Kraków, pp. 147–53.

Suski 2017 = Robert Suski, 'The Epitome – Passive Copying or a Creative Reinterpretation of the Abridged Text', *Res Gestae. Czasopismo Historyczne* 5, pp. 25–34.

Treadgold 2007 = Warren Treadgold, *The Early Byzantine Historians*, New York – Basingstoke.

Twardowska 2017 = Kamilla Twardowska, 'The Church Foundations of Empress Pulcheria in Constantinople According to Theodore Lector's Church History and Other Contemporary Sources', *Res Gestae. Czasopismo Historyczne* 5, pp. 84–95.

Kazdhan 1991 = *The Oxford Dictionary of Byzantium*, ed. by A. P. Kazhdan, New York – Oxford.

Abstract

As one knows the *Church History* of Theodore Anagnostes has preserved fragmentary to current times. Our knowledge about the original text, mostly based on the so called *Epitome*, which is a selective summary of Theodore's original work from the beginnings of the seventh century. My article focuses on this work. On the basis of a few survived fragments of the original – mostly on two texts from the acts of the Second Synod in Nicaea and some fragments from the work of John of Damascus – I present the work method of the anonymous epitomist, considering the question: in what extent the text of epitome mirrors the original, and on the other hand, in what extent could it be perceived as an independent work. Firstly, I compare the preserved fragments of the *Church History* by Theodore Anagnostes with the matching parts of the *Epitome*. Secondly, I look closely into the text of the *Epitome* itself to examine the infection, syntax and lexis. Lastly, I mention some interesting, to my mind, points which generally refer to the style of the *Epitome*.

HARTMUT LEPPIN

THEODORET VON KYRRHOS BEI THEODOR ANAGNOSTES

Theodor Anagnostes bzw. die Texte, die sich mit seinem Werk in Verbindung bringen lassen,[1] galt lange als Steinbruch, um historische Einzelinformationen zu gewinnen; heute versucht man stärker, sein Werk ideengeschichtlich zu erfassen, etwa das Kaiserbild zu erörtern, wie das in verschiedenen Aufsätzen dieses Sammelbandes geschieht. Mein Beitrag zielt, wenngleich der Titel etwas anderes vermuten lässt, ebenfalls nicht primär auf Quellenkritik, sondern auf die Frage der Konzeption der Kirchengeschichte, was dann allerdings durchaus Auswirkungen auf die Quellenkritik hat. Im Zentrum steht dabei eine Schlüsselgestalt, nämlich Theodoret von Kyrrhos.

Theodoret stellt einen Sonderfall unter den bei Theodor Anagnostes behandelten Personen dar, weil er zugleich als Akteur auftritt und der Verfasser einer zentralen Quelle, seiner Kirchengeschichte, ist. Er ist ferner ein komplizierter, damit wohl auch aufschlussreicher Fall, weil seine kirchengeschichtliche Rolle ambivalent war:[2] Von Kind an für den kirchlichen Dienst vor-

---

[1] Allgemein Nautin 1994, pp. 213–44; Greatrex 2015, pp. 121–42, der die Bedeutung des Epitomators unterstreicht; Blaudeau 2006, pp. 619–53; grundlegend jetzt Kosiński et al. 2021, deren Ergebnisse leider nicht mehr vollständig berücksichtigt werden konnten. Trotz der Vorbehalte von Pouderon 2014, der die Eigenständigkeit des Epitomators betont, scheint es mir weiter sinnvoll, insgesamt von Theodor Anagnostes zu sprechen; aber hier wären noch weitere Forschungen notwendig; vgl. zur Bedeutung Theodors in diesem Sinne für die Überlieferung der Kirchenhistoriker auch die Einleitungen zu den jeweiligen Editionen: für Theodoret Parmentier – Hansen, 1998 S. XVIII–LI; für Sokrates Hansen 1995a, pp. xxxvi-xxxvii; für Sozomenos Hansen 1995b, pp. xxix–xxxv.

[2] Urbainczyk 2002; Leppin 2003; Pásztori-Kupán 2006; Schor 2011.

Studies in Theodore Anagnostes, ed. by Rafał Kosiński & Adrian Szopa, STTA 19 (Turnhout 2021), pp. 63–79
© BREPOLS ❧ PUBLISHERS   DOI 10.1484/M.STTA-EB.5.127976

gesehen, trat er 415 in ein Kloster ein und wurde 423 Bischof in Kyrrhos, das kirchenpolitisch Antiochia am Orontes unterstand. In Kyrrhos und auch anderswo entfaltete er eine bemerkenswerte Aktivität als Patron, als Briefschreiber, als Autor theologischer Schriften und als Kirchenpolitiker. Beim (Ersten) Konzil von Ephesos 431 gehörte er zu den Verteidigern des Nestorios. Obwohl zu den schärfsten Gegnern Kyrills von Alexandria zählend, schloss er sich der Verständigungsformel von 433/4 an, die jedoch nicht zu einer dauerhaften Beilegung des Konfliktes führte.

Theodoret wurde nunmehr vor allem für Dioskoros von Alexandria, den Nachfolger Kyrills, zur Hauptzielscheibe in den christologischen Kämpfen und 449 durch das Zweite Konzil von Ephesos, das sogenannte Räuberkonzil, abgesetzt. Doch die Konzilsväter von Chalkedon rehabilitierten ihn 451 wieder, nachdem er es über sich gebracht hatte, Nestorios zu verdammen. Er konnte noch einige Jahre in Kyrrhos wirken, blieb aber eine umstrittene Gestalt. Auch nach seinem Tod ergingen immer wieder Verurteilungen gegen ihn, nicht zuletzt im Rahmen des Drei-Kapitel-Streits. Für Miaphysiten war er der Inbegriff einer dyophysitischen, nestorianischen Irrlehre. Zugleich gewann sein umfangreiches Werk durchaus Anerkennung; gerade seine Kirchengeschichte fand viele Nutzer, darunter eben auch Theodor Anagnostes.

In einem ersten Teil werde ich Theodorets Erwähnungen als Akteur bei Theodor Anagnostes besprechen, dann einige Stellen erörtern, an denen der Anagnostes Theodoret als Quelle heranzieht. Auf dieser Grundlage will ich verdeutlichen, dass Theodoret einen wesentlichen Einfluss auf die Geschichtskonzeption des Theodor Anagnostes ausübte, und zwar in dem Sinne, dass seine Kirchengeschichte ein besonderes Augenmerk auf Christen legt, die sich durch Rechtgläubigkeit auszeichneten und deswegen Opfer von Fehlentscheidungen wurden. Dies konnte die Bedrängnis des Rechtgläubigen in der eigenen Zeit plausibel machen – Theodor Anagnostes schrieb ja in der Verbannung.[3] Ebenso wenig wie im Falle von Theodorets Kirchengeschichte läuft Theodors Werk darauf hinaus, dass ein guter Zustand der Welt erreicht wird, vielmehr betont es die Fortdauer des Leidens,

---

[3] Thdr. Lect. *h.e.* praef (ed. Hansen 1995c).

das den Rechtgläubigen widerfährt. Einbeziehen möchte ich auch die Rolle des anonymen Epitomators aus dem Beginn des 7. Jahrhunderts, dessen Arbeit für unsere Überlieferung grundlegend ist, und zwar vor allem unter dem Gesichtspunkt, warum er einen Chalkedonier wie Theodor Anagnostes mit einem Miaphysiten wie Johannes Diakrinomenos in Verbindung bringen konnte. Es sind also, soweit möglich, fortwährend drei Ebenen zu unterscheiden: die Theodorets, die von Theodor Anagnostes und jene des Epitomators.

1. Die erste Erwähnung Theodorets in der Epitome bezieht sich auf das Zweite Konzil von Ephesos im Jahr 449.[4] Schon der Beginn der Passage macht klar, woher der Wind weht: ‚Eine Synode wurde nach Ephesos einberufen, an der keiner von den Bischöfen von Oriens teilnahm'. Dann schildert die Epitome des Theodor Anagnostes, der man ihren raffenden Charakter hier anmerkt, kurz den Verlauf:
Dioskor und die anderen, die die Dinge gegen die Orthodoxie zusammengeschustert hatten, setzten Flavian und Eusebios von Dorylaion ab, verliehen Eutyches die Würde des Priesters und die Verwaltung des Klosters. Sie enthoben ferner Theodoret, Ibas, Andreas und andere Bischöfe aus Oriens ihres Amtes, die alle abwesend waren, zudem Domnos von Antiochia.[5]

Aus der Sicht des Autors ist klar, dass dieses Konzil keine Ökumenizität besitzt. Dass der Bischof von Rom Leo wiederum Eutyches bereits verurteilt hatte, war vom Verfasser schon vorher festgestellt worden.[6]

Unklar ist, welcher Andreas hier gemeint ist; mir scheint Andreas von Samosata der wahrscheinlichste Kandidat zu sein, da dieser zum Umfeld Theodorets gehörte.[7] An anderer Stelle hatte Theodor Anagnostes offenbar eine Schrift dieses Andreas gegen Kyrill erwähnt,[8] ferner erscheint derselbe hinter Theodoret und

---

[4] Thdr. Lect. *h.e.* E 347 (ed. Hansen 1995c).
[5] Thdr. Lect. *h.e.* E 347 (ed. Hansen 1995c). Auffällig ist in der Passage der Wechsel zwischen Präsens und Aorist, für den ich keine Erklärung habe; vermutlich war dies eine Folgung der Kürzung.
[6] Thdr. Lect. *h.e.* E 345 (ed. Hansen 1995c).
[7] Zu Andreas von Samosata Schor 2011, pp. 102–09; Kosiński et al. 2021 p. 85.
[8] Thdr. Lect. *h.e.* E 530 (ed. Hansen 1995c).

Ibas in der Liste der durch eine spätere Synode Verurteilten,[9] wurde mithin als ein Opfer des Konzils betrachtet. Allerdings nahm an Ephesos II schon ein Rufin als Bischof von Samosata teil,[10] so dass diese Tradition irrtümlich sein muss. Möglich ist aber, wie Günther Christian Hansen[11] vorschlägt, an einen Priester und Archimandriten namens Andreas zu denken, der die Verurteilung des Eutyches unterschrieben hatte.[12]

Falls tatsächlich Andreas hier zu Unrecht genannt worden ist, könnte das durchaus auf den Epitomator zurückgehen, zumal wenn man auf den getrennt überlieferten, auf Theodor Anagnostes bezugnehmenden Bericht über das Konzil von Chalkedon blickt,[13] ein Neufund, den Hansen in den *Fontes minores* 10 vorgelegt hat. Er behandelt ebenfalls Ephesos II, erwähnt aber Andreas mit keinem Wort.[14] Trotz der Unklarheit in Hinblick auf Andreas, dürfte Theodoret bei Theodor Anagnostes definitiv als jemand erschienen sein, der zu Unrecht verurteilt worden war.

Dass der Anagnostes, wie zu erwarten, auch die Rehabilitierung Theodorets auf dem Konzil von Chalkedon 451 erwähnt hat, bestätigt Victor von Tunnuna.[15] Seine hohe Meinung von diesem Konzil belegt die *Epitome* selbst, die hier vergleichsweise ausführlich ist und vieles anführt, was die Bedeutung des Konzils herausstreicht:[16] Kaiser Markian orientierte sich am Beispiel Constantins; die Bischöfe, die von überall her kamen, versammelten sich in der Kirche der Märtyrerin Euphemia, beschlossen, was in Hinblick auf Dogma und Verhalten richtig war, und wurden vom Herrscherpaar mit hoher Ehre bedacht. Der getrennt überlieferte, von Hansen edierte Bericht über das Konzil von Chalkedon ist ausführlicher und setzt übrigens ganz andere Akzente, da er nah an den Akten bleibt – der Epitomator scheint hier also durchaus eigenständig verfahren zu sein. Theodoret behandelt der

---

[9] Vict. Tunn. ad a. 499 (ed. Hansen 1995c).

[10] ACO II i. 1 79, Z. 15.

[11] Hansen 1995 ad Thdr. Lect. *h.e.* E 347.

[12] ACO II i. 1. 146, Z. 25 f.

[13] Hansen 1998, p. 110, Z. 5; s. auch Kosiński et al. 2021, 545–83, die betonen, dass dies kein Fragment der Kirchengeschichte Theodorets war (545).

[14] Hansen 1998, p. 114, Z. 62–64.

[15] Vict. Tunn. ad a. 451 = Thdr. Lect. *h.e.* F 3 (ed. Hansen 1995c).

[16] Thdr. Lect. *h.e.* E 360 (ed. Hansen 1995c).

Autor des Konzilsberichts eingehender als jede andere Gestalt, sogar intensiver als Dioskoros und Ibas: Der Autor betont, dass Theodoret zwar die *Kephalaia* Kyrills angegriffen habe und deswegen verurteilt worden sei, dass Leo von Rom ihn aber als rechtgläubig anerkannt und Theodoret weiterhin vehement für seine eigene Anerkennung als Rechtgläubiger gestritten habe.[17] Ausführlich schildert er auch die Zulassung Theodorets zunächst als Ankläger zum Konzil.[18] Ferner erwähnt er, wie Theodoret Nestorios verdammt, den *Tomus Leonis* unterzeichnet, so wieder aufgenommen wird und sein Bistum zurückerhält.[19] Damit wird seine Rehabilitierung gewürdigt, die später immer wieder in Frage gestellt werden sollte.

Um zu mutmaßlichen Auszügen aus Theodor Anagnostes zurückzukehren: Die Verurteilung Theodorets und anderer, die als Dyophysiten galten, durch eine von Anastasius einberufene Synode von Konstantinopel im Jahr 499 scheint Victor von Tunnuna auf der Basis von Theodor Anagnostes erwähnt zu haben.[20] Eine weitere Verurteilung des Bischofs von Kyrrhos durch Flavian von Antiochia 511/2 erwähnte Theodor Anagnostes, falls man die entsprechende Passage aus Theophanes[21] auf ihn zurückführen darf. Das Verhalten des Antiochener Bischofs bezeichnet er ausdrücklich als kleinmütig.

Der Theodoret, den Theodor Anagnostes vorstellt, genießt eine hohe Autorität, fällt aber trotzdem einer verfehlten Politik zum Opfer und wird verurteilt. Das war natürlich eine klare Positionierung in der Zeit des Anastasius, als die Erinnerung an Theodoret gefährdet war und Theodor Anagnostes in Verbannung gehen musste.

Geoffrey Greatrex hat daran erinnert,[22] dass man auch den Epitomator bzw. Kompilator als Autor im Blick haben müsse, der sich ja bemerkenswerterweise nicht scheute, den Chalkedonier Theodor Anagnostes und den Antinestorianer Johannes Diakri-

---

[17] Hansen 1998, pp. 116, 89–96.
[18] Hansen 1998, p. 118, Z. 107–14, p. 120, pp. 133–39.
[19] Hansen 1998, p. 126, Z. 249–51.
[20] Vict. Tunn. ad a. 499 = Thdr. Lect. *h.e.* F 54 (ed. Hansen 1995c).
[21] Thphn. A.M. 6003, p. 153. 12–154. 2 (ed. De Boor 1883–1885), s. Kosiński et al. p. 430–31.
[22] Greatrex 2015, p. 138.

nomenos in einer Epitome zusammenzuführen. Daher scheint es mir wichtig, auch auf die Epitome des Johannes einen Blick zu werfen:

Das Epitomon aus Johannes schildert im Kontext des Konzils von Chalkedon die Szene, wie Theodoret normal Platz nehmen kann, während Dioskoros zornig auf dem Fußboden sitzen muss,[23] was eine Verschärfung des auf Theodor Anagnostes zurückgeführten Berichtes über Chalkedon darstellt. Ferner erwähnt Johannes ein Schreiben Theodorets an Souras von Germanikeia, in dem er sagt, dass das Konzil von Chalkedon 520 Teilnehmer gehabt habe,[24] wie es auch in einem Schreiben der Synode an Leo von Rom und einem kaiserlichen Brief heißt.[25] Theodoret war mithin in den Augen des Johannes oder des Epitomators ein wichtiger Gewährsmann für das Konzil von Chalkedon. Der erwähnte Brief Theodorets ist anderweitig nicht erhalten, so dass der Verfasser Zugang zu einer anderen Sammlung von Briefen gehabt haben muss, als wir sie kennen, was bei dem umfangreichen Briefcorpus Theodorets nicht überrascht. Auch Theodorets Schrift gegen Kyrill erwähnen die Auszüge, die Johannes Diakrinomenos zugeordnet werden, in der Form ohne Polemik, wenngleich es heißt, dass Kyrill unter den Heiligen weile.[26] Theodoret besitzt mithin durchaus Autorität, obgleich Johannes Diakrinomenos es mit den Miaphysiten hielt. Als Opfer erscheint er indes nicht.

2. Theodoret ist nicht die einzige Gestalt, der Theodor Anagnostes eine Rolle als Opfer einer verfehlten Kirchenpolitik zuschreibt. Theodor von Mopsuestia wird an einigen wichtigen Stellen erwähnt, interessanterweise auch mit einer Information, die in einem negativen Sinne gedeutet werden konnte. Bei Sozomenos fand der Anagnostes die Nachricht, dass Theodor von Mopsuestia als junger Mann Mönch geworden sei, diese Lebensform dann unter Vorwänden aufgegeben und eine Ehe angestrebt habe, dass Johannes Chrysostomos es aber gelungen sei, ihm dies

---

[23] Jo. Diacr. *fr. h.e.* E 533 (ed. Hansen 1995c).
[24] Jo. Diacr. *fr. h.e.* E 534 (ed. Hansen 1995c).
[25] ACO II 1. 3. 116, 34; II 1. 3. 122, 34.
[26] Jo. Diacr. *fr. h.e.* E 529 (ed. Hansen 1995c).

durch eine eigene Schrift auszureden.[27] Theodor Anagnostes nimmt die Passage auf und ergänzt sogar den Namen der Frau, der auf das entsprechende Werk des Johannes zurückgehen dürfte.[28] Der Kontext diente jedoch wohl vor allem dem Lob des Johannes Chrysostomos und nicht so sehr der Kritik an Theodor von Mopsuestia, dem man es ja auch positiv anrechnen konnte, wenn er sich überwunden hatte und zum asketischen Leben zurückgekehrt war. Doch Theodoret war offenbar vorsichtig und erwähnte diese Episode aus der Jugend seines Helden nicht.

In abträglichen Worten berichtet Theodor Anagnostes von Mönchen, die Theodosius und Pulcheria dazu drängen, Theodor von Mopsuestia nach dessen Tod als Häretiker zu verurteilen.[29] Er erwähnt jedoch ebenso, dass er und Nestorios – den der Anagnostes, wie wir sehen werden, ablehnt – bei persischen Christen anerkannt seien.[30] Auch die Verurteilungen Theodors von Mopsuestia unter Anastasius verschweigt Theodor Anagnostes nicht,[31] hebt aber hervor, dass Johannes von Antiochia[32] und sein Nachfolger Domnos[33] Theodor von Mopsuestia ausdrücklich als rechtgläubig verteidigten. Der Letztere habe sogar ein kaiserliches Reskript erwirkt, dass sich gegen die Feinde Kyrills richtete.[34] Wie im Falle Theodorets haben wir es also mit einer Gestalt zu tun, die großen Respekt genießt, aber verurteilt wird, gerade unter Anastasius, unter dem auch der Anagnostes ins Exil gehen musste. Theodor von Mopsuestia erscheint als ein weiteres Opfer der Macht der Falschgläubigen.

Wieder ein Blick auf den Epitomator: Ein Fragment aus dem Werk des Johannes Diakrinomenos erwähnt, dass Ibas die Übersetzung der Schriften des Theodor von Mopsuestia ins Syrische veranlasst[35] und Zenon die Schule von Edessa wegen der nesto-

---

[27] Soz. *h.e.* VIII. 2. 8–10 (ed. Hansen 1995b).

[28] Thdr. Lect. *h.e.* E 282 mit Joh. Chrys. *ad. Theodr.* 14 (PG 47, 297).

[29] Thdr. Lect. *h.e.* E 338 (ed. Hansen 1995c).

[30] Thdr. Lect. *h.e.* E 439 (ed. Hansen 1995c).

[31] Thdr. Lect. *h.e.* E 472–73; Vict. Tunn. ad a. 499 = Thdr. Lect. *h.e.* F 54. Ferner Thdr. Lect. *h.e.* E 497 (ed. Hansen 1995c).

[32] Thdr. Lect. *h.e.* E 339 (ed. Hansen 1995c).

[33] Thdr. Lect. *h.e.* E 341 (ed. Hansen 1995c).

[34] An einer Stelle ergänzt der Epitomator eine Glosse (Thdr. Lect. *h.e.* E 105 (ed. Hansen 1995c)).

[35] Jo. Diacr. *fr. h.e.* E 546 (ed. Hansen 1995c).

rianischen Sympathien geschlossen habe.[36] Liest man die beiden Notizen zusammen, entsteht der Eindruck, dass der Epitomator diese Maßnahme, die Johannes Diakrinomenos gefallen haben müssten, nicht billigte. Ein christliches intellektuelles Zentrum mit Ausstrahlung ging so zugrunde. Die Tatsache, dass der Epitomator ein Werk Theodor von Mopsuestias, die Schrift gegen Eunomios,[37] kennt, spricht zusätzlich für eine gewisse Nähe zu diesem.

Negativ geprägt ist hingegen das Bild des Nestorios bei Theodor Anagnostes. Kaum hat er die Wahl erwähnt,[38] kritisiert er ihn scharf: ‚Nestorios verursachte zugleich mit seiner Wahl unzählige Unruhen und zog aufgrund seiner Aufgeblasenheit (τῦφος) den Hass aller auf sich'. Einer seiner Presbyter beginnt mit Attacken auf die Theotokos, die Nestorios noch verstärkt.[39] Daraufhin tadelt ihn Eusebios von Dorylaion,[40] der ja seinerseits später als Nestorianer verurteilt werden sollte, und das Konzil von Ephesos I 431 verdammt ihn, so dass er elend in der Verbannung stirbt.[41] An verschiedenen Stellen kommt Theodor Anagnostes auf Versammlungen zu sprechen, die Nestorios verurteilten, bisweilen parallel mit Eutyches,[42] der das andere Extrem verkörperte.

Auch wenn Theodor Anagnostes sich deutlich von Nestorios absetzt, muss er einräumen, dass Pulcheria, die von Nestorios gegenüber ihrem Bruder verleumdet worden war, auch seine Freunde ablehnt,[43] darunter eben Theodor von Mopsuestia. Er macht diese Bemerkung, nachdem er betont hat, dass Johannes von Antiochia gegenüber dem Kaiser die Rechtgläubigkeit Theodor von Mopsuestias betont hatte.[44] Er verschweigt auch nicht, dass Theodor von Mopusestia für die Anhänger des Nestorios im Perserreich eine Autorität war.[45] Obwohl die Nähe des Bischofs von Mopsuestia zu Nestorios ihm wohlbekannt war, trennt er

---

[36] Jo. Diacr. *fr. h.e.* E 548 (ed. Hansen 1995c); Becker 2006, p. 55–56.
[37] Thdr. Lect. *h.e.* E 105 (ed. Hansen 1995c).
[38] Thdr. Lect. *h.e.* E 326 (ed. Hansen 1995c).
[39] Thdr. Lect. *h.e.* E 327 (ed. Hansen 1995c).
[40] Thdr. Lect. *h.e.* E 328 (ed. Hansen 1995c).
[41] Thdr. Lect. *h.e.* E 329 (ed. Hansen 1995c).
[42] Thdr. Lect. *h.e.* E 473, E 518 (ed. Hansen 1995c).
[43] Thdr. Lect. *h.e.* E 340 (ed. Hansen 1995c).
[44] Thdr. Lect. *h.e.* E 339 (ed. Hansen 1995c).
[45] Thdr. Lect. *h.e.* E 439 (ed. Hansen 1995c).

scharf zwischen den beiden, indem er Nestorios deutlich kritisiert, Theodor von Mopsuestia hingegen zu einem Opfer von Fehlentscheidungen macht.

3. Damit zum zweiten Teil, zur Benutzung Theodorets durch Theodor Anagnostes. In einigen Passagen setzt Theodor Anagnostes sich mit dessen Werk explizit auseinander: Als er in der *Praefatio* von seinen Quellen spricht, hebt er unter den sogenannten synoptischen Kirchenhistorikern Theodoret hervor, zum einen, indem er ihn als ersten nennt, zum anderen, indem er ihn als, den ‚Bischof von Kyrrhos heiligen Angedenkens' bezeichnet.[46]

In anderen Passagen seines Werks nimmt er ebenfalls explizit auf das Werk Theodorets Bezug: In seiner *Kirchengeschichte* hatte dieser Theophilos von Alexandria gepriesen, besonders dafür, dass er hart gegen Heiden vorging und das Serapeion zerstörte.[47] Aufgrund der Tatsache, dass Theophilos mütterlicherseits der Onkel Kyrills war, vermutet Theodor Anagnostes, dass Theodoret anfangs keine feindliche Gesinnung gegenüber Kyrill gehegt habe[48] – offenbar ist es für ihn selbstverständlich, dass eine Kritik an Kyrill hätte auf seine Verwandten abfärben müssen. In der Tat verzichtet Theodoret in der *Kirchengeschichte* auf jegliche Polemik gegen Kyrill,[49] wie er auch das Konzil von Ephesos I, an dem der Konflikt zwischen Antiochenern und Alexandrinern zum Ausbruch kam, im Gegensatz zu Sokrates unerwähnt lässt; offenbar wollte er, der doch allgemein als Gegner Kyrills bekannt war, nicht in Wunden bohren.

Der erwähnte Theodor von Mopsuestia hingegen spielt bei Theodoret eine wesentliche Rolle. Theodor Anagnostes hebt zu Recht hervor, das Theodoret ihn gemeinsam mit dessen Bruder Polychronios von Apameia sehr lobte,[50] wobei Theodoret vor allem die theologischen Qualitäten Theodor von Mopsuestias pries und seinen Kampf gegen Häresien, was ein indirekter Kommentar zu den aktuellen Streitigkeiten war.

---

[46] Thdr. Lect. *h.e.* praef., Z. 19–20 (ed. Hansen 1995c); zur *Praefatio* Nautin 1994, pp. 216–18, 233–40.

[47] Er wird lediglich in Thdt. *h.e.* v. 22 (ed. Hansen 1995c) knapp erwähnt.

[48] Thdr. Lect. *h.e.* E 269 (ed. Hansen 1995c).

[49] Thdt. *h.e.* v. 35. 1 (ed. Hansen 1995c).

[50] Thdr. Lect. *h.e.* E 318 zu Thdt. *h.e.* v. 40. 1–2 (ed. Hansen 1995c).

Der Tod Theodor von Mopsuestias markiert bei Theodoret sogar gemeinsam mit jenem des Theodotos von Antiochia, der durch seine Milde für eine Aussöhnung mit Apollinaristen gesorgt hatte,[51] das Ende der *Kirchengeschichte*. So setzt Theodoret einen letztlich anti-kyrillianischen Schlusspunkt, ohne ihn explizit zu machen. Zugleich verbindet er ihn mit einem verhüllten Plädoyer für Aussöhnung. Theodotos erwähnt Theodor Anagnostes in den erhaltenen Passagen nicht; doch das besagt angesichts des schlechten Erhaltungszustands seines Werks wenig.

Theodor Anagnostes stellt Theodoret ferner als Kritiker der Χριστιανικὴ ἱστορία des Philippos von Side hin, verwechselt ihn aber unter diesem Aspekt mit Sokrates.[52] Auch an einer anderen Stelle irrt Theodor Anagnostes, als er nämlich den Mönch Jakob, der unter den Empfängern des Rundschreibens Kaiser Leos war,[53] für Jakob von Nisibis hält, über den Theodoret in seiner *Mönchsgeschichte* (1) ausführlich geschrieben hatte, wie Theodor Anagnostes weiß. Interessanterweise scheint der Epitomator hier einzugreifen und Theodor Anagnostes mit der Formel zu korrigieren: ‚Man muss aber wissen [...]‘: nämlich, dass das Wunder, das der Autor hier erwähnt hatte, in die Zeit eben von Constantius II. gehört,[54] in die Theodor Anagonstes ihn an anderer Stelle zutreffend einordnet.[55]

Viel häufiger greift Theodor Anagnostes auf seinen Vorgänger Theodoret zurück, ohne sich mit dessen Einschätzungen ausdrücklich auseinanderzusetzen. Hier muss ich mich für die ersten zwei Bücher auf die Auswertung durch Günther Christian Hansen stützen, denn den *Codex Marcianus* gr. 344 konnte ich nicht einsehen – andererseits ist mein Vertrauern zu Hansens Zuverlässigkeit sehr groß.[56] Natürlich kann ich mich dabei nur auf einige signifikante Passagen konzentrieren.

---

[51] Thdt. *h.e.* v. 38. 2 (ed. Hansen 1995c).

[52] Thdr. Lect. *h.e.* E 324 mit Socr. *h.e.* vii. 26. 5–27. 8 (ed. Hansen 1995a).

[53] ACO II v. 23. 13.

[54] Thdr. Lect. *h.e.* E 374 (ed. Hansen 1995c).

[55] Thdr. Lect. *h.e.* E 111 (ed. Hansen 1995c); vgl. Kosiński et al. 2021, p. 237.

[56] Hansen 1995c, p. xiv verweist auch auf die Lücken der Theodoret-Benutzung. Vgl. allerdings für die Schwierigkeiten der Hansen'schen Ausgabe Kosiński 2017, pp. 111–24.

Theodor Anagnostes hält sich im ersten Buch, das Constantin dem Großen gewidmet ist, zunächst stärker an Sozomenos, doch für das theologisch entscheidende Ereignis, den Beginn des sogenannten Arianischen Streits, greift er auf Theodoret zurück.[57] Dessen Deutung war von dem öfters wiederkehrenden Gedanken bestimmt, dass der Frieden der Kirche stets durch den Satan gefährdet sei. Sokrates hingegen unterstreicht die individuelle Rolle des Areios[58] und Sozomenos benennt allgemein die Streitsucht als Ursache;[59] beide setzen also auf personale Faktoren, während bei Theodoret und dann auch bei Theodor Anagnostes ein grundsätzliches Bild der Bedrohung entsteht. Der Anagnostes übernimmt auch die Nennung der Träger apostolischer Charismata auf der Synode,[60] was dem Konzil eine zusätzliche Weihe verleiht. Auch sonst scheint Theodor Anagnostes sich besonders für Teilnehmer interessiert zu haben, die spezielle Charismata besaßen, von denen man somit erwarten konnte, dass sie dem Satan gewachsen waren.

Während Theodor Anagnostes den Tod Constantins wiederum auf der Grundlage des Sokrates schildert, übernimmt er die Apologie Constantins bei Theodoret und greift damit ein zentrales Motiv aus dessen Werk auf: Constantin habe sich täuschen lassen, weil er eben wie David ein Mensch gewesen sei und daher der Täuschung habe anheimfallen können.[61] Der für Theodoret charakteristische, anti-eusebianische Gedanke, dass ein vollendeter Zustand der Welt nicht möglich sei, schlägt hier durch. Im zweiten Buch ist Theodoret weniger prominent. Theodor Anagnostes greift auf ihn zurück, als es um das Versagen von Bischöfen geht, wie z. B. um die Grausamkeiten von Bischof Gregor in Alexandria[62] oder die Intrigen eines Stephanos in Antiochia.[63]

---

[57] Thdt. *h.e.* I. 2. 5–11 (ed. Parmentier – Hansen 1998); vgl. Pouderon 2014, p. 538.

[58] Socr. *h.e.* I. 5. 1 (ed. Hansen 1995c).

[59] Soz. *h.e.* I. 15. 1 (ed. Hansen 1995b).

[60] Thdt. *h.e.* I. 7. 3–6 (ed. Parmentier – Hansen 1998).

[61] Thdt. *h.e.* I. 33 (ed. Parmentier – Hansen 1998).

[62] Thdt. *h.e.* II. 4. 3 (ed. Parmentier – Hansen 1998).

[63] Thdt. *h.e.* II. 8. 54–10. 3 (ed. Parmentier – Hansen 1998).

Ab dem dritten Buch sind wir ganz auf die Arbeit des Exzerptors angewiesen, um den Bezug auf Theodoret zu bestimmen. Für die Zeit Julians und des Valens beziehen die Theodoret-Zitate bei Theodor Anagnostes sich vor allem auf Glaubenshelden, die für die Situation der bedrängten Kirche stehen. Aus der Herrschaft Theodosius des Großen findet der Tod des Markellos von Apameia Erwähnung, der stirbt, weil er die Heiden bekämpft.[64] Der Kaiser selbst erscheint, wie bei Theodoret, als ein gelehriger Schüler des mutigen Bischofs Ambrosius.[65] Auch die Christenverfolgungen in Persien zur Zeit von Theodosius II. entnimmt der Epitomator aus Theodoret,[66] erwähnt aber auch den gottgewirkten Sieg der Römer über die Perser[67] nach Sokrates.[68] An einer Stelle ändert Theodor Anagnostes aus theologischen Gründen den Wortlaut Theodorets, indem er ὑπόστασις in οὐσία ändert.[69]

Die bisherigen, sehr knappen Überlegungen erwecken den Eindruck, dass es sich lohnen würde, den Umgang von Theodor Anagnostes mit der Überlieferung der Synoptiker insgesamt genauer in Augenschein zu nehmen. Die Ergebnisse der entsprechenden Beobachtungen könnten genauere Auskunft über seine Konzeption und damit über seine Position in seiner eigenen Zeit geben. Denn offenkundig hat er vieles bewusst montiert. Doch diese Analyse kann ich hier nicht leisten.

4. Blicken wir zurück: Ein Teil der Kirchengeschichtsschreibung hatte seit Euseb eine triumphalistische Tendenz. Zwar werden unzählige Leiden der Frommen, der Märtyrer, geschildert, doch das Ganze mündete bei Euseb in ein großartiges Herrschertum. In diese Tradition stellt sich Sozomenos, wenn er Pulcheria, die

---

[64] Thdr. Lect, *h.e.* E 253 (ed. Hansen 1995c) nach Thdt. *h.e.* v. 21. 5–16 (ed. Parmentier – Hansen 1998), auch bei Soz. *h.e.* VII. 15. 12–14 (ed. Hansen 1995b).

[65] Thdr. Lect. *h.e.* E 270–E 271 (ed. Hansen 1995c).

[66] Thdr. Lect. *h.e.* E 313 nach Thdt. *h.e.* v. 39, mit kleineren Irrtümern, s. Hansen 1995c ad loc.

[67] Thdr. Lect. *h.e.* E 314 (ed. Hansen 1995c).

[68] Socr. *h.e.* VII. 18. 8–25 (ed. Hansen 1995a).

[69] Hansen 1995c, p. 36; vgl. Thdt. *h.e.* II.8 (ed. Parmentier – Hansen 1998) – das Synodalschreiben von Serdika.

Kaiserin seiner Zeit preist, aber auch Sokrates, wenn er am Ende seines Werks auf eine gute Bischofswahl verweist.

Bei Theodoret liegen die Dinge indes ganz anders. Gegen Ende seines Werkes, für die Zeit seines Kaisers Theodosius II., schilderte er die erwähnte Christenverfolgung im Persischen Reich und verdeutlichte damit, wie schlimm die Zeiten weiterhin waren. Damit akzentuiert er innerhalb seiner *Kirchengeschichte* die Opfergeschichte stark. Mit dem Ausdruck ‚Opfergeschichte‘ möchte ich keinen neuen Gattungsbegriff einführen und kann mich schon gar nicht auf eine antike Definition berufen. Doch scheint es mir einen wichtigen Unterschied auszumachen, ob ein Autor am Ende die Erfolge der Kirche im Zusammenwirken mit dem Kaiser rühmt oder die fortdauernde Gefährdung des wahren Glaubens betont. Natürlich spielen Opfer, Märtyrer und Verbannte, in allen Kirchengeschichten eine wesentliche Rolle, doch die Perspektive war höchst unterschiedlich.

Diese Tendenz kommt bei ganz unterschiedlichen Autoren zum Vorschein: so bei Barḥadbšabbā von Bet Arbaia, dem dyophysitischen Kirchenhistoriker (wenn diese gängige Bezeichnung wirklich zutrifft),[70] und beim Miaphysiten Johannes von Ephesos. Bei diesem steht die Kirchengeschichte unter apokalyptischen Vorzeichen; fortwährend spricht er von Streit und Verfolgung, doch kennt er immerhin Episoden einer gelungenen Herrschaft wie im Falle der Mission Justinians in Kleinasien, die Johannes von Ephesos selbst höchst erfolgreich durchführte.[71] Ein ähnlicher Fall könnte bei Theodor Anagnostes das Konzil von Chalkedon gewesen sein, in Abschnitten, auf die der Epitomator rekurriert, die allerdings für den separaten Bericht keine Bedeutung haben.

Es spricht einiges dafür, Theodor Anagnostes in diese Tradition einer die Opfer betonenden Kirchengeschichtsschreibung einzuordnen, zumal auch die *Kirchengeschichte* Theodorets, der ihn auf

---

[70] Zu ihm Debié 2015, pp. 599–601; Becker – Childers 2011, pp. 257–58; Becker 2008, pp. 11–16. Der Titel *Kirchengeschichte* geht auf Abdisho (Ebedjesu) zurück (Bibl. Or. III. 1. 1, 169 [Kap. 93]). Editionen: Nau 1913, pp. 19–32; Nau 1932, pp. 1–18.

[71] Ginkel 1995; Ashbrook-Harvey – Brakmann 1998, pp. 553–55; Richter 2002, pp. 29–41; Bruns 2006; Destephen 2008, pp. 494–519; Debié 2015, pp. 137–39, 535–42. Zu beiden Leppin 2019 und 2020.

jeden Fall massiv beeinflusst hat, unter den Vorzeichen einer Verfolgung stand: Beide schreiben aus der Verbannung; das dürfte ihren Blick gefärbt haben.

Günter Christian Hansen hat in seiner Edition betont, dass Politik bei Theodor Anagnostes nur eine geringe Rolle spiele,[72] während Geoffrey Greatrex hier eine Nuancierung angemahnt und etwa darauf hingewiesen hat, dass auch bei Theodor Anagnostes die Gliederung nach den Kaisern erfolgt, was indes schon lange dem Usus entsprach.[73] Die Kaiser und ihre Bewertung spielen bei Theodor Anagnostes eine wesentliche Rolle. Zugleich kennt er eine Reihe von Heldengestalten, die ungerechtes Leid erfahren und deren Gedächtnis noch zu seiner Zeit gefährdet ist. Obwohl sonst Konstantinopel so wichtig für Theodor Anagnostes ist, sind diese Gestalten nicht an Konstantinopel gebunden – Theodor von Mopsuestia und Theodoret von Kyrrhos, die beiden Opfer, mit denen wir uns näher befasst haben, stammen ja beide aus der Provinz.

Wenn die Verfolgungssituation eine so große Rolle für die Geschichtskonzeption von Theodor Anagnostes spielt, passt es sehr gut, dass er seine *Praefatio* damit beginnt, dass er sich als einen unerklärlicherweise Verbannten definiert. Damit schlägt er nämlich ein Thema an, das sich anscheinend durchgezogen hat. Diese *Kirchengeschichte* dürfte in einem hohen Maße eine Reflexion über die Bedrängnis der Rechtgläubigen gewesen sein.

Gut möglich, dass auch der Epitomator sich in dieser Tradition bewegte. Das könnte die eigenartige Spannung in seinem Werk erklären: Denn der Blick auf die Opfer kaiserlicher und bischöflicher Willkürmaßnahmen hätte es ihm erlaubt, konfessionell so verschiedene Autoren wie Theodor Anagnostes und Johannes Diakrinomenos zusammenzubinden. Gemeinsam hatten sie nämlich, dass ihre Konfessionen jeweils massive Verfolgungen hatten erdulden müssen und weiter erlitten. Die Opferrolle konnte, wenn diese Überlegungen zutreffen, bemerkenswerte Verbindungen jenseits konfessioneller Grenzen schaffen.

[72] Hansen 1995c, p. xviii.
[73] Vgl. Greatrex 2015, pp. 122–24.

Bibliographie

Quellen

De Boor 1883–1885 = Theophanes, Chronographia, recensuit Carolus de Boor, v. I–II, Leipzig.

Hansen 1995a = Sokrates, *Kirchengeschichte*, hrsg. von Günther Christian Hansen, GCS NF 1, Berlin.

Hansen 1995b = Sozomenos, *Kirchengeschichte*, hrsg. von Günther Christian Hansen, GCS NF 4, Berlin.

Hansen 1995c = Theodorus Anagnostes, *Kirchengeschichte*, hrsg. von Günther Christian Hansen, GCS NF 3, Berlin.

Hansen 1998 = Günther Christian Hansen, ‚Ein kurzer Bericht über das Konzil von Chalkedon‘, in *Fontes Minores 10*, hrsg. von Ludwig Burgmann (Forschungen zur Byzantinischen Rechtsgeschichte 22).

Nau 1913 = François Nau (Hrsg.), *La seconde partie de l'histoire de Barḥadbesabba ʿArbaïa*, Paris (PO 9,5).

Nau 1932 = François Nau (Hrsg.), *La première partie de l'histoire de Barḥadbesabba ʿArbaïa*, Paris (PO 23,2).

Parmentier – Hansen 1998 = Theodoret, *Kirchengeschichte* hrsg. von Léon Parmentier – Günther Christian Hansen, GCS NF 5, Berlin.

Literatur

Ashbrook-Harvey – Brakmann 1998 = Susan Ashbrook-Harvey – Heinzgerd Brakmann, ‚Johannes von Ephesus‘, *RAC,* 18, pp. 553–64.

Becker 2006 = Adam H. Becker, *Fear of God and the Beginning of Wisdom. The School of Nisibis and the Development of Scholastic Culture in Late Antique Mesopotamia*, Philadelphia.

Becker 2008 = Adam H. Becker (Hrsg.), *Sources for the Study of the School of Nisibis*, übers. und eingel. von Adam H. Becker (Translated Texts for Historians 50), Liverpool.

Becker – Childers 2011 = Adam H. Becker – Jeff W. Childers, s. v. ‚Barhadbeschabba ʿArbaya‘, in *Gorgias Encyclopedic Dictionary of the Syriac Heritage*, hrsg. von Sebastian P. Brock, Piscataway, pp. 257–58.

Blaudeau 2006 = Philippe Blaudeau, *Alexandrie et Constantinople 451–91. De l'histoire à la géo-ecclésiologie*, Bibliothèque des Écoles françaises d'Athènes et de Rome 327, Rom.

Bruns 2006 = Peter Bruns, ‚Kirchengeschichte als Hagiographie? Zur theologischen Konzeption des Johannes von Ephesus‘, *Studia Patristica*, 42, pp. 65–72.

Debié 2015 = Muriel Debié, *L'écriture de l'histoire en syriaque: transmissions interculturelles et constructions identitaires entre hellénisme et islam. Avec des répertoires des textes historiographiques en annexe*, Late Antique History and Religion 12, Leuven.

Destephen 2008 = Sylvain Destephen, ‚Iôannès 43‘, in *Prosopographie Chrétienne du Bas-Empire 3: Diocèse d'Asie (325–641)*, hrsg. von Sylvain Destephen, Paris, pp. 493–94.

Ginkel 1995 = Jan Jacob van Ginkel, *John of Ephesus. A Monophysite Historian in Sixth-Century Byzantium*, Groningen.

Greatrex 2015 = Geoffrey Greatrex, ‚Théodore Lecteur et son épitomateur anonyme du VIIe siècle‘, in *L'historiographie tardo-antique et la transmission des savoirs*, hrsg. von Philippe Blaudeau – Peter van Nuffelen, Millennium-Studien 55, Berlin – Boston, pp. 121–44.

Kosiński 2017 = Rafał Kosiński, ‚Corpus Theodorianum. Preliminary Propositions for a New Arrangement of Theodore Lector's Legacy‘, *Res gestae. Czasopismo Historyczne*, 5, pp. 111–24.

Kosiński et al. 2021 = Rafał Kosiński – Kamilla Twardowska – Aneta Zabrocka – Adrian Szopa, *The Church Histories of Theodore Lector and John Diakrinomenos*, Berlin.

Leppin 2003 = Hartmut Leppin, ‚The Church Historians. Socrates, Sozomenus, and Theodoretus‘, in *Greek and Roman Historiography in Late Antiquity. Fourth to Sixth Century A.D.*, hrsg. von Gabriele Marasco, Leiden, pp. 219–54.

Leppin 2019 = Hartmut Leppin, ‚The Roman Empire in John of Ephesus' *Church History*: Being Roman, Writing Syriac‘, in *Historiography and Space in Late Antiquity*, hrsg. von Peter van Nuffelen, Cambridge, pp. 113–35.

Leppin 2020 = Hartmut Leppin, Zwischen Bekennerstolz und Konsensfindung. Konzile und Konzilstheorie in der Geschichtsschreibung des ausgehenden sechsten Jahrhunderts, in *Konzilien und kanonisches Recht in Spätantike und frühem Mittelalter*, hrsg. von Wolfram Brandes – Alexandra Hasse-Ungeheuer – Hartmut Leppin. Forschungen zur byzantinischen Rechtsgeschichte NF 2, Berlin – Boston, pp. 107–32.

Nautin 1994 = Pierre Nautin, ‚Théodore Lecteur et sa „réunion de différentes Histoires" de l'Église‘, *REB*, 52, pp. 213–44.

Pásztori-Kupán 2006 = István Pásztori-Kupán, *Theodoret of Cyrus*, London – New York.

Pouderon 2014 = Bernard Pouderon, ‚Pour une évaluation de l'Epitome anonyme d'histoires ecclésiastiques. confrontation des trois historiens sources, de la Tripartite de Théodore le Lecteur et de celle de Cassiodore', in *Mélanges Jean-Pierre Mahé*, hrsg. von Aram Mardirossian – Agnès Ouzounian – Constantin Zuckerman, Travaux et Mémoires 18, Paris, pp. 527–45.

Richter 2002 = Siegfried G. Richter, *Studien zur Christianisierung Nubiens*, Sprachen und Kulturen des christlichen Orients 11, Wiesbaden.

Schor 2011 = Adam M. Schor, *Theodoret's People. Social Networks and Religious Conflict in Late Roman Syria*, The Transformation of the Classical Heritage 48, Berkeley.

Urbainczyk 2002 = Theresa Urbainczyk, *Theodoret of Cyrrhus. The Bishop and the Holy Man*, Ann Arbor.

Abstract

Theodoret of Cyrrhus was bishop of Cyrrhus, a small Syrian city. He is well-known as a church politician who was denounced as a friend of Nestorius by his foes; but he was also a widely read church historian, whose work covered the period from the last years of Constantine to his own time. In both roles, as a historical agent and as a source, he appears in Theodore Anagnostes' work. There is a common concept of history between Theodoret and Theodore: Both describe ecclesiastical history as a history of victimhood. Theodoret was a victim himself in Theodore's view as he condemns Theodoret's deposition at the council of Ephesus II as unjust; yet, he also narrates his rehabilitation by the Council of Chalcedon extensively. Theodore refers to Theodoret's *Church History* in various passages, starting from the *Praefatio*. He believes that Theodoret, who does not criticise Cyrillus in this work, originally had sympathy for the bishop of Alexandria and often quotes him explicitly as an important authority. In some cases, however, one gets the impression that he implicitly deviates from Theodoret's narrative. Thus, despite his Chalcedonian stance, Theodore draws a nuanced picture of Theodoret although his predecessor had the reputation of being a dyophysite.

PHILIPPE BLAUDEAU

VICTOR OF TUNNUNA AS USER
OF THE *ECCLESIASTICAL HISTORY*
OF THEODORE LECTOR:
CHOICES AND OBJECTIVES

Rather than write a *breviarum* like Liberatus of Carthage – with whose narrative he seems not to have been familiar[1] – Victor of Tunnuna makes a historiographical choice inspired by a different model for narrating ecclesiastical events. He sets himself the task of continuing the chronicle begun by Saint Jerome and continued by Prosper of Aquitaine. However, like the work of the Carthaginian deacon, the content of the African bishop's work indicates a certain kinship with the ecclesiastical histories – a kinship already noted, if not described, by Isidore of Seville.[2] While, as we shall see, Victor's borrowing from Theodore Lector's text provides the pattern, the final development of the *Chronicon* emphasizes its kinship with ecclesiastical histories. Indeed, the African bishop gives a predominant place to ecclesiastical material and inserts a certain letter (which happens to have been false) intended to destroy Vigilius' reputation.[3] Moreover, in his work, the fight over orthodoxy is updated and personalized: thus, Vic-

---

[1] Mommsen 1894, p. 183; Cardelle de Hartmann 2001, p. 112*–113*; see also Placanica 1997, p. xvii.

[2] Isidore of Seville, *De Viris illustribus 25* (ed. Codoñer Merino 1964): 'Victor Tunnunensis ecclesiae Africanae episcopus. Hic a principio mundi usque ad primum Iustini imperii annum breuem per consules annuos bellicarum ecclesiasticarumque rerum nobilissimam promulgavit historiam, laude et notatione illustrem ac memoria dignam'. ('Victor of Tunnuna, bishop of the Church of Africa. He published a very famous short history, illustrious through praise and notoriety and worthy of memory, which contains facts of war and deeds of the Church, from the beginning of the world until the first year of the reign of Justin II (organized) according to consular year').

[3] Victor of Tunnuna, *Chronicon*, § 130 (ed. Cardelle de Hartmann 2001). See also Blaudeau 2012, pp. 283–85.

Studies in Theodore Anagnostes, ed. by Rafał Kosiński & Adrian Szopa, STTA 19 (Turnhout 2021), pp. 81–99
© BREPOLS ❧ PUBLISHERS   DOI 10.1484/M.STTA-EB.5.127977

tor reminds the reader how much he suffered for his faith, to the point of being exiled (*c.* 554–55) to Alexandria along with Theodore of Cabarsussum (Byzacena [4]). He also mentions that he was put in the Praetorian prison and then imprisoned in Diocletian's castle. He further describes how he was brought to Constantinople to face a dispute with the patriarch Eutychius (564). Summoned to a monastery,[5] he specifies that he remained in the capital after sanctions were lifted by the new emperor, Justin II.[6] Thus, it was on the shores of the Bosporus that he composed his narrative (*c.* 568 or perhaps even 575), which has strong overtones of apology-polemic. This is the only work that can be attributed to him with certainty.[7]

Because of this particular context of his life, Victor incorporated considerable content from Church history in his chronicle while at the same time preserving the yearly framework of consular dating. His belonging to the African community and his fight for the Three Chapters caused him to commit further to this choice. As P. Bruns has emphasized, Victor shared with Facundus of Hermiane and Liberatus of Carthage three principles that are irreducible to either the model of the Imperial Church or that of the

---

[4] Maier 1973, p. 425.

[5] Victor of Tunnuna, *Chronicon*, § 153; § 156; § 169 (ed. Cardelle de Hartmann 2001). Isidore of Seville, *De viris illustribus* 25 (ed. Codoner Merino 1964): 'Hic pro defensione trium capitulorum [ecclesia sua pulsus] a Iustiniano Augusto exilio in Aegyptum transportatur. Unde rursus Constantinopolim evocatus, dum Iustiniano imperatori et Euthicio Constantinopolitanae urbis episcopo obtrectatoribus eorumdem trium capitulorum resisteret, rursus in monasterio eiusdem ciuitatis custodiendus mittitur, atque in eadem damnatione, ut dicunt, moritur'. 'Chased from his church because of his defense of the Three Chapters, Victor was exiled to Egypt by the Emperor Justinian. Then, called again to Constantinople because he resisted the Emperor Justinian and the Bishop of Constantinople Eutychius, who were detractors of the Three Chapters, he was again sent to a monastery in that city and kept there; it is said that he died during this punishment'.

[6] See Placanica 1999, p. 246. Isidore's belief that Victor was under punishment until his death (see above) very likely is a result of his interpretation of the last paragraphs of the chronicle, which ends with the advent of Justin II without mentioning his first acts.

[7] Mommsen 1894, p. 178, notes that two manuscripts of the *De paenitentia* attribute it to 'Victor Tonensis episcopus historiographus'. However, it is usually thought that Gennadius of Marseille is earlier referring to that work when he mentions the *libellus* of Victor of Cartenna (chap. 78). See *CPL* 854.

petrinology developed by the Apostolic See, in spite of his deep reverence for the long-standing decisions ratified by Rome: a certain conciliarism (which supposes Rome's demonstrated acceptance of synodal decisions), respect for the primacy of Rome, and a defense of traditions.[8] No doubt this orientation resulted from a particular history, one characterized by the Cyprian heritage, the memory of the Great Persecution, the impact of the Donatist schism, Augustine's legacy, and the painful experience of Vandal domination. Thus, Victor positions his work at the heart of a culture of voluntary resistance.[9] This proclaimed particularity rests on the need to consider the legacy of history, since each generation must submit to the past, rather than redefine it.[10] It also comes from a geographical awareness open to the Ecumene but for the most part joined to it through the Mediterranean domain alone. Thus, Latin-African Christianity tends to think of itself as a space that has been tested and has remained intact. This is why it considers itself justified in exhorting its sister-churches when they risk losing sight of the crucial integrity of Chalcedon. Should we still invoke a certain accumulated delay in the face of the miaphysite question to better understand Victor's intention?[11] One might, on the contrary, emphasize that Vigilius of Thapsus (*c.* 470–82) had mounted a refutation in his work *Against Eutyches.*[12] But Victor, like Facundus or Liberatus, does not seem to have used it. It would surely be more accurate to refer here to a feeling of having been separated for a time from what had happened in the East, or perhaps a vague fear of becoming incorporated into the Alexandrian patriarchy,[13] and, within the heat of controversy, a passionate quest for information, governed by a particular sensibility.

[8] See Bruns 1995, p. 157; see also Pewesin 1937, p. 28.

[9] See Markus 1972, pp. 34–5.

[10] According to Facundus of Hermiane, *Defense of the Three Chapters,* VI, 5, 46; see Eno, 1976, p. 101.

[11] Modéran 1999, p. 707.

[12] On the date, see Petri 2003, pp. 34–9.

[13] It is possible that this expansion of its jurisdictional remit was proposed, in vain, by Justinian to Theodosius of Alexandria in exchange for his support of the Council of Chalcedon. See Maspéro 1919, pp. 38–9.

Whatever the case may be, a specific attention to context – better, a new understanding of ecclesiastical history – is cultivated in the *Chronicon*. It is for these reasons, and not only because of availability, that Victor privileges Theodore Lector's account, to which neither Facundus nor Liberatus had access. Victor, perhaps sensitive to the similarities between his own life and that of Theodore – who was also an exile [14] – appreciates the compatibility of Theodore's work with his own fundamental model of historical-doctrinal representation, which contrasts *obtrectatores* [15] and *defensores* of the truth. [16] This system of division between *obtrectatores* and *defensores* is relevant to the opposition between Arians and Niceans (in particular due to the Vandals' long period of domination in Africa). Above all, it characterizes the opposition between opponents and supporters of the Council of Chalcedon, and then fully reveals its relevance with the narration, in the final part of the *Chronicon*, of the struggle surrounding the *Three Chapters*, since that controversy was sparked by the *subreptio* of the Acephali miaphysites. [17] Thus, Victor borrows from Theodore Lector's *Ecclesiastical History* a significant amount of material, which can be divided into 59 passages of unequal length. It must be emphasized that while this division, made by Hansen, is functional, it is also debatable:

[14] See Theodore Lector, *Historia Ecclesiastica (HE)* (ed. Hansen 1995), p. 1; see also E 492, p. 139 and E 515, p. 148 and Blaudeau 2006 a, pp. 550–51.

[15] Such as Timothy Aelurus, F. 7 (= § 19), in Theodore Lector, *HE*, p. 104; F. 19 (= § 49), p. 115 (ed. Hansen 1995). Note that the paragraph numbers refer to the location of the passage in Victor's *Chronicon*, whereas 'F.' refers to the number of what Hansen considers a fragment of Theodore's *Historia Ecclesiastica* translated by Victor.

[16] Among the *defensores* who are also presented as *custodes* of the council of 451 we find Proterius (*custos*), *ibid.*, F. 7 (§ 19), p. 104; Timothy Salophaciolus (F. 10, § 23), p. 107; F. 17 (§ 49), p. 113; F. 20 (§ 53), p. 115; Euphemius of Constantinople (*custos*), F. 32 (§ 63), p. 122; Calandion of Antioch, F. 38 (§ 68), p. 125 (ed. Hansen 1995). Regarding the latter, Victor indicates the aggravation of the punishment of exile decided by Anastasius. No doubt the African got this information from Theodore's text, whose sole witness he would be in this case.

[17] This corresponds closely to the argument developed by Facundus of Hermiane (*Defense of the Three Chapters*, I, 2 ed. Clément – vander Plaetse 1974), an understanding that also appears in Liberatus of Carthage's *Breviarium*, XXIV, p. 140 (ed. Schwartz – Cassingena-Trévedy – Blaudeau 2019, pp. 344–47); see Pewesin 1938, p. 95, Cardelle de Hartmann 2001, p. 113*, and Placanica, 1999, p. 134.

the number of passages may be higher.[18] It should be added that Hansen believed that the parallels between the *Chronicon* and the epitome of the *Ecclesiastical History* written by Theodore constituted proof of such servile borrowing that Victor's summaries can practically be considered fragments of Theodore's work. More accurately, Kosiński has demonstrated that they are better thought of as a rather drastic synopsis, or a Latin summarization, of Lector's text.[19] In any case, Victor of Tunnuna is the first writer we can be absolutely certain used the most personal section of Theodore's account.[20] It is true that according to Hansen,[21] the oldest evidence of use of Theodore comes from *The Life of Saint Sabas*, composed by Cyril of Scythopolis around 556.[22] However, the eight passages that demonstrate an incontestable

---

[18] For example, § 64, ed. Cardelle de Hartmann 2001, p. 20, which indicates the death of Peter Mongus of Alexandria, who was bound until the end by Roman condemnation ('incubator ecclesie sub damnatione moritur'), from whom Athanasius of Alexandria received the episcopate and the error at the same time. There is also § 31 a. 467, *ibid.*, p. 11, which describes a sign in the sky: a cloud in the shape of a pole that remained in the same place for 10 days. For Placanica (1997, p. 78), this indication comes from Theodore's account, since it is also found in Theophanus (AM 5958, ed. De Boor 1893, p. 115): there, the cloud is in the shape of trumpet (in this respect it comes close to the *Chronichon Paschale*, § 467, ed. Dindorf 1832, p. 597), and is said to have appeared in the evening. These facts do not appear the epitome and are not mentioned by Hansen. It is also possible that some political-military information (for example § 72, p. 22) came from Lector's account; see Kosiński 2017, p. 117.

[19] Kosiński 2017, pp. 113–17, 120.

[20] We know that Theodore's ample work was probably comprised of eight books, four of which were what could be called the *Tripartita* (covering the period from Constantine's reign until 439, the end of Socrates of Constantinople's account), and four of which were his own personal compositions (from 439 to 518). As Delacenserie 2016 has recently shown, it would be incorrect to consider the first part a simple compendium. On the contrary, it allowed Theodore to model negative imperial images (especially via Constance II) and to justify the promotion of the see of Constantinople, independent of the state's changing support (see Delacenserie 2016, especially p. 143). The desire to signify the actuality of such an understanding is the origin of the rather adroit combination, in the first part, of elements from Socrates' *Church History* and in particular from Theodoret of Cyrrhus. While maintaining the see of Rome in first place, Theodore intended to preserve Constantinople's centrality, where the combat for orthodoxy was at stake. To do this, he had to draw from the account of the Euphratesian bishop despite his Antiochian tropism, since the latter's Christological orientations were easily compatible with his own interpretations.

[21] See Hansen 1995, pp. xix–xxi.

[22] See Flusin 1983, pp. 32–33.

connection between the two accounts involve figures – most often Palestinians – whose actions are discussed during only a brief period (between 511 and 518). It is thus doubtful that Cyril, when he undertook to write the paragraphs in question, turned to an exiled Constaninopolitan historian. Flusin proposes another hypothesis: it is more likely that a common source, issued from the ranks of Palestinian monks, explains the resemblances between the two accounts.[23] In contrast, as I have said, Victor of Tunnuna's *Chronicon*, which was completed in 565, depends heavily on Theodore's work,[24] in particular for its treatment of the reigns of Zeno and Anastasius.[25] Of course, the African bishop makes no explicit mention of his source. His silence makes it impossible to be certain where he consulted it, but we have good reason to believe he may have done so during his stay in Constantinople, perhaps at the monastery to which he was sent around 564,[26] or in another library after having regained his freedom.

It is clear that Victor read Theodore in Greek. But, while Victor spoke Greek – no doubt because he learned it in Africa[27] and was able to perfect his mastery of it during his forced stay in the East – it still eluded him somewhat. This explains – unless it was a mere oversight – his attribution of the name Barbas to the Arian bishop who could not baptize because the springs had dried up, causing the candidate to flee to the Catholic Church.[28] In Theodore's version, it is the catechumen who is named Barbas. This relation to Greek – one of proximity, rather than familiarity – also explains why Victor prefers to transliterate rather than translate certain expressions, either because they are technical or because their meaning is highly polemical. Thus, he refers to the documents that made up Emperor Leo's general survey (carried out in 457–58) and the

---

[23] See Flusin 1983, pp. 60–67.

[24] See Placanica 1997, pp. xix–xxi.

[25] Cf. Hansen 1995, p. xxi.

[26] Cf. Placanica 1997, p. xii.

[27] Like Fulgentius of Ruspe, Facundus, and Liberatus, but not Corippus, nor, it would seem, Junillus. Unlike many other areas of the West, the teaching of Greek was in fact still widespread in Africa during late Antiquity. See Simonetti 1994.

[28] Theodore Lector, *HE* F. 55 (§ 82), p. 136 (ed. Hansen 1995).

responses to it (furnished by 65 recipients, mostly metropolitan bishops who were charged with discussing them with their suffragans) by saying that they are 'called inciclia in Greek'.[29] And Victor proceeds in the same way with the famous interpolated *trisagion*,[30] which he renders as 'Plato [...] et Marinus [...] et

---

[29] § 33, ed. Cardelle de Hartmann 2001, pp. 12, 175 for ἐγκύκλια, the name given by the imperial chancellery at the time of official publication, usually rendered *codex encyclius* in Latin. Let us recall that the questionnaire focused on recognition of Timothy Aelurus as the legitimate archbishop of Alexandria after the lynching of Proterius and acceptance or rejection of the decisions of Chalcedon. In the published file, after the imperial letter, one could find the supplications of the Proterians to the emperor as well as their letter to Anatolius, who had previously been deacon of the Alexandrian Church. It also included a *libellus* from the Timothians submitted to the emperor on his request. Duly indexed and preserved, the responses received through August 458 were soon combined with the documents submitted to the examination of their authors and then published by the imperial authority. Incompletely transmitted to us, they all rejected Aelurus, while one sole letter indicated a refusal of Chalcedon. See Blaudeau 2006a, pp. 151–61.

[30] A simple acclamation inspired by Isaiah (Is 6, 3). The formulation of the Christological *trisagion* ('Holy God, Holy Strong, Holy Immortal, who was crucified for us, have mercy on us') may have been created by Eustathius of Antioch in the context of the Arian controversy, but did not become established practice at that time. It seems that when the Nestorian controversy worsened, the hymn took on a clear anti-diphysite meaning, perhaps at the instigation of the monastic movement of the capital and surrounding area led by Dalmatios – who was from the East and was a disciple of Isaac, himself Syrian in origin – as well as by Hypatios, both of whom were in favor of the Cyrillian teaching. Indeed, in their petition to Theodosus II, the seven bishops sent by John of Antioch, who were forbidden from staying in Constantinople after the negotiations of Chalcedon (September 431), complained that 'currently, some are trying to adulterate...this terrible acclamation of sanctity' (ACO, I-1-7, pp. 72, 36–37). At Chalcedon (451), at the end of the first session, the bishops of the patriarch of Antioch intoned a *trisagion* that seemed to be addressed to the Logos specifically ('Holy God, Holy strong, Holy immortal, have mercy on us', ACO, II-1-1, p. 195). This brief formula is the first one that can be fully confirmed. It was seized on by akoimetic circles, who gave it a Trinitarian meaning and created the legend that Proclus was the author of the famous troparion. The textual sources revealing this process are quite complex. In any case, it seems that Peter the Fuller, the miaphysite archbishop of Antioch (471; 475–76; 485–88) sought to take advantage of the strongly polemical nature of the Eusthasian formula when he insisted on its Theopaschist meaning with the addition of ὁ σταυρωθεὶς δι'ἡμᾶς, ἐλέησον ἡμᾶς. No doubt this interpolated expression was known already at that time in Constantinople, but at first it did not spread far: in the capital, on the instigation of akoimetic circles in particular, the Trinitarian understanding of the *Trisagion* predominated. It must have been in this milieu – though it is not clear exactly when – that the legend that the Archbishop Proclus (434–46) propagated

ymno quem greci "trisagion" dicunt, "o staurotis di emas" noviter apponentes' in recounting the riot of 512.[31] He also uses topographical indications that correspond directly to local usage.[32] It may be that he thought this choice would be appreciated as a touch of exoticism rather than seen as a source of confusion by his least habituated readers.[33]

The superficiality that Hansen sometimes attributes to Victor's work ('Oberflächlichkeit Victors'[34]) should not be ascribed primarily to Victor's imperfect command of Greek. Hansen, as a philologist, invokes this levity to explain Victor's misinterpretation of the doctrinal position of the patriarch John III of Jerusalem. John was elected after Elias was deposed and exiled to Aila on 1 September 516,[35] for having strongly opposed Severus of Antioch and the imperial support he enjoyed. Whereas Theodore maintains that the new archbishop remained in communion with the Chalcedonian monastics gathered around Sabas and Theodore, refusing to yield to the emperor's attacks, Victor claims on the contrary that he did yield, receiving Severus in his communion and condemning the Synod of Chalcedon. No doubt

---

the *trisagion* was born, thus supposedly guaranteeing its authenticity. In fact, Proclus himself is said to have learned it from a child who was taught by the angels. Thus, all the ingredients combined to crystallize the conflicts over the troparion. Nevertheless, they didn't come to a head until 511, and then intensified further the following year.

[31] On this, see Meier 2007, pp. 161–72 and my piece 'Hymnes, tropaires et kontakia controversés: composition et emploi du chant partisan lors de la querelle christologique (451–565)' in *Polémique en chanson, IVᵉ–XVIᵉ s (BnF & Paris 3), 11–13 June 2015* (forthcoming).

[32] Thus, Constantinople was set on fire 'apo tis Calcis' to Constantine's forum in the context of the sedition of 512 (§ 94, ed. Cardelle de Hartmann 2001, p. 31); see F. 65 in Theodore Lector, *HE*, p. 144 (ed. Hansen 1995); Victor also refers to the plane tree estate ('in possessione Platani uocabulo') to which Flavian of Antioch withdrew for a time (§ 85, ed. Cardelle de Hartmann; p. 27 = Lector, F. 59, p. 141, ed. Hansen 1995): the event occurred in 512 (and not in 504 as the chronicle implies; see Alpi 2009, p. 49). In the latter case, the transparency between the terms in Greek and Latin is such that it can directly give the meaning in his maternal language.

[33] No doubt his first aim was to reach readers who were African opponents of the condemnation of the *Three Chapters*, as Placanica suggests (1997, p. xxvi). On the astonishing spatial trajectory of his work, which certainly was not part of its author's plan, see above.

[34] Hansen 1995, p. 149.

[35] Alpi 2009, II, p. 126.

this must be considered a simple misunderstanding. Victor's claim that Anastasius' mother was Arian may also have been such a misunderstanding – Theodore imputes that faith to Anastasius' uncle, Clearchus, whom Victor does not mention; Anastasius' mother was, rather, almost certainly Manichean.[36] We may also note numerous errors affecting the chronological ordering of facts. Most often, it is difficult to determine the cause of such errors. This is the case with the doctrinal training provided by Leo to Juvenal to help him combat the teachings of Eutyches and Dioscorus.[37] Victor wrongly states that this parenetic teaching was handed down during the consulship of Patricius and Remirus – that is, in 459. The same is true of Emperor Leo's initiative, mentioned above, to send out a questionnaire to bishops and publish it along with their responses (*codex encyclius*).[38] The date Victor gives, 468, is shocking with respect to the narration, correctly dated ten years earlier, of the events that accompanied it – unless this is to be understood as an attempt to isolate an unfortunate decision that he attributed to excessive and inappropriate attention to the complaint of the heretics.[39] If so, this ill-fated intervention, which was unanimously defeated by the bishops, would have presaged the comparable and much more grievous efforts of

---

[36] F 39 (§ 67) in Theodore Lector, *HE*, p. 126 (ed. Hansen 1995). See also the epitome E 448, *ibid.* p. 126 and Greatrex in the present volume. It is possible that Victor may have thought it more relevant to emphasize the emperor's Arian genealogy in order to better compare his reign to the brutal governance experienced by the African faithful under the domination of their Vandal persecutors.

[37] F. 6 (§ 22) in *ibid.*, p. 102. This passage has no specific corresponding passage in the epitome. No doubt its origin was a passage in the *HE* that discussed the letter sent from Leo to Juvenal (454), the content of which was strongly parenetic (ACO II, 4, pp. 91–93 and Blaudeau 2012, pp. 250–51). Recall that Juvenal died in 458.

[38] F. 9 (§ 33) in *HE*, p. 105 (ed. Hansen 1995). Note the specific inflection of the account: before deciding to launch the investigation, the Emperor Leo was touched by the supplication of Egyptians encouraging him to call a synod to judge the decisions of Chalcedon (an argument that doesn't appear in the epitome). In such a simplified form, this account is not without connection to the facts as they can be established. See Blaudeau 2006a, pp. 154–56.

[39] In that case, Victor rejects the evaluation of someone whom he praises elsewhere (§ 142 ed. Cardelle de Hartmann 2001, p. 46), that is to say Facundus of Hermiane, who interpreted this move by the emperor as an attempt to confirm rather than to question the status of the Council of Chalcedon (*Defense of the Three Chapters*, XII, 3, 17 ed. Clément – vander Plaetse 1974).

Justinian against the *Three Chapters*.[40] We may also note the example of the Constantinopolitan synod that Victor says was convened by Anastasius in 499 (it actually took place in 507) to condemn Leo and the Eastern leaders of diphysite thought (the causes and decisions of this council are confused with those of the Antioch assembly in 509).[41] This presentation seems to follow the same logic: to establish an outrageous imperial precedent to the retroactive condemnation of certain works or of the very character of hierarchs who died in peace with the Church.[42]

More generally, Victor abridges Theodore's text significantly,[43] proceeding by omission and selective cuts as well as reconfiguration. A representative selection of the most noteworthy information ignored by Victor but mentioned by Theodore includes the following: Victor says nothing of Pulcherius' or Marcian's proofs of piety, does not refer to the ignominious treatment of Proterius' body, makes no mention of the first stage of Aelurus' exile to Gangra,[44] gives no attention to the initiatives of Bishop Gennadius of Constantinople, who is mentioned only in one of the lists of hierarchs (the same is true for Martyrius of Antioch); there is nothing about Daniel's undertaking against Basiliscus[45] (E 406), nor about the latter's attempt to correct his religious policy through his anti-Encyclicals; absence of any mention of Marcianos' rebellion against Zeno; the surprising omission of the surname of the miaphysite (Peter) Mongus, whereas that of (Timothy) Aelurus is willingly brandished;[46] no accusation of

[40] § 132; § 137, ed. Cardelle de Hartmann 2001, p. 45.

[41] See Grumel 1972, no. 186, pp. 139–40 and especially Placanica's very detailed note (1997, p. 95).

[42] Theodore Lector, *HE*, F. 54 (§ 81), p. 135 (ed. Hansen 1995).

[43] A striking example is the account of the divine punishment of the Arian blasphemer Olympios and the consequences of the memory of this exemplary sanction (through the mediation of an image). The account is cited at length, it seems, by John of Damascus (= F. 52a, *ibid.*, pp. 131–33; that is, 85 lines), a tale from which Victor draws 3.5 lines (= F. 52b § 80, *ibid.*, p. 133). See also Kosiński 2017, pp. 113–17 and Greatrex in the present volume.

[44] F. 10 (§ 9) in Theodore Lector, *HE*, p. 107 (ed. Hansen 1995). Aelurus' exile is supposed to have been to Cherson initially, whereas the epitome (E 380, *ibid.*) states it was Gangra.

[45] This is however indicated in the epitome. See E. 406 in Theodore Lector, *HE*, p. 113 (ed. Hansen 1995).

[46] That of the catholic John (Talaia) is also omitted. Note also that in present-

collaboration with Acacius launched against the papal legates of 483, and nothing about many aspects of Macedonius' fight against Anastasius.[47] The site of Flavian of Antioch's exile (Petra) is ignored,[48] and nothing is said of the aborted council of Heraclea (515), to which Rome very belatedly sent its representatives.[49] Similarly, Victor relegates to oblivion the initiatives of Timothy of Constantinople, an *obtrectator* of the council.[50] While it is difficult to explain all of these choices, we may note several trends: significant simplification of imperial actions; a limit on reminders of the horrors committed by heretics; an attempt not to tarnish Roman initiatives as long as they fit within the general framework of a pontifical policy faithful to the Chaceldonian heritage and to the teaching of Leo; and a valorization of the role of the best representatives of institutional authority rather than an exaltation of the charismatic power of ascetics. Above all, Victor sought to preserve Constantinopolitan centralism, a characteristic demonstrated by Theodore's work, down to the topographical details. The Bishop of Tunnuna intended to balance his spatial distribution of events: thus, he tries not to lose sight of events in Carthage or in Africa more generally (the narration of which, for the most part, does not come from consulting Theodore's work).[51] He also emphasizes the importance of the situation in Alexandria, which he was able to personally observe. By contrast, his discussions of Antioch and Jerusalem are more limited and modest.

---

ing the Alexandrian succession, Victor gives surnames to the two Johns (Mula and Niceta; F. 47, § 73, *ibid.*, p. 129). On the importance of these sobriquets, see Blaudeau 2006a, pp. 354–60.

[47] Whereas Theodore wrote his church history to indicate the quality of his commitment. See Blaudeau 2006a, pp. 550–51.

[48] See F. 59 (§ 85) in Theodore Lector, *HE*, p. 141 (ed. Hansen 1995). No doubt this silence can be explained by the fact that he considered Flavian to be untrustworthy in matters of faith.

[49] Which, however, Theophanus and the *Synodicon vetus* note. See E. 511 in Theodore Lector, *HE*, p. 146 (ed. Hansen 1995).

[50] Ed. Cardelle de Hartmann 2001, § 99, p. 32.

[51] For example, the following passages: § 26, ed. Cardelle de Hartmann 2001, p. 10 (succession of the see of Carthage); § 50, 51, *ibid.*, p. 16 (persecutions of Huneric); § 78, Placanica 1991, p. 24 (Vandal royal succession); § 86, *ibid.*, p. 27 (death of the Catholic Archbishop of Carthage, Eugenius). On the other hand, Victor says nothing about the Synod of Carthage (February 484).

Significantly reducing Theodore's account – it is reduced even with respect to what has come down to us through the epitome tradition[52] – Victor's narration, as I have said, reveals a guiding intention that can be more precisely established in certain cases. Grouping together in a single paragraph, on the reign of Zeno, references to ascetics who were famous at the time but some of whom are unknown to us today,[53] Victor discusses only their healing powers and their prescience. He avoids reporting on the contact that the emperor sought to establish with them – with Severus the Paphlagonian in particular – as if he wanted to preserve their sanctity from what he seemed to consider an attempt at appropriation, whereas from the point of view of power, this will to establish communication was crucial. It was supposed to make manifest the dialogue between individuals chosen by God without any prior ecclesiastical mediation, and to be completely frank – that is, open to the possibility of failure. This characteristic trait of the theological-political consciousness developed by the Eastern Roman Empire, which is reflected in Theodore's account, seems to have no place in Victor's narrative demonstration. Similarly, while the Bishop of Tunnuna seems not to have wanted to dwell on prodigies,[54] he gives prominent place to the phenomenon of collective madness that struck the populations of Alexandria and Egypt in 507.[55] He identified this behavior more clearly than Theodore seems to have done in the original passage (E 515 P), and deliberately describes it as an episode of cynanthropy. Above all, whereas the Greek summary lists three competing interpretations of this singular and dramatic event proposed by contemporaries,[56] Victor retains only one, a doctrinal explana-

---

[52] See Blaudeau 2006a, pp. 536–37; Kosiński 2017.

[53] F. 36 (§ 66) in Theodore Lector, *HE*, p. 124 (ed. Hansen 1995). Anastasius, Annianus, and Manasseh cannot be identified; Vindiomalus only is if he is considered identical to Bendidianus (Auxentius's successor). Regarding Severus, an ascetic from Paphlagonia (not to be confused with his miaphysite homonym and the future archbishop of Antioch), we can consult a long fragment from the Athos Iviron Codex 497, fol. 25ᵛ (= F. 37 in *ibid.*, pp. 124–25). See also Placanica 1997, p. 90.

[54] *Ibid.*, pp. xv–xvi.

[55] F. 71 (§ 88) in Theodore Lector, *HE*, p. 148 (ed. Hansen 1995).

[56] Victor leaves aside two other explanations proposed by some according to Theodore Lector (*HE*, E 516, pp. 148–49 (ed. Hansen 1995)): 1. the fact of

tion, apparently intended to attest to the legitimacy of following the Council of Chalcedon. He reports the following words: 'while these things were occurring, an angel appeared to some of the people in the form of a man, saying that these things were happening because they had anathematized the Council of Chalcedon; he threatened them so that in the future they would not presume such a thing[57]'.

Thus, while Theodore's account does not dominate Victor's to the point that the latter becomes merely a condensed summary, this is because the bishop intended to bring out certain emphases that are not so strongly stressed in Lector. For example, Victor repeats that Timothy Aelurus murdered Proterius even if he notes a chronologically distant fact regarding miaphysitism. It is a matter of emphasizing how criminal heresy is.[58] Above all, the African reconfigures Theodore's teachings, in an attempt to summarize but also because his ecclesiological model does not completely agree with that of his source. More precisely, the paragraphs listing episcopal successions, which Victor draws from Theodore's text but organizes differently, are the result of his pedagogical intent. On the other hand, his suggestive re-shaping of the order of the major sees is a result of his geo-ecclesiological vision. When he has the opportunity to recall famous synods, even those that may have been disastrous, the Bishop of Tunnuna emphasizes the importance of such proceedings – but this is in order to place Constantinople, and its titular bishop, in fifth – rather than second – position.[59] The message is perfectly clear, and is reiterated in the paragraph concerning the council of 553.[60]

---

having dared to utter oaths; 2. having been prevented from attending the feast of the Exaltation of the Holy Cross in Jerusalem.

[57] § 88, ed. C. Cardelle de Hartmann 2001, p. 28: 'his evenientibus, angelus in viri specie quibusdam ex populo apparuit, dicens hos eis pro eo quod anathema synodo Calcidonensi dederint evenisse, comminatus deinceps nichil eos tale aliquid presumere' (= F 71 in Theodore Lector, *HE*, p. 148. (ed. Hansen 1995)).

[58] 'Interfector Proterii' (§ 23, § 49, ed. C. Cardelle de Hartmann 2001, p. 9 and p. 15), 'Proterii...peremptor' (§ 46, *ibid.*, p. 14), 'qui Proterium interfecit,' *ibid.* p. 17. There is reason to believe that Victor's insistence also comes, at least indirectly, from the pontifical discourse developed on the subject by Leo and, especially, by Simplicius. On the latter, see Blaudeau 2006b, pp. 184–87.

[59] The Council of Ephesus (449) as well as of Chalcedon (451). See F 1 (§ 4) in Theodore Lector, *HE*, p. 3; F 3 (§ 10), *ibid.*, pp. 5–6 (ed. Hansen 1995).

[60] § 147, ed. C. Cardelle de Hartmann 2001, p. 48.

It is indeed a matter of refusing the pentarchy as conceived by Justinian and his entourage. Despite Theodore's promotion of the see of Constaninople, it can only be placed last in the order of the main Churches, which must always be based on the traditional pre-eminence of the three Petrine sees (Rome, Alexandria, Antioch).

Thus, this historiographical discourse that one might at first glance think is completely dependent on Theodore's aims is discreetly reshaped. Indeed, among the few pieces of information that Victor includes in his account of the period between 449 and 519 which are not borrowed from Theodore,[61] we find a unique feature that contributes to the change of perspective Victor seeks: in discussing the beginning of Zeno's reign, the African bishop imputes to the Isaurian emperor a desire to eliminate his son, Leo II. The latter is said to have escaped death only through the subterfuge of his mother Ariadne, who put another child in his place and tonsured her son.[62] In recounting this, no doubt Victor gathers together a Constantinopolitan oral tradition sparked by the confusion surrounding the fates of Leo II and Basiliscus, son of Armatus. Ariadne convinced her husband Zeno to spare Basiliscus' life: he became bishop of Cyzicus.[63] For Victor this was a matter of sullying the reputation of Emperor Zeno, soon to be 'numbed by the blow of the Eutychian error'.[64] In this way, he prefigured the misdeeds and iniquities of Justinian, whose existence came to an end the very same day that Theodore of Cebarsussi, whom he had exiled far from his see, died in Constantinople.[65]

Thus, Theodore's *Historia Ecclesiastica*, which is strictly Chalcedonian in its orientation, does not always suffice for producing the lesson that Victor seeks to pass on: that the emperor claimed to be Chalcedonian but was in fact a persecutor. It made it possible, however, to celebrate the figure of Vitalian, master of the

---

[61] Or sometimes from Prosper of Aquitaine for the period through 455.
[62] § 42, ed. C. Cardelle de Hartmann 2001, p. 14.
[63] See Croke 1983, p. 90.
[64] F. 23 (§ 54) in Theodore Lector, *HE*, p. 118 a. 482.
[65] § 173, ed. C. Cardelle de Hartmann 2001, p. 54.

soldiers and the true defender of the council of 451.[66] The intensity with which Victor draws on Theodore here is not a matter of mere imitation: unlike Lector, Victor was very aware of how the life of the champion of diphytism came to an end – he even emphasizes in his account that his assassination within the palace walls was organized and carried out by Justinian's faction.[67]

Thus, Victor drew on Theodore's *Historia Ecclesiastica* in writing his chronicle not only because it offered abundant material but also because it is shaped by a dynamic suitable to the movement Victor hoped to give to his own account. Moreover, at the cost of a significant amount of reorientation, which was sometimes erroneous or confused, he placed his work rather logically within a wider perspective in which, as in Theodore's project, the author's life commitment and the sense of his account come together in a resolute defense of faith, that is here of the *Three Chapters*. In proceeding in this way, Victor both honors and appropriates the spirit of Theodore's narrative. Above all, he guarantees his personal composition an unexpected *Fortleben*. Indeed, his work, which was discovered by John of Biclar when the latter was in Constantinople in the 570s and then brought back, inspired the latter to continue it in his turn. Through this transmission, Victor's *Chronicon* enjoyed a true Hispanic posterity, which the manuscript tradition testifies to, though it is perhaps not exclusive.[68] It reached Isidore of Seville, who used it for his own *chronica maiora*. Thus, several paragraphs originally taken from Theodore's work ended up having significant influence in the Western Middle Ages.[69] They illustrate the remarkable journey

---

[66] F. 63 (§ 91) in Theodore Lector, *HE*, p. 143; F. 66 (§ 95), *ibid.*, p. 145 (ed. Hansen 1995).

[67] § 107, ed. C. Cardelle de Hartmann 2001, p. 35 (July 520); see *PLRE* 2, p. 1176.

[68] Contra C. Cardelle de Hartmann 2001, p. 108*. See Brandes 1999, 278.

[69] *Chronica maiora*, pp. 473–74 (see especially § 384 on the Alexandrian cynanthropy = Victor of Tunnuna, *Chronicon*, § 88, ed. C. Cardelle de Hartmann 2001, p. 28); § 388 on the discovery of the body of Barnaby; compare with Victor of Tunnuna, *Chronicon* § 60, p. 19; § 389 on the modification of the evangelical text, compare with Victor § 87, p. 27; § 392 on the blasphemy of the Arian Olympios, compare with Victor § 80, p. 25; § 393, the Barbas episode; compare with Victor, § 82, p. 36.

of a historiographical production that was more sophisticated than it appears. They are the result of a double passage within the Mediterranean world of late antiquity: from Greek to Latin and from Constantinople to Hispania, thanks to the efforts of an African bishop committed to a certain understanding of ecclesial history, as well as the curiosity of his Iberian brothers.

This paper was prepared with the support of *Basileia Imperial y Primatus Pontificio ad Orientem en epoca tardoantigua: las relaciones geo-eclesiales y politico-eclesiasticas entre roma y las iglesias patriarcales (451–536)*, Université de Santander (dir. Pr Silvia Acerbi), Programa Estatal de Fomento de la Investigación Científica y Técnica de Excelencia, Subprograma Estatal de Generación de Conocimiento (Espagne).

Bibliography

Sources

Cardelle de Hartmann 2001 = *Victoris Tunnunensis Chronicon cum reliquiis ex Consularibus Caesaraugustanis et Iohannis Biclarensis Chronicon*, ed. Carmen Cardelle de Hartmann with an Historical Commentary on the Consularia Caesaraugustana and Iohannis Biclarensis Chronicon by Roger Collins, CC SL 173A, Turnhout.

Clément – vander Plaetse 1974 = *Facundi episcopi ecclesiae Hermianensis opera omnia. I. Pro defensione triorum capitulorum*, ed. Jean-Marie Clément – Roel vander Plaetse, CC SL 90A Turnhout, pp. 1–378.

Codoñer Merino 1964 = *El De viris illustribus de Isidoro de Sevilla*, ed. C. Codoñer Merino, Salamanque.

De Boor 1883–1885 = Theophanes, *Chronographia*, recensuit Carolus de Boor, v. I–II, Leipzig.

Dindorf 1832 = *Chronicon Paschale*, recensuit Ludivicus Dindorfius, Lipsiae.

Hansen 1995 = Theodoros Anagnostes, *Kirchengeschichte. Zweite, durchgesehene Auflage*, ed. Günther Christian Hansen, GCS NF 3, Berlin.

Kosiński – Twardowska – Zabrocka – Szopa 2021 = *The* Church Histories *of Theodor Lector and John Diakrinomenos*, ed. Rafał Kosiński – Kamilla Twardowska – Aneta Zabrocka – Adrian Szopa, Berlin.

Mommsen 1894 = *Isidori Iunioris episcopi Hispalensis Chronica maiora*, ed. Theodor Mommsen, *MGH AA* XI, Berlin, pp. 391–481.

Mommsen 1894 = *Victoris Tonnonensis episcopi Chronica*, ed. Theodor Mommsen, *MGH AA* XI, Berlin, pp. 163–206.

Petri 2003 = Vigilio di Tapso, *Contro eutiche*, ed. Sara Petri, Brescia.

Placanica 1997 = Vittore da Tunnuna, *Chronica. Chiesa e impero nell'età di Giustiniano*, ed. Antonio Placanica, Florence.

Schwartz – Cassingena-Trévedy – Blaudeau 2019 = Liberatus de Carthage, *Abrégé de l'histoire des nestoriens et des eutychiens*, ed. Eduard Schwartz, transl. François Cassingena-Trévedy – Philippe Blaudeau, SC 607, Paris.

Schwartz 1936 = Liberatus of Carthage, *Breviarium. Causae nestorianorum et eutychianorum breviarium*, ed. Eduard Schwartz, ACO, II, 5, Berlin – Leipzig, pp. 98–141.

Literature

Alpi 2009 = Frédéric Alpi, *La route royale* (ὁδὸς βασιλική, *'ūrḥō malkoyītō*) *Sévère d'Antioche et les Églises d'Orient (512–18)*, I. *Texte*. II. *Sources et documents*, Beyrouth.

Blaudeau 2006a = Philippe Blaudeau, *Alexandrie et Constantinople (451–91). De l'histoire à la géo-ecclésiologie*, Rome.

Blaudeau 2006b = Philippe Blaudeau, 'Rome contre Alexandrie? L'interprétation pontificale de l'enjeu monophysite (de l'émergence de la controverse eutychienne au schisme acacien 448–84)', *Adamantius*, 12, pp. 140–216.

Blaudeau 2012 = Philippe Blaudeau, *Le Siège de Rome et l'Orient (448–536). Étude géo-ecclésiologique*, Rome.

Brandes 1999 = Wolfram Brandes, 'Bibliographie', *Byzantinische Zeitschrift*, 92, pp. 278–79.

Bruns 1995 = Peter Bruns, 'Zwischen Rom und Byzanz. Die Haltung des Facundus von Hermiane und der Nordafrikanischen Kirche während des Drei-Kapitel-Streits', *Zeitschrift für Kirchengeschichte*, 106, pp. 151–78.

Croke 1983 = Brian Croke, 'Basiliscus, the Boy-Emperor', *Greek, Roman and Byzantine Studies*, 24, pp. 81–91.

Delacenserie 2016 = Emerance Delacenserie, *L'histoire ecclésiastique de Socrate de Constantinople: banque de données et autorité historiographiques pour la création d'œuvres originales au VIe s. (Théodore le Lecteur, Cassiodore, la première version arménienne)*, thèse dactylographiée, Université d'Angers/Université de Gand.

Eno 1976 = Robert Eno, 'Doctrinal Authority in the African Ecclesiology of the Sixth Century: Ferrandus and Facundus', *Revue des études augustiniennes*, 22, pp. 95–113.

Flusin 1983 = Bernard Flusin, *Miracle et histoire dans l'œuvre de Cyrille de Scythopolis*, Paris.

Grumel 1972 = Venance Grumel, *Les regestes des actes du patriarcat de Constantinople*, I. *Les actes des patriarches*. 1. *Les regestes de 381 à 715*, Paris.

Kosiński 2017 = Rafał Kosiński, 'Corpus Theodorianum. Preliminary Propositions for a New Arrangement of Theodore Lector's Legacy', *Res gestae. Czasopismo Historyczne*, 5, pp. 111–24.

Maier 1973 = Jean-Louis Maier, *L'Épiscopat de l'Afrique romaine, vandale et byzantine*, Neuchâtel.

Maspéro 1923 = Jean Maspéro, *Histoire des patriarches d'Alexandrie depuis la mort de l'empereur Anastase iusqu'à la réconciliation des Églises jacobites (518–616), ouvrage revu et publié après la mort de l'auteur par Adrian Fortescue et Gaston Wiet*, Paris.

Meier 2007 = Mischa Meier, 'Σταυρωθεὶς δι'ἡμᾶς – der Aufstand gegen Anastasios im Jahr 512', *Millennium*, 4, pp. 157–238.

Placanica 1999 = 'Teologia polemica e storiografia ecclesiastica nella controversia dei Tre Capitoli', in *Res Christiana. Temi interdisciplinari di patrologia*, ed. Antonio Quacquarelli, Rome, pp. 129–254.

Modéran 1999 = Yves Modéran, *Les Églises et la reconquista byzantine. A. L'Afrique*, in *Histoire du christianisme. III. Les Églises d'Orient et d'Occident (432–610)*, ed. Charles Pietri (†) – Luce Pietri, Paris, pp. 699–717.

Markus 1972 = Róbert Imre Markus, 'Christianity and Dissent in Roman North Africa: Changing Perspectives in Recent Work', *Studies in Church History*, 9, pp. 21–36.

Pewesin 1937 = Wolfgang Pewesin, 'Imperium, ecclesia universalis, Rom. Der Kampf der afrikanischen Kirche um die Mitte des 6. Jahrhunderts', in *Gestige Grundlagen römischer Kirchenpolitik*, ed. Erich Seeberg – Wilhelm Weber – Robert Holtzmann, Stuttgart, pp. 53–84.

Simonetti 1994 = Manlio Simonetti, 'Di alcuni caratteri specifici della letteratura africana nei secoli V e VI', in *Cristianesimo e specificità regionali nel Mediterraneo latino (sec. IV–VI). XXII Incontro di studiosi dell'Antichità cristiana, Roma, 6–8 maggio 1993*, Rome, pp. 127–36.

Abstract

Victor uses Theodore Lector's *Historia Ecclesiastica* in writing his chronicle not only because it offers abundant material but also because it is driven by a dynamic which seems to him adaptable to the slant he wishes to give to his narration, in other words the preservation of the Council of Chalcedon and consequently, in his mind, the defense of the *Three Chapters*. Moreover, at the price of a quite significant reorientation, which sometimes proves wrong or confusing, it places it logically enough in a larger perspective or, as was already the case with Theodore's project, within the context of a congruency between his life's commitment and of the meaning of his story: for Victor, a resolute defense of the *Three Chapters*. In doing so, Victor honors as much as he appropriates the spirit of the Lector's story. Above all he assures an unexpected Fortleben to his personal composition.

RAFAŁ KOSIŃSKI

THE *LAUDATIO BARNABAE* BY ALEXANDER THE MONK AND ITS RELATION TO THEODORE LECTOR'S WORK

1. *The author, purpose, and time of composition*

The author of the panegyric in honour of the Apostle Barnabas was a monk named Alexander, who resided in Cyprus at the monastery founded in the proximity of Barnabas' grave, founded at the same time as the church by the emperor Zeno.[1] It was at this church that this panegyric was most probably delivered in the presence of the metropolitan of Salamis.[2] Alexander is also credited with the authorship of the *Inventio crucis*, a composition dedicated to the discovery of the Holy Cross relics during Constantine's reign. As this latter work contains an anathema against Origen, it is usually dated approximately to a period around the Second Council of Constantinople (553).[3]

Laudatio Barnabae is a text whose actual objective was not only to venerate the saint, recognized as the Apostle of Cyprus, but also in particular to communicate the justification for the Church of Cyprus' aspiration to independence from the other metropolitan sees of the Empire. The argument cited in favour of the *autocephalous* (self-governing) status of the local Church was its perceived apostolic tradition, namely the founding of the Cypriot Church by the Apostle whose grave was located on the island and who, even more significantly, miraculously confirmed his role of the patron saint of Cyprus. It was related to the efforts

---

[1] On this shrine, see esp. Roux 1998 and Megaw 2006, pp. 394–404.
[2] Van Deun 1993, p. 15.
[3] For this work, see Scott 2004, pp. 157–58 and Nesbitt 2003, pp. 23–39.

Studies in Theodore Anagnostes, ed. by Rafał KOSIŃSKI & Adrian SZOPA, STTA 19 (Turnhout 2021), pp. 101–130
© BREPOLS ❧ PUBLISHERS   DOI 10.1484/M.STTA-EB.5.127978

by the Patriarchate of Antioch under Peter the Fuller (in the late fifth century) to subordinate the Church of Cyprus to the jurisdiction of the See of Antioch on the strength of the argumentation of the Apostolic character of the Antiochene Church, coupled with the claim that Christianity arrived in Cyprus from the city on the Orontes. For this reason, the entire second part of the panegyrical work is devoted to the issue of ecclesiastical autocephaly, which is roughly one third of the whole composition.[4]

Such a strong concentration, on the author's part, on the question of the Church of Cyprus' independence may suggest that it indeed may have been in danger at the time of the composition of this panegyrical work. As a result, it may have been composed relatively shortly after the events described in the second part.[5] However, already in the nineteenth century that some scholars raised a number of arguments which would put the placement of the composition of this text at the turn of the fifth and sixth centuries in doubt, and suggested shifting it by as many as several centuries forwards.[6] Currently, the dating of the panegyric has been based generally on the arguments brought forward by Richard Lipsius in the late nineteenth century.[7] He refers to the numerous inaccuracies in Alexander's depiction of Zeno's reign, but especially in the timeline of Peter the Fuller's episcopate, which would rather invalidate dating the composition to a time just after the events under consideration.[8] It was reckoned

---

[4] Another work that originated from the Church of Cyprus' struggle for its ecclesiastical independence is the so-called *Voyages of Barnabas*, the text most likely dating back to the period between the Council of Ephesus and the discovery of Barnabas' relics at the close of the fifth century. For a relevant argumentation in detail, see Starowieyski 1994, pp. 193–98.

[5] According to Caesar Baronius' view (Baronius 1858, p. 454), Alexander composed his work in the late fifth century (cf. also Combefis 1662, pp. 1–2); on the contrary, Le Nain de Tillemont 1693, vol. I, pp. 438 and 646 found that the errors made by Alexander are proof that he authored it at a much later time. Likewise, Delehaye 1907, p. 236, was of the opinion that the work was not earlier than the latter half of the sixth century.

[6] For a recapitulation of earlier views on the dating of Alexander the Monk's works, see Salaville 1912, pp. 134–37 and Van Deun 1993, pp. 16–21.

[7] Lipsius 1884, pp. 298–304.

[8] For instance, Lipsius 1884, pp. 302–03. Also, the negative representation of Emperor Zeno, who was, as *magister militum per Orientem*, according to the

that the pivotal argument defining the *terminus post quem* was the author's referring to the Bishop of Constantinople as 'ecumenical patriarch,' which was used for the first time by Patriarch John II in the year 518, but would become more widespread only in the following decades.[9] A much greater problem was to determine the *terminus ante quem*. It was also noticed that the panegyric showed no trace of the theological controversies of the seventh century, such as Monoenergism and Monotheletism,[10] and mentioned no information on the capture and complete destruction of Salamis by the Arabic troops of Muawiyah, which is reported to have taken place in 648.[11] Consequently, it was somewhat tempting to assume that the *Laudatio* should have been written in the sixth century, without making the date more specific.

More recently, some scholars have attempted to narrow down the time-span for the composition of this work, but they seem to proceed from the incorrect assumptions. Notably, in his introduction to the critical edition, Peter Van Deun argues that the *terminus ante quem* for the composition of the *Laudatio* is 566, i.e., the final year up to which Victor of Tunnuna brought his *Chronicle*, placing the information about the discovery of Barnabas' relics and the Gospel of Matthew in Cyprus under the year 488. The scholar has assumed that Victor must have known the contents of the *Laudatio*, which is summarized in his anno-

---

panegyric, prone to corruption offered by the Fuller, would obviously attest to the fact that it could not have been written during this emperor's reign.

[9] Cf. Lipsius 1884, p. 303. This title was used on many occasions by the emperor Justinian in reference to Patriarch of Constantinople (e.g., in the title of *Novella* 3 of 535 addressed to Patriarch Epiphanios [ed. Schoell 1912, p. 18]), cf. Flusin 1998, p. 519. For more on this title, see Grumel 1908, pp. 161–71, V. Grumel 1945, pp. 212–18 and V. Laurent 1948, pp. 5–26.

[10] P. Van Deun 1993, pp. 20–21.

[11] Cf. R. A. Lipsius 1884, p. 304, esp. note 1. It should be noted that the precise date of the Arab conquest of Cyprus as well as the scale of the destruction at Salamis are both uncertain in view of the fact that the Byzantine and Arabic sources do not provide any details on this matter, while all the specific information that we have comes only from an account found in a Syriac chronicle by Pseudo-Dionysios of Tel-Mahre. According to this source, Muaviya plundered Salamis once again in 653, cf. A. Beihammer 2004, pp. 47–68 and L. Zavagno 2017, pp. 74–79.

tation,[12] whereas in actual fact Victor had drawn this particular information from Theodore Lector's *History* (which was written shortly after the year 518), not from the *Laudatio*, and therefore it cannot be of use in determining the dates of the latter work. It would not appear very likely either that the *terminus post quem*, as Bernd Kollmann argues,[13] could have been delimited by the riots at Constantinople in connection with the Theopaschite addition to the Trishagion, which broke out in the year 512. Although Kollmann holds the opinion that this Constantinopolitan controversy is actually reflected in the *Laudatio*, it does not seem to be correct. The addition issue was well known across the East, also outside Constantinople,[14] and we even know of some heated disputes over this question in Cyprus.[15] It is then evident that there is no need at all to connect the preoccupation with this problem only with the disturbances at the capital.

Peter Van Deun is correct, nevertheless, in his opinion that setting the general dating for the panegyric in Justinian's reign coincides with the dates proposed for the other work by Alexander, i.e., the above-named *Inventio Crucis*, encompassing the period 543–53.[16] It also seems reasonable to assume that dating the *Laudatio Barnabae* to this period could be supported by some

---

[12] P. Van Deun 1993, p. 21. Van Deun's suggestion was also followed by B. Kollmann 2007, p. 60.

[13] Cf. B. Kollmann 2007, p. 59.

[14] One of the examples may be a mention of the controversy in the *History* by John Diakrinomenos (*Epitome* 540, ed. Hansen 1995, p. 154, 17–19), who wrote his work in the Eastern part of the Roman Empire, most likely at Antioch, or in the *Vita Sabae* by Cyril of Scythopolis (*Vita Sabae* 32, ed. Schwartz 1939, pp. 117, 25–118, 14).

[15] Cf., e.g., Sophronios of Jerusalem's *Letter* to Arcadius of Cyprus, as cited by Van Deun, describing a controversy over Peter the Fuller's addition that broke out on the island, cf. Sophronios' *Letter* to Arcadius of Cyprus, 1–2, 20, 22, 33–35 (ed. Albert – von Schönborn 1978, pp. 188 [24]–191 [27], 206 [42]–209 [45], 210 [46]–211 [47] and 222 [58]–225 [61]) and P. Van Deun 1993, p. 20.

[16] Cf. Van Esbroeck 1975, pp. 271–72 and Van Esbroeck 1979, pp. 106–11. Nesbitt 2003, pp. 29–33, makes a cautious suggestion to date the *Inventio Crucis* back to the time before the conquest of the Holy Land by the Persians and Arabs during Heraclius' reign. Kollmann 2007, p. 60, argues that Alexander's writing should have been contemporaneous with the final years of Justinian's reign.

other arguments which would come from an internal analysis of the text.

First of all, in consideration of the actual purpose of the presently discussed work, one should ask when, in the period following the attempts to subordinate Cyprus to the jurisdiction of Antioch under the episcopate of Peter the Fuller (as represented in the *Laudatio* account), the Church of Cyprus had once again seen it as necessary to reassert their rights to the autocephaly.[17] The problem is that the sources refer to the question of the ecclesiastical independence of Cyprus only during the period of the Constantinopolitan council *In Trullo* in the year 692,[18] in order to clarify the status of the Church on the island in a completely new political situation at the time. This is, in any event, a period that is definitely later than the time of the composition of Alexander's panegyric. It is still possible that the growing concern in Cyprus may have been caused by the efforts to rearrange the structure of the Church whose introduction had already begun under Justinian, in the 530s and 540s, in connection with the so-called pentarchy system, i.e., of the five patriarchates whose jurisdictions were to encompass all the territories of the Christian *oikoumene* within the framework

[17] Alexander's work was written at the request of the hegumen of the Barnabas shrine and was delivered in the presence of the metropolitan of Salamis, cf. P. Van Deun 1993, p. 15.

[18] Cf. canon 39 of the council *In Trullo* (ACO 2, ii, iv, pp. 40, 8–25; ed. Schwartz 1929), where it is said that the status of the Church of Cyprus is based on the decrees of the Council of Ephesus: Τοῦ ἀδελφοῦ καὶ συλλειτουργοῦ ἡμῶν Ἰωάννου τοῦ τῆς Κυπρίων νήσου προέδρου, ἅμα τῷ οἰκείῳ λαῷ ἐπὶ τὴν Ἑλλησπόντιον ἐπαρχίαν διά τε τὰς βαρβαρικὰς ἐφόδους διά τε τὸ τῆς ἐθνικῆς ἐλευθερωθῆναι δουλείας καὶ καθαρῶς τοῖς σκήπτροις τοῦ χριστιανικωτάτου κράτους ὑποταγῆναι τῆς εἰρημένης μεταστάντος νήσου, προνοίᾳ τοῦ φιλανθρώπου θεοῦ καὶ μόχθῳ τοῦ φιλοχρίστου καὶ εὐσεβοῦς ἡμῶν βασιλέως συνορῶμεν, ὥστε ἀκαινοτόμητα διαφυλαχθῆναι τὰ παρὰ τῶν ἐν Ἐφέσῳ τὸ πρότερον συνελθόντων θεοφόρων πατέρων τῷ θρόνῳ τοῦ προγεγραμμένου ἀνδρὸς παρασχεθέντα προνόμια, ὥστε τὴν Νέαν Ἰουστινιανούπολιν τὸ δίκαιον ἔχειν τῆς Κωνσταντιέων πόλεως καὶ τὸν ἐπ᾽ αὐτῇ καθιστάμενον θεοφιλέστατον ἐπίσκοπον πάντων προεδρεύειν τῶν τῆς Ἑλησποντίων ἐπαρχίας καὶ ὑπὸ τῶν οἰκείων ἐπισκόπων χειροτονεῖσθαι κατὰ τὴν ἀρχαίαν συνήθειαν· τὰ γὰρ ἐν ἑκάστῃ ἐκκλησίᾳ ἔθη καὶ οἱ θεοφόροι ἡμῶν πατέρες παραφυλάττεσθαι διεγνώκασι, τοῦ τῆς Κυζικηνῶν πόλεως ἐπισκόπου ὑποκειμένου τῷ προέδρῳ τῆς εἰρημένης Ἰουστινιανουπόλεως, μιμήσει τῶν λοιπῶν ἁπάντων ἐπισκόπων τῶν ὑπὸ τὸν λεχθέντα θεοφιλέστατον πρόεδρον Ἰωάννην, ὑφ᾽ οὗ χρείας καλούσης καὶ ὁ τῆς αὐτῆς Κυζικηνῶν πόλεως ἐπίσκοπος χειροτονηθήσεται.

of the Roman Empire.[19] The emperor's attempts may have been a cause for concern to the hierarchy of the Church in Cyprus, who would strive, in terms of propaganda actions, to buttress their claim for complete independence from the Patriarchate of Antioch, especially in view of the fairly ambiguous resolution achieved during the Council of Ephesus in 431.[20] In this specific situation, invoking the discovery of Barnabas' relics in Cyprus during the emperor Zeno's reign as well as to the privilege of autocephaly reputedly bestowed on the Church of Cyprus by this ruler would have further reinforced the claim stated by the Cypriot hierarchy.[21]

Secondly, it should be stressed that Alexander the Monk, as we shall see later on, makes an attempt at diminishing the impact

---

[19] The concept of one emperor and five patriarchs was already emphasized in *Novella* 6, 8 of the year 535 (ed. Schoell 1912, p. 46), where it is stated that metropolitans should be subject to patriarchs. The idea of pentarchy is clearly defined in the *proemium* of the *Novella* 109 of 541 (ed. Schoell 1912, pp. 517–18: ὅ τε τῆς ἑσπερίας Ῥώμης καὶ ταύτης τῆς βασιλίδος πόλεως καὶ Ἀλεξανδρείας καὶ Θεουπόλεως καὶ Ἱεροσολύμων, καὶ πάντες οἱ ὑπ᾿ αὐτοὺς τεταγμένοι ὁσιώτατοι ἐπίσκοποι) and is also present in later legislation, e.g., in *Novella* 123, 3 of 546 (ed. Schoell 1912, p. 597). Cf. also Kuźma 2011, pp. 115–16.

[20] In a special proclamation, the Council of Ephesus (431) granted independence to the Church of Cyprus only on the condition that there was no ancient custom of consecrating bishops in Cyprus by Patriarch of Antioch. The Church of Antioch was therefore in position to question this act, while the emperor Zeno's privilege, as reported by Alexander the Monk, was supposed to have been unconditional. For the Council of Ephesus, see *Gesta de episcopis Cypriis* (ACO i, i, 7, pp. 122, 5–10 [ed. Schwartz 1929]): εἰ μηδὲ ἔθος ἀρχαῖν παρηκολούθησαν, ὥστε τὸν ἐπίσκοπον τῆς Ἀντιοχέων πόλεως τὰς ἐν Κύπρῳ ποιεῖσθαι χειροτονίας, καθαδιὰ τῶν λιβέλλων καὶ τῶν οἰκείων φωνῶν ἐδίδαξαν οἱ εὐλαβέστατοι ἄνδρες οἱ τὴν πρόσοδον τῇ ἁγίᾳ συνόδῳ ποιησάμενοι, ἕξουσιν τὸ ἀνεπηρέαστον καὶ ἀβίαστον οἱ τῶν ἁγίων ἐκκλησιῶν τῶν κατὰ τὴν Κύπρον προεστῶτες, κατὰ τοὺς κανόνας τῶν ὁσίων πατέρων καὶ τὴν ἀρχαίαν συνήθειαν δι᾿ ἑαυτῶν τὰς χειροτονίας τῶν εὐλαβεστάτων ἐπισκόπων ποιούμενοι). In this regard, cf. also Hackett 1901, pp. 20–21; Hill 1949, pp. 275–76 (who closely follows John Hackett's narration concerning church matters) and Starowieyski 2007, p. 1125.

[21] There is now no point in deciding on the authenticity of Alexander's account regarding the autocephaly privilege conferred on the Church of Cyprus by Zeno, yet it should be noted that the text of *Laudatio* is the only one that communicates this information, apparently in an attempt to serve as an element of the propaganda campaign of the local Church. In any event, it seems to be beyond dispute that the relics of Barnabas had been found during this ruler's reign and the Church of Cyprus used it as a pretext to voice their claim to independence, as passed on in the tradition drawing on Theodore Lector's *History*.

of Theopaschite overtones in Peter's activity in favour of crediting him with a firmly anti-Chalcedonian attitude, which may be proof that the work was written in Justinian's reign, following his adoption of the so-called Theopaschite formula ('One of the Trinity crucified in the flesh' / *unus ex Trinitate crucifixum est carne*); in 533, the emperor promulgated the edicts according to which the formula was incorporated into the body of Chalcedonian orthodoxy.[22] An excessively critical approach to Theopaschism at that time may have been viewed with reluctance in Constantinople, having a negative impact on the fulfilment of Cypriot aspirations.[23]

To sum up, it seems that the safest bet is to put the date of the *Laudatio Barnabae* within the limits of the emperor Justinian's reign, most probably sometime around the middle of that period. Perhaps, some unspecified controversies over the ecclesiastical independence of Cyprus would have once again reappeared at the time, a possible trace of which may be Nikephor Kallistos' mention to the effect that the emperor had reaffirmed the independence of the Church of Cyprus.[24]

---

[22] CJ I, 1, 6 of 15 March 533 (ed. Krueger 1892, pp. 7–8); CJ I, 1, 7 of 16 March 533 (ed. Krueger 1892, pp. 8–10); CJ I, 1, 8 of 6 June 533 (ed. Krueger 1892, pp. 10–11). *Chronicon paschale*, s.a. 533 (ed. Dindorf 1832, pp. 630–33).

[23] Even when he explains why Peter the Fuller's addition to the *Trishagion* hymn is something wrong, Alexander does not say anything about its theologically erroneous contents, but only that the hymn was revealed miraculously, so consequently nothing should be added to or removed from it; cf. *Laudatio Barnabae* 639–64 (ed. Van Deun 1993). The only moment when the author of the panegyric ventures into a greater criticism of Theopaschism is a passage which accuses the Apollinarists of 'professing a morbid view that God had suffered' (*Laudatio Barnabae* 629 (ed. Van Deun 1993, p. 110): θεοπασχίαν νοσοῦσι). Still, there is an obvious theological difference between asserting that God suffers and stating that One of the Trinity suffered (or was crucified) in the body.

[24] Nikephos Kallistos Xanthopoulos, xvi, 37 (PG 147, col. 200 CD): Ἐκράτυνε δ' ἐπὶ μᾶλλον τοῦτο καὶ Ἰουστινιανὸς ὕστερον ἐπὶ δόξῃ τῆς γαμετῆς Θεοδώρας Κύπρον λαχούσης πατρίδα· καθὰ δὴ καὶ ἐπὶ τὴν Ἀχριδῶ τὴν ἑαυτοῦ πατρίδα ἐποίει, ἣν δὴ πρώτην ἐκάλεσεν Ἰουστινιανήν. It is well worth remembering however that the extant laws from the emperor Justinian's period do not refer to any information on the autocephaly of Cyprus. On this question, cf. also Downey 1958, p. 228, where the author argues that the issue of the independence of the Church of Cyprus had only resurfaced during the above-mentioned council *in Trullo* in the year 691/92. As we know, Justinian would make numerous references to his vision of one emperor and five patriarchs, the so-called pentarchy. Even though

2. *Parallels between the accounts in the* Laudatio Barnabae *and the* History *by Theodore Lector and other sources*

The panegyric in honour of Barnabas contains two accounts, which can also be found in the tradition related to the *Church History* by Theodore Lector. The first one deals with the story of Peter the Fuller and his activity as Patriarch of Antioch, while the other one treats of the discovery of the relics of Apostle Barnabas in Cyprus and the related question of the autocephaly of Cyprus. Unfortunately, both accounts survive only in the sources which draw on Theodore's *History*, while the original work is lost. This circumstance obviously makes it very difficult to compare the *Laudatio* with the Theodorean tradition, especially as all the extant works connected with it are later than Alexander the Monk's panegyric. The Theodorean tradition is primarily the *Epitome* of various church histories,[25] written in the early seventh century, the dependent works from the ninth century: the *Chronography* by Theophanes,[26] George the Monk's *Chronicle*,[27] and the *Synodicon Vetus*,[28] as well as the much later works, whose authors had also directly or indirectly drawn

these do not hint at any formal subordination of the island to the Patriarchate of Antioch, the emperor's policy may have caused some alarm in Cyprus, as possibly reflected in the drawing up of the propaganda document in support of the argumentation for the autocephaly of the Church of Cyprus.

[25] For the dating of the *Epitome*, see Hansen 1995, pp. xxxvii–xxxix, who dates the compilation to the period 610–15 (which is followed by Ph. Blaudeau 2006, p. 536). Cf. also Pouderon 1998, pp. 178–85; Nautin 1994, p. 242, who argues for a general dating at around the year 600.

[26] Theophanes (died 817/18) was the founder of the monastery of Megas Agros on Mt Sigriane (where he was also a monk). His *Chronicle* covers the period from 284 to 813, cf. Mango – Scott 1997, pp. xliii–lxiii and Treadgold 2013, pp. 38–77.

[27] George was a monk at some unidentified monastery in Constantinople. His *Chronicle* begins with the Creation and ends in the year 843 with the reestablishment of icons veneration, yet it was actually written somewhat later on, most likely after 870; cf. Hunger 1978, pp. 347–51 and Treadgold 2013, pp. 115–19.

[28] The *Synodicon Vetus* is an anonymous author's concise history of church synods spanning the period from the Apostolic times up to the year 886, ending with the final deposition of Patriarch Photios of Constantinople. The *Synodicon* was composed probably not much later, at the turn of the ninth and tenth centuries; cf. Duffy, Parker 1979, pp. xiii–xv.

from the *Epitome*, such as the works by Kedrenos,[29] Simeon Logothetes,[30] Nikephos Kallistos Xanthopulos,[31] and the *Souda*.[32] Only the *Chronicle* by Victor of Tunnuna, who derives his information directly from Theodore's *History*, is temporally coincident with the period when the *Laudatio* was composed. Also, as a source independent from the *Epitome*, it helps in verifying this latter account.[33]

Certain elements from the story of Peter the Fuller and the discovery of Barnabas' relics can also be found in sources independent of Theodore's work (even though a common original source is not out of the question), such as the *Gesta de nomine Acacii*, *Vita Sabae* by Cyril of Scythopolis, and the *Letters* by Severus of Sozopolis.

Finally, it should be stressed that the accounts of Theodore and Alexander are different in terms of their literary genre. While the composition of the Cypriot monk was a panegyric (even if it contains some elements of historical narrative), Theodore wrote a historical work, which would also bear on certain differences between the two accounts.

The narrative of Peter the Fuller

The following listing presents the text of the *Laudatio* alongside the parallel accounts from the other sources relevant to Peter the Fuller's career.

---

[29] Kedrenos was most probably a monk who penned his work (*Compedium historiarum*) in the late eleventh or early twelfth century. It encompasses the period from the Creation to the accession of the emperor Isaac I Komnenos in 1057; cf. Hunger 1978, pp. 393–94.

[30] Simeon Logothetes was active in the mid-tenth century. His *Chronicle* covers a period up to the year 948; cf. Hunger 1978, pp. 354–57.

[31] Nikephor Kallistos Xanthopoulos was a presbyter at the Hagia Sophia in Constantinople, becoming a monk near the end of his life. It appears that he may have died shortly after the year 1326. He was the author of liturgical works as well as of a *Church History* written after 1317, whose 18 surviving books encompass a period from Christ's time to the year 610; cf. Beck 1956, pp. 705–07 and Gentz 1966.

[32] The precise date of the composition of the *Souda* lexicon is unknown, but it must have been written certainly later than the mid-tenth century, perhaps around the year 1000, cf. Adler 1932, cols 675–717.

[33] On the author, see Placanica 1989, pp. 327–36.

Laudatio Barnabae	Theodore Lector's *Epitome*	*Gesta de nomine Acacii*	Sources dependent on the *Epitome*
584–600 (ed. Van Deun 1993, p. 108) Τοῦ δὲ μακαρίου Μαρκιανοῦ καταπαύσαντος τὴν ἀρχήν, παρέλαβε τὴν βασιλείαν ὁ τῆς θείας λήξεως Λέων· τούτῳ ὑπῆρχε γαμβρός, Ζήνων τίς ὀνόματι, Ἴσαυρος τῷ γένει, ὅστις καὶ ἐβασίλευσε μετ' αὐτόν. Κατ' ἐκεῖνον δὲ τὸν καιρὸν εὑρέθη ἐν τῇ εὐαγεστάτῃ μονῇ τῶν Ἀκοιμήτων διάβολος τίς μονάζων, ὥσπερ ἐν ἀποστόλοις Ἰούδας, τοὔνομα Πέτρος, τὸ ἐπιτέδευμα κναφεύς· οὗτος δὲ τὴν ἐν Καλχηδόνι ἁγίαν σύνοδον ἀποστρεφόμενος, τῶν Εὐτυχιανιστῶν ὑπερεμάχει δογμάτων. Τοῦτον οἱ τῆς ἁγίας μονῆς ἐκείνης, ὡς λυμεῶνα καὶ φθορέα καὶ τῶν ἀποστολικῶν δογμάτων ἐχθρόν, ἐδίωξαν τοῦ μοναστηρίου· αὐτὸς δὲ καταλαβὼν τὴν Κωνσταντινούπολιν, τὸν τῶν κολάκων βίον ἐζήλωσεν, ἐξ οἰκίας εἰς οἰκίαν περιερχόμενος καὶ γαστριζόμενος· εὑρὼν δέ τινας τῶν ἐν τέλει τῆς βδελυρᾶς αὐτοῦ αἱρέσεως ὄντας, ἐκολλήθη αὐτοῖς καὶ δι' αὐτῶν γίνεται γνώριμος τῷ γαμβρῷ τοῦ βασιλέως, πατρικίῳ ὄντι τὸ τηνικαῦτα καὶ κόμητι ἐξκουβιτόρων·	**390 (ed. Hansen 1995, p. 109, 20–22)** [...] Ζήνων ὁ στρατηλάτης ὁ γαμβρὸς ἐπὶ θυγατρὶ Ἀριάδνῃ τοῦ βασιλέως Λέοντος. τούτῳ Πέτρος πρεσβύτερος τοῦ ἐν Χαλκηδόνι ναοῦ Βάσσης τῆς μάρτυρος, ὁ ἐπίκλην Κναφεύς, ἠκολούθησεν ἐπὶ Ἀντιόχειαν.	**25 (ed. Günther 1895, p. 450, 2–3)** Petrum apud Constantinopolim monasterium gubernasse [...]	**Theophanes AM 5956 (ed. de Boor 1883, p. 113, 17–18. 20–22)** Τούτῳ τῷ ἔτει Λέων ὁ βασιλεὺς Ζήνωνα τὸν γαμβρὸν στρατηγὸν τῆς ἑῴας πάσης πεποίηκε [...] Πέτρος δὲ ὁ Κναφεὺς ἠκολούθει τῷ Ζήνωνι πρεσβύτερος ὢν τοῦ ἐν Χαλκηδόνι ναοῦ Βάσσης τῆς μάρτυρος. **Synodicon Vetus 98 (ed. Duffy – Parker 1979, p. 84, 1–3)**[34] Τοῦ βασιλέως οὖν Λέοντος γαμβρὸν αὐτοῦ Ζήνωνα τὸν ἐπὶ θυγατρὶ Ἀριάδνῃ οἰκείᾳ ἐν Ἀντιοχείᾳ τῆς Συρίας ἐξαποστείλαντος, μοναχός τις μονῆς τῶν Ἀκοιμήτων ἐπηκολούθησεν, ...

Contrary to the opinion prevailing in historiography since the time of Richard Lipsius,[35] Alexander delivers some fairly accurate information about the emperor Zeno. He knows that the ruler

[34] The present text aims to discuss, in the first place, the earlier longer recension of the *Synodicon Vetus*. The shorter one is its later 'remake' which made a thorough revision of it, in the passage under consideration, as based on Theodore's *Epitome*, whose content it essentially repeats. In this particular recension, the anonymous editor knows that Peter was a presbyter of the Church at Chalcedon (SV² 98 [ed. Duffy – Parker 1979, p. 178, 2–3]: Ἀνιὼν δὲ Πέτρος τις τῆς ἐν Χαλκηδόνι ἐκκλησίας ἐπίκλην Κναφεὺς συνείπετο...), but he does not refer to the latter figure's roots in the *Akoimetoi* monastery.

[35] Cf. Lipsius 1884, p. 303. This view is reiterated in all the later studies dealing with the *Laudatio*.

was of Isaurian origin, served as *comes* of the *excubitores*, and was the son-in-law of the emperor Leo I (although he does not give his wife's name). On the other hand, the *Epitome* relates that Zeno held the office of *magister militum*, but it states the name of his wife, Ariadne (and the *Synodicon Vetus* repeats this piece of information), which cannot be found in Theophanes' *Chronography*. Alexander's work and the tradition related to Theodore also share many similarities, depicting the events in a similar sequence: the figure of Zeno comes first, his role at the court being defined, then passing on to the details on Peter the Fuller. This is clearly not how the Roman tradition represents it, where there is virtually no link between the figures of Zeno and Peter the Fuller, which seems to be understandable after all. First of all, the Roman sources had drawn their information about Peter the Fuller from Patriarch Acacius of Constantinople (which they do not fail to notice in some incisive remarks),[36] who certainly would not have drawn a link between the then reigning ruler and the incriminated heretic. It also seems to be obvious that even if the papal milieu had known about such a relation from some other sources, they would not have alluded to it in the late 480s in the formal correspondence with Constantinople, as the popes would never direct their attack on Zeno himself in their letters, focusing on the charges addressed to Acacius. On the other hand, the very mentioning of Peter the Fuller, the then incumbent Patriarch of Antioch accepted by the ruler, in the *Gesta*, may have been a certain form of hidden criticism towards the emperor. In any case, it would have been reasonable to expect a greater similarity between the Roman and Theodorean traditions, as essentially both of them present the information derived from the milieu of the Constantinopolitan patriarchate.

---

[36] *Gesta de nomine Acacii* are a summary of the development of the Christological dispute in the Eastern part of the Roman Empire with the aim of clarifying the question of the Roman synod's deposition of Acacius in 485. The source was written most likely in the later years of Pope Felix III's pontificate; cf. Günther 1894, pp. 146–49; Schwartz 1934, pp. 265–66 and Nautin 1966–1967, p. 139. Acacius' letter which is cited in some Roman sources, dating most probably from the year 477/78, is lost, and its content is known only from some sources of papal provenance; cf. Grumel 1972, pp. 113–14 (no. 151).

As regards the question of Peter the Fuller, the *Laudatio* gives us many more details than the Theodorean tradition does. According to Alexander's account, Peter came from the monastery of the *Akoimetoi*, from which (and likewise from several other monastic establishments later on), he was expelled. Subsequently, he would lead the life of an itinerant monk in Constantinople, where he finally became acquainted with Zeno through the Miaphysite circles. The author points out that Peter was a follower of Eutyches' teachings and an opponent of Chalcedon. In contrast, the *Epitome* (followed by Theophanes) provides a completely different version of his background: Peter was a presbyter at the church dedicated to the female martyr Bassa at Chalcedon. In the Theodorean tradition, it is only the *Synodicon* that gives a version convergent with the *Laudatio*, also mentioning that Peter came from the monastery of the *Akoimetoi*, but it does not say anything about his service as a presbyter of that church at Chalcedon. The Roman tradition, on the other hand, is once again different from the remaining sources, as it recounts that Peter the Fuller was not only a monk but also the head of a monastery near Constantinople. Unfortunately, since no name is given, we do not know if it really refers to the monastery of the *Akoimetoi* mentioned in the *Laudatio* and the *Synodicon*. Incidentally, a possible intentional omission of the name of that monastery would be easy to understand in view of the then current alliance between the papacy and the *Akoimetoi*.[37] Besides the *Laudatio*, no other source makes an association between Peter and the Eutychian teachings at that point in time.

Laudatio Barnabae	Theodore Lector's *Epitome*	Gesta de nomine Acacii	Sources dependent on the *Epitome*
601–20 (ed. Van Deun 1993, pp. 108-109) καὶ περιθέμενος εὐλαβείας πρόσωπον, ἣν σὺν αὐτῷ ἀδιαλείπτως, μὴ τολμῶν δημοσιεῦσαι τὴν ἰδίαν ἀσέβειαν. Ἀπαίροντι δὲ τῷ Ζήνωνι ἐπὶ τὰ μέρη τῆς ἀνατολῆς, συνείπετο ὁ Κναφεὺς ἕως	390 (ed. Hansen 1995, pp. 109, 19–20. 110, 1–6) Μαρτυρίου τὴν Ἀντιοχείας ἐπισκοποῦντος ἐκκλησίαν κατέλαβε τὴν Ἀντιόχειαν Ζήνων [...] ἐποφθαλμίσας δὲ τῷ	25 (ed. Günther 1895, p. 450, 3–7) [...] sed hoc propter crimina derelicto Antiochiam fugisse; ibi pulso Martyrio catholico episcopo per uilissimum populum et ha-	Theophanes, AM 5956 (ed. de Boor 1883, p. 113, 22–34) [...] ὃς καὶ πείσας Ζήνωνα συνεργῆσαι αὐτῷ μισθοῦται τῶν Ἀπολιναρίου τινὰς ὁμοδόξαν καὶ θορύβους μυρίους ἐγείρει κατὰ

[37] For the relations between the *Akoimetoi* and the papacy in the mid-480s, see Kosiński 2010, pp. 180–82.

THE *LAUDATIO BARNABAE* BY ALEXANDER THE MONK

Laudatio Barnabae	Theodore Lector's *Epitome*	*Gesta de nomine Acacii*	Sources dependent on the *Epitome*
Ἀντιοχείας. Εὑρὼν δὲ ἐκεῖ πολλοὺς τῶν Ἀπολιναριστῶν, κατὰ τοῦ πατριάρχου λοιπὸν ἐνεανιεύσατο, διεγείρων κατ' αὐτοῦ τοὺς ἀτάκτους τοῦ λαοῦ καὶ λοιδορῶν τὴν ἐν Καλχηδόνι σύνοδον καὶ Νεστοριανὸν καλῶν τὸν πατριάρχην. Ἐν πολλῇ δὲ ἀκαταστασίᾳ καὶ θορύβῳ τῆς Ἀντιοχέων ὑπαρχούσης, προσῆλθεν ὁ Κναφεὺς τῷ κόμητι, μετὰ δόλου λέγων· Ἐὰν μὴ διαδεχθῇ ὁ ἐπίσκοπος τῆσδε τῆς πόλεως, ἀμήχανον ἐσυχίαν ἄγειν τὸν δῆμον', ἄμα καὶ ταξάμενος αὐτῷ χρυσίου ποσότητα πολλήν, εἴπερ τύχοι τοῦ αἰτουμένου· ἐξέφανε γὰρ αὐτῷ καὶ τοῦ ἰδίου σκοποῦ τὰ κεκρυμμένα. Τότε πείθει ὁ Κναφεὺς τοὺς τὰ ὅμοια αὐτῷ νοσοῦντας καί τινας θυμελικοὺς καὶ ἑτέρους τῶν δημοτῶν πονηροὺς ἄνδρας, καὶ ἀναφέρει τῷ βασιλεῖ, πάνδεινα κατὰ τοῦ ἐπισκόπου ψευδόμενος· ἀλλ' οὐδὲν ὤνησεν ἡ αὐτοῦ δεινότης, τοῦ βασιλέως τῶν ἀποστολικῶν δογμάτων ὑπερασπίζοντος.	θρόνῳ τῆς πόλεως πείθει τὸν Ζήνωνα συνεργῆσαι αὐτῷ· καὶ τῆς λώβης τοῦ Ἀπολιναρίου τινὰς μισθωσάμενος μυρίους θορύβους κατὰ τῆς πίστεως καὶ Μαρτυρίου τοῦ ἐπισκόπου εἰργάσατο, ἀναθέματι δῆθεν βάλλων τοὺς μὴ λέγοντας ὅτι θεὸς ἐσταυρώθη· ἐν οἷς καὶ τὸν λαὸν εἰς διαίρεσιν ἤγαγε καὶ ἐν τῷ τρισαγίῳ προσέθηκε Πέτρος τὸ 'ὁ σταυρωθεὶς δι' ἡμᾶς'.

391 (ed. Hansen 1995, p. 110, 7–11)
Μαρτύριος πρὸς βασιλέα ἐλθὼν σὺν πολλῇ τιμῇ ἀπελύθη σπουδῇ καὶ παραινέσει Γενναδίου· ἐλθὼν δὲ εἰς Ἀντιόχειαν καὶ βλέπων Ἀντιοχεῖς ταραχαῖς καὶ στάσεσι χαίροντας καὶ Ζήνωνα τούτοις συμπράττοντα, ἀπετάξατο τῇ ἐπισκοπῇ ἐπ' ἐκκλησίας εἰπών· 'κλήρῳ ἀνυποτάκτῳ καὶ λαῷ ἀπειθεῖ καὶ ἐκκλησίᾳ ἐρρυπωμένῃ ἀποτάττομαι, φυλάττων ἐμαυτῷ τῆς ἱερωσύνης ἀξίωμα'.

392 (ed. Hansen 1995, p. 110, 12–16)
Μαρτυρίου ἀναχωρήσαντος τυραννικῶς ὁ Κναφεὺς τῷ θρόνῳ ἐπεπήδησεν· καὶ χειροτονεῖ εὐθὺς ἐπίσκοπον Ἀπαμείας Ἰωάννην τινὰ ἀπὸ καθαιρέσεως. γνοὺς δὲ ταῦτα Γεννάδιος διδάσκει πάντα τὸν βασιλέα. ὁ δὲ κελεύει τὸν Κναφέα πεμφθῆναι εἰς ἐξορίαν· ὅπερ προμαθὼν φυγῇ χρησάμενος τὴν ἐξορίαν | ereticos sedem ipsium occupasse continuoque damnatum ab episcopis atque a Leone principe Oasam deportatum; | τῆς πίστεως καὶ Μαρτυρίου τοῦ ἐπισκόπου. καὶ ἀναθεματίζει τοὺς μὴ λέγοντας τὸν θεὸν σταυρωθῆναι, καὶ σχίσας τὸν λαὸν Ἀντιοχείας προστίθησιν ἐν τῷ τρισαγίῳ ὕμνῳ τό· 'ὁ σταυρωθεὶς δι' ἡμᾶς'. ὅπερ ἕως σήμερον ἔκτοτε καιροῦ παρὰ τοῖς Θεοπασχίταις ἐκράτησε λέγεσθαι. Μαρτύριος δὲ πρὸς Λέοντα τὸν βασιλέα παρεγένετο, καὶ ἀπεδέχθη μετὰ πολλῆς τιμῆς σπουδῇ Γενναδίου ἐπισκόπου Κωνσταντινουπόλεως. ἐπανελθὼν δὲ εἰς Ἀντιόχειαν καὶ εὑρὼν τοὺς λαοὺς στασιάζοντας καὶ Ζήνωνα τούτοις συμπράττοντα ἐπ' ἐκκλησίας τῇ ἐπισκοπῇ ἀπετάξατο εἰπών· 'κλήρῳ ἀνυποτάκτῳ, καὶ λαῷ ἀπειθεῖ, καὶ ἐκκλησίᾳ ἐρρυπωμένῃ ἀποτάττομαι, φυλάττων ἑαυτῷ τὸ ἀξίωμα τῆς ἱερωσύνης'.

George the Monk (ed. de Boor 1978, p. 618, 10–14)
Ἐφ' οὗ Μαρτύριος Ἀντιοχείας διὰ τὴν τοῦ Ζήνωνος περὶ τὴν ὀρθόδοξον πίστιν διαστροφὴν ἀποταξάμενος τῆς ἐπισκοπῆς ἐπ' ἐκκλησίας ἔφη· κλήρῳ ἀνυποτάκτῳ καὶ λαῷ ἀπειθεῖ καὶ ἐκκλησίᾳ ῥερυπωμένῃ ἀποτάσσομαι φυλάττων ἐμαυτῷ τὸ τῆς ἱερωσύνης ἀξίωμα.

Synodicon Vetus 98 (ed. Duffy – Parker 1979, p. 84, 2–9)
[...] μοναχός τις μονῆς τῶν Ἀκοιμήτων ἐπηκολούθησεν, ὃς τῷ θρόνῳ |

(cont.)

Laudatio Barnabae	Theodore Lector's Epitome	Gesta de nomine Acacii	Sources dependent on the Epitome
	διέφυγεν. ψήφῳ δὲ κοινῇ Ἰουλιανός τις εἰς ἐπίσκοπον προχειρίζεται.		ἐποφθαλμήσας τῆς πόλεως πείθει τὸν Ζήνωνα συνεργεῖν αὐτῷ· καὶ τῆς λώβης Ἀπολιναρίου τινὰς μισθωσάμενος τὸν θρόνον Ἀντιοχείας καθήρπασε, καὶ μιαρὰν ποιησάμενος σύνοδον προσθήκην τοῦ τρισαγίου «ὁ σταυρωθεὶς δι' ἡμᾶς» καινοτομεῖ ὁ ἀνόσιος. Ὅπερ μαθὼν αὐτοκράτωρ Λέων ὁ μέγας καὶ εὐσεβέστατος ἐξοπισθῆναι αὐτὸν διετάξατο· ὃς προφθάσας εἰς τὴν μονὴν τῶν Ἀκοιμήτων κατέφυγε.

The differences in reporting on the first period of Peter the Fuller's activity at Antioch can be seen already in the circumstances of how he appeared in the city. According to the *Laudatio*, Peter the Fuller joined Zeno, who had been staying there at the time, whereas the Theodorean tradition has it that he had accompanied Zeno from the beginning. It should also be noted that the *Gesta* accuse Peter of some unspecified crimes (*propter crimina derelicto*), which is not mentioned in the other sources (hostile to him) at all. It is possible that this enigmatic *crimen* may have been somehow connected with his heterodox teachings.

In his account of Peter the Fuller's beginnings in Antioch, the panegyrist once again underscores Peter's actions in opposition to the Council of Chalcedon, which led to the disturbances in the city, although a mention of his associations with the Antiochene Apollinarists is certainly noteworthy. A similar transmission can be found in the *Epitome*, yet the emphasis is laid somewhere else completely: the epitomator does not refer to Peter's anti-Chalcedonian activity in the first place, stressing that he espoused Apollinarist (or, rather, Theopaschite) views instead, which is not mentioned *de facto* by Alexander, who only noted some connections between Peter and the Apollinarists. Still, the *Epitome* quotes Peter's Theopaschite addition to the *Trishagion*, suggesting that it was the key point of his teachings. Possibly, the panegyrist shifts back to an earlier period the information of

Peter's anathematization of Chalcedon during his third episcopate, with no interest in the question of the addition to the hymn at that point.

Laudatio and *Epitome* agree on the point that Peter's actions, directed primarily against the then incumbent bishop of the city (unlike the other sources, the *Laudatio* makes no mention of Martyrios by name), would lead to the outbreak of the riots in Antioch. The latter fact is also mentioned in the Roman tradition. Both the panegyrist and the epitomator make a note of Zeno's support for Peter the Fuller. As the *Laudatio* reports, Zeno received a bribe in gold from Peter. Finally, both of the sources report the intervention made by the emperor Leo, who had given his support to Martyrios, with only the *Epitome* referring to the decisive role allegedly played by Patriarch Gennadios of Constantinople, while the *Laudatio* makes no mention of him at all (just like the Roman tradition, which is well informed about Peter's eventual place of exile, i.e., the Oasis in Egypt). Theophanes also notes Gennadios' role in the rehabilitation of Martyrios, generally repeating the transmission found in the *Epitome*. The *Synodicon*, on the other hand, departs from the other works related to the Theodorean tradition and is closer to the *Laudatio*, only referring to the emperor's decision with no mention of any participation by the Bishop of Constantinople.[38]

Laudatio Barnabae	Theodore Lector's *Epitome*	Other sources
621–38 (ed. Van Deun 1993, pp. 109–10) Τοῦ δὲ τὰ τῇ δεκαταλείψαντος καὶ εἰς τὴν ἀγέρω βασιλείαν μετατεθέντος, τῆς βασιλείας διάδοχος γίνεται ὁ Ζήνων. Εὐθέως δὲ οἱ προειρημένοι Ἀντιοχείας δεητικὸν ἀνέγαγον τῷ βασιλεῖ, αἰτούμενοι τὸν Κναφέα ἐπίσκοπον· ὃ δὴ καὶ γέγονε, τοῦ χρυσίου πείθοντος πάντας τοὺς τῆς βασιλικῆς αὐλῆς εἰς τὴν ὑπὲρ αὐτοῦ συνεγορίαν. Εὐθέως οὖν ἅματῇ	**410 (ed. Hansen 1995, p. 114, 13–16)** Ἰουλιανὸς ὁ μετὰ Μαρτύριον Ἀντιοχείας ἐπίσκοπος ὑπὸ λύπης τῶν κινουμένων ἀπέθανεν. ὁ δὲ Κναφεὺς καταλαβὼν τὸν θρόνον εἰς ἀναθεματισμοὺς καὶ ταραχὰς ἐσχόλαζεν· ἐν οἷς καὶ φόνοι καὶ ἁρπαγαὶ διὰ τὴν προσθήκην δῆθεν τοῦ τρισαγίου γεγόνασιν.	**Theophanes AM 5967 (ed. de Boor 1883, p. 121, 1–2. 5–6. 13–14. 23–26)** Βασιλίσκος δὲ ἐν τῷ Κάμπῳ ἀνηγορεύθη βασιλεὺς [...]. Τιμόθεον δὲ τὸν Ἐλοῦρον ἀνεκαλέσατο διὰ τύπον, καὶ Πέτρον τὸν Κναφέα κρυπτόμενον ἐν τῇ μονῇ τῶν Ἀκοιμήτων, [...] Βασιλίσκος δὲ τοῦτον [Timothy] εἰς Ἀλεξάνδρειαν μετὰ τύπων κατὰ τῆς συνόδου ἐξέπεμψεν, καὶ Πέτρον Κναφέα εἰς Ἀντιόχειαν, [...] Πέτρος δὲ ὁ Κναφεὺς καταλαβὼν τὸν θρόνον εἰς ἀναθέματα καὶ ταραχὰς ἐχώρησεν. ὅθεν φόνοι καὶ ἁρπαγαὶ διὰ τὴν προσθήκην τοῦ τρισαγίου γεγόνασιν.

(cont.)

---

[38] SV² 98 (ed. Duffy – Parker 1979, p. 178, 3–9) reiterates faithfully the transmission of the longer version, likewise ignoring Gennadios' role and referring only to the emperor's intervention.

Laudatio Barnabae	Theodore Lector's Epitome	Other sources
χειροτονίᾳ ἀνεθεμάτισε δημοσίᾳ τὴν ἁγίαν ἐν Καλχηδόνι σύνοδον· θέλων δὲ ἀρέσαι τοῖς Ἀπολιναρισταῖς, θεοπασχίαν νοσοῦσι, καινοτομίαν κακίστην ἐπενόησε τοῦ εἰπεῖν ἐν τῷ Τρισαγίῳ ἐπιτέλει τοῦ ὕμνου· Ὁ σταυρωθεὶς δι' ἡμᾶς'. Ταῦτα μαθόντες οἱ ἅγιοι ἐπίσκοποι καὶ πατέρες ἡμῶν, διηγέρθησαν γενναίως κατὰ τῆς αὐτοῦ κακοδοξίας· καὶ πρῶτον μὲν ἐπειράθησαν διὰ παραινετικῶν γραμμάτων ἀνακαλέσασθαι αὐτὸν ἐκτοῦ βαράθρου τῆς ἀσεβείας, ὡς δὲ εἶδον αὐτὸν ἀντιλέγοντα καὶ μᾶλλον θρασυνόμενον κατὰ τῆς ὀρθοδόξου πίστεως, τότε ἀπεφήναντο κατ' αὐτοῦ καὶ ἀνεθεμάτισαν αὐτὸν πάντες οἱ κατὰ τὴν οἰκουμένην ἐπίσκοποι.		**Synodicon Vetus 100 (ed. Duffy – Parker 1979, p. 86, 1–4)** [39] Ἰωάννης δὲ Κύρου ἐπίσκοπος ὁ μακάριος τὸν Γναφέα Πέτρον καὶ πάλιν ἐν Ἀντιοχείᾳ ὁρῶν ἀθέως πολιτευόμενον καὶ Βασιλίσκου τὸ κράτος ἐρχόμενον πρὸς ἀσθένειαν, σύνοδον θείαν καὶ ἱερὰν ἐν τῇ πόλει αὐτοῦ συνεκρότησε καὶ τὸν Γναφέα Πέτρον ἀνεθεμάτισε. **101 (ed. Duffy – Parker 1979, p. 86, 1–3)** Καὶ Βασιλίσκου Ζήνων τὸν τύραννον χειρωσάμενος ἐν Ἀντιοχείᾳ σύνοδον ἁγίαν συναθροισθῆναι προσέταξεν, ἣ τὴν ἁγίαν ἐν Χαλκηδόνι κυρώσασα σύνοδον τὸν Γναφέα Πέτρον ἐξορίᾳ καὶ ἀναθέματι καθυπέβαλεν, [...] **Cyril of Scythopolis, _Vita Sabae_ 32 (ed. Schwartz 1939, pp. 117, 25–118, 8)** ἐπειδὴ δὲ τινες αὐτῶν [Armenian] λέγειν ἐπεχείρησαν τὸν τρισάγιον ὕμνον μετὰ τῆς ὑπὸ Πέτρου τοῦ ἐπίκλην Κναφέως ἐπινοηθείσης προσθήκης τοῦ ὁ σταυρωθεὶς δι' ἡμᾶς, ἀγανακτήσας εἰκότως ὁ θεῖος πρεσβύτης [Sabas] Ἑλληνιστὶ τοῦτον αὐτοὺς ψάλλειν τὸν ὕμνον ἐκέλευσεν κατὰ τὴν ἀρχαίαν τῆς καθολικῆς ἐκκλησίας παράδοσιν καὶ οὐ κατὰ τὴν τοῦ ῥηθέντος Πέτρου καινοτομίαν τοῦ τὰ Εὐτυχοῦς φρονήσαντος καὶ ἐκ δευτέρου τυραννικῶι τρόπωι τοῦ Ἀντιοχείας θρόνου κρατήσαντος καὶ ὑπὸ τῶν ἐκκλεσιαστικῶν θεσμῶν ἐκβληθέντος [...]

In this part, Alexander proceeds to focus on the period of Zeno's reign. It is worth noting that the two episcopates of Peter the Fuller are merged into one: the first one from the time of Basiliskos' rule, the other one in the later period of Zeno's reign. Once again, the author highlights the venal character of the latter emperor and his court. He also repeats the information about Peter the Fuller's condemnation of Chalcedon. This time, however, the panegyrist mentions (just as Theophanes does) the notorious addition to the *Trishagion*, explaining that Peter announced it because he wanted to satisfy his supporters from the Apollinarist circles, but it did not reflect his actual views on the matter. Finally, the author mentions the anathemas against Peter the Fuller by pronounced 'all the bishops of the world'. The Theodorean tradition, on the other hand, is focused more on the violence and the civil unrest which had broken out as

---

[39] SV² 100–01 (ed. Duffy – Parker 1979, p. 179) restates essentially the transmission of the longer version, without adding anything new thereto.

a consequence of the introduction of the *Trishagion* addition. In contrast, the *Synodicon Vetus* makes reference to the anathematization of Peter, here also departing from the other sources of the Theodorean tradition, being the only one to mention the name of a bishop who condemned Peter, whilst Cyril of Scythopolis gives a brief description of Peter the Fuller's career as Bishop of Antioch. In his account, Cyril concentrates his attention on the addition to the *Trishagion*, referring to Peter as Eutychian but making no connection between this epithet and any specific period of his public activity.

Laudatio Barnabae	Theodore Lector's *Epitome*	Other sources
665–82 (ed. Van Deun 1993, pp. 111–12) Οὕτως τοιγαποῦν ὁ Κναφεὺς Πέτρος ἀναθεματισθείς, ὡς εἴρηται, ὑπὸ πάντων τῶν ἐπισκόπων καὶ τοῦ Ζήνωνος φυγόντος ἐκτῆς βασιλείας διὰ τὴν ἐπανάστασιν Βασιλίσκου, φυγὰς ᾤχετο εἰς ἀγνώστους τόπους. Ὡς δὲ ἐπανῆλθεν ὁ Ζήνων εἰς τὴν ἑαυτοῦ βασιλείαν, Πέτρον μὲν τὸν Κναφέα ἀναζητήσας, ἀπεκατέστησε τῇ Ἀντιοχέων ἐπίσκοπον, τῶν ἐπ' αὐτῷ ἀναθεματισμῶν μεδαμῶς λυθέντων, τὸν δὲ μακάριον Καλανδίωνα τὸν πατριάρχην εἰς Ὄασιν ἐξωστράκισε. Τοῦ Κναφέως βίᾳ ἀπολαβόντος τὸν θρόνον, ἅτε ἀπεγνωσμένος λοιπὸν καὶ μηδεμίαν ἐλπίδα ἔχων, ἀδεῶς μᾶλλον δὲ ἀθέως ἐχρέσατο τῇ τυραννίδι, φονεύων καὶ δημεύων καὶ φυγαδεύων πάντας τοὺς μὴ βουλομένους κοινωνεῖς αὐτοῦ τῇ ἀσεβείᾳ. Ἀλλὰ ταῦτα μὲν παρέσω, πολλὰ ὄντα καὶ ἰδίας συγγραφῆς δεόμενα, βαδιοῦμαι δὲ πρὸς τὸ κατεπεῖγον, δεικνὺν πᾶσι τοῦ ἁγίου ἀποστόλου Βαρνάβα τὴν ἀμέτρητον χάριν καὶ ὅσην ἔχει περὶ τὴν ἰδίαν πατρίδα φροντίδατε καὶ κηδεμονίαν.	**427 (ed. Hansen 1995, p. 118, 23–26)** Πέτρου προσθήκην ‹ἤδη πρότερον› ποιησαμένου ἐν τῷ τρισαγίῳ ‘ὁ σταυρωθεὶς δι' ἡμᾶς' {ἤδη πρότερον} Καλανδίων ὁρῶν πολλοὺς σκανδαλιζομένους προσέθηκε ‘Χριστέ βασιλεῦ, ὁ σταυρωθεὶς δι' ἡμᾶς'. Πέτρος δὲ πάλιν ἐλθὼν περιεῖλεν τὸ ‘Χριστέ βασιλεῦ'.	**Theophanes 5982 (ed. de Boor 1883, pp. 133, 30–134, l. 6–9)** Ζήνων δὲ ὁ βασιλεὺς ἀνεθεὶς τῶν τυράννων ἐξέβαλε τῆς ἐκκλησίας Ἀντιοχέας Καλανδίωνα καὶ ἐξώρισεν εἰς Ὄασιν, Πέτρον δὲ τὸν Κναφέα κατέστησεν. [...] Πέτρος δὲ ὁ Κναφεὺς εἰσελθὼν εἰς Ἀντιόχειαν πολλὰ κακὰ πέπραχεν, ἀναθεματισμοὺς τῆς συνόδου καὶ ἐκβολὰς ἐπισκόπων ἀνεπιλήπτων ἀντεισαγωγάς τε καὶ χειροτονίας ἀθέσμους καὶ τὰ τούτοις ὅμοια. **Synodicon Vetus 105 (ed. Duffy – Parker 1979, p. 90, 1–4)[40]** Ζήνων τοίνυν ὁ βασιλεὺς χειρωσάμενος Ἰλλοῦν τε καὶ Λεόντιον κατὰ τῶν τῆς ἀνατολῆς ἐπισκόπων ἐχώρησε, καὶ Ἀντιοχείας τὸν Καλανδίωνα ἐξορίσας εἰς Ὄασιν τὸν Γναφέα Πέτρον πάλιν ἀποκατέστησεν· ὃς αἱρετικὴν συστησάμενος σύνοδον τὴν ἐν Χαλκηδόνι ἁγίαν ἀνεθεμάτισε σύνοδον. [...] **Cyril of Scythopolis, Vita Sabae 32 (ed. Schwartz 1939, p. 118, 8–14)** [...] καὶ πάλιν ἐκ τρίτου μετὰ τὴν ἐν Ἰσαυρίαι γεγενημένην τοῦ Ἰλλοῦ τυραννίδα ἐπὶ τῆς βασιλείας Ζήνωνος βασιλικῆι αὐθεντίαι τοῦ αὐτοῦ θρόνου κρατήσαντος ἀθέσμως μὴ λυθέντων τῶν κατ' αὐτοῦ γεγονότων ἀναθεμάτων καὶ πᾶσαν τὴν Ἀνατολὴν ἐκταράξαντος καὶ ὑπὸ τοῦ πάπα Ῥώμης Φιλικος ἀναθεματισθέντος δία τε τὴν ἑτεροδοξίαν καὶ τὴν εἰρημένεν τῶι τρισαγίωι προσθέκην.

[40] SV² 105 (ed. Duffy – Parker 1979, p. 180) states only that Zeno banished Kalandion and had him replaced with Peter.

Comparing the conclusion of the story of Peter the Fuller with the Theodorean tradition shows once again that Alexander merged the events from Peter's two episcopates into one narrative, combining all that happened after Basiliskos' usurpation with the events that ensued after the revolt of Illus. Zeno's restoration of Peter the Fuller to the See of Antioch following the defeat of Illus and the removal of Kalandion is situated chronologically, according to Alexander's account, after the defeat of Basiliskos, with the consequence that his narration shortens Peter the Fuller's story to two episcopates, both of which Peter owed, as the *Laudatio* recounts, to the emperor Zeno. Actually, in the former case, Zeno removed, rather than elevated, Peter upon his return to power, and would give him support once again only several years later, after the fall of Illus. It is Alexander's confusing of those two rebellions that is the main cause of this incorrect chronology.[41] For his part, Cyril of Scythopolis uses a 'construction' which is similar to Alexander's in that he puts an emphasis on the unlawful nature of Peter's final episcopate, stressing that he had not been cleared of the church anathemas placed upon him.

It should also be said that the Theodorean tradition links Peter's acting against the Council of Chalcedon only with his last episcopate. Both the *Laudatio* and the *Synodicon Vetus*, but also Theophanes, report on Kalandion's banishment to Oasis.

The narrative of the discovery of Barnabas' relics and the affirmation of the autocephaly of the Church of Cyprus

The fairly detailed *Laudatio* account on Peter the Fuller is followed by a lengthy treatment (encompassing as many as ten chapters: 37–46 [682–853], which we shall not cite here) of his

---

[41] The tradition that Peter the Fuller owed his second episcopate to Zeno, not to Basiliskos, must have nonetheless been alive in the East, as it is mentioned by John Malalas (*Chronographia* XV, 1 and 5–6, pp. 301–04; ed. Thurn 2000). In any case, Alexander could not have drawn on this author in his own narrative on Peter the Fuller, because the two accounts are different in a number of details; for instance, Malalas gives the information that Peter was a *paramonarios* of St Euphemia's Church at Chalcedon (*Chronographia* XV, 1, p. 301, 7–8; ed. Thurn 2000).

efforts to bring the Church of Cyprus under the Antiochene patriarchate's control, the finding of the Apostle Barnabas' relics and the Gospel of Matthew handwritten by the saint during the episcopate of Bishop Anthemios of Salamis, and finally of the positive settlement of the matter during the *endemousa* synod and the emperor Zeno's final decision on the granting of ecclesial autonomy to Cyprus, which involved the presentation of the Gospel of Matthew manuscript, found inside Barnabas' grave, to the emperor. The emperor deposited the Gospel at the palace, where it was read out each year on the Thursday before Easter (Maundy Thursday). He also ordered the building of a church in the name of the Apostle Barnabas at the site of his grave.

The account of this particular event in the Theodorean tradition is much more succinct and can be basically reduced to one brief sentence derived from the transmission of the *Epitome*. An exception is the transmission found in the chronicle by Victor of Tunnuna, who draws on the original version of Theodore's *History*, although his account is even shorter than the *Epitome*'s transmission. Let us have a look at all the specific excerpts:

Theodore Lector's *Epitome*	Other sources
436 (ed. Hansen 1995, p. 121, 19–23) Βαρνάβα τοῦ ἀποστόλου τὸ λεί-ψανον εὑρέθη ἐν Κύπρῳ ὑπὸ δέν-δρον κερατέαν, ἔχον ἐπὶ στήθους τὸ κατὰ Ματθαῖον εὐαγγέλιον ἰδιόγραφον τοῦ Βαρνάβα. ἐξ ἧς προφάσεως καὶ περιγεγόνασι Κύπριοι τοῦ αὐτοκέφαλον εἶναι τὴν κατ' αὐτοὺς μητρόπολιν καὶ μὴ τελεῖν ὑπὸ Ἀντιόχειαν. τὸ δὲ τοιοῦτον εὐαγγέλιον Ζήνων ἀπέ-θετο ἐν τῷ παλατίῳ ἐν τῷ ἁγίῳ Στεφάνῳ.	**Victor of Tunnuna s.a. 488.1 (ed. Placanica 1997, p. 20)** Corpus sancti Barnabae apostoli in Cypro et evangelium secundum Matthaeum eius manu scriptum ipso eodem revelante inventum est. **Souda θύϊνα (ed. Adler 1931, p. 733, 19–21)** Θύϊνα: ἐπὶ Ζήνωνος βασιλέως εὑρέθη ἐν Κύπρῳ τὸ λείψανον Βαρνάβα τοῦ ἀποστόλου, τοῦ συνεκδήμου Παύλῳ. ἔκειτο δὲ ἐπὶ τὸ στῆθος Βαρνάβα τὸ κατὰ Ματθαῖον εὐαγγέλιον, ἔχον πτυχία θύϊνα. **George the Monk (ed. de Boor 1978, pp. 618, 21–619, 8)** καὶ Βαρνάβα τοῦ ἀποστόλου τὸ λείψανον εὑρέθη ἐν Κύπρῳ ὑπὸ δένδρον κερατέαν ἔχον ἐπὶ στήθους τὸ κατὰ Ματθαῖον εὐαγγέλιον ἰδιόγραφον τοῦ Βαρνάβα. ἐξ ἧς προφάσεως καὶ περιγεγόνασι Κύπριοι τοῦ ἀκέφαλον εἶναι τὴν κατ' αὐτοὺς μητρόπολιν καὶ μὴ τελεῖν ὑπὸ Ἀντιόχειαν. ὅπερ εὐαγγέλιον ἀποθέμενος Ζήνων ἐν τῷ παλατίῳ εἰς τὸν ναὸν τοῦ ἁγίου Στεφάνου κατ' ἐνιαυτὸν ἀναγινώσκεται τῇ ἁγίᾳ καὶ μεγάλῃ πέμπτῃ.

(cont.)

Theodore Lector's *Epitome*	Other sources
	Simeon Logothetes, *Chronicon* 101.6 (ed. Wahlgren 2006, p. 133, 17–21) ἐφ᾽ οὗ τὸ τοῦ ἀποστόλου Βαρνάβα λείψανον εὑρέθη ἐν Κύπρῳ ὑπὸ δένδρον κερατέαν, ἔχον ἐπὶ στήθους τὸ κατὰ Ματθαῖον εὐαγγέλιον ἰδιόγραφον τοῦ Βαρνάβα· ἐξ ἧς προφάσεως γέγονε μητρόπολις καὶ μὴ τελεῖν ὑπὸ Ἀντιόχειαν.[42] τὸ δὲ τοιοῦτον εὐαγγέλιον Ζήνων ἀπέθετο εἰς τὸ παλάτιον ἐν τῷ ἁγίῳ Στεφάνῳ. **Kedrenos 385.2 (ed. Tartaglia 2016, p. 603, 7–13).** τούτῳ τῷ χρόνῳ τὸ τοῦ ἁγίου ἀποστόλου Βαρνάβα λείψανον εὑρέθη ἐν Κύπρῳ ὑπὸ δένδρον κερατέαν ἱστάμενον, ἔχον ἐπὶ τοῦ στήθους τὸ κατὰ Ματθαῖον εὐαγγέλιον ἰδιόγραφον αὐτοῦ τοῦ ἀποστόλου Βαρνάβα. ἐξ ἧς προφάσεως ἔκτοτε γέγονε μητρόπολις ἡ Κύπρος, καὶ τοῦ μὴ τελεῖν ὑπὸ Ἀντιόχειαν, ἀλλ᾽ ὑπὸ Κωνσταντινούπολιν. τὸ δὲ τοιοῦτον εὐαγγέλιον Ζήνων ἀπέθετο ἐν τῷ Παλατίῳ, ἐν τῷ ναῷ τοῦ ἁγίου Στεφάνου ἐν τῇ Δάφνῃ. **Nikephoros Kallistos XVI, 37 (PG 147, col. 200 C)** Ἐπὶ δὲ τῆς αὐτοῦ [Anastasius] ἡγεμονίας καὶ τὸ λείψανον Βαρνάβα τοῦ ἀποστόλου εὑρέθη ἐν Κύπρῳ ὑπὸ δένδρον ὃ Κεράτιον λέγεται κείμενον· οὗ ἐπιστρέρνιον τὸ θεῖον καὶ ἱερὸν Εὐαγγέλιον Ματθαίου τοῦ εὐαγγελιστοῦ ἐτύγχανεν ὄν, χερσὶν οἰκείαις τῷ Βαρνάβᾳ γραφέν. Ἐκ ταύτης τοίνυν προφάσεως καὶ Κύπριοι τὸ καταρχὰς περιγεγόνασιν αὐτοκέφαλον ἔχειν τὴν κατ᾽ αὐτοὺς μητρόπολιν, καὶ μὴ τελεῖν ὑπὸ Ἀντιόχειαν ᾗ καὶ ὑπέκειτο πρότερον.

A relation similar to the above sources can be found in Severus of Sozopolis' *Letter* 108, addressed to Thomas, Bishop of Germanicea:[43]

> This question was examined with great carefulness when my meanness was in the royal city, at the time when the affair of Macedonius was being examined, who became archbishop of that city, and there was produced the Gospel of Matthew, which was written in large letters, and was preserved with great honour in the royal palace, which was said to have been found in the days of Zeno of honourable memory in a city of the island Cyprus buried with the holy Barnabas, who went about with Paul and spread the divine preaching; and,

[42] The following added phrase can be found in the CPHK manuscripts (no such addition in the F1): ἀλλ᾽ ὑπὸ Κωνσταντινούπολιν.

[43] Severus of Antioch, *Letter 108* (ed. Brooks 1920, pp. 266–67).

when the Gospel of Matthew was opened, it was found to be free from the falsification contained in this addition, of the story of the soldier and the spear.

In spite of its concise character, the passage from the *Epitome* contains most of the information from the *Laudatio Barnabae*, except for the one that referred to the emperor Zeno's validation of the autocephaly of Cyprus and Peter the Fuller's role in those events. It is now impossible to determine if the epitomator passed over these details or if they were not in Theodore's work at all. It is also possible that Alexander the Monk complemented Theodore's account with exactly the fundamental (for him) question of the emperor's affirmation of the Church of Cyprus' status. In my opinion, the latter possibility seems to be the most plausible one. In this context, it is notable that Victor of Tunnuna makes no mention of the autocephaly at all, even in the form that can be found in the *Epitome* and all the dependent sources, despite the fact that this piece of information would have probably been present in the original version of Theodore's *History*. Severus does likewise, but in his case this information might have been omitted on purpose. *Letter* 108, though undated, was written at the time when Severus had already been expelled from the See of Antioch.[44] Besides, the issue of Cyprus was completely beyond the subject matter of his epistle. Thus, as we can see, the *Laudatio* remains the only source that refers to Peter the Fuller in the context of this affair.

3. *Conclusions*

The above-stated points of convergence between the work of Alexander the Monk and the *Epitome* or, more broadly, the tradition related to Theodore hint at the existence of the relation between the *Laudatio* and Theodore's *History*. It appears to be very likely that Alexander the Monk would have drawn on Theodore's *History*, either directly or not, in composing the section on Peter the Fuller. It is evident that he had access to well-informed

---

[44] Cf. Severus of Antioch, *Letter 108* (ed. Brooks 1920, p. 264): Of the holy Severus patriarch of Antioch, from the 27th of the 9th book after exile which was addressed to Thomas bishop of Germanicea.

121

sources on the subject, but the various items of information derived (and perhaps extracted directly) from his source were wrongly arranged in the process of composing his work. Besides, the panegyrist is not very much concerned with providing a great deal of detailed information, which would not have contributed, as he saw it, anything of use to the main storyline. Alexander was not very much concerned with chronological accuracy, often giving no names of protagonists, especially if he regarded them as of secondary importance. He does not mention the names of the bishops of Constantinople (except for Proklos, who is mentioned at *Laudatio Barnabae* 35) and Antioch (save for Peter the Fuller and Kalandion), but he tends to focus his attention on the roles of the successive emperors. It would seem then that the prevailing view, according to which Alexander the Monk had very little knowledge about Zeno's reign is not correct, as he did possess some fairly detailed information on this matter, but he was quite likely confused in this respect, misinterpreting the proper chronology of the facts. Alexander's most conspicuous error was the merging of Peter's second episcopate, following Basiliskos' usurpation, and his third one, which came after Illus' rebellion, into one. Besides, the panegyrist diminishes the Theopaschite elements in Peter the Fuller's teaching and delivers a sequence of events which is in reverse order compared with the Theodorean tradition: in the *Laudatio*, Peter had been opposed to the Council of Chalcedon from the very beginning, and would have reportedly introduced the Theopaschite addition to the *Trishagion* only later on, apparently in an attempt to win favour with the Apollinarist circles. On the contrary, in the transmission related to the *Epitome*, this addition had been at the forefront of the Antiochene bishop's teachings, while his acting against the council would take place only during the years of his final episcopate.

The issue of the Church of Cyprus' autocephaly in the *Laudatio*'s account is the key point linking the story of Peter the Fuller and that of the finding of Barnabas' relics, but in the surviving extracts from Theodore's composition the two narratives are in no way connected with one another. It is worth noting that the epitomator does not seem to be very much concerned with the Cypriot question, providing just a brief annotation on the miraculous nature of the relics discovery. A trace of a connection between Peter the Fuller and Cyprus in the Theodorean tradition may be perhaps identified only in the *Chronicle* by Victor of Tunnuna, who includes a note on the finding of Barnabas' relics and a fairly obscure mention referring to Peter's death, both under the same year entry, showing very clearly his misunderstanding of the Greek text which he used or his inadequate representation of the information obtained from it.[45] However, since Victor makes no mention of any insidious attempt by Peter (or by any other Bishop of Antioch) to bring the Church of Cyprus under his control, it is possible that Theodore might not have elaborated on this subject.

It must be emphasized that the transmission which is the closest to the *Laudatio* is the one in the *Synodicon Vetus*, which departs from the *Epitome* in many significant details. The *Synodicon*, like the *Laudatio*, reports that Peter the Fuller came from the monastery of the *Akoimetoi*. It also passes over Bishop Gennadios' role in the deposition of Peter, which is accentuated in the Theodore-based tradition. It may be that the anonymous author represents a branch of the Theodorean tradition which is different from that of the *Epitome*, or he may have used a different (hitherto unidentified) source in the matters connected with Peter the Fuller's episcopacy.

Likewise, the Constantinopolitan tradition connected with the discovery of Barnabas' grave (but first of all, with the translation of Matthew's Gospel to Constantinople) is very similar to the version in the *Laudatio*, even though it is narrated in a very concise manner, without any details relating to the *inventio* of the Apostle's relics. Another figure who may be recognized as an exponent of the generally understood Constantinopolitan tradition is Severus of Antioch. The matter of the discovery of a Gospel handwritten by Barnabas must have been widely commented

---

[45] Victor of Tunnuna, *Chronica*, ad a. 488 (1) (ed. Placanica 1997, p. 20): Corpus sancti Barnabae apostoli in Cypro et evangelium secundum Matthaeum eius manu scriptum ipso eodem revelante inventum est. [...] (3): Petrus Antiochenus episcopus sub damnatione moritur et eius loco Stephanus ordinatur; quem Acacius Constantinopolitanus per suos satellites necat et in eius loco Calendionem ordinat. orientales autem episcopi tamquam nescientes Iohannem cognomento Campaneum eidem Antiochenae ecclesiae consecrant episcopum. cui Petrus succedit haereticus.

during the episcopate of Macedonius as this particular version of the Gospel was consulted on in the theological dispute described in Severus' letter.

It appears that Theodore Lector would have drawn the pieces of information on the events in the diocese of the East from a source that was focused on this region, namely from the *History* by John Diakrinomenos. This latter author devotes much space to the activities of Peter the Fuller, his usurpation of the metropolitan throne of the See of Antioch,[46] as well as to the liturgical novelties he introduced.[47] Therefore, it would be fair to venture a hypothesis that the prototype of the story known from the Theodorean tradition as well as from the *Laudatio Barnabae* can be traced to John's work, while the information about the discovery of the Apostle's grave and the Gospel of Matthew, as derived from the Constantinopolitan tradition, had probably no relation with that work. It may be the reason why Theodore's account, in its extant form, does not link the question of the finding of the saint's relics and the autocephaly of Cyprus with the figure of Peter the Fuller. For this reason, we cannot be sure whether the person behind the attempt to subordinate the Church of Cyprus to Antioch was indeed Peter or someone else. Victor's dating is mostly correct, as it is based on the fairly precise dating system of Theodore Lector. As may be concluded from the extant fragments of his *History*, Theodore would most probably date the events on the basis of the consular system.[48] As Victor also made use of consular dating, setting the timeline of the events he draws from Theodore's *History* should be correct. Still, we should bear in mind that Victor's chronology relating to the Antioch

---

[46] Cf. John Diakrinomenos, *Epitome* 540 (ed. Hansen 1995, p. 154, 17–19): Πέτρος ὁ Κναφεὺς ἐν Σελευκείᾳ τῇ ἐν Συρίᾳ ἐχειροτονήθη Ἀντιοχείας ἐπίσκοπος ὑπὸ τῶν ἐκεῖ εὑρεθέντων ἐπισκόπων, τούτους βιασαμένου τοῦ Πέτρῳ ἐπαμύναντος Ζήνωνος.

[47] Cf. John Diakrionomenos, *Epitome* 547 (ed. Hansen 1995, p. 155, 17–20): Πέτρον φησς τὸν Κναφέα ἐπινοῆσαι τὸ μύρον ἐν τῇ ἐκκλησίᾳ ἐπὶ παντὸς τοῦ λαοῦ ἁγιάζεσθαι καὶ τὴν ἐπὶ τῶν ὑδάτων ἐν τοῖς θεοφανίοις ἐπίκλησιν ἐν τῇ ἑσπέρᾳ γίνεσθαι καὶ ἐν ἑκάστῃ εὐχῇ τὴν θεοτόκον ὀνομάζεσθαι καὶ ἐνπάσῃ συνάξει τὸ σύμβολον λέγεσθαι.

[48] Cf. Theodore Lector, fr. 2 (ed. Hansen 1995, p. 99, 8): ἐπράττετο δὲ ταῦτα κατὰ τὴν ὑπατείαν Πρωτογένους καὶ Ἀστερίου and fr. 52a (ed. Hansen 1995, p. 131, 10) Ὑπὸ δὲ ταύτην τὴν ὑπατείαν κατὰ τὸν μῆνα τὸν Δεκέμβριον.

issues is often incorrect. Notably, under the year 490, he provides the information on Kalandion's bringing of Eustathius' relics to Antioch, which must have taken place at least five years earlier, as this patriarch had been deposed by the emperor Zeno in the year 485.[49] Likewise, the content of Victor's entry s. a. 488 is quite odd and possibly indicative of his misunderstanding of the Greek text. Besides, he accumulates events of various years under one and the same year, which may put the accuracy of his time-line sequence in doubt.[50] For this reason, we cannot be certain of the correctness of the year 488 as the date of the discovery of Barnabas' relics.[51] Based on the order in the *Epitome*, it can be assumed that in Theodore's *Church History* this narrative was placed after the account of the translation of Eustathius' relics to Antioch (*Epitome* 435), but before the mention of the outbreak of Illus' revolt (*Epitome* 437), namely during the episcopate of Kalandion, not that of Peter the Fuller. Of course, Theodore may have combined the entries referring to the relics, omitting their proper time sequence, but even in that case the dating as proposed by Victor (who would have surely drawn the information of the *inventio* from Theodore's *History*) would have very likely been coincidental. The passages of the *Epitome* 435–37 come from one manuscript B, which would suggest that the correct order was preserved therein. Therefore, the finding of Barnabas' remains should probably have taken place prior to the year 485. Furthermore, Kalandion's support for the revolt of Illus at that time might have encouraged Zeno to give his backing to the Cypriot aspirations, while Kalandion's well-known dedication to the Council of Chalcedon may have in turn induced the author of the *Laudatio* to attribute his possible claim to the ecclesiastical jurisdiction over Cyprus to a person allied with the anti-Chalcedonian movement.

[49] Cf. Kosiński 2010, pp. 152–53.

[50] On the question of the discrepancies among the sources reporting on the time of Fuller's death and the succession on the throne of the See of Antioch, see Kosiński 2010, pp. 196–97.

[51] By contrast, Kedrenos gives the fourth year of Zeno's reign, i.e., 478, as the year of the discovery of Barnabas' relics, cf. Kedrenos, 385.2 (ed. Tartaglia 2016, p. 603, 7–13).

Bibliography

Sources

Adler 1931 = *Lexiconographi Graeci*, vol. 1, *Suidae Lexicon*, edidit Ada Adler, pars II, 1, Lipsiae.

Albert – von Schönborn 1978 = Micheline Albert – Christoph von Schönborn, *Lettre de Sophrone de Jérusalem à Arcadius de Chypre. Version syriaque inédite du text grec perdu*, Patrologia Orientalis 39, Turnhout.

Brooks 1920 = *A Collection of Letters of Severus of Antioch from numerous Syriac manuscripts*, ed. Ernest Walter Brooks, Patrologia Orientalis, vol. 14, Paris, pp. 1–310.

De Boor 1883 = *Theophanis Chronographia*, recensuit Carolus de Boor, vol. 1–2, Lipsiae.

De Boor 1978 = *Georgii Monachi Chronicon*, edidit Carolus de Boor, editionem anni MCMIV correctirem curavit Peter Wirth, volumen I–II, Stutgardiae.

Dindorf 1832 = *Chronicon paschale: Chronicon paschale ad exemplar Vaticanum*, recensuit Ludivicus Dindorfius, vol. I, Bonnae.

Duffy – Parker 1979 = *The Synodicon Vetus*, ed. John Duffy – John Parker, Washington.

Günther 1895 = *Epistulae imperatorum pontificum aliorum inde ab. a. CCCLXVII usque ad a. DLIII datae, Avellana quae dicitur collectio*, recensuit commentario critico instruxit indices adiecit Otto Günther, pars 1, *Prolegomena. Epistulae I-CIV*, Corpus Scriptorum Ecclesiasticorum Latinorum 35, Vindobonae.

Hansen 1995 = John Diakrinomenos, *Epitome*, in Theodoros Anagnostes, *Kirchengeschichte*, ed. Günther Christian Hansen, zweite, durchgesehene Auflage, Berlin, pp. 152–57.

Hansen 1995 = Theodoros Anagnostes, *Kirchengeschichte*, ed. Günther Christian Hansen, zweite, durchgesehene Auflage, Berlin.

Krueger 1892 = *Corpus Iuris Civilis*, vol. II, *Codex Iustinianus*, recognovit Paulus Krueger, Berlin.

Migne 1904 = *Nicephori Callisti Xanthopuli Ecclesiasticae Historiae Libri XVIII*, Patrologia Graeca, vol. 145–47, Paris.

Ohme 2013 = *Acta Conciliorum Oecumenicorum*, ser. 2, vol. II, pars IV, *Concilium Constantinopolitanum a. 691/2 in Trullo habitum (Concilium Quinisextum)*, ed. Heinz Ohme, Berlin – Boston.

Placanica 1997 = Vittore da Tunnuna, *Chronica. Chiesa e Impero nell'età di Giustiniano*, ed. Antonio Placanica, Firenze.

Schoell 1912 = *Corpus Iuris Civilis*, vol. III, *Novellae*, recognovit Rudolfus Schoell, opus Schoellii morte interceptum absolvit Guilelmus Kroll, Berlin.

Schwartz 1929 = *Acta Conciliorum Oecumenicorum*, tomus I, *Concilium universale Ephesenum*, vol. I, 7, edidit Eduard Schwartz, Berlin – Leipzig.

Schwartz 1939 = *Kyrillos von Skythopolis*, ed. Eduard Schwartz, Leipzig, pp. 85–200.

Tartaglia 2016 = *Georgii Cedreni Historiarum Compendium*, edizione critica a cura di Luigi Tartaglia, 2 vols, Roma.

Thurn 2000 = *Chronographia*: *Ioannis Malalae Chronographia*, recensuit Hans Thurn, Berlin.

Van Deun 1993 = *Hagiographica Cypria. Sancti Barnabae Laudatio auctore Alexandro Monacho et Sanctorum Bartholomaei et Barnabae Vita e Menologio imperiali deprompta*, editae curante Peter Van Deun, *Vita Sancti Auxibii*, edita curante J. Noret, Turnhout – Leuven.

Wahlgren 2006 = *Symeonis Magistri et Logothetae Chronicon*, recensuit Staffan Wahlgren, Berolini et Novi Eboraci.

Literature

Adler 1932 = Ada Adler, 'Suidas', in *Paulys Realencyclopädie der classischen Altertumswissenschaft*, Zweite Reihe, vol. 4, Stuttgart, cols 675–717.

Baronius 1858 = Caesar Baronius, *Annales ecclesiastici a Christo nato ad annum 1198*, Paris.

Beck 1956 = Hans-Georg Beck, *Kirche und theologische Literatur in byzantinischen Reich*, Münich.

Beihammer 2004 = Alexander Daniel Beihammer, 'The First Naval Campaigns of the Arabs against Cyprus (649–53)', *Graeco-Arabica*, 9–10, pp. 47–68.

Blaudeau 2006 = Philippe Blaudeau, *Alexandrie et Constantinople (451–91). De l'histoire à la géo-ecclésiologie*, Roma.

Combefis 1662 = François Combefis, *Bibliotheca Patrum Concionatoria*, vol. VII, Paris.

Delehaye 1907 = Hippolyte Delehaye, 'Saints de Chypre', *Analecta Bollandiana*, 26, pp. 161–297.

Downey 1958 = Glanville Downey, 'The Claim of Antioch to Ecclesiastical Jurisdiction over Cyprus', *Proceedings of the American Philosophical Society*, 102, pp. 224–28.

Duffy – Parker 1979 = John Duffy – John Parker, 'Introduction', in *The Synodicon Vetus*, Text, Translation, and Notes by John Duffy – John Parker, Washington, pp. xiii–xxvii.

Flusin 1998 = Bernard Flusin, 'Évêques et patriarches. Les structures de l'Église impériale', in *Histoire du christianisme des origines à nos jours*, sous la direction de Jean Marie Mayeur – Charles Pietri – Luce Pietri – André Vauchez – Marc Venard, vol. 3, *Les Églises d'Orient et d'Occident (432–610)*, sous la responsabilité de Luce Pietri, Paris, pp. 485–543.

Gentz 1966 = Günter Gentz, *Die Kirchengeschichte des Nicephorus Callistus Xanthopulos und ihre Quellen*, überarbeitet und erweitert von Friedhelm Winkelmann, Berlin.

Grumel 1908 = Venance Grumel, 'Le titre de patriarche oecuménique avant saint Grégoire le Grand', *Echos d'Orient*, 11, pp. 161–71.

Grumel 1945 = Venance Grumel, 'Le titre de patriarche oecuménique sur les sceaux byzantins', *Revue des études grecques*, 58, pp. 212–18.

Grumel 1972 = Venance Grumel, *Les regestes des actes du patriarcat de Constantinople*, vol. I, *Les actes des patriarches*, fasc. I, *Les regestes de 381 à 715*, deuxième edition, Paris.

Günther 1894 = Otto Günther 1894, 'Zu den "Gesta de nomine Acacii"', *Byzantinische Zeitschrift*, 3, pp. 146–49.

Hackett 1901 = John Hackett, *A History of the Orthodox Church of Cyprus from the Coming of the Apostles Paul and Barnabas to the Commencement of the British Occupation*, London.

Hansen 1995 = Günther Christian Hansen, 'Einleitung', in *Theodoros Anagnostes, Kirchengeschichte*, herausgegeben von G. Ch. Hansen, Zweite, durchgesehene Auflage, Berlin.

Hill 1949 = George Hill, *A History of Cyprus*, vol. I, *To the Conquest by Richard Lion Heart*, Cambridge.

Hunger 1978 = Herbert Hunger, *Die Hochsprachliche profane Literatur der Byzantiner*, 1. Band, *Philosophie, Rhetorik, Epistolographie, Geschichtsschreibung, Geographie*, München.

Kollmann 2007 = Bernd Kollmann, *Einleitung*, in Alexander Monachus, *Laudatio Barnabae. Lobrede auf Barnabas*, eingeleitet von Bernd Kollmann, übersetzt von Bernd Kollmann – Werner Deuse, Turnhout, pp. 7–60.

Kosiński 2010 = Rafał Kosiński, *Emperor Zeno. Religion and Politics*, Cracow.

Kuźma 2011 = Andrzej Kuźma, 'Prymat w Kościele w korespondencji papieża św. Grzegorza Wielkiego z patriarchami wschodnimi', *Rocznik Teologiczny*, 53, pp. 107–21.

Laurent 1948 = Vitalien Laurent, 'Le titre de patriarche oecuménique et la signature patriarcale. Recherches de diplomatique et de sigillographie byzantines', *Revue des études byzantines*, 6, pp. 5–26.

Le Nain de Tillemont 1693 = Louis-Sébastien Le Nain de Tillemont, *Mémoires pour servir à histoire ecclésiastique*, vol. I, Paris.

Lipsius 1884 = Richard Adelbert Lipsius, *Die apokryphen Apostelgeschichten und Apostellegenden. Ein Beitrag zur altchristlichen Literaturgeschichte*, II, 2.

Mango – Scott = Cyril Mango – Roger Scott, 'Introduction', in *The Chronicle of Theophanes Confessor. Byzantine and Near Eastern History AD 284–813*, Translated with Introduction and Commentary by Cyril Mango – Roger Scott with the assistance of G. Greatrex, Oxford, pp. xliii–c.

Megaw 2006 = Arthur H. S. Megaw, 'The Campanopetra reconsidered: the pilgrimage church of the Apostle Barnabas?', in *Byzantine Style, Religion and Civilization. In Honour of Sir Steven Runciman*, ed. by Elisabeth Jeffreys, Cambridge, pp. 394–404.

Nautin 1994 = Pierre Nautin, 'Théodore Lecteur et sa "Réunion de différentes histoire" de l'Église', *Revue des Études Byzantines*, 52, pp. 213–43.

Nautin 1966–1967 = Pierre Nautin, 'L'ecclésiologie romaine à l'époque du schisme d'Acace', in *Annuaire de l'École Pratique des Hautes Études, Section des Sciences Religieuses*, 74, pp. 138–41.

Nesbitt 2003 = John Nesbitt 2003, 'Alexander the Monk's Text of Helena's Discovery of the Cross (BHG 410)', in *Byzantine authors: literary activities and preoccupations, Texts and Translations Dedicated to the Memory of Nicolas Oikonomides*, ed. by John Nesbitt, Leiden, pp. 23–39.

Placanica 1989 = Antonio Placanica, Da Cartagine a Bisanzio: per la biografia di Vittore Tunnunense, *Vetera Christianorum*, 26, pp. 327–36.

Pouderon 1998 = Bernard Pouderon, Le codex Parisinus graecus 1555 A et sa récension de l'Épitomè byzantin d'histoires ecclésiastiques, *Revue des études byzantines*, 56, pp. 169–91.

Roux 1998 = Georges Roux, *La basilique de la Campanopétra*, Paris.

Salaville 1912 = Sévérien Salaville, Le moine Alexandre de Chypre (VIᵉ siècle), *Echos d'Orient*, 15, pp. 134–37.

Schwartz 1934 = Eduard Schwartz, *Publizistische Sammlungen zum acacianischen Schisma*, München.

Scott 2004 = Roger Scott, 'Discovery of the True Cross', in *Metaphrastes, or gained in translation: essays and translations in hon-*

our of Robert H. Jordan, ed. by Margaret M. Mullett, Belfast, pp. 157–84.

Starowieyski 1994 = Marek Starowieyski, 'Datation des Actes (Voyages) de S. Barnabé (BGH 225; ClAp 285) et du Panégyrique de S. Barnabé par Alexandre le Moine (BGH 226; CPG 7400; ClAp 286)', in *Philohistor. Miscellanea in honorem Caroli Laga septuagenarii*, ed. by Antoon Schoors – Peter Van Deun, Leuven, pp. 193–98.

Starowieyski 2007 = Marek Starowieyski, *Apokryfy Nowego Testamentu*, vol. II, *Apostołowie*, part 2, *Bartłomiej, Filip, Jakub Mniejszy, Jakub Większy, Judasz, Maciej, Mateusz, Szymon i Juda Tadeusz, Ewangeliści, Uczniowie Pańscy*, ed. by Marek Starowieyski, Kraków.

Treadgold 2013 = Warren Treadgold, *The Middle Byzantine Historians*, Basingstoke.

Van Deun 1993 = Peter Van Deun, 'Préliminaires', in *Hagiographica Cypria. Sancti Barnabae Laudatio auctore Alexandro Monacho et Sanctorum Bartholomaei et Barnabae Vita e Menologio imperiali deprompta*, editae curante Peter Van Deun, *Vita Sancti Auxibii*, edita curante Jacques Noret, Turnhout – Leuven, pp. 15–21.

Van Esbroeck 1975 = Michel Van Esbroeck, *Les plus anciens homéliaires géorgiens. Études descriptive et historique*, Louvain.

Van Esbroeck 1979 = Michel Van Esbroeck, 'L'opuscule 'sur la croix' d'Alexandre de Chypre et sa version géorgienne', *Bedi Kartlisa*, 37, pp. 106–11.

Zavagno 2017 = Luca Zavagno, *Cyprus between Late Antiquity and the Early Middle Ages (ca. 600–800). An Island in Transition*, London – New York.

Abstract

The present article deals with the dependence relation between the *Laudatio Barnabae* by Alexander the Monk and Theodore Lector's *Ecclesiastical History*. As our analysis has demonstrated, there are many points of convergence between Alexander's panegyric and Theodore's *History*, which hint at the existence of the relation between them. It appears to be very likely that Alexander the Monk would have drawn on Theodore's *History* in composing the section on Peter the Fuller. Likewise, the Theodorean tradition connected with the discovery of Barnabas' grave and with the translation of the Matthew's Gospel to Constantinople is very similar to the version in the *Laudatio*, even though it is narrated in a very concise manner.

THE EMPEROR AND
POLITICAL AUTHORITIES IN
THEODORE LECTOR'S WORK

CHRISTOPH BEGASS

KAISERWECHSEL UND KAISERERHEBUNGEN IN DER *KIRCHENGESCHICHTE* DES THEODOROS ANAGNOSTES

1. *Problemstellung*

‚Es fällt auf', schreibt Günther Christian Hansen über die Konzeption der Kirchengeschichte des Theodoros Anagnostes, ‚daß die politische Geschichte in geringerem Maße als bei Sokrates und Sozomenos und später bei Euagrios berücksichtigt zu sein scheint, und anscheinend nur, soweit sie unmittelbare Ursachen oder Auswirkungen im kirchenpolitischen Bereich hat'.[1] Sollte diese Feststellung zutreffen, wäre eine Quelle ersten Ranges für die zweite Hälfte des 5. Jahrhunderts nur für die dezidiert kirchenpolitischen Belange von Bedeutung. Tatsächlich konzentrierte sich Theodoros im zweiten Teil seiner *Kirchengeschichte*, die schon ‚bald nach 610' nur noch in einer epitomisierten Fassung kursierte, auf die Zeitgeschichte und legte dabei den Fokus auf das Geschehen in Konstantinopel.[2] Da er nah am berichteten Geschehen war und überdies mit vielen zentralen Akteuren in engem persönlichen Austausch stand, verfügte er über viele Informationen aus erster Hand. Vor diesem Hintergrund möchte ich die Probe machen, inwieweit uns Theodoros' *Kirchengeschichte* helfen kann, die Eigenheiten der Kaisererhebungen in der Spätantike zu rekonstruieren und zu systematisieren.[3] Da die *historia tripartita* eine Kompilation aus Sokrates, Sozomenos und Theodoret ist,[4] wird sich die Untersuchung auf die *Kirchenhistorische*

---

[1] Hansen 1995, p. xviii.
[2] Hansen 1995, p. xxii; xxxix.
[3] S. unten Abschnitt 5.
[4] Vgl. Hansen 1995, pp. xiii–xvi.

Studies in Theodore Anagnostes, ed. by Rafał Kosiński & Adrian Szopa, STTA 19 (Turnhout 2021), pp. 133–160
© BREPOLS ❦ PUBLISHERS   DOI 10.1484/M.STTA-EB.5.127979

Epitome konzentrieren. Bevor ich die von Theodoros geschilderten Erhebungen eingehender untersuche, ist noch kurz zu erläutern, warum die Frage, *wer* in der Spätantike *wie* Kaiser wurde und es nach Möglichkeit auch blieb, nach wie vor eines der großen Probleme der Spätantike darstellt.

2. *Kaisererhebungen in der Spätantike als Forschungsproblem*

Durch die zentrale Stellung des Kaisers im politischen System der Spätantike konnte kein Kirchenhistoriker die Erhebung eines neuen Kaisers ausblenden. Daher widmet sich selbstverständlich auch Theodoros allen Kaisererhebungen in dem von ihm behandelten Zeitraum. Wichtig ist daher die Frage, wie er diese Krönungen schildert, welche Schwerpunkte er setzt, wie er die Prätendenten beurteilt und welche Informationen er bietet. Kaisererhebungen sind zwar in der Geschichte der römischen Kaiserzeit, der Spätantike und selbstverständlich auch der byzantinischen Geschichte ein zentrales Problem der politischen Geschichte, zugleich wissen wir aber erstaunlich wenig über die Mechanismen, derer es bedurfte, um einen Kaiser zu ‚machen‘.[5] Da es seit der Etablierung der Monarchie durch Augustus nie eine rechtliche Fixierung des Kaisertums gegeben hatte, mußte zwangsläufig auch der Weg zur Erlangung der Kaiserwürde weitgehend undefiniert bleiben. Am besten zu fassen sind die Mechanismen noch in der Zeit der sog. Soldatenkaiser, da hier die Machtverhältnisse eindeutig sind: Das erfolgreiche Heer ruft seinen Feldherren zum neuen Kaiser aus, der sich freilich zumeist gegen mindestens einen, bereits etablierten Kaiser zu erwähren hat. Dieser weitgehend militärische Akt ist auch insofern gut zu fassen, als der Kaiser in der Tradition des Augustus in erster Linie als *imperator* verstanden wurde.[6] Die Erhebung eines erfolgreichen Feldherrn zum Augustus war somit ein dem System inhärenter Schritt.

---

[5] Der folgende Abschnitt fußt auf Überlegungen, die ich an anderer Stelle ausführlicher dargelegt habe, vgl. Begass (im Druck). Jüngst legte Lilie einen Querschnitt der Erhebungen durch die gesamte byzantinische Geschichte vor, vgl. Lilie 2017, pp. 21–41.

[6] Vgl. zuletzt Hebblewhite 2017, pp. 8–12.

KAISERWECHSEL UND KAISERERHEBUNGEN IN DER *KIRCHENGESCHICHTE*

Vor nunmehr 25 Jahren hat Egon Flaig mit dem Modell der ,Akzeptanzgruppen' versucht, dem Problem des Kaisertums in der früheren Kaiserzeit, jenseits von staats- und verfassungsrechtlichen Erklärungen, Herr zu werden.[7] Sein Modell hat sich trotz mancher Kritik bewährt und in der Folge etabliert, so daß es als in den Grundzügen bekannt vorausgesetzt werden kann. Der früher allmächtig gedachte römische Kaiser, so hat Flaig herausgestellt, war gefangen in einem System von Verpflichtungen gegenüber verschiedenen gesellschaftlichen Gruppen. Neben Heer und Senat durfte er in der Hohen Kaiserzeit vor allem die Akzeptanz der stadtrömischen Bevölkerung nicht verlieren. Trotz einiger Ähnlichkeiten liegen die Dinge im spätantiken oströmischen Reich anders. Anknüpfend an Flaigs Modell hat vor allem Rene Pfeilschifter in seiner eindrucksvollen Studie gezeigt, worin die Unterschiede zur Hohen Kaiserzeit liegen.[8] Gleiches gilt, *cum grano salis*, für die Kaisererhebungen im östlichen Reichsteil – und auf diesen werde ich mich in der Folge konzentrieren. Über die Kaisererhebungen im Konstantinopel des 5. und 6. Jahrhunderts sind wir durch die Protokolle im sog. ,Zeremonienbuch' außergewöhnlich gut unterrichtet. Diese Dokumente, die, wie seit J. B. Burys Untersuchung allgemein angenommen wird, von Justinians langjährigem *magister officiorum* Petros Patrikios stammen,[9] sind in der Exzerptsammlung *de cerimoniis* des Konstantinos VII. Porphyrogenntos aus dem 9. Jahrhundert überliefert. Erhalten sind die Protokolle der Krönungen – in chronologischer Reihenfolge – von Leo I. 457 (I 91), Leo II. 473 (I 94), Anastasius 491 (I 92), Justin I. 518 (I 93) und Justinian 527 (I 95). Der Bericht über die Erhebung des Nikephoros Phocas (reg. 963–69; I 96) ist offensichtlich ein späterer Zusatz, da hier die Erhebung des Nachfolgers von Konstantins VII. (reg. 913–59) Sohn Romanos II. (reg. 959–63) beschrieben wird.[10] Auffällig ist zudem die Reihen-

---

[7] Vgl. Flaig 1992/2019.

[8] Pfeilschifter, 2013, pp. 1–38 (zum Akzeptanzmodell); vgl. auch Trampedach 2005, pp. 275–90.

[9] Bury 1907, pp. 209–27, 417–39; zu Leben und Werk des Petros Patrikios vgl. PLRE IIIB 993–98 und zuletzt Banchich 2015, pp. 1–3. Die neue französische Ausgabe des Zeremonienbuches (ed. G. Dagron † – B. Flusin) war mir leider noch nicht zugänglich.

[10] Vgl. Kresten 2000, pp. 474–89.

folge, in der die Protokolle überliefert sind,[11] sowie der Umstand, daß Berichte der Krönungen Zenos (474)[12] und Basiliscus' (475)[13] fehlen.

Da das ‚Zeremonienbuch' eine besonders günstige Quellenlage suggeriert, haben die dort berücksichtigten Krönungen jeweils mehrere Einzeluntersuchungen erfahren. Diese betrachten ihren Gegenstand jedoch jeweils recht isoliert, ohne den Anspruch zu erheben, die Krönungen im spätantiken Konstantinopel in einem größeren Rahmen zu erfassen. Vor diesem Hintergrund ist es bemerkenswert, daß bis heute keine systematische Untersuchung der Kaisererhebungen in der Spätantike vorliegt.[14] Eine weitere Kehrseite der durch das Zeremonienbuch außergewöhnlich guten Quellenlage ist eine starke Konzentration auf diese Berichte. Da diese einen in sich geschlossenen Zugang bieten, wird die Parallelüberlieferung oftmals vernachlässigt, ohne daß dieses Vorgehen weiter begründet würde. Hiermit sind wir bei der *Kirchengeschichte* des Theodoros Anagnostes und deren möglichem Wert für die spätantiken Kaisererhebungen. Mit Theodoros haben wir einen Gewährsmann in Konstantinopel, der über Wissen aus erster Hand verfügte. Er war zwar nicht im Palast bei den Händeln zugegen, aus denen der neue Kaiser hervorging, doch verfügte er durch seine Stellung über Zugang zu Patriarch Macedonius (496–511), der ihn mit Informationen versorgen konnte.[15] Anders als das Zeremonienbuch berichtet die *Kirchengeschichtliche Epitome* von allen sieben Krönungen im Zeitraum zwischen 450 und 518, inklusive der geglückten Usurpation des Basiliscus.[16]

[11] So ist die Krönung Leos II. (I 94), die im Jahre 474 stattfand, nach der Justins (I 93) des Jahres 518 eingeordnet.

[12] Vgl. Kosiński 2010, pp. 70–72.

[13] Vgl. Redies 1997, pp. 213–15; Prostko-Prostyński 2000, pp. 259–65; Kosiński 2010, pp. 79–82.

[14] Vgl. Begass (im Druck).

[15] Hansen 1995, p. x erwägt sogar, daß Theodoros möglicherweise mit Macedonius 511–18 in die Verbannung gegangen sein könnte.

[16] Es handelt sich um die Krönungen Marcians (450), Leos I. (457), Leos II. (473), Zenos (474), Basiliscus' (475), Anastasius' (491) und Justins (518).

3. *Die Kaiserkrönungen in der Kirchenhistorischen Epitome*

Die erste Erhebung, die die *Kirchenhistorische Epitome* referiert, ist die Marcians, der dem plötzlich bei einem Reitunfall verstorbenen Theodosius II. 450 folgte. Auf engstem Raum, der wahrscheinlich mit der Epitomisierung zu erklären ist, bietet Theodoros einige Informationen, die wir nur durch ihn kennen:

> Μαρκιανὸς Ἰλλυριὸς τὸ γένος τριβοῦνος ὤν, προβεβηκὼς ἐν ἡλικίᾳ, ἐν πολέμοις γενόμενος ἄριστος, ἀνηγορεύθη βασιλεὺς ἐν τῷ Ἑβδόμῳ ὑπὸ παντὸς τοῦ στρατοῦ.[17]

Dariusz Brodka hat eindrücklich gezeigt, wie verschlungen die Quellenlage zu Marcians Biographie bis zur Etablierung seiner Herrschaft ist.[18] Über die unterschiedlichen Versionen der Legende, daß der Flug eines Adlers dem jungen Soldaten in den 420er Jahren die Kaiserwürde vorausgesagt habe, müssen wir hier nicht weiter handeln. Hinsichtlich Theodoros' Bericht über die Erhebung Marcians ist vielmehr von Bedeutung, daß er auf knappem Raum wichtige Informationen bietet, die sonst nur von deutlich späteren Autoren geboten werden, die sicher von Theodoros abhängen. So bietet Theodoros zwar nur die generelle Angabe, Marcian sei schon ‚im fortgeschrittenen Alter' Kaiser geworden, diese wird aber durch die Osterchronik ebenso bestätigt wie ergänzt, wenn sie angibt, er sei 457 ‚im Alter von 65 Jahren' gestorben.[19] Nach dieser Angabe wäre er mit 58 Jahren Kaiser geworden. In weiten Teilen beruht das Chronicon Paschale zwar auf Malalas, ist aber, wie Pia Carolla jüngst gezeigt hat, für die Zeit Theodosius' II. und Marcians nicht vollständig von ihm abhängig.[20] Kommen wir zu Theodoros' Bericht zurück. Es ist zunächst bemerkenswert, daß Theodoros (bzw. der Epitomator) sogleich hervorhebt, der neue Kaiser sei entschieden gegen den Ämterkauf

---

[17] Theod. Anagn. 354, p. 100,11–13 (ed. Hansen 1995).

[18] Brodka 2012, pp. 145–62; Begass 2019; vgl. auch PLRE II 714–16.

[19] Chron. Pasch. p. 592,16–17 (ed. Dindorf 1832): ἐτελεύτησεν Μαρκιανὸς Αὔγουστος, ὢν ἐτῶν ξε΄.

[20] Carolla 2016, p. 52: ‚the section of the Chronicon paschale about the emperors Theodosius II (408–50 AD) and Marcianus (450–57 AD) does not show a direct dependence on, but a complex relationship with Malalas' book 14: sometimes they are identical, sometimes close, sometimes very different'.

vorgegangen (ὃς εὐθὺς ἐκέλευσεν ἄρχοντα ἐπὶ δόσει χρημάτων μὴ γίνεσθαι). Indem diese Maßnahme als einzige sofort ergriffene erwähnt wird, rückt sie den neuen Kaiser sogleich in ein äußerst positives Licht. Dieser Eindruck, den Marcian mit allen ‚orthodoxen' Kaisern bei Theodoros teilt, ist Marcians Einberufung des Konzils von Chalcedon geschuldet, das für Theodoros einen Sieg der Orthodoxie bedeutete.

Im Bericht über die Erhebung wird das Mitte des 5. Jahrhunderts noch starke militärische Element korrekt wiedergegeben. Nicht nur wird hier ein aktiver Offizier ausgewählt, er wird auch auf dem Hebdomon vom, wie es ausdrücklich heißt, ‚ganzen Heer' ausgerufen (ἐν τῷ Ἑβδόμῳ ὑπὸ παντὸς τοῦ στρατοῦ). Theodoros gibt hier ein knappes Bild einer Krönung, die, so scheint es in seinem Bericht, als eine der letzten noch nach den Spielregeln des Militärs vonstatten ging. Auffallend an seinem Bericht ist aber vor allem, was fehlt – nämlich die entscheidende Rolle Pulcherias und Aspars.[21] Nach Malalas gebot der sterbende Theodosius seiner Schwester, den weitgehend unbekannten Offizier mittleren Ranges zu heiraten und damit als Kaiser zu legitimieren.[22] Um 450 führte aber auch an Aspar kein Weg vorbei. Seine erfolgreiche Thronbesteigung zeigt folglich, daß Marcian die Unterstützung Pulcherias und Aspars genoß.[23] Daneben finden wir bei Theodoros zudem keinen Hinweis auf die Mitwirkung des Patriarchen Anatolius (449–58) bei der Krönung. Diese ist für Marcian erst im 10. Jahrhundert bei Symeon Magistros (bzw. Leon Grammatikos) belegt.[24] Da die Epitome des Theodoros über die Krönungszeremonie selbst überhaupt nichts sagen, mag dies nicht

[21] Vgl. Begass (im Druck).

[22] Malal. 14,27, pp. 288, 27–33 (ed. Thurn 2000); Evagr. 1,22, p. 32,31–33,5 (ed. Bidez – Parmentier 1898).

[23] Gegen Holum 1982, pp. 208–09, der Pulcherias Rolle betonte, hat Burgess 1993/94, pp. 47–68 vorgebracht, Marcian sei Aspars Kandidat gewesen, den Pulcheria in der Öffentlichkeit habe legitimieren müssen. Plausibler ist es freilich anzunehmen, Pulcheria und Aspar hätten die Nachfolge unter sich ausgehandelt, vgl. Sickel 1898, p. 517 und Pfeilschifter 2013, pp. 151–52, 514–16.

[24] Leon Gramm. 111,4–5 (ed. Bekker 1842) = Symeon Mag. Chron. 98,1, p. 128,2–3 (ed. Wahlgren 2006): Μαρκιανὸς ἐβασίλευσεν ἔτη ἓξ καὶ μῆνας πέντε, στεφθεὶς ὑπὸ Ἀνατολίου πατριάρχου. Nachdem diese Passage lange als Beweis für die erste Krönung durch den Patriarchen angesehen wurde, konnte Enßlin 1947, p. 3 zeigen, daß die Parallelüberlieferung gegen eine solche Interpretation spricht; vgl. auch Winkelmann 1978, pp. 468–70.

KAISERWECHSEL UND KAISERERHEBUNGEN IN DER *KIRCHENGESCHICHTE*

als Argument gegen eine Krönung durch den Patriarchen gelten, doch hat Friedhelm Winkelmann vor nunmehr vierzig Jahren dafür plädiert, daß wir eine aktive Rolle des Patriarchen bei der Krönung erst für Anastasius 491 annehmen dürften.[25]

Auch die Krönung Leos I. 457 wird in der *Kirchengeschicht-lichen Epitome* nur mit einem Satz bedacht. Nachdem Marcians Tod vermerkt wurde, berichtet Theodoros nur trocken, daß ,ein gewisser Leo' (Λέων τις) die Kaiserwürde übernahm, er aus Thrakien stammte und ,den Rang eines Tribunen innehatte':

προχειρίζεται δὲ εἰς βασιλέα Λέων τις, Θρᾷξ μὲν τῷ γένει, τρι-βοῦνος δὲ τὴν ἀξίαν.[26]

Zwei Dinge springen hier sofort ins Auge: Zunächst ist der kurze Kommentar genau gleich aufgebaut wie der zu Marcian. Auch bei diesem wurde seine Herkunft angegeben (Μαρκιανὸς Ἰλλυριὸς τὸ γένος), dann sein militärisches Amt als Tribun (τριβοῦνος ὤν). Ist bei Marcian die genaue Stellung nicht genau zu klären,[27] bestätigen Iordanes und Michael Syrus unabhängig voneinander das Amt des Tribunen für Leo.[28] Wie bei Marcian ist aber auch bei Leo weniger das bemerkenswert, was der Text bietet, sondern vielmehr das, was er offensichtlich verschweigt. Entscheidend für Leos Aufstieg zur Kaiserwürde war einmal mehr Aspar, der hier erneut nicht erwähnt wird. Daß er aber die alles entscheidende Instanz war, belegen viele zeitnahe Quellen unabhängig voneinander, etwa Candidus und Priscus,[29] Iordanes und Pro-

[25] Winkelmann 1978, p. 468; dazu ausführlich unten Abschnitt 4.

[26] Theod. Anagn. 367, p. 103,19–20 (ed. Hansen 1995) = Theoph. a. m. 5950, p. 110,19–21 (ed. de Boor 1883) (dazu unten).

[27] Vgl. PLRE II 715.

[28] Iord. Rom. 335, p. 43,16 (ed. Mommsen 1882); Mich. Syr. IX 1, p. ii 126 (ed. Chabot 1899–1924); Cedr. p. i 608,5 (ed. Bekker 1838–1839) = p. 594,17 (ed. Tartaglia 2016); Theoph. a.m. 5950, p. 110,19–20 (ed. de Boor 1883).

[29] Cand. fr. 1,26 (ed. Blockley 1981–1983): διέρχεται δὲ ἐν τῷ πρώτῳ λόγῳ ... τὴν ἀνάρρησιν διὰ Ἀσπαρος Λέοντος; Prisc. fr. 20 (ed. Müller 1851) = fr. 19 (ed. Blockley 1981–1983) (= Suda A 3803 [I 343,9–11 (ed. Adler 1967)]): Μαρκιανοῦ δὲ τοῦ βασιλέως χρηστοῦ μὲν γεγονότος, θᾶττον δὲ ἐκβεβιωκότος, αὐτο-κελεύστῳ γνώμῃ Ἄσπαρ Λέοντα διάδοχον αὐτοῦ γενέσθαι παρεσκεύασεν. Diese Passage findet sich im Lemma zu Aspar (Suda A 4201, s. v. Ἄσπαρ [I 387,12–14 (ed. Adler 1967)]): ὅτι Μαρκιανοῦ τοῦ βασιλέως χρηστοῦ μὲν γεγονότος, θᾶττον δὲ ἐκβεβιωκότος, αὐτοκελεύστῳ γνώμῃ Ἄσπαρ Λέοντα διάδοχον αὐτοῦ γενέσθαι παρε-σκεύασεν.

kop.[30] Auch viele der byzantinischen Historiographen berichten davon.[31] Theophanes hingegen erwähnt zwar nicht Aspars Rolle bei der Krönung Leos, hebt aber wie die übrigen Quellen dessen überragenden Einfluß auf den Kaiser in dessen ersten Jahren hervor, der letztlich zur Ermordung Aspars und seiner Söhne geführt habe.[32] Um den Gang der Untersuchung hier nicht zu unterbrechen, wird die Frage, welche Rolle der Patriarch bei der Krönung Leos. I. einnahm, unten gesondert behandeln werden.[33]

Im Spätsommer 473 erhob Leo seinen Enkel zum Mitregenten, zu Leo II. Neben Malalas bietet Theodoros den einzigen Bericht der Erhebung Leos des Jüngeren (die Schilderung bei Theophanes ist wiederum größtenteils aus Theodoros übernommen):

Λέων ὁ βασιλεὺς προεβάλετο Καίσαρα Λέοντα τὸν μικρὸν τὸν υἱὸν Ἀριάδνης τῆς ἑαυτοῦ θυγατρὸς καὶ Ζήνωνος τοῦ γαμβροῦ αὐτοῦ. ἡ κόνις τούτῳ τῷ χρόνῳ κατῆλθεν μηνὶ Νοεμβρίῳ πυρακτούντων νεφῶν φανέντων ἐν οὐρανῷ πρότερον, ὡς πάντας πιστεῦσαι ὅτι πῦρ ἦν τὸ μέλλον καταφέρεσθαι.[34]

Bemerkenswert ist hier zunächst die ausführliche Beschreibung des Himmelszeichens der brennenden Staubwolken, die auch Theophanes mit ganz ähnlichen Worten beschreibt, das Omen aber von der Erhebung Leos des Jüngeren abtrennt und in das nächste Jahr (a. m. 5966 = 474 n. Chr.) verlegt:

τούτῳ τῷ ἔτει ἡ κόνις κατῆλθε πυρακτούντων τῶν νεφῶν προφανέντων, ὡς πάντας νομίζειν, ὅτι πῦρ βρέχει.[35]

---

[30] Iord. Rom. 335 (ed. Mommsen 1882): *Leo Bessica ortus progeniae Asparis patricii potentia ex tribuno militum factus est imperator*; Proc. BV I 5,7; 6,3 (ed. Haury – Wirth 1962–1964).

[31] So etwa Symeon Magister: Leon Gramm. 113,2–5 (ed. Bekker 1842) = Symeon Mag. Chron. 99, p. 129,1–130,5 (ed. Wahlgren 2006; ich folge dieser Ausgabe): Λέων ὁ μέγας, ὁ πληθεὶς παρὰ Ἄσπαρος καὶ Ἀρδαβουρίου. τούτων γὰρ βουληθέντων τὴν βασιλείαν κρατῆσαι οὐκ εἴασεν ἡ σύγκλητος ὡς Ἀρειανῶν ὄντων.

[32] Krönung: Theoph. a.m. 5949, p. 109,23–24 (ed. de Boor 1883); Ermordung: Theoph. a. m. 5963, p. 117,11–13 (ed. de Boor 1883). Zu Leos Krönung vgl. Boak 1919, pp. 37–38; Lilie 1998, 395–408; Croke 2005, pp. 149–52; Siebigs 2010, pp. 194–215 (Wahl und Krönung), pp. 657–81 (Diskussion des Quellenbefundes).

[33] S. unten Abschnitt 4.

[34] Theod. Anagn. 398, p. 111,13–16 (ed. Hansen 1995).

[35] Theoph. a. m. 5966, p. 119,29–30 (ed. de Boor 1883). Bei Theophanes

Im übrigen sind die biographischen Angaben – was keinesfalls selbstverständlich ist – bei Theodoros korrekt: Leo II. war der Sohn Ariadnes und Zenos, des späteren Kaisers. Im Gegensatz zu Theodoros bietet Malalas jedoch mehrere wichtige Informationen, die bei Theodoros fehlen, etwa die, daß Ariadne diejenige war, die ‚Leo zur Herrschaft gebracht‘ habe.[36] Vielleicht steckt der Kern dieser Information aber in Theodoros' Bemerkung, Leo I. sei zu diesem Zeitpunkt bereits ‚krank gewesen und kurz darauf gestorben‘ (Λέοντος τοῦ μεγάλου ἀρρωστήσαντος καὶ μετὰ βραχὺ τελευτήσαντος).[37] Theodoros (bzw. sein Epitomator) berichtet dies bereits im Zusammenhang mit der Krönung Zenos, die Rafał Kosiński in seiner Biographie dieses Kaisers detailliert untersucht hat.[38] Daß die Berichte der Krönungen Leos II. und Zenos ursprünglich deutlich länger waren, darauf deutet m. E. auch die Bemerkung des Victor Tunnunnensis zur Krönung Zenos hin, der in seiner stark von Theodoros abhängigen *Kirchengeschichte* hervorhebt,[39] der Vater sei vom Sohn *contra consuetudinem* gekrönt worden.[40] Es ist in der Tat schwer vorstellbar, daß ein aufmerksamer Berichterstatter wie Theodoros diese besondere Konstellation nicht zumindest vermerkt hätte. Als Vergleich kann wiederum Malalas dienen, der glaubt, die schon durch die Familiensituation der handelnden Personen unübersichtliche Situation ausführlich zu erklären müssen.[41] Für Zeno fehlt, wie eingangs erwähnt, das Protokoll im Zeremonienbuch, so daß eine wichtige Kontrollinstanz nicht zur Verfügung steht. Die Passage bei Theodoros lautet:

> Λέων ὁ μικρὸς ὁ Ζήνωνος υἱὸς ἀνηγορεύθη βασιλεὺς Λέοντος τοῦ μεγάλου ἀρρωστήσαντος καὶ μετὰ βραχὺ τελευτήσαντος. Λέων ὁ μικρὸς τὸν ἴδιον πατέρα Ζήνωνα βασιλέα ἐν τῷ ἱππο-

folgt auf die Erhebung Leos II. der Tod des Westkaisers Olybrius und die Umtriebe Rikimers.

[36] Malal. 14,47, p. 299,19 (ed. Thurn 2000): ὑπεβλήθη δὲ ὑπὸ τῆς ἰδίας μητρὸς τῆς ἐπιφανεστάτης Ἀριάδνης (danach Chron. Pasch. p. 599,8–9 ed. Dindorf 1832).

[37] Theod. Anagn. 400, pp. 112, 11–12 (ed. Hansen 1995).

[38] Kosiński 2010, pp. 70–72.

[39] Zum Verhältnis des Victor Tunnunnensis zu Theodoros vgl. Hansen 1995, p. xxi.

[40] Vict. Tunn. ad ann. 474,2, p. 112,5 (ed. Hansen 1995).

[41] Vgl. zu Malalas' Bericht aber Kosiński 2010, p. 71 Anm. 88: ‚but he [*sc.* Malalas] again turns out to be a doubtful source here‘.

δρομίῳ ἀνηγόρευσεν. δέκα μόνους μῆνας αὐτὸς βασιλεύσας <...>
[hier vermutet Hansen eine Lücke] εὐθὺς ἐτελεύτησεν.[42]

Vergleicht man diesen kurzen Abriß mit den zahlreichen Berichten der anderen antiken Autoren, so bietet allein Theodoros (und der von ihm abhängige Theophanes)[43] die Nachricht, Leo habe Zeno ‚im Hippodrom' zum Kaiser erhoben. Weder Marcellinus Comes noch Malalas, um nur die wichtigsten zu nennen, erwähnen überhaupt einen Ort.[44] Victor von Tunnunna hebt zwar, wie oben erwähnt, die außerordentliche Konstellation hervor, daß der Sohn den Vater gekrönt habe, einen Ort nennt er aber nicht. Die Ortsangabe finden wir hingegen auch bei Theophanes, der sogar weitere Details bietet:

Λέων ὁ μικρὸς [...] ἔστεψε Ζήνωνα τὸν ἴδιον πατέρα Ζήνωνα βασιλέα ἐν τῷ καθίσματι τοῦ ἱπποδρομίου.[45]

Leo habe seinen Vater also im Kathisma des Hippodroms ‚bekränzt' (ἔστεψε). Auf den ersten Blick mögen diese Details dafür sprechen, daß, wie Hansen meinte, Theophanes ‚die vollständige Epitome vor sich gehabt und benutzt' habe.[46] Inwieweit Theophanes hier aber möglicherweise anachronistischer Weise Motive erwähnt, die zu seiner Zeit selbstverständlich waren, ist heute nicht mehr zu entscheiden. Die Information, Zeno sei vor der größtmöglichen Öffentlichkeit, nämlich im Hippodrom, gekrönt worden, steht zudem in gewissem Widerspruch zu einer Bemerkung des Kandidos, Zeno sei als Isaurier so unbeliebt bei der Bevölkerung gewesen, daß Leo I. zunächst seinen gleichnamigen Enkel, nicht seinen Schwiegersohn zum Mitregenten gewählt habe.[47]

---

[42] Theod. Anagn. 400, p. 112,11–14 (ed. Hansen 1995).

[43] Vgl. unten Anm. 46.

[44] Marc. Com. ad ann. 474,1, p. 91,2–5 (ed. Mommsen 1894); Malal. 14,47, p. 300,17–301,25 (ed. Thurn 2000) (unter Berufung auf Nestorianus [p. 301,30]); Chron. Pasch. p. 599,8–16 (ed. Dindorf 1832) (aus Malalas); Evagr. HE 2,17, p. 67,5–15 (ed. Bidez – Parmentier 1898); Cedr. p. i 615,4–7 (ed. Bekker 1838–1839) = p. 600,36–39 (ed. Tartaglia 2016); Zonar. 14,2, p. 154,29–255,5 (ed. Dindorf 1869); zum Bericht des Theophanes vgl. die folgende Anm.

[45] Theoph. a.m. 5966, p. 120,1–5 (ed. de Boor 1883).

[46] Zur Benutzung durch Theophanes vgl. Hansen 1995, pp. xxix–xxx (das Zitat p. xxix).

[47] Kosiński 2010, p. 70.

KAISERWECHSEL UND KAISERERHEBUNGEN IN DER *KIRCHENGESCHICHTE*

Von den zwei Überlieferungssträngen zu Zenos Erhebung ist, wie Rafał Kosiński zu Recht hervorgehoben hat, jener Tradition der Vorzug zu geben, die die Wahl Zenos mit dem Umstand in Verbindung bringt, daß der junge Leo nicht alleine habe herrschen können, sondern einen erwachsenen Mitkaiser benötigt habe.[48] Wie Kosiński gezeigt hat, wird der Einfluß des Senats auch bei Kandidos und der Daniels-Vita erwähnt, wobei letztere dem Senat eine entscheidende Rolle zuschreibt, wenn sie behauptet, es habe gar einen Senatsbeschluß gegeben.[49] Ein solches Dekret war jedoch keinesfalls das Ergebnis einer erbitterten Debatte unter den Senatoren; vielmehr stimmte der Senat hier nur einer Entscheidung zu, die eine kleine Gruppe hochrangiger Magistrate – in diesem Fall gemeinsam mit Kaiserin Ariadne – getroffen hatte.[50] Damit löst sich der zuvor angesprochene Widerspruch zwischen Kandidos und Theodoros weitgehend auf: Wenn die wichtigsten Senatoren zum Entschluß gekommen waren, Zeno zum neuen Mitkaiser zu erheben, war es nur folgerichtig, den neuen Kaiser im Rahmen des *consensus omnium* der Öffentlichkeit zu präsentieren. Die Bühne dafür bot der Hippodrom. Ich halte daher diese Information, die Theodoros als erster überliefert, für unbedingt plausibel.

In der *Kirchengeschichtlichen Epitome* folgt auf die Erhebung Zenos sofort die Usurpation des Basiliscus, die Ernennung seines Sohnes Marcus und die Flucht Zenos.[51] Durch die Arbeiten von Michael Redies, Jan Prostko-Prostyński und Rafał Kosiński sind die Hintergründe dieser Usurpation – oder Machtübernahme – mittlerweile gut bekannt.[52] Der eigentliche Bericht des Theodoros ist knapp und genauso formelhaft wie die bisher betrachteten:

---

[48] Kosiński 2010, p. 71.

[49] V. Dan. Styl. 67, p. 65,12–14 (ed. Delahaye 1923). καὶ ἐγένετο συμβούλιον ὑπὸ τῆς συγκλήτου ἕνεκεν τοῦ νήπιον ὑπάρχειν τὸν βασιλέα καὶ μὴ δύνασθαι ὑπογραφὰς ποιεῖν. Vgl. auch Cand fr. 1,49 (ed. Blockley 1981–1983): συναινέσει τῆς βουλῆς. Die von Kosiński 2010, p. 71 angeführte Stelle Proc. BV 1,7,3 (ed. Haury – Wirth 1962–1964) trägt nichts zur Frage nach der Rolle des Senats bei.

[50] Vgl. ausführlich Begass (im Druck); so auch Kosiński 2010, p. 71: ‚This decision, of such a great weight and significance, must have been made by the most influential people in the state, and such people were in the senate'. Vgl. dazu Beck 1966; Begass 2018.

[51] Theod. Anagn. 112,19–22 (ed. Hansen 1995).

[52] Vgl. Redies 1997, pp. 211–21; Prostko-Prostyński 2000, pp. 259–65; Kosiński 2010, pp. 79–97.

143

Βασιλίσκος ἐν τῷ Κάμπῳ ἀνηγορεύθη βασιλεύς, καὶ ποιήσας Καίσαρα Μᾶρκον τὸν ἴδιον υἱὸν κτλ.[53]

Er gewinnt lediglich Gewicht als Einleitung zu einer – sogar noch in der epitomisierten Form – langen Passage über die religionspolitischen Streitigkeiten, in die sich Basiliscus mit den Alexandrinern um Timotheus Aelurus verstrickte.[54] Auch den Maßnahmen des zurückgekehrten Zeno widmete Theodoros auffallend viel Raum.[55]

Die Erhebung des Anastasius im Frühjahr 491 wird zwar anfänglich nach dem üblichen Schema dargestellt, Theodoros ist sich aber der besonderen Situation bewußt, die nach Zenos Tod entstanden war:

Ζήνων ὁ βασιλεὺς ἐτελεύτησεν. ἀναγορεύεται δὲ εἰς βασιλέα ὑπὸ Ἀριάδνης τῆς Αὐγούστης Ἀναστάσιος ὁ σιλεντιάριος ἐκ τοῦ Δυρραχίου ὁρμώμενος. περὶ οὗ ἀντέστη Εὐφήμιος ὁ ἐπίσκοπος αἱρετικὸν καλῶν καὶ τῶν Χριστιανῶν ἀνάξιον.[56]

Ariadne kam als Kaiserin eine Schlüsselrolle zu, die von allen beteiligten Parteien anerkannt wurde.[57] Die komplizierten Aushandlungsprozesse, in die alle wichtigen Personen der Zeit eingebunden waren, müssen hier nicht erneut aufgearbeitet werden.[58] Vor dem Hintergrund der reichen Parallelüberlieferung läßt sich aber festhalten, daß Theodoros' Bericht auch hier die Verhältnisse durchaus korrekt widerspiegelt, wenn er die außergewöhnliche Situation und die daraus resultierende Rolle der Kaiserin betont. Anastasius ist für Theodoros ein Häretiker der schlimmsten Sorte. Folgerichtig weist bereits die Notiz zur Krönung auf den Konflikt mit Patriarach Euphemius hin, und der Vorwurf der Häresie durchzieht den Rest der Darstellung. So denunziert Theodoros

---

[53] Theod. Anagn. 402, p. 112,19–20 (ed. Hansen 1995); Zonaras 14,2, p. 255,14–15 (ed. Dindorf 1869).

[54] Theod. Anagn. 403–12, pp. 113–14 (ed. Hansen 1995).

[55] Theod. Anagn. 413–17, pp. 114–15 (ed. Hansen 1995).

[56] Theod. Anagn. 446, p. 125,25–27 (ed. Hansen 1995).

[57] In der Forschung ist ihre Rolle kontrovers diskutiert worden, vgl. zuletzt Meier 2010, pp. 277–91 und Pfeilschifter 2013, p. 154 (mit weiterer Literatur).

[58] Vgl. Boak 1919, pp. 38–39; Treitinger 1956, pp. 10–11; Lilie 1995, pp. 3–12; Ballaira 2003, pp. 267–92; Haarer 2006, pp. 1–6; Meier 2009, pp. 63–75; Begass (im Druck).

den Kaiser, der mit Patriarch Macedonius (496–511) Theodoros' Gönner in die Verbannung trieb,[59] als ‚Zögling von Manichäern und Arianern'.[60] Aus diesem Jammertal scheint dann Justin gleichsam als Retter aufzusteigen:

προήχθη δὲ βασιλεὺς Ἰουστῖνος, ἀνὴρ πρεσβύτης ἀπὸ σταρτιωτῶν ἀρξάμενος καὶ μέχρι τῆς συγκλήτου προκόψας, τῆς ὀρθῆς πίστεως ἔμπυρος ζηλωτής, τὸ γένος Ἰλλυριός κτλ.[61]

Hier finden wir die üblichen Angaben über Herkunft und Ämter. In erster Linie erscheint Justin aber als der ‚feurige Eiferer für den rechten Glauben' (τῆς ὀρθῆς πίστεως ἔμπυρος ζηλωτής). Der Schwerpunkt liegt hier wieder auf der Religionspolitik, wird nun aber, da Theodoros Justins religiöse Einstellung billigt, ins Positive gewendet. Mit diesem Eindruck endet die *Kirchengeschichtliche Epitome*.

4. Die Rolle des Patriarchen bei der Krönung Leos I.

Kommen wir nun noch einmal auf die Frage zurück, welche Rolle der Patriarch bei Kaisererhebungen zu dieser Zeit spielte und ob bereits Leo I. vom Patriarchen gekrönt wurde. Nach Enßlins gründlicher Untersuchung galt lange Zeit als gesichert, daß bei Marcians Krönung 450 Patriarch Anatolius zwar anwesend war, aber noch keine tragende Rolle spielte.[62] Enßlin wandte sich damit dezidiert gegen die prominent von Wilhelm Sickel vertretene These, Marcian sei als erster Kaiser vom Bischof gekrönt worden, eine These, die in der Folgezeit lange Zeit das Feld behaupten konnte.[63] Enßlin selbst kam zum Schluß, bei der vermeintlichen

---

[59] Frend 1979, pp. 183–95; Dijkstra – Greatrex 2009, pp. 230–39; Greatrex 2010, pp. 125–29.

[60] Theod. Anagn. 448, p. 126,18 (ed. Hansen 1995): Μανιχαῖοι καὶ Ἀρειανοὶ ἔχαιρον Ἀναστασίῳ.

[61] Theod. Anagn. 524, p. 151,24–29 (ed. Hansen 1995).

[62] Vgl. Enßlin 1947.

[63] Sickel 1898, pp. 517–18. Zahlreiche Forscher, die Sickel folgten, darunter Stein und Kornemann, Alföldi oder Treitinger 1956, p. 8, nennt Enßlin 1947, p. 1. Später folgte dieser Interpretation etwa MacCormack 1981, p. 243; unentschieden bleibt Ballaira 2003, p. 275 Anm. 282. Hingegen änderte der von Enßlin zitierte G. Ostrogorsky aufgrund von Enßlins Untersuchung seine Meinung und folgte in der dritten Auflage seines Handbuches ausdrücklich Enßlins These, vgl. Ostrogorsky 1963, p. 51 Anm. 2.

Krönung Marcians durch Anatolius[64] handele es sich um eine falsche Rückprojizierung späterer Entwicklungen: ‚Und weil dann die späteren Chronisten wußten, daß inzwischen ja die Mitwirkung des Patriarchen beim Krönungszeremoniell zur Regel geworden war, so verknüpften sie mit der ersten Erwähnung des Bischofs bei einer solchen Gelegenheit die Vorstellung, daß er der Koronator gewesen sein müsse'.[65] Enßlin selbst plädierte dafür, daß als erster Kaiser Leo I. 457 vom Patriarchen gekrönt worden sei.[66] Es gebe weder, so betont er zu Recht, einen chronologischen noch einen inhaltlichen Grund, den Bericht des Zeremonienbuches (bzw. die zugrunde liegende Darstellung des Petros Patrikios) der Schilderung des Theodoros vorzuziehen.[67] In der Folgezeit konnte diese Deutung einige Anhänger für sich verbuchen,[68] bevor sie 1978 von Friedhelm Winkelmann verworfen wurde. Dieser plädierte dafür, dem Bericht des Zeremonienbuchs unbedingt den Vorzug zu geben.[69] Da aber Theodoros durch die zeitliche Nähe zum berichteten Geschehen besonderes Gewicht zukommt, erscheint es angebracht zu rekonstruieren, inwieweit Theodoros als Gewährsmann für eine Kaiserkrönung durch den Patriarchen gelten kann. Wie wir bereits gesehen haben, berichtet die *Kirchengeschichtliche Epitome* in der Fassung, wie Hansen sie bietet, nichts von einer Krönung durch den Patriarchen:

προχειρίζεται δὲ εἰς βασιλέα Λέων τις, Θρᾷξ μὲν τῷ γένει, τριβοῦνος δὲ τὴν ἀξίαν.[70]

---

[64] Cramer 1839, p. 311,2–3; Leon Gramm. 111,4–5 (ed. Bekker 1842) = Symeon Mag. Chron. 98, p. 128,1–2 (ed. Wahlgren 2006): Μαρκιανὸς ἐβασίλευσεν ἔτη ἓξ καὶ μῆνας πέντε, στεφθεὶς ὑπὸ Ἀνατολίου πατριάρχου.

[65] Enßlin 1947, p. 13.

[66] Enßlin 1947, p. 16 mit Anm. 6. Er kannte freilich Theodoros' Bericht nur in der unzureichenden Fassung der *Patrologia Graeca* (PG 86, p. 216A), die weitgehend auf Nikephoros Kallistou Xanthopoulos fußt; dazu das Folgende.

[67] Enßlin 1947, p. 16.

[68] Vgl. Ostrogorsky 1963, p. 51 Anm. 2; Maier 1973, p. 24: ‚Die Akklamation bedurfte der kanonischen Bestätigung durch Krönungsriten, die seit Leon I. (474 [*recte* 457]) der Patriarch von Konstantinopel durchführte'. Vor Enßlin vertrat diese Ansicht bereits Charanis 1937, p. 194: ‚Just exactly what the role of the patriarch was in the coronation of Marcian in 450 is not entirely clear, but that he actually crowned Leo I is absolutely certain'.

[69] Winkelmann 1978, p. 472, 479; unergiebig ist Szidat 2003, 51–61, der die Untersuchung Winkelmanns nicht berücksichtigt.

[70] Theod. Anagn. 367, p. 103,19–20 (ed. Hansen 1995).

Von großer Bedeutung ist daher Theophanes' Notiz. Er bietet den exakt gleichen Text, den er offensichtlich von Theodoros übernommen hat, jedoch mit einem Zusatz: [71]

τούτῳ τῷ ἔτει Λέων ἐβασίλευσεν, Θρᾷξ μὲν τῷ γένει, τριβοῦνος δὲ τὴν ἀξίαν, μηνὶ Φεβρουαρίῳ, ἰνδικτιῶνι ι΄. στεφθεὶς ὑπὸ Ἀνατολίου τοῦ πατριάρχου.[72]

Woher stammen aber die Information, wie die genaue Datierung und die Nachricht, Patriarch Anatolius habe Leo gekrönt, Informationen also, die Theophanes bietet, die bei Theodoros (in Hansens Edition) aber fehlen? Enßlin hatte aus dieser Stelle folgern wollen, daß bei der Krönung Leos der Patriarch zum ersten Mal eine entscheidende Rolle ,als Koronator' gespielt habe.[73] Sicher ist, daß Anatolius bei der Krönung anwesend war, wie auch das Krönungsprotokoll bestätigt.[74] Fraglich ist daher, welche Funktion er übernommen hat. Da die ,lakonische Aussage des Theophanes [...] durch keine andere Quelle, auch nicht durch das Zeremonienbuch gestützt' werde, hat sie Friedhelm Winkelmann in seiner Untersuchung verworfen und dafür plädiert, auf Basis des Zeremonienbuches erst für die Krönung des Anastasius 491 dem Patriarchen eine entscheidende Rolle zuzugestehen.[75] Wenn aber, wie Winkelmann selbst konstatiert, die Theophanes-Stelle tatsächlich auf Theodoros zurückgeht,[76] liegt die Annahme nahe, daß auch der Zusatz στεφθεὶς ὑπὸ Ἀνατολίου τοῦ πατριάρχου von Theodoros stammt. Durch die zeitliche Nähe des Theodoros zum Geschehen erhält die Theophanes-Stelle daher deutlich größeres Gewicht. Zudem ist die Theophanes-Stelle – entgegen Winkelmanns Befund – keineswegs ohne Parallele. In der Kirchenge-

---

[71] Dies nimmt auch Winkelmann 1978, p. 470 an.

[72] Theoph. a. m. 5950, p. 110,19–21 (ed. de Boor 1883) = Cedr. p. i 608,5 (ed. Bekker 1838–1839) = p. 594,17 (ed. Tartaglia 2016). Vgl. Winkelmann 1978, p. 470.

[73] Enßlin 1947, p. 19.

[74] De cerim. I 91, p. 410,10 (ed. Reiske 1828).

[75] Winkelmann 1978, p. 472 mit De cerim. I 92, p. 418,12–13 (ed. Reiske 1828). Dieser Deutung ist die Forschung weitgehend gefolgt, vgl. etwa Lilie 1995, pp. 9–11; ders. 1998, pp. 402–03; Meier 2009, p. 70; Ballaira 2003, p. 275 Anm. 282.

[76] Vgl. Winkelmann 1978, p. 470.

schichte des Nikephoros Kallistou Xanthopoulos (PG 145–47),[77] die Winkelmann nicht berücksichtigt hat, findet sich ebenfalls eine Passage, die von der Krönung Leos I. durch den Patriarchen spricht:

> ἐκείνου δὲ πρὸς ἀμείνω λῆξιν μεταχωρήσαντος, ψήφῳ κοινῇ τῆς συγκλήτου Λέων ὁ ἀπὸ τριβούνων, Θρᾷξ καὶ αὐτὸς τῷ γένει, βασιλεὺς Ῥωμαίων ἀναγορεύεται, τοῦ πατριάρχου Ἀνατολίου τὸ διάδημα περιθέντος κτλ.[78]

Dieser Paragraph weist nicht nur eine große inhaltliche wie sprachliche Nähe zu Theodoros und Theophanes auf, sondern bietet zugleich auch über die beiden früheren Chronisten hinausgehende Informationen. So sei Leo ἀπὸ τριβούνων (statt dem präsentischen τριβοῦνος δὲ τὴν ἀξίαν) gewesen, und Anatolius habe ihm das Diadem aufgesetzt. Um diese Stelle einordnen zu können, ist es nötig, einen Schritt zurückzutreten und die Überlieferungsgeschichte der *Kirchengeschichtlichen Epitome* zu berücksichtigen, die durch Gentz und Hansen intensiv aufgearbeitet ist.[79] Die *Epitome* ist in vier HSS überliefert.[80]

---

[77] Bei der Namensform Nikephoros *Kallistou* Xanthopoulos, d. h. ‚Nikephoros Xanthopoulos, Sohn des Kallistus‘, folge ich Gastgeber 2015, p. 141 Anm. 1. A. Berger, Chr. Gastgeber und S. Panteghini bereiten eine kritische Edition der Kirchengeschichte des Nikephoros Xanthopoulos vor, die in der *Series Vindobonensis* des CFHB erscheinen und die Ausgabe der PG ersetzen wird.

[78] Nikeph. Kall. Xanth. HE XV 15 (PG 147, p. 48B).

[79] Wie nötig es ist, die Überlieferung zu berücksichtigen, hat Lilie 1998, p. 402 Anm. 27 gezeigt. Er hat korrekt erkannt, daß die betreffende Theophanes-Stelle von Theod. Anagn. 367,103,19–20 (ed. Hansen 1995) abhängt, dabei aber übersehen, daß Hansen als Grundlage für den schlechten Text der Theodoros-Ausgabe, den PG 86, p. 216A bietet, den Codex Parisinus gr. 1440 (eine Abschrift von **B**, d. h. Nikephoros) identifiziert hat (dazu unten). Der Theodoros-Ausgabe in PG 86 liegt diejenige des Henri Valois (Paris 1673 [*non vidi*]) zugrunde, deren Text zuerst in der Ausgabe von Reading (Theodoriti Episcopi Cyri et Evagrii Scholastici Historia Ecclesiastica item excerpta ex historiis Philostorgi et Theodori lectoris ... ed. Reading, Cambridge 1720, p. 585) und dann in PG 86, p. 216A reproduziert wurde, vgl. Hansen 1995, p. xxviii. Hier findet sich neben der Passage προχειρίζεται δὲ εἰς βασιλέα Λέων τις, Θρᾷξ μὲν τῷ γένει, τριβοῦνος δὲ τὴν ἀξίαν (PG 86, p. 169 = Theod. Anagn. 367, p. 103,19–20 ed. Hansen 1995) auch ein Paragraph, der größere Nähe zu Theophanes als zu Nikephoros' *Kirchengeschichte* aufweist: ἐβασίλευσεν ἰνδικτιῶνος δεκάτης, μηνὶ Φεβρουαρίῳ στεφθεὶς ὑπὸ τοῦ αὐτοῦ πατριάρχου (PG 86, p. 216).

[80] Vgl. Hansen 1995, pp. xxiv–xxix und das Stemma p. xxxv; Gentz 1966, 187; Nautin 1994, pp. 213–43; Pouderon, 1997, pp. 178–80.

1) **M** = Codex Parisinus suppl. gr. 1156 (10./11. Jh.): enthält E 477–96 und 520–61[81]

2) **P** = Codex Parisinus gr. 1155A (13./14. Jh.),[82] eine ‚stark exzerpierende Abschrift von **M**‘.[83]

3) **V** = Codex Athous Vatopedi 286, fol. 91^r–218^v (13. Jh.): enthält lückenhaft E 5 bis E 458.[84]

4) **B** = Codex Baroccianus 142, fol. 216^v–224^r und fol. 236^v– 240^r (‚Anfang des 14. Jhs.‘).[85]

Da die HSS **B** auf fol. 236^v (Exzerpte aus Theodoros) am Rand jeweils in roter Tinte mit der Angabe ἀπὸ φωνῆς Νικηφόρου Καλλίστου τοῦ Ξανθοπούλου versehen ist, stammt sie eindeutig von Nikephoros.[86] Gentz hat mit guten Gründen dafür plädiert, daß Nikephoros ‚vielleicht eine umfangreichere Epitome kannte und diese für den Cod. Barocc. exzerpierte‘.[87] Dagegen hat Hansen eingewandt, Nikephoros habe lediglich **B** ‚und nicht etwa dessen Vorlage‘ benutzt; seine Begründung fußt jedoch allein auf der Auslassung des in **B** unleserlichen Namens Ἰωάννης an einer einzigen Stelle und kann m. E. Gentz' These daher keinesfalls entkräften.[88]

---

[81] Publiziert von Miller 1873, 273–88; 396–403 (= Miller 1876, 45–67).

[82] Publiziert von Cramer 1839, pp. 87–114. Bei der Datierung folge ich Hansen 1995, p. xxv gegen Gentz 1966, p. 187, der sie in das 10. Jh. setzt.

[83] Hansen 1995, p. xxv: ‚**P** ist eine (allerdings stark exzerpierende) Abschrift von **M**. Das ergibt sich daraus, daß **P** fast alle Sonderfehler und orthographischen Eigenheiten von **M** teilt‘. Ebd. p. xxxv stellt Hansen ergänzend fest, daß es sich bei **P** um ‚eine recht getreue Abschrift‘ handele.

[84] Publiziert von Papadopoulos-Kerameus 1901, p. 14, berichtet nichts von Leos Krönung. Zur Datierung: Hansen 1995, p. xxvi; vgl. auch Pouderon, 1997, p. 178.

[85] Nikeph. Kall. Xanth. HE XV (PG 147, pp. 9–116). Zu den überlieferten Textmassen und zur Datierung vgl. Hansen 1995, p. xxviii sowie Wilson 1974, p. 438. Zum Baroccianus 142 vgl. auch Pouderon 1997, pp. 169–92 (mit der älteren Literatur). Ein Scan des Baroccianus 142 ist online einsehbar (https:// digital.bodleian.ox.ac.uk/inquire/p/7e1a7a81-c8e7-42fb-926d-3230eefdf43d [zuletzt eingesehen 4. Oktober 2018]).

[86] Gentz 1966, p. 187; Hansen 1995, p. xxxiii und vor allem Wilson 1974, pp. 438, 440. Auch der *codex unicus* von Nikephoros' *Kirchengeschichte* (ÖNB hist. gr. 8) bietet Anzeichen dafür, daß ihn der Autor selbst annotiert hat, vgl. Gastgeber 2015, pp. 153–54.

[87] Gentz 1966, p. 189.

[88] Hansen 1995, p. xxxiv mit Theod. Anagn. Epit. 507, p. 144,19 (ed. Hansen 1995).

Die Krönung Leos I. wird überhaupt nur in **P** und **B** (d. h. dem ‚vorbereitenden Arbeitsexemplar‘ des Nikephoros [89]) überliefert. In **V** wird die Krönung Leos überhaupt nicht erwähnt [90] und **M** ist für diesen Zeitraum nicht erhalten; [91] da **P** aber eine ‚stark exzerpierende‘, zugleich aber ‚recht getreue Abschrift‘ von **M** ist, muß diese Information auch in **M** – Hansens Leitcodex – gestanden haben.[92] Hansens Ausgabe folgt daher wörtlich **P** (= Cramer p. 102,11–12), weshalb die Krönung durch den Patriarchen nicht aufgenommen ist. Inhaltlich wird das dort Gebotene durch **B** (= Nikeph. Kall. Xanth. HE XV 15 [PG 147, p. 48B]) bestätigt, der den Passus aber sprachlich modifiziert hat und sowohl mehr als auch präzisere Informationen bietet.[93]

Daß die Krönung durch Anatolius in der ursprünglichen Fassung der *Epitome* gestanden haben muß, zeigen sowohl **P** (als Apograph von **M**) als auch Nikephoros (**B**) und Theophanes. Dieser hatte, als er nach 810 seine Chronik schrieb, wohl noch ‚die vollständige Epitome vor sich gehabt und benutzt‘,[94] und möglicherweise nutzte noch Nikephoros eine solche umfangreichere HSS für seine Abschrift.

Da Theophanes den ersten Teil des Satzes wörtlich aus Theodoros übernommen hat (wie **P** bestätigt), wird, soweit wir Theophanes’ Methode kennen, auch die zweite Hälfte des Satzes aus Theodoros stammen. Nikephoros (bzw. die Vorlage, aus der er schöpft) [95] übernimmt offensichtlich einige Informationen aus Theodoros, modifiziert sie aber sprachlich. Die eigentliche Krönung durch Anatolius wird hier durch das Aufsetzen des Diadems vollzogen: τοῦ πατριάρχου Ἀνατολίου τὸ διάδημα περιθέντος. Die Änderung ist leicht zu erklären: Zum einen war zu Nikephoros’

---

[89] Vgl. Gastgeber 2015, p. 141 Anm. 2; ähnlich ebd. p. 153: ‚Arbeitsvorbereitungsexemplar‘.

[90] Vgl. die Wiedergabe bei Papadopoulos-Karameus 1901, p. 14; Pouderon 1997, p. 178.

[91] Vgl. die Wiedergabe bei Miller 1873, p. 61.

[92] Zu den Zitaten s. oben Anm. 83.

[93] Dieser Befund paßt zu jüngeren Untersuchungen, die Nikephoros’ Arbeitsweise genauer beleuchtet haben und zeigen konnten, daß er sowohl Passagen wörtlich übernimmt als auch andere paraphrasiert, kürzt oder weiterdichtet, vgl. Berger 2015, pp. 10; 15 Anm. 52; Schneider 2015, p. 35; Bleckmann 2015, 71–72; 77.

[94] Hansen 1995, p. xxix.

[95] S. oben Anm. 87–88.

KAISERWECHSEL UND KAISERERHEBUNGEN IN DER *KIRCHENGESCHICHTE*

Zeiten das Aufsetzen des Diadems Kernbestandteil der Krönung,[96] zum anderen findet sich die von ihm verwendete Formel schon früher in der byzantinischen Historiographie, etwa bei Skylitzes' Schilderung der Krönung Konstaninos VII. (913–59).[97] Nikephoros bietet aber auch weitere Informationen, die weder in den Theodoros-HSS noch bei Theophanes überliefert sind.[98] So nennt Nikephoros ein Amt präziser – ἀπὸ τριβούνων (*ex tribuno*) statt τριβοῦνος δὲ τὴν ἀξίαν (*tribunus*) sowie die Auskunft, Leos Krönung sei ein Senatsbeschluß (ψήφῳ κοινῇ τῆς συγκλήτου) vorausgegangen, der im übrigen auch im Zeremonienbuch vermerkt ist.[99] Lediglich die genaue Datierung, die Theophanes übernommen hat,[100] tradiert Nikephoros nicht. All dies spricht für Nikephoros' Glaubwürdigkeit. Woher diese Angaben stammen, läßt sich nicht sicher beantworten; daß sie aus einer ausführlicheren Fassung der *Epitome* – vielleicht sogar der ursprünglichen – stammen, ist aber, wie schon Gentz vermutet hat, sehr wahrscheinlich.[101]

Fassen wir zusammen: In allen vier Theodoros-HSS ist der Text der ursprünglichen *Epitome*, die ihrerseits schon eine Kurzfassung der *Kirchengeschichte* darstellte, stark gekürzt. Von den HSS berichten nur zwei (**P** und **B**) überhaupt von der Krönung Leos I. Während **P** die Krönung durch den Patriarchen nicht erwähnt, bieten Theophanes und Nikephoros (der Urheber von **B**), einen vollständigeren Text, der eindeutig mehr Material aus Theodoros gerettet hat, als die übrigen HSS überliefern. Zu diesem Ergebnis paßt der positive Befund der HSS: Wenn **M** tatsächlich den ‚spärlichen Überrest einer Handschrift der vollständigen Epitome'

---

[96] Treitinger 1956, p. 15; 26 Anm. 77.

[97] Skylitzes (Georgios Kedrenos, p. ii 321,12–13 [ed. Bekker 1839] = p. 233,10–11 [ed. Thurn 2000], der die Formel als τοῦτο δὴ τὸ Ὁμηρικόν bezeichnet); Hans Thurn hat im Apparat z. St. als Vorbild dieser Anspielung Il. 4,43 identifizieren wollen.

[98] Die leichte sprachliche Variante Θρᾷξ καὶ αὐτὸς τῷ γένει statt Θρᾷξ μὲν τῷ γένει bedarf keiner weiteren Erklärung.

[99] De cerim I 91, p. 410,7–8 Reiske: καὶ τοῦ ψηφίσματος εἰς Λέοντα τὸν τῆς εὐσεβοῦς λήξεως γινομένου παρὰ τῆς συγκλήτου. Hierbei handelt es sich jedoch keinesfalls um eine eigene Entscheidung des Senats; vielmehr bestätigt der Senat eine Wahl, die zuvor Aspar getroffen hatte, vgl. Pfeilschifter 2013, p. 152; Begass (im Druck) und oben Anm. 50.

[100] Theoph. a. m. 5950, p. 110,19–21 (ed. de Boor 1883): μηνὶ Φεβρουαρίῳ, ἰνδικτιῶνι ι´ στεφθεὶς ὑπὸ Ἀνατολίου τοῦ πατριάρχου.

[101] Gentz 1966, p. 189.

darstellt, von dem **P** ‚eine stark exzerpierende Abschrift' darstelle,[102] muß die Krönung in **M** gestanden haben, wurde in der knappen Form, wie wir sie in **P** fassen können, aber weggelassen.

Es spricht folglich vieles dafür, daß nicht erst Theophanes im 9. Jahrhundert, sondern bereits Theodoros im ersten Viertel des 6. Jahrhunderts von einer Krönung Leos I. durch den Patriarchen berichtete. Entgegen Winkelmanns Verdikt ist es also sehr wahrscheinlich, daß mit Theodoros ein zeitnaher und zuverlässiger Historiker eine solche Erhebung belegt. Hinzu kommt, daß auch das ‚Zeremonienbuch' für die Krönung Leos II. 473 zumindest eine deutlich herausgehobene Stellung des Patriarchen betont: Im Kathisma steht Leo I. in der Mitte, umrahmt von Patriarch Acacius auf der rechten und seinem Enkel Leo II. auf der linken Seite.[103] Der Patriarch spricht den Segen, dann übergibt der *praepositus sacri cubiculi* Leo I. die Krone, der sie Leo II. aufsetzt.[104] Für Zeno ist kein Krönungsprotokoll erhalten und der Bericht des Theodoros ist – in der vorliegenden Fassung – bis aufs äußerste verkürzt. Die Situation, in der Zeno 474 erhoben wurde, war so ungewöhnlich, daß Victor Tunnunnensis, dessen Bericht auf Theodoros zurückgeht, betont, diese Krönung sei *contra consuetudinem* vollzogen worden.[105] Daß in einer solch außergewöhnlichen Konstellation, in der der Sohn den Vater krönt, der Patriarch als zusätzliche Instanz mitwirkte, ist zumindest wahrscheinlich.[106] Sollte der Bericht des Zeremonienbuches korrekt sein, widerspräche die Rolle des Patriarchen, wie wir sie hier fassen, nicht unserer Interpretation: Sowohl Leo II. als auch Zeno erlangten die Kaiserwürde, als es bereits mit Leo I. bzw. Leo II. einen anerkannten Kaiser gab. Dessen Wahl eines Nachfolgers wurde nie in Frage gestellt, und auch bei der Krönung

---

[102] Hansen 1995, pp. xxiv–xxv.

[103] De cerim I 94, p. 432,5–13 (ed. Reiske 1828); Winkelmann 1978, p. 471.

[104] De cerim I 94, p. 432,8–10 (ed. Reiske 1828): καὶ εὐχὴν ἐποίησεν καὶ ὑπήχησαν πάντες τὸ ἀμήν. καὶ ὁ πραιπόσιτος ἐπέδωκεν τῷ βασιλεῖ στέφανον καὶ ἐπιτέθηκεν εἰς τὴν κεφαλὴν τοῦ καίσαρος.

[105] Vict. Tunn. ad ann. 474,2, p. 112,5 (ed. Hansen 1995).

[106] Eine einzige Symeon-HSS überliefert den Passus: [Ζήνων] ἐστέφθη δὲ ὑπὸ Ἀκακίου πατριάρχου[·] ἐν τῷ καθίσματι τοῦ ἱπποδρομίου (gedruckt bei Cramer 1839, p. 314,14–15 = Leon Gramm. 116,7–8 ed. Bekker 1842). Wegen der zweifelhaften Überlieferung hat Wahlgren diesen Satz nicht in den Text seiner Ausgabe übernommen, vgl. den Apparat zu Symeon Mag. Chron. 101, p. 132,1 (Wahlgren 2006).

wird er, nicht der Patriarch, die führende Rolle gespielt haben. Als Anastasius an die Macht kam, lag wieder die Situation einer ‚freien Wahl' vor.[107] Jetzt wirkte, wie das Zeremonienbuch belegt,[108] Patriarch Euphemius bei der Krönung aktiv mit, doch wird dies keineswegs als Besonderheit oder Neuerung vermerkt.[109] Euphemius spielt hier nicht nur während des Aushandlungsprozesses zwischen Ariadne und den Magistraten eine wichtige Rolle, sondern krönte laut dem offiziösen Protokoll Anastasius mit Kaisermantel und Diadem.[110]

5. *Fazit*

Bei der Zusammenschau der Kaisererhebungen bei Theodoros Anagnostes, wie sie in der *Kirchengeschichtlichen Epitome* erhalten sind, fällt auf, daß sie stark schematisch aufgebaut sind. Inwieweit dies der ursprünglichen Form entspricht oder ob dies auf den Epitomator zurückzuführen ist, läßt sich jedoch nicht mehr klären. Die Berichte folgen einem festen Schema:

1. Der alte Kaiser stirbt (ἐτελεύτησεν Ν Αὔγουστος, ὢν ἐτῶν Τ)
2. Der Prätendent X wird durch Z zum Kaiser erhoben.[111]
3. Der neue Kaiser wird kurz näher vorgestellt, wobei drei Faktoren herausgehoben werden:

   3.1. Die geographische Herkunft des neuen Kaisers: Marcian ist Ἰλλυριὸς τὸ γένος, Leo I. ist Θρᾷξ μὲν τῷ γένει, Anastasius ἐκ τοῦ Δυρραχίου ὁρμώμενος, Justin τὸ γένος Ἰλλυριός. Zenos isaurischer Hintergrund wird nicht eigens angeführt, offenbar weil er als hochrangiger Offizier und Vater Leos II. schon als bekannt vorausgesetzt wird.

---

[107] Vgl. Beck 1966, p. 13 und Pfeilschifter 2013, p. 148, der diesen Fall als ‚ungeregelten Herrschaftsübergang' bezeichnet.

[108] S. unten Anm. 110.

[109] De cerim. I 92, pp. 417–18 (ed. Reiske 1828). Vgl. auch Evagr. HE 3,29, p. 125,6–31 (ed. Bidez – Parmentier 1898); Theoph. a. m. 5983, p. 136,3–12 (ed. de Boor 1883); Zon. 14,3,1, p. 133,6–16 (ed. Pinder – Büttner-Wobst 1841).

[110] De cerim. I 92, pp. 423, 12–15 (ed. Reiske 1828).

[111] Das Schema X ἀνηγορεύθη βασιλεύς Z bei Marcian (354, p. 100,12), Zeno (400, p. 112,11) und Basiliscus (p. 112,19); ähnlich bei Leo II. (Λέων ὁ βασιλεὺς προεβάλετο Καίσαρα Λέοντα τὸν μικρόν [398, p. 111,13]) und Marcus (Βασιλίσκος ... ποιήσας Καίσαρα Μᾶρκον τὸν ἴδιον υἱόν [402, p. 112,19–20]).

3.2. Die bisherige Funktion des neuen Kaisers: Marcian und Leo I. sind Tribunen (τριβοῦνος ὤν und τριβοῦνος δὲ τὴν ἀξίαν bzw. ἀπὸ τριβούνων), Anastasius ὁ σιλεντιάριος, Justin wird unpräzise als ἀνὴρ πρεσβύτης ἀπὸ σταρτιωτῶν eingeführt.

3.3. Bei einigen Kaisern folgt eine kurze Beurteilung ihrer religiösen Orientierung, die die folgende Schilderung der Herrschaft bereits *in nuce* enthält und eine Bewertung der folgenden Jahre vorwegnimmt.

Welchen Wert haben nun die *Kirchengeschichte* bzw. die *Kirchengeschichtliche Epitome* des Theodoros Anagnostes für die Frage nach Kaisererhebungen? Ihr Wert ist hoch, und dies aus zwei Gründen: Zum einen sind Theodoros' Informationen, die sich anhand von Parallelquellen überprüfen lassen, sehr zuverlässig. Theodoros ist zwar durchweg meinungsstark, durch die zeitliche Nähe zum Geschehen erhält seine Darstellung aber eine besondere Bedeutung. Zum anderen ist die *Kirchengeschichte* gerade dort wichtig, wo sie Nachrichten bietet, die anderswo nicht überliefert sind, etwa die, daß Zeno von Leo II. im Hippodrom gekrönt wurde.[112] Gleiches gilt für die Mitwirkung des Patriarchen bei der Krönung. Daß Theophanes' Bericht der Krönung Leos I., bei der Patriarch Anatolius aktiv mitwirkte, aus dem Werk des Theodoros stammt, spricht gegen Winkelmanns These, nach der der Patriarch erst bei Anastasius 491 eine zentrale Rolle einnahm. Den Patriarchen gelang es vielmehr, in der hochdynamischen Phase zwischen 450 und 500 ihren Einfluß auch bei den Krönungen so zu festigen, daß die Krönung durch Euphemius 491 in den Quellen bereits nicht mehr als Besonderheit vermerkt wurde.[113] Gerade ein Patriarch wie Anatolius, der bereits 450 bei der Krönung Marcians anwesend gewesen war, mußte, als sich wenige Jahre später die nächste Gelegenheit ergab, darauf drängen, den zentralen Akt nun selbst zu übernehmen.[114]

---

[112] Theod. Anagn. 400, p. 112,13 (ed. Hansen 1995).

[113] Vielleicht ist so die Anwesenheit des Anatolius bei der Krönung Marcians zu erklären, wie sie bei Symeon Magister überliefert ist (s. oben Anm. 24).

[114] Für Lilie 1995 p. 11 gelang erst Patriarch Euphemius mit der Krönung des Anastasius 491 eine solche ‚Aufwertung seiner Rolle'.

Bibliographie

Quellen

Adler 1967 = Lexiconographi Graeci, vol. 1, Suidae Lexicon, ed. Ada Adler, Stuttgart.

Bekker 1838–1839 = *Georgii Cedreni Compendium historiarum*, ed. Immanuel Bekker, Bonn.

Bekker 1842 = *Leonis Grammatici Chronographia*, ed. Immanuel Bekker, Bonn.

Bidez – Parmentier 1898 = *The Ecclesiastical History of Evagrius with the scholia*, ed. Joseph Bidez – Léon Parmentier, London.

Blockley 1981–1983 = *The Fragmentary Classicising Historians of the Later Roman Empire. Eunapius, Olympiodorus, Priscus and Malchus*, ed. Roger C. Blockley, vol. I–II, Liverpool.

Chabot 1899–1924 = *Michael Syrianus Chronicon*, ed. Jean-Babtiste Chabot, Paris.

Cramer 1839 = *Anecdota Graeca*, ed. John Anthony Cramer, vol. 2, Oxford.

De Boor 1883 = *Theophanis Chronographia*, ed. Carolus de Boor, vol. 1–2, Leipzig.

Delahaye 1923 = *Vita S. Danielis Stylitae*, ed. Hyppolite Delahaye, Brüssel.

Dindorf 1832 = *Chronicon paschale ad exemplar Vaticanum*, ed. Ludwig Dindorf, Bonn.

Dindorf 1869 = *Ioannis Zonarae Epitome Historiarum*, ed. Ludwig Dindorf, Leipzig.

Hansen 1995 = Theodoros Anagnostes, *Kirchengeschichte*, ed. Günther Christian Hansen, Berlin, New York.

Haury – Wirth 1962–1964 = *Procopii Caesarenis opera omnia*, ed. Jakob Haury – Gerhard Wirth, vol. I–III, Leipzig.

Migne 1904 = Nikephor Kallistos Xanthopoulos: *Ecclesiasticae Historiae Libri XVIII*, Patrologia Graeca, vol. 145–47, Paris.

Mommsen 1882 = *Iordanis Romana et Getica*, ed. Theodor Mommsen, Berlin.

Mommsen 1894 = *Marcellinus Comes, Chronicon*, ed. Theodor Mommsen, MGH XI, Berlin.

Müller 1851 = *Prisci Panitae Fragmenta*, ed. Karl Müller, FHG IV, Paris.

Pinder – Büttner-Wobst 1841 = *Ioannis Zonarae epitome historiarum*, ed. Moritz Pinder – Theodor Büttner-Wobst, Bonn.

Reiske 1828 = *Constantini Porphyrogeniti Imperatoris De Cerimoniis Aulae Byzantinae libri duo*, ed. Johann Jacob Reiske, Bonn.

Tartaglia 2016 = *Georgii Cedreni Historiarum Compendium*, ed. Luigi Tartaglia, 2 vols, Rom.

Thurn 1973 = *Ioannis Scylitzae Synopsis Historiarum*, ed. Hans Thurn, Berlin.

Thurn 2000 = *Ioannis Malalae Chronographia*, ed. Hans Thurn, Berlin – New York.

Wahlgren 2006 = *Symeonis Magistri et Logothetae Chronicon*, ed. Staffan Wahlgren, Berlin – New York.

Literatur

Ballaira 2003 = Guglielmo Ballaira, ‚L'incoronazione dell'imperatore Anastasio I (491 d.C.) e la testimonianza del Panegirico di Prisciano', *Quaderni del Dipartimento di Filologia, Linguistica e Tradizione Classica Augusto Rostagni*, 2, pp. 267–92.

Banchich 2015 = Thomas M. Banchich, *The Lost History of Peter the Patrician. An Account of Rome's Imperial Past from the Age of Justinian*, Routledge Classical Translations, London – New York.

Beck 1966 = Hans-Georg Beck, *Senat und Volk von Konstantinopel. Probleme der byzantinischen Verfassungsgeschichte*, Sitzungsberichte der Bayerischen Akademie der Wissenschaften, philosophisch-historische Klasse 1966, 6, München.

Begass 2018 = Christoph Begass, *Die Senatsaristokratie des oströmischen Reichs, ca. 457–518. Prosopographische und sozialgeschichtliche Untersuchungen*, Vestigia, vol. 71, München.

Begass 2019 = Christoph Begass, ‚Kaiser Marcian und Myra. Ein Beitrag zu Geschichte und Epigraphik Lykiens in der Spätantike', *Chiron* 49, pp. 215–250.

Begass (im Druck) = Christoph Begass, ‚Die Rolle des Senats bei Kaisererhebungen in Konstantinopel von Konstantin bis Justinian', in *Das Zeitalter Konstantins. Bilanz und Perspektiven der Forschung.*, hrsg. von Andreas Goltz – Heinrich Schlange-Schöningen, Berlin – Boston.

Berger 2015 = Albrecht Berger, ‚Nikephorus Kallistou Xanthopoulos und seine Quellen in den Büchern I bis VI', in *Ecclesiastical History and Nikephoros Kallistou Xanthopoulos. Proceedings of the International Symposium*, Vienna 15th–16th December 2011, hrsg. von Christian Gastgeber – Sebastiano Panteghini (Veröffentlichungen zur Byzanzforschung, vol. 37), Wien, pp. 9–16.

Bleckmann 2015 = Bruno Bleckmann, ‚Nikephoros Xanthopoulos und Philostorgios‘, in *Ecclesiastical History and Nikephoros Kallistou Xanthopoulos. Proceedings of the International Symposium*, Vienna 15th–16th December 2011, hrsg. von Christian Gastgeber – Sebastiano Panteghini (Veröffentlichungen zur Byzanzforschung, vol. 37), Wien, pp. 71–80.

Boak 1919 = Arthur Edward Romilly Boak, ‚Imperial Coronation Ceremonies of the Fifth and Sixth Centuries‘, *Harvard Studies in Classical Philology*, 30, pp. 37–47.

Brodka 2012 = Dariusz Brodka, ‚Priskos von Panion und Kaiser Marcian. Eine Quellenuntersuchung zu Procop. 3,4,1–11, Evagr. HE 2,1, Theoph. AM 5943 und Nic. Kall. HE 15,1‘, *Millennium*, 9, pp. 145–62.

Burgess 1993/94 = Richard W. Burgess 1993/94, ‚The Accession of Marcian in the Light of Chalcedonian Apologetic and Monophysite Polemic‘, *Byzantinische Zeitschrift* 86/87, 1993/94, pp. 47–68 (= R. W. Burgess, 2011, *Chronicles, Consuls, and Coins. Historiography and History in the Later Roman Empire*, Aldershot, Nr. XII).

Bury 1907 = John Bagnell Bury, ‚The Ceremonial Book of Constantine Porphyrogennetos‘, *English Historical Review*, 22, pp. 209–27, pp. 417–39.

Carolla 2016 = Pia Carolla, ‚Priscus of Panion, John Malalas and the Chronicon Paschale (CP). A Complex Relationship‘, in *Byzanz und das Abendland IV: Studia Byzantino-Occidentalia*, hrsg. von Erika Juhász (Bibliotheca Byzantina 4), Budapest, pp. 51–70.

Charanis 1937 = Peter Charanis, ‚The Imperial Crown Modiolus and Its Constitutional Significance‘, *Byzantion*, 12, pp. 189–95.

Croke 2005 = Brian Croke, ‚Dynasty and Ethnicity. Emperor Leo I and the Eclipse of Aspar‘, *Chiron*, 35, pp. 147–203.

Dijkstra – Greatrex 2009 = Jitse Dijkstra – Geofferey Greatrex, ‚Patriarchs and Politics in Constantinople in the Reign of Anastasius (with a Reedition of O.Mon.Epiph 59)‘, Millennium, 6, pp. 223–64.

Enßlin 1947 = Wilhelm Enßlin, *Zur Frage nach der ersten Kaiserkrönung durch den Patriarchen und zur Bedeutung dieses Aktes im Wahlzeremoniell*, Würzburg.

Flaig 1992/2019 = Egon Flaig, *Den Kaiser herausfordern. Die Usurpation im Römischen Reich*, Frankfurt am Main (2. Auflage 2019).

Frend 1979 = William Hugh Clifford Frend, ‚The Fall of Macedonius 511. A Suggestion‘, in *Kerygma und Logos. Beiträge zu den geistesgeschichtlichen Beziehungen zwischen Antike und Christentum. Festschrift für Carl Andresen zum 70. Geburtstag*, hrsg. Adolf Martin Ritter, Göttingen, pp. 183–95.

Gastgeber 2015 = Christian Gastgeber, ‚Nikephoros Xanthopoulos und der codex unicus seiner Historia ecclesiastica (ÖNB, Cod. historicus graecus 8)‘, in *Ecclesiastical History and Nikephoros Kallistou Xanthopoulos. Proceedings of the International Symposium*, Vienna 15th–16th December 2011, hrsg. von Christian Gastgeber – Sebastiano Panteghini (Veröffentlichungen zur Byzanzforschung, vol. 37), Wien, pp. 141–73.

Gentz 1966 = Günter Gentz, *Die Kirchengeschichte des Nicephorus Callistus Xanthopulus und ihre Quellen,* nachgelassene Untersuchungen überarbeitet und erweitert von Friedhelm Winkelmann, Texte und Untersuchungen zur Geschichte der altchristlichen Literatur, vol. 98, Berlin.

Greatrex 2010 = Geoffrey Greatrex, ‚The Fall of Macedonius Reconsidered‘, *Studia Patristica*, 44, pp. 125–29.

Haarer 2006 = Fiona Haarer 2006, *Anastasius I. Politics and Empire in the Late Roman World*, Arca 46, Cambridge.

Hansen 1995 = Günther Christian Hansen, ‚Einleitung‘, in *Theodoros Anagnostes, Kirchengeschichte*, hrsg. von Günther Christian Hansen, Die griechischen christlichen Schriftsteller der ersten Jahrhunderte, Neue Folge, vol. 3, Berlin – New York, pp. ix–xxxix.

Hebblewhite 2017 = Mark Hebblewhite, *The Emperor and the Army in the Later Roman Empire, AD 235–395*, London – New York.

Holum 1982 = Kenneth G. Holum, *Theodosian Empresses. Women and Imperial Dominion in Late Antiquity*, The Transformation of the Classical Heritage, vol. 3, Berkeley.

Kosiński 2010 = Rafał Kosiński 2010, *The Emperor Zeno. Religion and Politics*, Byzantina et Slavica Cracoviensia 6, Cracow.

Kresten 2000 = Otto Kresten, ‚Beobachtungen zu Kapitel I 96 des „Zeremonienbuches“‘, *Byzantinische Zeitschrift* 93, pp. 474–89.

Lilie 1995 = Ralph-Johannes Lilie, ‚Die Krönung des Kaisers Anastasios I. (491)‘, *Byzantinoslavica*, 56, pp. 3–12.

Lilie 1998 = Ralph-Johannes Lilie, ‚Die Krönungsprotokolle des Zeremonienbuches und die Krönung Kaiser Leons I.‘, in *Dissertatiunculae criticae. Festschrift für Günther Christian Hansen*, hrsg. von Christian-Friedrich Collatz – Jürgen Dummer – Jutta Kollesch – Marie-Luise Werlitz, Würzburg, pp. 395–408.

Lilie 2017 = Ralph-Johannes Lilie, 2017, ‚Erbkaisertum oder Wahlmonarchie? Zur Sicherung der Herrschaftsnachfolge in Byzanz‘, in *Die mittelalterliche Thronfolge im europäischen Vergleich*, hrsg. von Matthias Becher, Vorträge und Forschungen, vol. 84, Ostfildern, pp. 21–41.

MacCormack 1981 = Sabine MacCormack, *Art and Ceremony in Late Antiquity*, The Transformation of the Classical Heritage, vol. 1, Berkeley.

Maier 1973 = Franz Georg Maier, *Byzanz*, Fischer-Weltgeschichte, vol. 13, Frankfurt am Main.

Meier 2009 = Mischa Meier, *Anastasios I. Die Entstehung des Byzantinischen Reiches*, Stuttgart.

Meier 2010 = Mischa Meier, ‚Ariadne. Der „Rote Faden" des Kaisertums', in *Augustae. Machtbewußte Frauen am römischen Kaiserhof?*, hrsg. von Anne Kolb, Berlin, pp. 277–91.

Miller 1873 = E. Miller, ‚Fragments inédits de Théodore le lecteur et de Jean d'Égée', *Revue archéologique*, 26, pp. 273–88, 396–403 (= E. Miller 1876, Mélanges de philologie et d'épigraphie, vol. 1, Paris, pp. 45–67).

Nautin 1994 = Pierre Nautin, ‚Théodore Lecteur et sa „réunion de différentes Histoires" de l'Église', *Revue des Études Byzantines*, 52, pp. 213–43.

Ostrogorsky 1963 = George Ostrogorsky, *Geschichte des byzantinischen Staates*, Handbuch der Altertumswissenschaft, vol. 12, 1, 2, München[3].

Papadopoulos-Kerameus 1901 = Athanasios Papadopoulos-Kerameus, ‚Νέα τεμάχη τῆς ἐκκλησιαστικῆς ἱστορίας Θεοδώρου ἀναγνώστου τοῦ ἐντολέως', *Журнал Министерства народного просвещения*, 333, pp. 1–24.

Pfeilschifter 2013 = Rene Pfeilschifter, *Der Kaiser und Konstantinopel. Kommunikation und Konfliktaustragung in einer spätantiken Metropole*, Millennium-Studien, vol. 44, Berlin – Boston.

Pouderon 1997 = Bernard Pouderon, ‚Les fragments anonyms du Baroc. gr. 142 et les notices consacrées à Jean Diacrinoménos, Basile de Cilicie et l'Anonyme d'Héraclée', *Revue des Études Byzantines*, 55, pp. 169–92.

Prostko-Prostyński 2000 = Jan Prostko-Prostyński, ‚Basiliskos. Ein in Rom anerkannter Usurpator', *Zeitschrift für Papyrologie und Epigraphik*, 133, pp. 259–65.

Redies 1997 = Michael Redies, ‚Die Usurpation des Basiliskos (475–76) im Kontext der aufsteigenden monophysitischen Kirche', *Antiquité Tardive*, 5, pp. 211–21.

Schneider 2015 = Horst Schneider, ‚Die Rezeption der Vita Constantini des Eusebios bei Nikephorus Kallistou Xanthopoulos', in *Ecclesiastical History and Nikephoros Kallistou Xanthopoulos. Proceedings of the International Symposium*, Vienna 15th–16th

159

December 2011, hrsg. von Christian Gastgeber – Sebastiano Panteghini, Veröffentlichungen zur Byzanzforschung, vol. 37, Wien, pp. 17–42.

Sickel 1898 = Wilhelm Sickel, ‚Das byzantinische Krönungsrecht bis zum 10. Jahrhundert', *Byzantinische Zeitschrift*, 7, pp. 511–57.

Siebigs 2010 = Gereon Siebigs, *Kaiser Leo I. Das oströmische Reich in den ersten drei Jahren seiner Regierung (457–60 n. Chr.)*, Beiträge zur Altertumskunde, vol. 276, Berlin – New York.

Szidat 2003 = Joachim Szidat, ‚Zur Rolle des Patriarchen von Konstantinopel bei der Erhebung eines Kaisers im 5. und 6. Jhd.', *Göttinger Forum für Altertumswissenschaft*, 16, pp. 51–61.

Trampedach 2005 = Kai Trampedach, ‚Kaiserwechsel und Krönungsritual im Konstantinopel des 5. bis 6. Jahrhunderts', in *Investitur- und Krönungsritual. Herrschaftseinsetzungen im kulturellen Vergleich*, hrsg. von Marion Steinicke – Stefan Weinfurter, Köln – Weimar – Wien, pp. 275–90.

Treitinger 1956 = Otto Treitinger, *Die oströmische Kaiser- und Reichsidee. Vom oströmischen Staats- und Reichsgedanken*, Darmstadt.

Wilson 1974 = Nigel Guy Wilson, ‚The Autograph of Nicephorus Callistus Xanthopoulos', *Journal of Theological Studies*, N.S. 25, pp. 437–42.

Winkelmann 1978 = Friedhelm Winkelmann, ‚Zur Rolle der Patriarchen von Konstantinopel bei Kaiserwechseln in frühbyzantinischer Zeit', *Klio. Beiträge zur alten Geschichte*, 60, pp. 467–81.

Abstract

Although the second part of Theodore Lector's ‚Church History' survived only in an abridged version, this ‚Epitome' offers brief accounts of all coronations which took place between 450 and 518. First, the article examines these reports and asks how reliable they are. Furthermore, it can be shown that Theodore offers some detailed information which can be found only here; thus, Theodore must be regarded as an important source for imperial appointments. Second, the paper takes a fresh look on the problem of when the patriarch took an active part in the coronation ceremony. Theophanes, who, in the ninth century, excerpted a longer version of Theodore's works, allows us to assume that, despite Winkelmann's generally accepted thesis, the patriarch played an important role in the coronation ceremony as early as 457.

MICHEL KAPLAN

LA LÉGISLATION DE ZÉNON ET ANASTASE CONCERNANT L'ÉGLISE ET LES MONASTÈRES

Après l'autorisation du culte chrétien par Galère (311) et Constantin (312), il est apparu indispensable de prendre des mesures législatives concernant ce culte et son clergé. Même chose dès lors que les ermitages et monastères ont commencé à se multiplier. Zénon et Anastase viennent donc s'inscrire dans une longue tradition et leur production est comparativement peu importante.

Dès 325, Constantin convoque le concile de Nicée ; il en préside la séance d'ouverture et plusieurs autres ; il intervient de façon décisive pour faire condamner les derniers résistants. Les actes des conciles généraux, œcuméniques, font l'objet d'une promulgation impériale et deviennent donc des lois d'Empire d'un type particulier. Ils ne sont d'ailleurs pas repris par les codifications. La législation concernant l'Église, les églises particulières et les établissements religieux commence donc dès cette époque ; dans le code Théodosien, un livre entier, le livre XVI[1], est consacré aux sujets ecclésiastiques, même si d'autres lois liées à ceux-ci se trouvent dispersées dans d'autres livres. Dans le Code Justinien, les sujets proprement ecclésiastiques n'occupent que les titres 2 et 3 du livre I[2]. Les lois attribuées à Zénon et Anastase sont au nombre de quatre dans le titre 2 et de cinq dans le titre 3[3]. Elles

---

[1] Mommsen – Krueger 1990. Traduction française et commentaire : Magnou-Nortier 2002.

[2] Krueger 1997, pp. 12–39.

[3] CJ I, 2, 15-18, pp. 14–16 (ed. Krueger 1997) ; CJ I, 3, 35–39, pp. 23–25 (ed. Krueger 1997).

Studies in Theodore Anagnostes, ed. by Rafał KOSIŃSKI & Adrian SZOPA, STTA 19 (Turnhout 2021), pp. 161–181
© BREPOLS ❧ PUBLISHERS
DOI 10.1484/M.STTA-EB.5.127980

sont donc peu nombreuses et n'ont pas toujours recueilli l'attention qu'elles méritaient[4].

Pour bien comprendre ce qui se passe sur le plan législatif dans la deuxième moitié du Vᵉ siècle et les premières années du VIᵉ siècle jusqu'en 518, il faut revenir à cet événement majeur que fut le concile de Chalcédoine. Deux aspects majeurs, la condamnation du monophysisme et la définition des patriarcats accordant à Constantinople la seconde place derrière Rome, « la ville honorée de la présence de l'empereur et du sénat et jouissant des mêmes privilèges civils que Rome, l'ancienne ville impériale, devait aussi avoir le même rang supérieur qu'elle dans les affaires d'Église, tout en étant la seconde après elle »[5], retiennent généralement l'attention. Mais c'est oublier un peu vite qu'un autre souci avait poussé Marcien à convoquer un concile : mettre un peu d'ordre dans l'organisation de l'Église et mettre au pas ceux qui avaient entretenu le désordre dans la capitale, les moines.

Sur trente canons, huit seulement échappent à une préoccupation purement organisationnelle : le concile de Chalcédoine est avant tout un concile disciplinaire et la législation ultérieure se préoccupe de l'appliquer. Elle constitue avant tout les décrets d'application des canons conciliaires.

Bien sûr, le concile de Chalcédoine est surtout connu pour sa position sur le monophysisme et les conséquences qu'il eut pour l'histoire de l'Empire Romain d'Orient. C'est particulièrement le cas pour les règnes de Zénon et Anastase qui nous intéressent aujourd'hui. S'agissant de la législation concernant les établissements ecclésiastiques, les clercs et les moines, on ne trouve toutefois que peu de mention de ces débats, et notamment de ce

---

[4] L'ouvrage le plus important sur la politique religieuse de Zénon est Kosiński 2010. Il insiste autant que faire se peut sur les sources juridiques : pp. 106–08 ; 198–201. Mais il souligne le faible nombre qui nous est parvenu (p. 223) : « We should remember, however, that little is known about Zeno's legislation, as we have got very few extant legal acts, pertaining to religious matters, issued by that emperor ; in Justinian's Code, there are only five laws of that nature that can be unquestionably attributed to Zeno ». Derniers ouvrages généraux sur Anastase : Haarer 2006, Meier 2010. Aucun de ces deux ouvrages ne s'intéresse sérieusement à la législation d'Anastase concernant l'Église et les monastères.

[5] Schwartz – Schieffer 1933, p. 447 : τὴν βασιλείᾳ καὶ συγκλήτῳ τιμηθεῖσαν πόλιν, καὶ τῶν ἴσων ἀπολαύουσαν πρεσβείων τῇ πρεσβυτέρᾳ βασιλίδι Ῥώμῃ, καὶ ἐν τοῖς ἐκκλησιαστικοῖς ὡς ἐκείνην μεγαλύνεσθαι πράγμασι, δευτέραν μετ'ἐκείνην ὑπάρχουσαν.

qu'aurait pu entraîner sur ce plan l'Hénotique de Zénon. Ce dernier eut à souffrir de l'usurpation de Basiliskos (475–76), lors de laquelle un moine éminent, Daniel le Stylite, joua un rôle important contre l'usurpateur et sa position monophysite extrémiste[6]. C'est le seul événement dont on retrouve la trace dans la législation. Dans la loi CJ I, 2, 16, du 17 décembre 476[7], Zénon annule

> toutes les innovations faites par les tyrans tant contre les vénérables églises et leurs ministres dont le sacerdoce était sous la responsabilité du bienheureux et très religieux évêque et patriarche Akakios, père de notre pieuse personne, que contre les autres églises situées dans les différentes provinces et contre leurs vénérables évêques, s'agissant de l'ordination de prêtres et de la déposition d'évêques entreprises par qui que ce soit durant cette période, sur les prérogatives des évêques dans les assemblées d'évêques ou hors de celles-ci et sur celles des métropolites et du patriarche en ces temps impies. Ces ordres criminels, pragmatiques sanctions et constitutions impies sont abolies, quoique revêtues de formes légales. Nous ordonnons que celles qui ont été faites et établies par les souverains nos prédécesseurs de divine mémoire et celles qui ont promues depuis par notre majesté impériale concernant les saintes églises, les *martyria*, les évêques, les clercs et les moines soient inviolablement observées[8].

Bref, Zénon se place résolument dans la continuité de Marcien (450–57) et Léon Ier (457–74) et nous devons examiner la législation-

---

[6] Kosiński 2010, pp. 91–92. Kaplan 2016.

[7] Kosiński 2010, pp. 106–08 et n. 51 démontre que la datation (477) indiquée dans l'édition de Krueger 1997 est erronée. Il rétablit la bonne datation. Nous suivons sa démonstration sur la filiation entre les lois de Zénon et celles de ses deux prédécesseurs, Marcien et Léon Ier.

[8] CJ I, 2, 16, p. 14 (ed. Krueger 1997) : *his, quæ contra hæc tempore tyrannidis innovata sunt tam contra venerabiles ecclesias, quarum sacerdotium gerit beatissimus ac religiossimus episcopus patriarcha nostræ pietatis pater Acacius, quam ceteras, quæ per diversas provincias collocatæ sunt, nec non et reverentissimos earum antistites seu de jure sacerdotalium creationum seu de expulsione cuiusquam episcopi a quolibet illis temporibus facta seu de prerogativa in episcoporum concilio vel extra concilium ante alios residenti vel de privilegio metropolitano vel patriarchico seu isdem impiis temporibus, penitus antiquandis, ut cassatis et rescissis, quæ per huiusmodi sceleratas iussiones aut pragmaticas sanctiones aut constitutiones impias sive formas subsecuta sunt, quæ a divæ recordationis retro principibus ante nostrum imperium et deinceps a nostra mansuetudine indulta vel constituta sunt super sanctis ecclesiis et martyriis et religiosis episcopis, clericis aut monachis, inviolata serventur.*

lation en matière ecclésiastique de ces deux empereurs avec celle de Zénon et Anastase pour mieux comprendre cette dernière. Au-delà des convictions dogmatiques des unes et des autres, c'est tout un corpus de droit qui se met en place, que viendra couronner et amplifier Justinien, par son Code et ses Novelles.

Commençons par ceux, ou plutôt celles qui donnent lieu à peu de législation. Le concile s'intéresse aux diaconesses (canon 15) et aux vierges consacrées (canon 16). Les diaconesses ne seront pas ordonnées avant l'âge de quarante ans, gage de leur engagement ; après leur ordination et leur entrée en fonction, elles ne peuvent se marier, sous peine d'anathème contre elles et leur mari. Quant aux moniales, comme les moines, c'est le célibat qui est protégé, sous peine d'excommunication, peine que l'évêque peut toutefois moduler. Compte tenu de la limitation des droits des femmes, il importe de savoir quelle est leur capacité. Une loi de Marcien de 455 est plus diserte et montre la diversité des femmes consacrées à Dieu. L'empereur « ordonne par une loi générale qu'une femme, soit veuve, soit diaconesse, soit vierge consacrée à Dieu, soit *sanctimonialis*, ou encore une femme qui jouisse de quelque honneur ou dignité religieuse » si, par testament ou codicille légal, elle « a jugé bon ou jugera bon de léguer à une église, à un *martyrium*, ou à un clerc, ou à un moine, ou aux pauvres quelque bien, en tout ou en partie » ceci sera valide et effectif, de quelque façon que soit fait le don, que le testament soit écrit ou non écrit [9].

Comme l'a bien montré Gilbert Dagron [10], l'un des points essentiels des canons de Chalcédoine est d'établir l'autorité des évêques, et d'abord sur les moines. Notons d'abord que, comme pour la cléricature, seuls les hommes libres peuvent se faire moines. Pour autant, Zénon n'exclut pas totalement les autres :

---

[9] CJ I, 2, 13, p. 13 (ed. Krueger 1997) : *Generali lege sancimus sive vidua sive diaconissa vel virgo deo dicata vel sanctimonialis, sive quocumque alio nomine religione honoris vel dignitatis femina nuncupatur, testamento vel codicillo suo, quod tamen alia omni juris ratione munitum sit, ecclesiæ vel maryrio vel clerico vel pauperibus aliquid vel ex integro vel ex parte in quacumque re vel specie credidit seu crediderit relinquendum, id modis omnibus ratum firmumque consistat, sive hoc institutione sive substitutione seu legato aut fideicommisso per universitatem seu speciali, sive scripta sive non scripta voluntate duerit derelictum.* Sur les rapports patrimoniaux entre les femmes et l'Église, Beaucamp 2000.

[10] Dagron 1976, pp. 272–76.

Nous ne dénions pas aux esclaves le droit de participer à la vie solitaire, pourvu qu'ils bénéficient du consentement de leurs maîtres ; ceux-ci ne doivent pas ignorer que, s'ils donnent à leurs esclaves le droit de joindre le culte monastique, ils seront privés de leur propriété sur eux aussi longtemps que ceux-ci conserveront l'habit monastique ; mais, assurément, que si les esclaves abandonnent la vie solitaire et modifient leur condition, ils retourneront au joug de la servitude auquel ils auront échappé par l'observance de la condition monastique [11].

Quelques jours avant, le même Zénon avait pris la même disposition pour les colons adscrits [12].

D'une façon générale, la législation impériale n'est pas hostile aux moines, qui bénéficient d'un certain nombre de protections accordées aux membres du clergé. Or la plupart des moines ne sont pas clercs, et donc pas soumis *ex officio* aux évêques ; c'est l'objet des canons de Chalcédoine de les soumettre malgré tout à l'autorité épiscopale. Comme le montre le mouvement d'afflux de reliques à Constantinople à cette époque, il se passait des choses étranges avec ces objets supposés saints, pas seulement du fait des moines, mais le plus souvent par leur entremise, ce qui leur donnait un ascendant sur la population de la ville. C'est ce que montre la loi de Léon Ier de 459, selon laquelle ni un moine ni personne de quelque condition ne doit tenter d'apporter de façon illicite dans des bâtiments publics ou dans quelque endroit érigé pour les plaisirs du peuple ni de vénérables croix ni des reliques de saints martyrs. En effet, les édifices religieux (*religiosæ sedes*) ne manquent pas, ils peuvent, après due consultation des évêques, y placer les reliques des martyrs non de façon usurpée, mais avec

---

[11] CJ I, 3, 37 (484), p. 24 (ed. Krueger 1997) : *Servis, si dominorum fuerint voluntate muniti, solitariam vitam participandi licentia non denegetur, dum tamen eorum domini non ignorent, quod, si servis suis ad monasteriorum cultum migrandi tribuerint facultatem, eorundem servorum dominio, donec servi in eodem monachorum habitu duraverint, spoliandos : alioquin si relicta forte vita solitaria ad aliam se condicionem transtulerint, certum eos ad servitutis jugum quam monachicæ professionis cultu evaserant, reversuros.* Kosiński 2010, p. 198.

[12] CJ I, 3, 36, p. 24 (ed. Krueger 1997). Il s'agit d'éviter un mouvement de fuite de la main d'œuvre rurale vers les monastères, tout en préservant le droit de propriété. Kosiński 2010, p. 198.

l'approbation épiscopale, les moines et autres personnes religieuses se tenant ainsi à leur place[13].

Le reste de ce qui concerne les moines n'est qu'une application du quatrième canon de Chalcédoine. Léon Ier a promulgué une loi spéciale adressée au *magister militum per Orientem* en charge du diocèse (civil) d'Orient, mais qui contient un message plus général. Selon celle-ci, ceux qui vivent dans des monastères n'ont pas le droit de les quitter pour s'établir à Antioche ou d'autres cités, sauf ceux qui ont les fonctions d'apocrisiaires, et seulement pour les tâches qui leur ont été confiées, évidemment par leur higoumène et pour traiter les affaires du monastère. Mais ils ne devront pas se mêler de discuter de foi ou de dogme (περὶ θρησκείας ἢ δόγματος) ni mener à la sédition et au trouble les esprits simples de la population, à peine d'être sévèrement punis[14]. On ne saurait être plus clair. D'autant que l'abandon pur et simple du monastère est chose fréquente : ceux qui abandonnent leur monastère ne reprendront pas les biens meubles qu'ils y ont apportés, même si [le don] n'avait pas été enregistré[15], a fortiori les biens immeubles qu'ils ont pu donner et qui sont devenus inaliénables en principe et sont protégés par la loi. Léon Ier étend à tout ce qu'il appelle « les vénérables établissements » (σεβασμίοις οἴκοις) la protection éclairée qu'il accorde aux biens ecclésiastiques au sens strict, y compris l'autorisation de donner des biens en location, voire de les échanger ou même de les aliéner en cas de nécessité[16]. Parmi ces σεβασμίοις οἴκοις, outre les établissements de charité, on trouve les monastères. Pour ceux-ci, ces opérations foncières, qui doivent être dument enregistrées dans les bureaux des administrations, notamment fiscales, s'agissant des monastères, « il faut la présence des higoumènes et des autres moines »[17]. Les monastères et les biens qui

---

[13] CJ I, 3, 26, p. 21 (ed. Krueger 1997).

[14] CJ I, 3, 29, p. 22 (ed. Krueger 1997).

[15] CJ I, 3, 38, de Zénon ou d'Anastase, pp. 24–25 (ed. Krueger 1997).

[16] CJ I, 2, 17, pp. 15–16 (ed. Krueger 1997).

[17] *Ibid.*, c. 2 (ed. Krueger 1997) : δεῖ παρεῖναι τοὺς ἡγουμένους καὶ τοὺς ἄλλους μοναχούς. Le texte intégral du Code Justinien en latin ne nous est pas parvenu. L'édition Krueger 1997 supplée ici, comme pour tous les textes cités par la suite, par le Nomocanon des 14 titres, sans doute compilé sous Héraclius, dans l'édition Pitra 1868.

en relèvent (*rebus juris eorum*), du moins ceux de Constantinople, sont inclus dans la dispense du « droit de logement » (*metatorum*), dans la foulée des orphelinats. « En effet, il semble à tous égards nécessaire que de là vienne l'entretien et l'éducation pour les orphelins, les pauvres, et pour l'usage des églises, des asiles de pauvres et des lieux d'ascèse [18] ».

Ajoutons une autre décision importante, due à Zénon ou Anastase : l'empereur ordonne que personne ne soit en charge de deux monastères. C'est à l'évêque du territoire où ils sont situés, de s'en occuper. Chaque monastère aura son propre higoumène ; l'évêque sera responsable de la nomination et des actes de l'higoumène, celui-ci pour les actes des moines [19].

S'agissant des clercs de tout grade, les mêmes conditions de liberté valent que pour les moines. Pour les esclaves, la loi de Zénon de 484 est encore plus explicite : il est interdit d'enrôler un esclave dans le clergé même avec le consentement du propriétaire ; celui-ci doit d'abord affranchir l'esclave.

Sur le plan fiscal, le clergé a été exempté depuis longtemps de la plupart des impôts : dès le milieu du IVe siècle de la *collatio lustralis* et de la capitation [20] ; cela vaut pour toute leur famille. Ces mêmes lois exemptent les mêmes bénéficiaires des obligations de logement des militaires et surtout fonctionnaires (*hospitium*), des corvées pour les routes et ponts (*parangariæ*) [21] et des impôts personnels (*munera personalia*) [22]. En revanche, les clercs restent

---

[18] CJ I, 3, 34, p. 23 (ed. Krueger 1997) : *valde etenim hoc videtur esse necessarium, cum exinde sustentatio vel educatio orphanis atque egenis et usibus ecclesiasticis vel ptochiis vel asceteriis comparetur.*

[19] CJ I, 3, 39, p. 25 (ed. Krueger 1997). Le cas du propriétaire de deux monastères situés dans deux évêchés différents n'est pas évoqué.

[20] La *collatio lustralis*, impôt urbain, en grec χρυσάργυρον, sera abolie par Anastase pour l'ensemble de la population ; pour ce faire, il détache de la fortune impériale (*Res Privata*) des biens constituant le *Sacrum Patrimonium*, sous les ordres lui aussi d'un comte, dont les revenus compensent la suppression du χρυσάργυρον (CJ 1, 34, c. 1 et 2, pp. 82–84; ed. Krueger 1997). Cf. Kaplan 1976, pp. 11–12. Pour la capitation : CTh XVI, 2, 10 (346) (ed. Mommsen – Krueger 1990).

[21] Pour ces deux charges, CTh XVI, 2, 8 (343) (ed. Mommsen – Krueger 1990) = CJ 1, 3, 1, p. 19 (ed. Krueger 1997) ; CTh XVI, 2, 14 (356) = CJ I, 3, 2, p. 19 (ed. Krueger 1997) ; CTh XIII, 1, 1 (356) (ed. Mommsen – Krueger 1990).

[22] Pour ce dernier point, CTh XVI, 2, 24 (ed. Mommsen – Krueger 1990) = CJ I, 3, 7, p. 19 (ed. Krueger 1997).

soumis au principal, c'est-à-dire l'impôt foncier pour les biens-fonds, les *juga*, qu'ils possèdent[23] ; ils sont donc soumis à la *jugatio*.

Les clercs disposent également de privilèges judiciaires. Dans les procès impliquant uniquement des ecclésiastiques, c'est le tribunal épiscopal qui tranche. En revanche, dès lors que l'une des parties est laïque, les procès se déroulent devant les tribunaux civils ; toutefois, les ecclésiastiques ou moines seront jugés dans leur province, et non dans une province autre, même si la partie laïque est originaire d'une autre province, de façon à pouvoir accomplir leurs obligations religieuses en dehors des séances du procès[24]. Pour ne pas avoir à verser de caution, ils bénéficient de la garantie de l'économe ou des *defensores ecclesiæ*. Si le fond du procès est non civil, mais religieux, l'évêque, qui est responsable pour son clergé, se fait représenter par l'économe, le *defensor* servant de caution[25]. Si le procès se déroule dans la capitale, les ecclésiastiques ne peuvent être jugés que devant le tribunal du préfet du prétoire[26]. En cas d'accusation infondée, dans la capitale comme en province, l'accusateur remboursera les frais et sera condamné aux dépens[27]. Ce privilège ecclésiastique n'est toutefois pas poussé à l'extrême, comme le montre une loi de Zénon : évêques, clercs et moines doivent obéir aux ordres du gouverneur et se rendre à son tribunal, et non l'inverse ; le gouverneur peut envoyer des mandataires enquêter sur place[28].

Mais, depuis une loi de Marcien de 456, si les plaignants contre un membre du clergé l'acceptent, la juridiction de l'évêque sera valable, y compris à Constantinople. Sinon, ils le poursuivront au tribunal du préfet du prétoire, sans pouvoir le traduire devant aucune autre cour. Les ecclésiastiques n'ont pas à prêter serment. Devant le tribunal du préfet du prétoire, ils bénéficient d'un traitement de faveur, tant pour la somme à donner à l'huissier (limitée à deux *solidi*) ou pour les convocations ou pour le

---

[23] CTh XVI, 2, 15 (360) (ed. Mommsen – Krueger 1990) = CJ I, 3, 3, p. 19 (ed. Krueger 1997).

[24] CJ I, 3, 32 (Léon Ier, 472), pr., pp. 22–23 (ed. Krueger 1997).

[25] CJ I, 3, 32, c. 2 et 4, p. 23 (ed. Krueger 1997).

[26] CJ I, 3, 32, c. 1, pp. 22–23 (ed. Krueger 1997).

[27] CJ I, 3, 32, c. 8, p. 23 (ed. Krueger 1997).

[28] CJ I, 3, 36, pp. 23–24 (ed. Krueger 1997).

recrutement d'un procureur s'ils veulent continuer le procès par l'intermédiaire de ce dernier. Et l'empereur ordonne « que cela vaudra aussi pour les autres divers représentants de ton éminence dans le cas du susdit clergé, en lien avec les affaires dans lesquelles des versements sont effectués, de façon que les dépens et frais pour les procès soit plus faibles et légers quand ils sont versés par des clercs »[29].

Léon Ier a pris des dispositions pour que les clercs de tout rang puissent disposer librement de leurs biens, même s'ils sont potentiellement encore sous la dépendance de leurs ascendants.

> Les évêques, prêtres et diacres de la sainte église orthodoxe, qui ont mérité par leur moralité et leur irréprochable pureté d'obtenir leur rang, tout ce qu'ils ont pu acquérir et posséder pendant qu'ils occupaient leur rang et leur poste, même s'ils étaient au pouvoir de leur père, grand-père ou aïeul toujours vivants, ils le revendiquent comme leurs biens propres : sur ces biens, s'ils le désirent, ils ont le droit et la libre faculté de tester, de donner ou de les aliéner à quelque autre titre ; et ces biens ne deviendront en aucun cas propriété de leurs frères, sœurs ou de leurs descendants, mais celle de leurs propres enfants ou autres descendants ou d'héritiers extérieurs [choisis par eux]. Ils ne pourront pas être revendiqués par leurs pères, grands-pères ou arrière-grands-pères, mais par les enfants des clercs comme leur propriété. Sans conteste, cela deviendra la propriété de ceux à qui elle a été concédée durant leur vie ou par une dernière volonté ou testament, pourvu que ce vœu ait été clairement exprimé[30].

Zénon s'est montré soucieux de garder le contrôle des circonscriptions ecclésiastiques : personne ne conteste au pouvoir impérial le droit de modifier le découpage provincial. Zénon entend donc maintenir le principe selon lequel il y a un évêque par cité et une cité par évêque (Chalcédoine, canon 12).

> Nous ordonnons que toutes les cités, soit auparavant restaurées, soit des cités qui ne l'étaient pas auparavant mais qui ont

---

[29] CJ I, 3, 25, p. 21 (ed. Krueger 1997) : *circa alios quoque diversos apparitores eminentiæ tuæ in his, quæ ex consuetudine præbentur officio, observari in causis prædictorum clericorum iubemus, ut litis sumptus vel expensæ a clericis pauciores et humanioresve præstentur.*

[30] CJ I, 3, 33 (472), p. 23 (ed. Krueger 1997).

été promues par bienfait impérial, aient leur propre évêque, qui y gérera les affaires ecclésiastiques. Donc personne n'a d'aucune façon le droit, même en vertu d'un ordre impérial, de priver une cité de sa dotation épiscopale ou d'un territoire qui lui a été concédé, ni d'aucun autre droit, ni de la rendre à cet égard ou d'une autre façon sujette d'autres cités.

Si quelqu'un ose agir contrairement à cela à l'égard de ce type de cité en la privant du droit d'avoir son évêque ou d'un privilège qui lui a été ou lui sera concédé, cela sera nul et non avenu et celui qui le tentera subira l'infamie et la confiscation[31]. Zénon prévoit toutefois une exception : dans la province de Scythie, zone située autour du delta du Danube qui subit d'incessantes invasions barbares, les églises locales ne peuvent être préservées que par l'évêque métropolitain de Scythie de Tomis (Constanza, en Roumanie)[32]. Autre exception : « nous exceptons de cette loi la cité des Isauriens, récemment érigée en cité en l'honneur de Konôn, qui y subit le martyr, à savoir Léontopolis, qui gardera son présent statut. On a discuté si ce devait être le cas ou si elle devait rester sous l'autorité du pieux évêque d'Isauropolis (Isaura). Elle restera une cité, avec tous ses droits, mais gérée par le dit évêque »[33]. L'évêque d'Isauropolis exerce donc simultanément son autorité dans cette cité et celle Léontopolis ; il y a donc un seul évêque pour deux cités.

L'un des abus dénoncés par le concile de Chalcédoine était la simonie (canon 2). En 469, Léon Ier édicte une loi importante que l'on peut résumer ainsi. Toute personne élevée à la dignité épiscopale dans la capitale ou en province le sera avec pureté

---

[31] CJ I, 3, 35, pr. et c. 1, pp. 23–24 (ed. Krueger 1997) : Πᾶσαν πόλιν εἴτε ἀνανεωθεῖσαν κατὰ τοὺς προλαβόντας χρόνους εἴτε οὐκ οὖσαν μὲν πρότερον, διὰ δὲ βασιλικῆς φιλοτιμίας ἀποδειχθεῖσαν πόλιν ἔχειν ἐκ παντὸς τρόπου ἀχώριστον καὶ ἴδιον τὸν ἐπιμελησόμενον τῶν ἐκκλησιαστικῶν πραγμάτων ἐπίσκοπον θεσπίζομεν· μηδενὶ παντάπασιν οὔσης ἀδείας δι'οἱουδήποτε τρόπου, μηδὲ μὴν διὰ θείας βασιλικῆς κελεύσεως ἀφαιρεῖσθαι πόλιν οἱανδήποτε τοῦ τῆς ἰδιαζούσης ἐπισκοπῆς ἢ καὶ τῆς ἀφορισθείσης αὐτῇ περιοικίδος ἢ ἄλλου τινὸς δικαίου καὶ κατὰ τοῦτο τὸ μέρος ἢ καὶ ἄλλως ὁπωσδήποτε πόλεσιν ἑτέραις ὑποτελῆ ποιεῖν. Sur cette loi, Kosiński 2010, pp. 199–200.

[32] CJ I, 3, 35, c. 2, i (ed. Krueger 1997). Jones 1986, pp. 877–78.

[33] CJ I, 3, 35, c. 3, p. 24 (ed. Krueger 1997). Léontopolis (ou Isaura Palaia) et Isauropolis (ou Isaura) semblent être en Lycaonie : Métivier 2005, pp. 69, n. 222, 250, n. 24 et 291 n. 280 ; Belke 1984, pp. 180–81 (Isauropolis) et pp. 180 et 198 (Léontopolis).

d'esprit, libre choix et par le jugement incorrompu de tous. Personne n'achètera un grade sacerdotal, mais le devra au mérite ; rien ne sera assuré si la sainteté incorruptible est corrompue. L'on choisira comme évêque un homme chaste et humble, quelqu'un dont la vie irréprochable puisse tout purifier où qu'il se trouve. Qu'il soit ordonné non par l'argent, mais par les prières qu'on lui fait d'accepter cette dignité, dépourvu de brigue. Sinon, il est indigne de la prêtrise. Celui qui a obtenu la sainte et vénérable position d'évêque à l'aide d'argent, ou dont on découvre qu'il a accepté quoi que ce soit pour ordonner ou choisir une autre personne, sera radié de la prêtrise, condamné à une perpétuelle infamie, avec tous ses complices [34].

Le problème de l'argent et de la richesse est sous-jacent à bien des moments et les titulaires de postes ecclésiastiques ont tendance à forcer les fidèles à fournir continuellement des offrandes. Une loi de Zénon ou Anastase tente de limiter cet abus.

> Nous ordonnons de plus qu'aucun évêque, chôrévêque, périodeute ou clerc ne force des laïcs qui s'y refusent à fournir des produits en offrande expiatoire que, dans les provinces, on appelle prémices ou dons qu'ils exigent comme une sorte d'impôt, ni aux cultivateurs, qu'ils admettent dans le clergé, et en particulier ceux qui sont sous la juridiction des pieux évêques ou des saintes églises qui leur appartiennent, pas plus que ce que l'on appelle des corvées, ou d'autres fardeaux ou servitudes de ce type, et ne leur infligent pas des interdits ou anathèmes, les privant ainsi – un sujet que l'on ne peut mentionner sans offense – de la communion aux saints mystères et du vénérable et salvifique baptême.

Les empereurs savent que cela s'est fait et que des villages entiers, clercs et laïcs ont été ainsi traités. Voilà qui fait détester la foi orthodoxe ; c'est interdit et aucune coutume ne l'imposera. Chacun devrait offrir ce qui lui semble bon du fruit de son travail, sans qu'on le force, notamment un pauvre ou quelqu'un qui par malchance n'a rien tiré de sa culture. En tout état de cause, l'offrande doit être volontaire [35].

---

[34] CJ I, 3, 30, p. 22 (ed. Krueger 1997).

[35] CJ I, 3, 38, pp. 24–25 (ed. Krueger 1997) : Καὶ τοῦτο δὲ θεσπίζομεν ὥστε μηδένα τῶν θεοφιλεστάτων ἐπισκόπων ἢ χωρεπισκόπων ἢ περιοδευτῶν ἢ κληρικῶν

L'une des obligations charitables majeures est le rachat des captifs. Il est fréquent que ce soit l'objet d'un testament, mais que les bénéficiaires ou chargés de le faire appliquer négligent cette tâche, ce qui motive une loi de Léon Ier de 468.

> Il n'est permis à personne, s'il a été institué héritier soit par testament soit ab intestat soit comme fidéicommis, soit comme légataire, de ne pas respecter les dispositions du testateur ou de les violer de façon malhonnête en affirmant incertain le legs ou fidéicommis qui a été fait pour le rachat des prisonniers : de toute façon, il aboutira selon la volonté du testateur en action pieuse[36].

Les dispositions suivent. Si le testateur a désigné la personne chargée du rachat des captifs, elle aura le droit de réclamer le legs et devra exécuter scrupuleusement le vœu du testateur. Si aucune personne n'a été désignée, le vénérable évêque de la cité de naissance du testateur pourra réclamer la somme et accomplir sans délai la volonté du testateur. L'évêque procède ainsi immédiatement et en fait rapport au recteur (gouverneur) de la province. Au bout d'un an, il fera connaître le nombre de captifs rachetés et le prix payé, en exécution des volontés des personnes décédées. Il ne lèvera pas de frais. Si le légataire n'a pas désigné d'exécuteur et qu'il est d'origine barbare, qu'il y a un doute sur sa patrie, le vénérable évêque de la cité où la personne est décédée aura le droit de se réclamer du testament et de l'exécuter. Si le testateur est mort dans un *vicus* ou un *territorium*, l'évêque de la cité dont il dépend réclamera l'héritage[37].

ἄκοντας τοὺς λαϊκοὺς συνελαύνειν πρὸς τὴν τῶν καρποφοριῶν τῶν ἐν τοῖς τόποις καλουμένων ἀπαρχῶν ἤτοι προσφορῶν ἔκτισιν ὥσπερ τι τέλος ταῦτα μεθοδεύοντας, ἢ καὶ γεωργοῖς μέν, ἐν κλήρῳ δὲ καταλεγομένοις, καὶ μάλιστα ἐκείνοις, οἳ μηδ᾽ ὑπὸ δεσποτείαν εἰσίν τῶν θεοφιλεστάτων ἐπισκόπων ἢ τῶν κατ᾽ αὐτοὺς ἁγιωτάτων ἐκκλησιῶν, ἢ τὰς καλουμένας ἀγγαρείας ἢ ἑτέρας τοιουτοτρόπους ἀπαχθείας ἢ ὑπηρεσίας ἐπεφέρειν, μηδ᾽ ἀφορισμοὺς τούτων ἕνεκα τῶν αἰτιῶν ἢ ἀναθεματισμοὺς τούτοις ἐπάγειν καὶ τῆς τῶν ἁγίων μυστηρίων μεταλήψεως καὶ αὐτοῦ τοῦ σεβασμίου καὶ σωτηριώδους βαπτίσματος. Kosiński 2010, pp. 199 et 201.

[36] CJ I, 3, 28, p. 21 (ed. Krueger 1997) : *Nulli licere decernimus, si testamento heres sit institutus seu ab intestato succedat seu fideicommissarius vel legatarius inveniatur, dispositionem pii testatoris infringere vel improbas mente violare, adserendo incertum esse legatum vel fideicommissum, quod redemptioni relinquitur captivorum, sed modis omnibus exactum pro voluntate testoris piæ rei negotio proficere.* Jones 1986, p. 895.

[37] CJ I, 3, 28, pp. 21–22 (ed. Krueger 1997).

L'Église peut compter sur la générosité de fondateurs dont la volonté doit être exécutée. Une loi de Zénon [38] y veille.

Si quelqu'un donne des biens meubles, immeubles ou auto-meubles ou quelque autre droit au profit de quelque martyr, apôtre, prophète ou saint ange pour y édifier un oratoire, à qui que ce soit qu'il ait fait la pieuse donation, pourvu que ce don ait été acté conformément aux dispositions sacrées, comme c'est obligatoire en ce cas, que ce don soit valide et soit exigé de toute manière, que l'édifice ait été ou non commencé, même si le donateur a seulement manifesté son intention par la promesse d'un don. Lui et ses héritiers sont liés par la pieuse promesse et devront, comme indiqué, non seulement édifier le pieux oratoire, promis par la donation, mais devront aussi, quand il aura été édifié ou sera en cours de construction, lui remettre sans tarder les revenus (de la donation). c. 1. Ces dispositions s'appliqueront également à ce que l'on appelle des hôpitaux, hospices ou asiles de pauvres que quiconque aura, de la manière susdite, promis d'édifier à titre de donation. c. 2. Les évêques très aimés de Dieu de l'endroit ou les pieux économes auront le droit de mener, conformément à notre divine impériale disposition, une action contre eux concernant ce qu'ils ont pieusement promis, si en effet – ce qu'il est inconvenant de dire – une action en justice s'avérait nécessaire. c. 3. Mais dès lors que cette loi aura été respectée et que la promesse de donation

---

[38] CJ I, 2, 15, p. 14 (ed. Krueger 1997). Εἴ τις δωρεὰν κινητῶν ἢ ἀκινήτων ἢ αὐτοκινήτων πραγμάτων ἢ οἱουδήποτε δικαίου ποιήσοιτο εἰς πρόσωπον οἱουδήποτε μάρτυρος ἢ ἀποστόλου ἢ προφήτου ἢ τῶν ἁγίων ἀγγέλων, ὡς μέλλων εὐκτήριον οἶκον οἰκοδομεῖν εἰς μνήμην, οὕπερ ὀνόματι τὴν εὐσεβῆ διατυποῖ δωρεάν εἰ μόνον τὴν πρᾶ-ξιν τῶν ὑπομνημάτων κατὰ τὰς θείας διατάξεις ἐνεφάνισεν, εφ'ὧν τοῦτο ἀναγκαῖόν ἐστι μαθεῖν, κρατεῖν καὶ ἐν ἀπαιτήσει ἐκ παντὸς εἶναι τρόπου, κἂν ἀρχθέντος ἢ καὶ μὴ ἀρχθέντος, ἀλλὰ προδηλωθέντος μόνον διὰ τῆς δωρεᾶς τοῦ εὐαγοῦς οἰκοδομήματος ὁ φιλοτιμούμενος τὴν οἰκείαν δηλώσῃ γνώμην, ὥστε καὶ αὐτὸν καὶ τοὺς αὐτοῦ κληρο-νόμους τοῖς εὐσεβῶς ἐπηγγελμένοις ἐνόχους ὄντας καὶ προδηλούμενον, ὡς εἴρηται, ἐκ τῆς δωρεᾶς εὐαγὲς εὐκτήριον οἰκοδομεῖν καὶ οἰκοδομηθέντι ἢ οἰκοδομουμένῳ τὴν ἐκ τῆς αὐτῆς φιλοτιμίας ἀνελλιπῶς παρέχειν ἀπόλαυσιν. c. 1 Τὰ δὲ αὐτὰ καὶ ἐπὶ ταῖς τῶν καλουμένων ξενοδοχείων ἢ νοσοκομείων ἢ πτωχείων οἰκοδομεῖσθαι καθ'ὃν προείρη-ται τρόπον ἐπαγγελθέντων δωρεαῖς κατὰ πάντα τρόπον κρατείτω. c. 2 Ἀδείας διδο-μένης τοῖς κατὰ τόπον θεοφιλεστάτοις ἐπισκόποις ἤτοι τοῖς εὐλαβεστάτοις οἰκονόμοις τὴν ἐκ ταύτης ἡμῶν διατάξεως ἁρμόζουσαν ἀγωγὴν κινεῖν κατ'αὐτῶν εφ'οἷς εὐσεβῶς ἐπηγγείλαντο δικαστικῆς, ὅπερ καὶ λέγειν ἀπρεπές, δεομένους ἀνάγκης. c. 3 Ἐπὶ τούτῳ μέντοι τῷ ὅρῳ, εφ'ᾧ τε πληρωθέντων τῶν δοκούντων τούτῳ τῷ νομῳ καὶ τῆς εὐσεβοῦς τῶν δωρησαμένων ἐπαγγελίας ἔργῳ παραδοθείσης συγχωρεῖσθαι κατὰ τὰ δόξαντα, τοῖς φιλοτιμησαμένοις καὶ κατὰ τοὺς ἐπιτεθέντας αὐτοῖς ὅρους προβαίνειν τὴν τῶν δωρηθέντων διοίκησιν.

aura été accomplie, que la gestion du bien donné soit assurée conformément aux directives du donateur et aux conditions qui y sont énoncées.

Ces donations ou fondations viennent agrandir la fortune ecclésiastique. Celle-ci est considérée comme inaliénable, d'une façon a priori immuable, ce qui ne facilite pas la gestion. En 470, Léon Ier doit donner des consignes pour conférer un minimum de souplesse et d'efficacité à la gestion des biens ecclésiastiques[39].

> Nous ordonnons que désormais aucun archevêque gouvernant la sacrosainte église de cette ville impériale, aucun économe, a qui été déléguée la gestion de la fortune ecclésiastique n'aura le pouvoir de transférer à qui que ce soit, sous quelque forme d'aliénation que ce soit des biens-fonds ou propriétés urbaines ou rurales, en un mot des biens immeubles, ni les colons ou esclaves installés sur ces biens ou des annones civiles, concédés à la sainte église, par la dernière volonté ou de testament de qui que ce soit, ou par la volonté d'une personne vivante ; il pourra diviser ces biens, les cultiver, les accroître, les augmenter, mais non oser aliéner rien de ces biens.

Si quelqu'un par testament ou don de son vivant, ou par vente, donation ou autre a souhaité que ses propriétés ou une partie définie de celles-ci, que ce soit des biens-fonds ou propriétés urbaines ou rurales, des annones, des esclaves, des colons avec leur pécule appartienne à la susdite vénérable église, ils (l'archevêque et l'économe) maintiendront l'intégrité de ces biens, sans avoir à aucun moment ni sous aucun prétexte le pouvoir, en échange d'un prétendu bienfait ou faveur, d'aliéner en faveur de qui que ce soit, même si la totalité du clergé, avec le pieux évêque et l'économe agréent cette aliénation.

---

[39] CJ I, 2, 14, pp. 13–14 (ed. Krueger 1997). Prologue : *Jubemus nulli posthac archiepiscopo in hac urbe regia sacrosanctæ ecclesiæ præsidenti, nulli œconomo, cui res ecclesiastica gubernanda mandatur, esse facultatem fundos vel prædia urbana seu rustica, res postremo immobiles aut in his prædiis colonos vel mancipia constituta aut annonas civiles cujuscumque suprema vel superstitis voluntate ad religiosam ecclesiam devolutas sub cuiuscumque alienationis specie ad quamcumque transferre personam, sed ea prædia dividere quidem, colere augere et ampliare nec ulli isdem prædiis audere cedere.*

Cela ne va pas de soi. Ce qui relève des droits de la bienheureuse église, présents et à venir, tout comme l'église elle-même doit être conservé sans diminution. Qui que ce soit qui ait osé le faire, celui qui acquerra un bien ecclésiastique, par don, achat, échange ou autre contrat, à part ce que nous allons décider perdra ce qu'il aura acquis, car ce qui est contraire à la loi et nul et non avenu. Ces biens fonds et tout ce qui s'y trouve, et aussi les revenus et améliorations, le clergé et les économes les réclameront comme s'ils n'avaient jamais été cédés. L'économe qui aura permis une telle aliénation, à l'exception de ce que la présente loi permet, sera déchu et la perte sera remboursée sur ses biens, ainsi que par ses héritiers, successeurs et descendants. Les notaires qui auront acté seront définitivement exilés. Les juges qui auront enregistré ces actes seront subiront révocation et confiscation.

Encore faut-il joindre à la rigueur un minimum de souplesse. Comme il semblerait que cela interdise aux pieux économes d'agir dans l'intérêt de l'Église, ils pourront précautionneusement agir pour le bien de celle-ci :

> néanmoins, si un pieux économe de l'Église de la ville impériale estime avantageux la détention temporaire en usufruit de certains biens fonds ou propriétés urbaines ou rurales appartenant à l'Église au bénéfice d'un demandeur pour la durée convenue entre eux, ou pour la vie du demandeur, que l'économe passe un contrat écrit avec le demandeur pour la durée convenue [40].

Ce contrat précise les conditions matérielles de sa réalisation. Le délai convenu écoulé, ce qui a été détenu de façon temporaire revient de façon absolue sous le contrôle de l'Église. Une fois le temps écoulé ou le preneur décédé, la personne qui a reçu une propriété ecclésiastique pour lui fournir un certain revenu rendra au moins le double du revenu concédé en même temps que le

---

[40] CJ I, 2, 14, c. 9, p. 14 (ed. Krueger 1997) : *Si quando igitu vir religiosus œconomus huius regiæ urbis ecclesiæ perspexerit expedire, ut desideranti cuiquam certarum possessionum atque prædiorum, urbanorum scilicet sive rusticorum, ad jus ecclesiasticum pertinentibus temporaria usus fructus possessio pro ipsius petitione præstetur, tunc eius temporis, quod inter utrosque convenerit, sive in diem vitæ suæ ab eo qui desiderat postuletur, pacta cum eo qui hoc elegerit œconomus atque conscribat, per quæ et tempus, intra quod hoc præstari placuerit, statuatur.*

bien-fonds lui-même, le bien immeuble, les colons et les esclaves qui s'y trouvent. Tout accord qui ne serait pas conforme à cela sera nul et non avenu ; la possession et le droit de propriété resteront à l'Église ; le clergé ou l'économe le réclameront, au titre d'un transfert illégal.

Les biens ecclésiastiques ne se limitent pas à ceux de l'église cathédrale ; s'y ajoutent les fondations pieuses, pour lesquelles nous avons une loi de Zénon ou plus vraisemblablement d'Anastase, en application du canon 8 de Chalcédoine[41]. La loi confirme ce qui touche la Grande Église de la capitale, mais se penche sur les établissements de charité, valable pour tout l'Empire.

> c. 1. Nous ordonnons que l'aliénation de biens immeubles ou d'annones civiles appartenant ou venant à appartenir aux σεβασμίοις οἴκοις soit nulle et non avenue, de quelque façon qu'elle ait été faite ou tentée ou conçue, sauf s'il se trouve qu'une vente, une hypothèque ou l'échange d'une telle propriété puisse se faire à l'avantage ou en raison de quelque nécessité ou utilité qui pourrait exister s'agissant de ces maisons, à savoir, si le prix de la propriété est utilisé pour payer des dettes, non pas de celles qui existent naturellement ou ordinairement, mais celles qui proviennent de l'acceptation de successions ou héritages, ou proviennent de raisons nécessaires ou avantageuses aux susdites σεβασμίοις οἴκοις, ou bien pour acquérir ou acheter une autre propriété qui s'avère plus utile ou même nécessaire pour celles-ci, ou encore en vue de la rénovation ou de l'entretien des dites maisons urgents et ne pouvant souffrir de délai. Les mêmes raisons à consentir une exception existent en lien avec l'interdiction de contracter une dette ou consentir des hypothèques qui en découleraient. Ainsi, un échange peut être fait si, de la même façon, il concerne une propriété plus utile, voire nécessaire, et qui puisse procurer un revenu adéquat pour une vénérable maison qui ne soit pas inférieur à celui de ce qui est aliéné. Même chose pour une emphytéose, pourvu que le revenu ne soit en aucune manière diminué ou également si ce qui est concédé est totalement stérile. Car nous n'interdisons pas à ces maisons de se séparer de leurs biens par donation ou aliénation

---

[41] CJ I, 2, 17, pp. 15–16 (ed. Krueger 1997). Sur les différentes catégories d'établissements ecclésiastiques, Kaplan 1976, pp. 17–21. Sur leurs propriétés, Jones 1986, pp. 901–03.

si, vu leur *ἀπορίαν*, ils n'apportent aucun revenu mais plutôt des pertes[42].

c. 2. Ce qui est opéré ne sera pas valide sauf si les raisons susdites sont enregistrées dans les registres (*ὑπομνήμασιν*) à Byzance auprès du maître du cens (*μαγιστρόκηνσος*), dans les provinces auprès des défenseurs [des églises] (*παρὰ τοῖς ἐκδίκοις*), en présence des saintes écritures, les églises étant représentées par leurs économes et les clercs qui y siègent ; pour les monastères, il faut la présence des higoumènes et des autres moines ; pour les *πτωχείων*, du gérant (*διοικητοῦ*), de ses subordonnés et des pauvres ; pour les *ξενώνων*, du gérant et de tous ceux qui seront ses subordonnés ; même chose pour les orphelinats. Ainsi, tout ce qui est agréé par la majorité peut être fait, avec en tout état de cause le consentement de l'évêque de l'endroit où ces transactions s'opèrent d'ordinaire[43].

c. 2a. Le maître du cens ou le défenseur ne peut pas refuser de se rendre dans la *σεβάσμιον οἶκον* où se déroule la tran-

---

[42] Θεσπίζομεν, ὥστε πᾶσαν ἐκποίησιν πραγμάτων ἀκινήτων ἢ πολιτικῶν σιτηρεσίων τοῖς σεβασμίοις οἴκοις διαφερόντων ἢ διοισόντων καθ'οἱονδήποτε τρόπον γινομένην ἢ μελετωμένην ἢ ἐπινοεῖσθαι δυναμένην σχολάζειν πλὴν εἰ μήπου χρείας τινὸς ἀναγκαίας καὶ ἐπωφελοῦς τοῖς αὐτοῖς σεβασμίοις οἴκοις ἀνακυπτούσης λυσιτελὴς εἴη τούτοις ἡ πρᾶσις τοῦ τοιούτου πράγματος ἢ ὑποθήκη ἢ ἀπαλλαγὴ ἢ διηνεκὴς ἐμφύτευσις, τουτέστιν ἐπειδὰν τὰ τιμήματα τοῦ πιπρασκομένου πράγματος εἰς διευλύτωσιν χρεῶν, οὐχ ἁπλῶς οὐδ'ὡς ἔτυχε συστάντων, ἀλλ'ἐκ διαδοχῶν τινων ἤτοι κληρονομιῶν ἢ ἐξ αἰτιῶν ἀναγκαίων καὶ χρειωδῶν ἑνὶ τῶν προδηλωθέντων σεβασμίων οἴκων ἐπικειμένων, ἢ καὶ εἰς πράγματος αὐτοῖς ἑτέρου χρειωδεστέρου τε καὶ ἐναγκαιοτέρου κτῆσιν καὶ ἀγορασίαν μέλλοι προχωρεῖν, ἢ καὶ εἰς ἀνανέωσιν ἤτοι ἐπιμέλειαν τοῦ αὐτοῦ οἴκου κατεπείγουσαν καὶ μακρᾶς ἀναβολῆς οὐκ ἀνεχομένην δαπανᾶσθαι· τῶν αὐτῶν αἰτιῶν καὶ ἐπὶ τοῖς δανείσμασι καὶ ταῖς ἐπ'αὐτοῖς ὑποθήκαις τῆς κωλύσεως ἐξῃρημένων. Τὰ δὲ τῆς ἀνταλλαγῆς, ὅταν ἐπὶ χρειωδεστέρῳ κατὰ τὸ ἴσον τρόπον καὶ ἀναγκαιοτέρῳ καὶ πρόσοδον ἀξίαν καὶ οὐκ ἐλάττονα τοῦ διδομένου πράγματος ἑνὶ τῶν αὐτῶν σεβασμίων οἴκων περιποιεῖν δυναμένῳ ἐπιζητεῖται· τὰ δὲ τῆς ἐμφυτεύσεως, ἡνίκα ἡ τῆς προσόδου μηδαμῶς ἀπομειοῖτο ποσότης ἢ καὶ ἄπορον εἴη παντελῶς τὸ διδόμενον· ἐπὶ γὰρ τοῖς τοιούτοις πράγμασι τοῖς μηδὲν μὲν κέρδος δι'ἀπορίαν προσφέρουσι, ζημίαν δὲ προστριβομένοις οὐδὲ δωρεὰς τοῖς αὐτοῖς οἴκοις ἢ ἐκχωρήσεις ἀπαγορεύομεν.

[43] Τὸ δὲ γινόμενον οὐκ ἄλλως ἰσχύει, εἰ μὴ μία τῶν εἰρημένων αἰτιῶν ἐν ὑπομνήμασι φανερωθῇ, ἐν μέν Βυζαντίῳ παρὰ τῷ μαγιστροκήνσῳ, ἐν δὲ ταῖς ἐπαρχίαις παρὰ τοῖς ἐκδίκοις, προκειμένων τῶν ἁγίων γραφῶν, καὶ ἐπὶ μὲν τῶν ἐκκλησιῶν παρόντων τῶν οἰκονόμων καὶ τῶν ἐνδημούντων κληρικῶν, ἐπὶ τῶν μοναστηρίων δεῖ παρεῖναι τοὺς ἡγουμένους καὶ τοὺς ἄλλους μοναχούς, ἐπὶ δὲ τῶν πτωχείων τοῦ διοικητοῦ καὶ τῶν ὑπουργούντων καὶ τῶν πτωχῶν, ἐπὶ τῶν ξενώνων τοῦ διοικητοῦ καὶ τῶν εὑρισκομένων ὑπουργῶν τῆς διοικήσεως καὶ ὁμοίως ἐπὶ τῶν ὀρφανοτροφείων, ὥστε κρατεῖν τὸ τοῖς πλείοσιν ἀρέσκον· συναινοῦντος καὶ τοῦ ἐπισκόπου τῶν τόπων, ἐν οἷς τοῦτο σύνεθες ἐπιγίνεσθαι.

saction, sans lui créer de préjudice ni la faire payer. Sinon, ils encourent une peine de 20 livres d'or[44].

c. 2b. Par la suite, des contrats seront dressés qui rappelleront les raisons et la manière dont auront été établis les actes, ainsi que les noms des contractants et celui de la personne auprès de qui les contrats ont été passés[45].

c. 3. Si quoi que ce soit de cette procédure a été omis, le créditeur et l'acheteur perdront le bien, la dette et le prix ; celui qui aura conclu un échange perdra tant ce qu'il a donné que ce qu'il a reçu ; quiconque aura reçu une propriété en emphytéose à vie, ou par cadeau ou par aliénation, rendra ce qu'il a reçu et un montant égal à ce qui aura été donné[46].

c. 4. Ces clauses s'appliqueront également aux propriétés des églises et des fondations pieuses acquises dans le futur[47].

c. 5. Si ces établissements détiennent des biens meubles, en dehors de la vaisselle sacrée, d'un montant suffisant pour les dépenses nécessaires aux besoins susmentionnés, aucune aliénation ou hypothèque d'une propriété immobilière nécessaire ou de « pains (politiques) » ne sera pratiquée[48].

On voit donc (c. 4) qu'il s'agit autant des églises que des établissements de charité, mais aussi que de nombreux établissements ecclésiastiques préféraient aliéner des biens immeubles plutôt que dépenser leurs biens meubles. En fait, c'est la situation générale, et notamment la multiplication des biens incultes et néanmoins imposés, qui rend ces procédures d'aliénation inévitables ; les établissements ecclésiastiques n'échappent pas aux conditions éco-

---

[44] Μὴ δυναμένου τοῦ μαγιστροκήνσου ἢ τοῦ ἐκδίκου παραιτεῖσθαι καραλαμβάνειν τὸν σεβάσμιον οἶκον, ἐν ᾧ ἡ τοιαύτη συνίσταται πρᾶξις, ἀζημίως καὶ ἐκδικούντων αὐτήν. Ὑπόκεινται γὰρ ἐκ παραβασίας ποινῇ χρυσίου λιτρῶν κʹ.

[45] Καὶ μετὰ ταῦτα γίνεται συμβόλαια μνημονεύοντα τῶν αἰτιῶν καὶ τῆς τῶν ὑπομνημάτων πράξεως καὶ τῆς προσηγορίας τῶν παραγενομένων καὶ παρ' ᾧ συνέστη.

[46] Εἰ δέ τι τῶν εἰρημένων παροφθείη, ὁ μὲν δανειστὴς καὶ ὁ ἀγοραστὴς ἐκπίπτει τοῦ πράγματος λαὶ τοῦ χρέους καὶ τῶν τιμῶν· ὁ δὲ λαβὼν εἰς ἀνταλλαγὴν καὶ οὗπερ ἔδωκε καὶ οὗπερ ἔλαβεν ἐκπίπτει· ὁ δὲ εἰς ἐμφύτευσιν ὑπὲρ τὴν ἰδίαν ζωὴν λαβὼν ἢ δωρεὰν ἢ ἐκχώρησιν ἀπηγορευμένην ἀναδίδωσιν ὅπερ εἴληφε καὶ ποσότητα ἑτέραν, ἧς ἄξιόν ἐστι τὸ δοθέν.

[47] Χώραν δὲ ἔχει τὰ εἰρημένα καὶ ἐπὶ τοῖς μέλλουσι γίνεσθαι ἐκκλησιαστικοῖς καὶ τοῖς ἐσομένοις εὐαγέσιν.

[48] Ὑπόντων δὲ κινητῶν ἔξωθεν τῶν ἱερῶν σκευῶν καὶ ἀρκούντων εἰς τὰς εἰρημένας αἰτίας ἀργεῖ τῶν ἀναγκαίων ἀκινήτων καὶ ἄρτων ἡ ἐκποίησις καὶ ἡ ὑποθήκη·

nomiques générales, marquées notamment par une oliganthropie qui rend difficile le maintien de la main d'œuvre rurale, fût-elle constituée de colons adscrits[49].

La dernière loi étudiée montre en outre une réalité complexe, car elle établit une claire distinction entre d'une part les églises, donc l'évêché et les églises qui en dépendent, et les établissements de charité, dont il est clair qu'ils ont leur propre dotation et leur propre personnel, qui ne dépendent pas, ou pas entièrement de l'évêque. Pour autant, et malgré sa clarté, la loi d'Anastase ne couvre pas tous les cas de figure. Sans doute trop confiant dans le canon 4 de Chalcédoine soumettant les moines et leurs monastères aux évêques ou peu soucieux de créer un nouveau motif d'affrontement entre moines et évêques, les empereurs n'ont pas légiféré sur les biens monastiques. Justinien s'en chargera, mais ceci est une autre histoire ; il développe et systématise les principes et dispositions énoncés par Zénon et Anastase.

Bibliographie

Sources

Krueger 1997 = *Corpus Juris Civilis, vol. 2, Codex Justinianus*, éd. Paul Krueger, Hildesheim.

Magnou-Nortier 2002 = *Le Code Théodosien, Livre XVI, et sa réception au Moyen Âge*, éd. Élisabeth Magnou-Nortier, Sources canoniques, 2, Paris.

Mommsen – Krueger 1990 = *Codex Theodosianus, Volumen I, Theodisiani libri XVI cum constitutionibus Sirmondinis*, éd. Theodor Mommsen – Paul Krueger, Bodenheim.

Pitra 1868 = Jean-Baptiste Pitra, *Iuris ecclesiastici graecorum historia et monumenta iussu Pii IX Pontificis Maximi*, vol. 2, Rome, pp. 453–640.

Schwartz – Schieffer 1933 = *Acta conciliorum oecumenicorum 2,1, Concilium Universale Chalcedonense*, Eduard Schwartz – Rudolf Schieffer, Berlin.

---

[49] Kaplan 1992, notamment pp. 180–83. Pour une interprétation différente, voir Sarris 2009.

Littérature secondaire

Beaucamp 2000 = Joëlle Beaucamp, « Donne, patrimonio, Chiesa (Bizantio, IV–VII secolo) », in *Il Tardoantico alle soglie del Duemila. Diritto, religione, società*, éd. Giuliana Lanata, Pise, pp. 249–65, repris en français dans Ead., *Femmes, patrimoines, normes à Byzance*, Bilans de Recherche 6, Paris, 2010, pp. 335–48.

Belke 1984 = Klaus Belke, *Galatien und Lykaonien*, Tabula Imperii Byzantini 4, Wien.

Dagron 1976 = Gilbert Dagron, « Les moines et la ville, Le monachisme à Constantinople jusqu'au concile de Chalcédoine », *Travaux et Mémoires* 4, pp. 229–76 repris dans *Id., La romanité chrétienne en Orient : héritages et mutations*, Variorum collected Studies Series 193, VIII, Londres, 1984.

Haarer 2006 = Fiona Haarer, *Anastasius I. Politics and Empire in the late Roman World*, Arca 46, Cambridge.

Jones 1986 = Arnold Hugh Martin Jones, *The Later Roman Empire, Baltimore. A social, economic and administrative Survey* (réédition de l'édition Oxford 1964).

Kaplan 1976 = Michel Kaplan, *Les propriétés de la Couronne et de l'Église dans l'Empire byzantin (Vᵉ–VIIᵉ siècles)*, Byzantina Sorbonensia 2, Paris.

Kaplan 1992 = Michel Kaplan, *Les hommes et la terre à Byzance du VIᵉ au XIᵉ siècle : propriété et exploitation du sol*, Publications de la Sorbonne, Byzantina Sorbonensia 10, Paris.

Kaplan 2016 = Michel Kaplan, « Un saint stylite et les pouvoirs : Daniel le Stylite († 493) », in *Figures de l'autorité médiévale, Mélanges offerts à Michel Zimmermann*, éd. Pierre Chastang – Patrick Henriet – Claire Soussen, Histoire ancienne et médiévale 142, Paris, pp. 183–97.

Kosiński 2010 = Rafał Kosiński, *The Emperor Zeno. Religion and Politics*, Byzantina et Slavica Cracoviensia VI, Cracow.

Meier 2010 = Mischa Meier, *Anastasios I. Die Entstehung des Byzantinischen Reiches*, Stuttgart.

Métivier 2005 = Sophie Métivier, *La Cappadoce (IVᵉ–VIᵉ siècle). Une histoire provinciale de l'Empire romain d'Orient*, Byzantina Sorbonensia 22, Paris.

Sarris 2009 = Peter Sarris, « Aristocrats, Peasants and the Transformation of Rural Society, c.400–800 », *Journal of Agrarian Change*, 9.1, pp. 3–22.

Abstract

After the granting of permission for Christian worship, it appeared essential to take legislative measures concerning this worship and its clergy. The same thing happened when hermitages and monasteries began to multiply. Zeno and Anastasios are therefore part of a long tradition and their production is comparatively small. The legislation of these two emperors is in line with the Council of Chalcedon (451), which is above all a disciplinary council, and subsequent legislation is concerned with its observance. It constitutes above all the decrees for the application of the conciliar canons. In general, imperial legislation is not hostile to monks, who benefit from a number of protections granted to members of the clergy. However, most monks are not clerics, and therefore not subject *ex officio* to the bishops. And their activity must be regulated. Zeno or Anastasios ordered that no one should be in charge of two monasteries. It is up to the bishop of the territory where they are located to take care of them. Each monastery shall have its own higoumen ; the bishop shall be responsible for the appointment and acts of the higoumen, the latter for the acts of the monks. Zeno was concerned to keep control of the ecclesiastical circumscriptions and to maintain the principle that there is one bishop per city and one city per bishop. The problem of money and wealth is underlying in many cases and the holders of ecclesiastical positions tend to force the faithful to continually provide offerings. A Zeno or Anastasios law attempts to limit this abuse. Our two emperors deal with ecclesiastical wealth, which is constantly increasing and remains inalienable, which does not facilitate management. The ecclesiastical property is not limited to that of the cathedral church ; there are also the pious foundations, for which we have a law of Zeno or more probably of Anastasos, in application of canon 8 of Chalcedon. The law confirms what concerns the Great Church in the capital, but looks at charitable institutions, and is valid for the entire Empire. Many ecclesiastical institutions preferred to dispose of real estate rather than to spend their movable property. In fact, it is the general situation, and in particular the multiplication of uncultivated and nevertheless imposed goods, that makes these procedures of alienation unavoidable ; ecclesiastical establishments do not escape the general economic conditions, marked in particular by oliganthropy that makes it difficult to maintain the rural workforce, even if it is made up of registered settlers.

DARIUSZ BRODKA

REBELLEN UND USURPATOREN –
ZUR BENUTZUNG
DER THEODOR-LECTOR-EPITOME
DURCH THEOPHANES

Die Frage nach der Benutzung der Kirchengeschichte des Theodor Lector durch Theophanes wurde schon mehrmals erörtert. Besonders wichtige Erkenntnisse lieferte in dieser Hinsicht G. Ch. Hansen in seiner Edition der erhaltenen Exzerpte und Fragmente des Theodor Lector. Hansen ging mit guten Gründen davon aus, dass Theophanes bei der Abfassung seiner Chronik eine vollständige Epitome vor sich gehabt und diese als eine seiner Hauptquellen für die Zeit von Konstantin bis Anastasios benutzt habe.[1] Die Art der Benutzung hielt Hansen für nicht sklavisch – Theophanes habe den Wortlaut der Epitome verändert, indem er stilistische Änderungen, Kürzungen oder Umstellungen vorgenommen habe. Erkennbar seien auch Verwechslungen und Ungenauigkeiten.[2] Hansen nahm dabei an, dass Theophanes in vielen Fällen den verlorenen Originaltext der Epitome ersetzen könne. So stehen zahlreiche Theophanes-Abschnitte in Hansens Ausgabe als Theodor-Lector-Exzerpte.[3] Beachtenswert sind auch die Erörterungen von B. Pouderon, der jüngst zum Schluss kam, dass Theophanes nicht nur die Theodor-Lector-Epitome, sondern auch die Originalfassung der Kirchengeschichte des Theodor Lector habe benutzen können. Darauf könnten diejenigen Stellen bei Theophanes hinweisen, die mehr Details als die entsprechenden

---

[1] Hansen 1971, p. xxix.
[2] Hansen 1971, p. xxix.
[3] Die Passagen aus Theophanes sind in Hansens Ausgabe durch Kleindruck gekennzeichnet.

Studies in Theodore Anagnostes, ed. by Rafał Kosiński & Adrian Szopa, STTA 19 (Turnhout 2021), pp. 183–203
© BREPOLS 🕮 PUBLISHERS   DOI 10.1484/M.STTA-EB.5.127981

Theodor-Lector-Exzerpte enthalten.[4] Es stellt sich allerdings die Frage nach der Herkunft dieser Zusätze: Gehen sie auf den Urtext der Kirchengeschichte, oder auf eine andere Vorlage zurück?[5]

Im Folgenden möchte ich mich auf den Umgang des Theophanes mit seinen Quellen konzentrieren, wobei die Theodor-Lector-Epitome im Fokus der Untersuchung steht. Um gewisse Flexibilität und unterschiedliche Vorgehensweise des Theophanes bei der Verarbeitung der Theodor-Lector-Epitome zeigen zu können, sollen hier diejenigen Theophanes-Stellen analysiert werden, die die Usurpationen bzw. die Aufstände gegen die Kaiser Zeno und Anastasios thematisieren. Dadurch lässt sich erkennen, dass sich Theophanes bei der Behandlung einzelner Ereignisse häufig nicht auf eine einzige Hauptquelle beschränkt, sondern an manchen Stellen diese mit Hilfe anderer Texte ergänzt, modifiziert oder verändert. Deswegen scheint die Methode Hansens, der viele Theophanes-Stellen für echte Theodor-Lector-Exzerpte hält, höchst problematisch zu sein.[6]

1. *Basiliskos*

Der Usurpation des Basiliskos widmete Theophanes drei Einträge: zu AM 5967, 5968 und 5969.[7] Theodor Lector schilderte sie ziemlich umfangreich, wie sich dies aus den erhaltenen Exzerpten ablesen lässt. In der Theodor-Lector-Epitome behandeln insgesamt dreizehn Exzerpte die Herrschaft des Basiliskos (vgl. Th.Lect. 401–13). Sie berichten ausführlich über wichtige Aspekte der innenpolitischen Situation im oströmischen Reich. Der Bericht des Epitomators ist sachlich und unparteilich. Es gibt hier keine scharfe Kritik an Basiliskos. Es ist nur die Rede davon, dass Basi-

---

4 Pouderon 2015, pp. 279–314.

5 Die Frage danach, inwiefern die Theodor-Lector-Epitome als zuverlässiger Textzeuge des Originaltextes gelten kann, diskutiert Greatrex 2015, pp. 121–42. Greatrex kommt zum Schluss, bereits der Epitomator habe seinen Bericht mit dem Material aus anderen Quellen ergänzen können. So gehe die Theodor-Lector-Epitome nicht nur auf die *Kirchengeschichte* des Theodor Lector, sondern auch auf andere Quellen zurück. Dieser Meinung ist völlig zuzustimmen.

6 Zum Umgang des Theophanes mit der Theodor-Lector-Epitome vgl. auch Greatrex 2015, p. 122–25.

7 Vgl. dazu Kosiński 2010, pp. 91–97.

liskos ein Komplott gegen Zeno geschmiedet habe, und dass seine Schwester Verina daran teilgenommen habe. Mit ihrer Hilfe habe er für sich die Unterstützung einiger Senatoren gewonnen. Auf die Nachricht von der Verschwörung sei der Kaiser Zeno zusammen mit seiner Frau Ariadne nach Isaurien geflohen (Th. Lect. 401). Bald nach der Übernahme der Kaisermacht habe Basiliskos die Orthodoxie angegriffen, wobei seine Frau ihn zu diesem Angriff veranlasst habe (Th. Lect. 402). Theodor Lector hob in seinem Bericht den Widerstand hervor, auf den die Religionspolitik des Basiliskos in Konstantinopel stieß, wo sich das Volk, die Kleriker und die Mönche für das Chalcedonense entschieden einsetzten.

Theophanes stellt diese Ereignisse zuerst im Eintrag zum Welt-jahr 5967 dar (Theoph. AM 5967, pp. 120–21). Dieser erste Eintrag geht fast völlig auf die Theodor-Lector-Epitome zurück, wobei der Chronist die Reihenfolge der Exzerpte in seiner Darstel-lung teilweise veränderte. In diesem ersten Eintrag zu Basiliskos' Herrschaft verwendete Theophanes insgesamt 9 Theodor-Lector-Exzerpte als seine Vorlage. Theophanes übernimmt hier fast skla-visch den Wortlaut der Vorlage und korrigiert diese nur in Kleinig-keiten. Stellenweise modifiziert er seine Vorlage, um den Bericht über das Geschehen klarer zu machen. Bei der Darstellung der Umstände, unter denen sich Timotheos Ailuros das Bein brach, ergänzt Theophanes seine Vorlage um die Notiz, dass dies in Byzanz geschehen sei. Die Auslassungen sind sehr selten: Bei der Widergabe des Exzerpts 410, das über den Tod des Bischofs von Antiochia Julian und die Rückkehr des Petrus Fullo nach Antio-chia berichtet, läßt Theophanes nur die Information darüber aus, dass Julian der Nachfolger des Martyrios gewesen sei. Theophanes verändert die Reihenfolge der benutzten Exzerpte, um ein klares Bild der innenpolitischen Situation darzustellen: Er beginnt mit der Übernahme der Kaisermacht durch Basiliskos und Flucht des Zeno und dann berichtet über die Religionspolitik des neuen Herrschers, über die Abberufung der Bischöfe Timotheos Ailuros und Petrus Fullo aus der Verbannung, über die Situation in Antio-chia und Alexandria. Zum Schluss konzentriert er sich wieder auf Basiliskos und dessen Angriff gegen Chalcedon und auf den religiösen Widerstand gegen Basiliskos in Konstantinopel. Nur an einer einzigen Stelle geht er über seine Hauptquelle hinaus – es geht nämlich um die Information über den Aufenthaltsort des Zeno. Zeno sollte zuerst nach Urba, dann nach Sbide fliehen und sei dort von Illus und Trocundes zwei Jahre belagert worden. Diese Information findet keine Parallele in der Theodor-Lector-Epitome. Diese gibt sich nur mit einer bloßen Angabe zufrieden, dass Zeno nach Isaurien geflohen sei. Aller Wahrscheinlichkeit nach wusste Theodor Lector nichts mehr über den Aufenthaltsort des Zeno, denn Victor von Tunnuna, der für diese Ereignisse wohl auf die Kirchengeschichte des Theodor Lector zurückgreift, spricht auch nur allgemein über Isaurien (vgl. Vict. Tun. 44).

Für das nächste Jahr, d. h. AM 5968, benutzte Theophanes die Exzerpte 406 und 408. Auch in diesem Fall übernimmt er sie fast wörtlich. Diesmal thematisiert er den Widerstand, den die Chalcedonier gegen die religionspolitischen Maßnahmen des Basiliskos in Konstantinopel leisteten (Theoph. AM 5968, p. 122). Die letzten zwei Theodor-Lector-Exzerpte, die sich auf Basiliskos' Herrschaft beziehen, verwendete Theophanes als seine Vorlage im Eintrag zum Weltjahr 5969. Diesmal geht er aber über die Theodor-Lector-Epitome hinaus. Theophanes muss erkannt haben, dass die Darstellung der Umstände, unter denen Zeno nach Konstantinopel zurückkehrte, in der Epitome wenig ausführlich ist. So greift er hier auf eine andere Vorlage zurück und macht wieder auf Zeno aufmerksam. Im Eintrag zum Weltjahr 5967 hatte Theophanes erwähnt, dass Zeno von Illus und Trocundes in Sbide belagert worden sei. Nun nimmt er diesen Faden erneut auf und stellt fest, dass Illus und Trocundes auf die Seite des Zeno gewechselt hätten. Zum Einen habe die Politik des Basiliskos' sie tief enttäuscht – dieser habe seine Versprechungen nicht erfüllt – zum Anderen hätten sie erkannt, wie schwach die Position des Usurpators sei – er habe die Unterstützung des Senats verloren. Unter diesen Umständen konnte Zeno zusammen mit Illus und Trocundes nach Konstantiopel zurückkehren (Theoph. AM 5969, p. 124). Auf ähnliche Weise stellt diese Ereignisse Euagrios dar, der überliefert, dass Zeno die Belagerer durch Bestechung für sich gewonnen habe. Euagrios gibt aber nicht die Namen dieser Belagerer an (Evagr. HE 3,8). Es bleibt dahingestellt, woher Theophanes sein Wissen über die Belagerung des Zeno durch Illus und Trocundes schöpft. Er geht hier weder auf die Theodor-Lector-Epitome noch auf Euagrios zurück. Infrage kämen somit zwei Geschichtswerke, die Theophanes häufig für die politischen

Ereignisse der zweiten Hälfte des 5. Jahrhunderts als Vorlage verwendet: Es ginge dabei um die ursprüngliche Version der Weltchronik des Johannes Malalas, d. h. den sog. Ur-Malalas, und die *Chronike Epitome* des Eustathios von Epiphaneia.

Der anschließende Bericht über den Verrat des Armatus und die Rückkehr des Zeno geht auf Malalas 15,5, pp. 302–03 zurück. Theophanes AM 5967, p. 124 stimmt hier mit Malalas in meisten Details überein. Beide Chronisten berichten übereinstimmend darüber, dass Basiliskos den Heermeister Armatus mit ‚seiner gesamten Heeresmacht' gegen Zeno ausgeschickt habe, dass Armatus ihm einen Eid auf die Taufe geschworen, er würde keinen Verrat üben, und dass Armatus von Zeno bestochen worden sei: Zeno habe ihm versprochen, er werde ihn zum lebenslänglichen *magister militum* machen und seinen Sohn zum Caesar erheben. Theophanes ist aber weit davon entfernt, den Malalas-Text direkt zu übernehmen, sondern gestaltet ihn fortwährend um. Er verfährt also anders als im Fall der Theodor-Lector-Exzerpte. Zum Verfügung stand ihm allerdings eine umfangreichere Textvariante des Malalas als diejenige, die heute erhalten ist. Er kennt nämlich zusätzliche Details, die bei Malalas fehlen. Er weiß z. B. dass Armatus' Sohn den Namen Basiliskos trug. Gewisse Abweichungen können aus der Arbeitsweise des Theophanes resultieren – beim Abkürzen seiner umfangreichen Vorlage konnte er solche Details wie die Ämter des Armatus verwechseln. Bei Malalas trägt dieser den Titel des *magister militum praesentalis*, bei Theophanes des *magister militum per Thracias*. Diese Sektion schließt Theophanes mit der Notiz ab, dass Zeno mit seiner Frau Ariadne nach Konstantiopel zurückgekehrt sei und vom Senat und Volk freudig angenommen worden sei. Es fällt auf, dass Theophanes über einen wichtigen Aspekt der Ereignisse schweigt: Außer Acht lässt er den Wechsel des religionspolitischen Kurses durch Basiliskos, der in der Endphase seiner Herrschaft seine antichalcedonischen Maßnahmen wiederrief (vgl. Evagr. HE 3,7). Dies wurde im Exzerpt 412 der Theodor-Lector-Epitome thematisiert. Es ist möglich, dass Theophanes dies absichtlich ausließ, um Basiliskos als Häretiker in ein schlechtes Licht rücken zu können.

Die nächste Sektion widmet sich dem Ende der Usurpation des Basiliskos (Theoph. AM 5969, pp. 125–26). Sie geht auf einige historiographische Traditionen zurück. Zuerst folgt Theophanes dem Theodor-Lector-Exzerpt 413: Basiliskos und seine Frau hätten im Baptysterium einer Kirche Zuflucht gesucht, und Basiliskos habe auf dem Altar sein kaiserliches Diadem niedergelegt. Zeno habe die Kirche und dann den Palast betreten. Auch in diesem Fall übernimmt Theophanes seine Vorlage ohne größere Veränderungen. Er ergänzt sie nur um einen Vermerk, dass Zenodia (Baisliskos' Frau) eine Häretikerin gewesen sei. Nun wechselt er seine Quelle und greift wieder auf Malalas zurück, wobei er dessen Bericht deutlich abkürzt: Zeno habe in die Kirche seine Boten ausgesandt und Basiliskos versprochen, er werde ihn und seine Familie nicht umbringen (vgl. Malal. 15,5, p. 303). Laut Theophanes wurde Basiliskos nach Kukusos in Kappadokien verbannt, und an diesem Punkt weicht er sowohl von Malalas, der auf das Kastell Limna als Verbannungsort verweist,[8] als auch von der Theodor-Lector-Epitome, die über Busamoi spricht, ab. Victor von Tunnuna zufolge wurden Basiliskos und seine Familie nach Sasemis in Kappadokien gesandt (Vict. Tunn. 47). Interessanterweise erscheint Kukusos bei Euagrios HE 3,8, der möglicherweise hier Eustathios als seine Vorlage verwendete. Es ist somit plausibel, dass Theophanes das Geschichtswerk des Eustathios als eine seiner Vorlagen bei der Darstellung der Usurpation des Basiliskos benutzte. Der Hungertod des Basiliskos und seiner Familie geht aller Wahrscheinlichkeit nach wieder auf Malalas zurück (vgl. Malal. 15,5 p. 303). Theophanes betont seine Kenntnisse auch anderer historiographischen Traditionen, indem er feststellt, dass andere Autoren die Todesumstände des Basiliskos anders dargestellt hätten.

Dies führt zum Schluss, dass sich Theophanes' Bericht über die Herrschaft des Basiliskos zumindest auf zwei Vorlagen stützt – über weite Strecken verwendet er die Theodor-Lector-Epitome als seine Hauptquelle, wobei er die meisten Exzerpte fast wörtlich übernimmt. Nichts weist darauf hin, dass er hier die originelle Fassung der Kirchengeschichte des Theodor Lector hätte benutzen können, denn den Rest des Quellematerials schöpft

---

[8] Die meisten Quellen stimmen in diesem Punkt mit Malalas überein; vgl. z. B. Marc. Com 476 (ed. Mommsen 1894), Iord. Rom., 343 (ed. Mommsen 1882), Joh. Nik. 88,42 (ed. Charles 1916), Chron. Pasch. 477 (ed. Dindorf 1832). Vgl. dazu Kosiński 2010, p. 96 n. 106.

er aus der Weltchronik des Johannes Malalas, dessen Bericht er abkürzt und stellenweise deutlich modifiziert. Sein Umgang mit Malalas und Theodor-Lector-Epitome ist also sehr unterschiedlich: Wenn er eine kurze, auf das Wesentliche beschränkte Darstellung zur Verfügung hat, übernimmt er sie fast wörtlich, wenn er einen umfangreichen Bericht benutzt, gestaltet er ihn um, kürzt ab und modifiziert. Es ist sehr plausibel, dass er noch eine weitere Nebenquelle benutzte – darauf wäre die Information über Illus und Trocundes sowie über Kukusos zurückgegangen. Dabei ginge es um die *Chronike Epitome* des Eustathios von Epiphaneia.[9]

2. *Marcian*

Den Aufstand Marcians im Jahr 479 behandeln nur zwei Theodor-Lector-Exzerpte (Th. Lect. 419–20). Beide wurden von Theophanes berücksichtigt. In diesem Fall beschränkt sich der Chronist nicht darauf, den Text der Exzerpte zu wiederholen, sondern er versucht aufgrund mehrerer Vorlagen seine originelle Fassung des Geschehens zu schaffen. Bei der Darstellung der Ursachen des Aufstands scheint sich Theophanes auf die Theodor-Lector-Epitome zu stützen – sowohl Theophanes als auch der Epitomator sagen übereinstimmend, dass sich Marcian gegen Zeno erhoben habe, weil seine Frau Leontia, im Gegensatz zur Frau Zenos Ariadne, in Purpur geboren sei, als Leo I. schon Kaiser gewesen sei. Anders als im Bericht über Basiliskos gibt es hier nur allgemeine Ähnlichkeiten zwischen Theophanes und der Epitome, und sie erstrecken sich nicht mehr auf die Wortwahl. Dieser Anfangsteil geht jedoch über die Theodor-Lector-Epitome hinaus. In der Theodor Lector-Epitome 419 wird Marcian als Zenos Schwager bezeichnet, während bei Theophanes als Sohn des Anthemius, des ehemaligen Westkaisers, dessen Frau Leontia Tochter der Verina und Schwester der Ariadne war. Diese Einführung deckt sich teilweise mit dem Anfang der parallelen Passage bei Euagrios – stellenweise erstrecken sich die Ähnlichkeiten auf die Wort-

---

[9] Mehr dazu in der nächsten Sektion.

wahl.[10] Euagrios macht auch auf die Familienbande aufmerksam, durch die Marcian mit dem Kaiser Leo I. verbunden war, weil er erwähnt, dass Marcians Frau Leontia die jüngste Tochter des Leo I. gewesen sei. Obwohl Theophanes die Kirchengeschichte des Euagrios als seine Vorlage nicht verwendete, griff er jedoch an manchen Stellen auf Euagrios' Quelle, d. h. auf Eustathios von Epiphaneia, zurück.[11] Man darf also annehmen, dass der Anfangsteil des Theophanes-Eintrags zum Weltjahr 5971 zwei Quellen kombiniert: die Theodor-Lector-Epitome und Eustathios von Epiphaneia. Die nächste Sektion behandelt den Verlauf des Aufstands, wobei das Geschehen nur in vagen Umrissen dargestellt wird. Es sei zu einem heftigen Kampf zwischen Marcian und Zeno gekommen, und Zeno sei besiegt worden. Der geschlagene Kaiser und seine Anhänger seien im Kaiserpalast eingeschlossen bzw. belagert worden. Marcian sei von seinen Brüdern Romulus und Pompeius unterstützt worden. Diese kurze Darstellung deckt sich fast wörtlich mit dem Theodor-Lector-Exzerpt 420.[12] Anschließend erscheint aber ein kurzer Kommentar: ‚Marcian hätte beinahe die Kaisermacht ergriffen'. Eine solche Feststellung gibt es im Theodor-Lector-Exzerpt nicht. Die verpasste Gelegenheit steht im Fokus der daran anschließenden Ausführungen des Theophanes. Theophanes bemerkt nämlich, dass Marcian seinen Erfolg nicht ausgenutzt habe – anstatt seine Gegner endgültig zu schlagen, habe er den Angriff unterbrochen, um sich zu erholen. In der Nacht kam eine Wende – Illus habe die Anhänger des Marcian bestochen, und Marcian habe in der Kirche der Heiligen Apostel Zuflucht suchen müssen. Diese Details gehen nicht auf die Theodor-Lector-Epitome zurück, weil sie das Geschehen

---

[10] Teoph. AM 5971, p. 126 (ed. De Boor 1883): Μαρκιανός, ὁ παῖς Ἀνθεμίου τοῦ κατὰ τὴν Ῥώμην βασιλεύσαντος, Evagr. HE 3,26 (ed. Bidez – Parmentier 1898): Μαρκιανός, ὁ παῖς Ἀνθεμίου τοῦ Ῥώμης βασιλεύσαντος.

[11] Euagrios selbst behauptet, dass sein Bericht über die Rebellion Marcians auf Eustathios zurückgehe (Evagr., HE 3,26; ed. Bidez – Parmentier 1898). Zum Umgang des Theophanes mit Eustathios von Epiphaneia vgl. Brodka 2017, p. 166–80.

[12] Theoph. AM 5971, pp. 126–27 (ed. De Boor 1883): Μαρκιανός, ὁ παῖς Ἀνθεμίου τοῦ κατὰ τὴν Ῥώμην βασιλεύσαντος, ἀνὴρ δὲ Λεοντίας, τῆς Βερίνης μὲν θυγατρός, ἀδελφῆς δὲ Ἀρεάδνης τῆς βασιλίδος· Evagr. 3,26 (ed. Bidez – Parmentier 1898): Μαρκιανός, παῖς μὲν Ἀνθεμίου τοῦ Ῥώμης βασιλεύσαντος, κῆδος δὲπρὸς Λεοντατὸν βεβασιλευκότα πρότερον ἐσχηκώς.

anders darstellt, indem sie vermerkt, dass Marcian und seine Brüder im Zeuxippos-Bad festgenommen worden seien. Die deutlichen Parallelen zu den Ausführungen des Theophanes lassen sich hingegen bei Euagrios erkennen. Euagrios behandelt das Thema der günstigen Gelegenheit (*kairos*), die von Marcian nicht ausgenutzt wurde (vgl. Euagr. HE 3,26). Er stellt fest ‚Hätte er die günstige Gelegenheit nicht vorübergehen lassen, und hätte er die Tat nicht auf den nächsten Morgen verschoben, hätte er sich der Herrschaft bemächtigt' (Übersetz. Hübner 2007). Euagrios schweigt aber über Illus und sagt nicht, was Marcian nach der Einstellung des Kampfes machte. Es ist somit klar, dass Euagrios nicht die Quelle des Theophanes ist. Theophanes stimmt aber mit Euagrios darin überein, dass Marcian von seinen Anhängern verraten und allein gelassen wurde und in die Kirche der Heiligen Apostel floh. Aller Wahrscheinlichkeit nach gehen Theophanes und Euagrios auf eine gemeinsame Vorlage, d. h. auf Eustathios, zurück. Zum Schluss wechselt Theophanes erneut seine Quelle und greift wieder auf die Theodor-Lector-Epitome zurück und berichtet, dass Marcian von Akakios zum Priester geweiht und vom Kaiser zur Verbannung in der Festung Papyrios verurteilt worden sei.[13] Er lässt hingegen die Fakten aus, die er aus Eustathios hätte gewinnen können. Bei Eustahios/Euagrios wurde Marcian zuerst ins Exil nach Caesarea in Kappadokien verbannt und nachdem er geflohen war, ließ ihn Zeno nach Tarsus bringen und zum Priester weihen. Theophanes schließt seine Darstellung mit der Nachricht über die Verhaftung des Pompeios und des Romulus im Zeuxippos-Bad sowie über ihre Flucht nach Westen ab. Sie dürfte als eine Überarbeitung des Theodor-Lector-Exzerpts interpretiert werden, denn im Zeuxippos-Bad wurden laut Theodor Lector nicht nur Romulus und Pompeios, sondern auch Marcian gefangen genommen. Es stellt sich aber die Frage danach, woher Theophanes weiß, dass Illus es war, der die Brüder verhaftete. Es ist plausibel, dass der Chronist diese Information

---

[13] Th. Lect. 420 (ed. Hansen 1995): Μαρκιανὸν χειροτονηθῆναι ὑπὸ Ἀκακίου πρεσβύτερον παρασκεύασαν καὶ εἰς τὸ Παπυρίου καστελλίον ἐξέπεμψαν, Theoph. AM 5971, p. 127 (ed. De Boor 1883): καὶ ὑπὸ Ἀκακίου χειροτονηθῆναι πρεσβύτερον κατὰ κέλευσιν Ζήνωνος· καὶ ἐξορίζεται εἰς τὸ Παπυρίου καστελλίν εἰς Καππαδοκίαν.

bei Eustathios fand, denn die Theodor-Lector-Epitome schweigt über die Teilnahme des Illus an der Bekämpfung des Aufstands.

Insgesamt darf man feststellen, dass der Aufstand Marcians in der Chronik des Theophanes aufgrund zwei Hauptquellen dargestellt wird.[14] Diesmal ändert Theophanes seine Arbeitsmethode und gibt sich nicht mit der bloßen Wiedergabe des Quellenmaterials zufrieden. Stattdessen verfährt er selektiv, wählt das Faktenmaterial aus beiden Traditionen aus und stellt durch entsprechende Auswahl und Anordnung des Stoffes neue Verbindungslinien und sein eigenes Bild des Hergangs des Geschehens her. In diesem Fall überlagern sich beide Quellen – deutlich ist das Bestreben, alles Erreichbare wiederzugeben: Theophanes lässt relativ wenig aus, er ist aber weit davon entfernt, beide Vorlagen direkt zu übernehmen, sondern er gestaltet sie stark um.

3. *Illus und Leontios*

Ein weiterer Aufstand, der sowohl von Theodor Lector als auch von Theophanes berücksichtigt wurde, ist die Rebellion des Illus und des Leontios. Die Theodor-Lector-Epitome widmet diesem Thema zwei Exzerpte: 437 und 438. Einen Parallelbericht, der ebenfalls auf die Kirchengeschichte des Theodor Lector zurückgeht, bietet der Chronist Victor von Tunnuna, der diese Geschehnisse in zwei Einträgen erwähnt. Weil ich dieses Thema an anderer Stelle ausführlich behandelt habe, beschränke ich hier auf das Wichtigste.[15] Theophanes bietet insgesamt eine ausführliche Darstellung des Konflikts des Zeno mit Illus und der anschließenden Usurpation des Leontios. Die Informationen darüber sind verteilt auf sieben Einträge (Theoph. AM 5972, 5973, 5974, 5975, 5976, 5977 und 5980). Betrachtet man die gesamte umfangreiche Darstellung der Rebellion bei Theophanes, so kommt man zum Schluss, dass der Chronist hier größtenteils auf Malalas beruht. Er ergänzt das aus Malalas gewonnene Material um einige Informationen aus dem Werk des Eustathios. Erst bei der Darstellung des Todes von Illus und Leontios wechselt er wieder seine Vorlage

---

[14] Vgl. dazu auch Greatrex 2015, p. 138.
[15] Brodka 2017, pp. 169–77.

und greift auf die Theodor-Lector-Epitome zurück, die er um Details aus Malalas ergänzt.[16] Es ist auch plausibel, wie Mango und Scott vermuten,[17] dass die kurze Notiz ‚in Antiochia rebellierte Illus offen (gegen Zeno)' (Theoph. AM 5972 pp. 127–28) auf die Theodor-Lector-Epitome 437 zurückgeht. Dies lässt sich aber mit Sicherheit nicht feststellen, weil das Thema ‚einer offenen Rebellion' in mehreren historiographischen Traditionen greifbar ist, wie Johannes von Antiochia dies belegt (Ioh. Ant. fr 306 Roberto). Abgesehen von dieser Notiz, lässt Theophanes das Exzerpt 437 außer Acht. Auf Theodor Lector geht erst die Information über die Umstände des Todes des Illus und des Leontios zurück (Theoph. AM 5980 p. 132): Nach der vierjährigen Belagerung seien sie durch die List des Schwagers des Trocundes besiegt worden. Diese Information geht in erster Linie auf die Theodor-Lector-Epitome zurück, die um einige Details aus der Chronik des Malalas ergänzt wird.[18] Die Theodor-Lector-Epitome sagt nur kurz, dass Illus und Trocundes enthauptet worden seien, während Malalas weitaus mehr über ihre Hinrichtung weiß und angibt, dass die Häupter der hingerichteten Rebellen zu Kaiser Zeno geschickt worden seien. Als dieser beim Pferderennen zugeschaut habe, habe man sie auf Spießen hereingetragen. Diese Details übernimmt Theophanes von Malalas. Es bleibt dahingestellt, woher Theophanes von den Umständen des Todes der Verina sowie von der Hinrichtung des Trocundes durch Johannes den Skythen weiß (Theoph. AM 5975, p. 129; AM 5976, p. 130). In Frage kämen meines Erachtens entweder Ur-Malalas oder Eustathios von Epiphaneia.

4. *Vitalian*

Besonders kontrovers ist die Frage danach, in welchem Maß Theophanes auf die Theodor-Lector-Epitome für die Darstellung der Rebellion Vitalians gegen Anastasios in den Jahren 513–15

---

[16] Mango – Scott 1997, p. 196.

[17] Mango – Scott 1997, p. 196.

[18] Theoph. AM 5980 p. 132 (ed. De Boor 1883) ~ Theod. Lect. 438 (ed. Hansen 1995); Malal. 15, 14 p. 315,61–66; p. 315,*46–*53 (ed. Thurn 2000); *Excerpta de insidiis* pp. 166, 13–28 (De Boor 1905).

zurückgreift.[19] In der erhaltenen Auffassung der Epitome wird kein Exzerpt diesem Thema gewidmet. Theophanes behandelt es in drei Einträgen – Theoph. AM 6005, 6006, 6007. Es ist sicher, dass Theodor Lector in seiner Kirchengeschichte den Aufstand Vitalians darstellte, wobei er zwischen dem Aufstand und der Religionspolitik des Kaisers eine enge Verbindung herzustellen suchte. Die Schrift *Über die Schismen* überliefert nämlich, sich auf Theodor Lector berufend, Vitalian habe sich gegen Anastasios wegen der Verfolgung der Orthodoxen durch den Kaiser erhoben. Darüber hinaus habe er die Einberufung des Konzils in Herakleia erzwungen, an dem 200 Bischöfe teilgenommen hätten (De schism. 8). Aller Wahrscheinlichkeit nach geht auch Victor von Tunnuna an den relevanten Stellen auf Theodor Lector zurück, so dass seine Chronik den Anhaltspunkt für die Untersuchung der Abhängigkeit des Theophanes von der Theodor-Lector-Epitome darstellen kann.

Schon auf den ersten Blick sind die Ähnlichkeiten zwischen dem Eintrag des Victor von Tunnuna zum Jahr 510 und dem Anfangsteil des Berichtes des Theophanes erkennbar. Victor von Tunnuna sagt, dass sich der Komes Vitalian, Sohn des Patriciolus, gegen Anastasios erhoben habe, weil der Kaiser die katholische Religion unterdrückt, die Anordnungen des Konzils von Chalcedon bekämpft, die orthodoxen Bischöfe verbannt und durch die Häretiker ersetzt habe (Vict.Tunn. 91). Theophanes deutet die Motive Vitalians auf ähnliche Weise: Vitalian, Sohn des Patriciolus, der Föderatenkomes habe sich empört, weil die Orthodoxen aus Mösien, Skythien und anderen Provinzen ihn zum Vorgehen gegen den gottlosen Anastasios aufgerufen hätten (Theoph. AM 6005, p. 157).[20] Beide Autoren stellen aber die Ereignisse aus einer anderen Perspektive dar. Bei Victor von Tunnuna handelt Vitalian aus eigener Initiative heraus, während er bei Theophanes die Impulse zum Handeln von außen bekommt. Der folgende Teil des Berichtes des Theophanes findet keine Parallele bei Victor: Vitalian habe viele Feinde vernichtet und viel Geld gewonnen. Erst der anschließende Satz hat seine Parallele bei Victor von

---

[19] Zum Aufstand Vitalians Meier 2009, pp. 295–310, Haarer 2006, p. 164–81. Zu Vitalian vgl. auch jüngst Laniado 2015, pp. 349–70.

[20] Zu den Motiven Vitalians Meier 2009, p. 309–10.

Tunnuna: Es sei zu einer Schlacht gekommen, in der 65 000 Soldaten des Kaisers von Vitalian vernichtet worden seien, und Hypatios, der Neffe des Anastasios, in die Gefangenschaft geraten sei. Victor von Tunnuna bietet dieselbe Zahl der Toten und spricht ebenfalls von der Gefangennahme des Hypatios. Er weiß aber auch darüber zu berichten, wie Vitalian ihn behandelte: Hypatios sollte misshandelt und im eisernen Käfig gehalten werden. Diese Details kennt Theophanes nicht mehr (Vict. Tunn. 92).

Zwischen Theoph. AM 6005 und Vict. Tunn. 91–92 gibt es deutliche Ähnlichkeiten, die vermuten lassen, dass beide Berichte zumindest teilweise auf dieselbe Quellentradition zurückgehen. Für eine solche Vermutung spricht vor allem die Figur von 65 000 Toten.[21] Diese gemeinsame Tradition muss den Grund für den Aufstand Vitalians in der Unzufriedenheit mit der Religionspolitik des Anastasios gesehen haben. Es stellt sich hier die zentrale Frage danach, in welchem Maß Theophanes' Bericht auf eine vollständigere Version der Theodor-Lector-Epitome zurückgehen könnte. Wie schon mehrmals angedeutet, benutzt Theophanes für die innenpolitischen Unruhen im 5. Jahrhundert nicht nur die Theodor-Lector-Epitome, sondern ergänzt sie häufig um die Details aus Malalas oder Eustathios. Für den Aufstand Vitalians kommt allerdings Eustathios nicht mehr in Frage, da sein Werk bis ins diese Zeit nicht reichte. Malalas liefert hingegen eine umfangreiche Darstellung der Revolte. Auch er verweist auf die religionspolitischen Faktoren, die Vitalian zur Tat motivierten: ‚als Grund wies er (sc. Vitalian) die verbannten Bischöfe vor' (Malal. 16,16, p. 329, Übersetz. Thurn/Meier 2009). Bei der Darstellung der ersten Kämpfe schweigt er hingegen über die verwandtschaftlichen Beziehungen des Hypatios.[22] Malalas gibt

---

[21] Andere historiografische Erzählstränge bieten ähnliche Zahlen – Johannes von Antiochia spricht in diesem Kontext über 60 000 Toten. Interessanterweise erscheint auch bei ihm der eiserne Käfig. Es gibt aber starke Abweichungen. Johannes von Antiochia behauptet, dass Anastasios' Neffe in Gefangenschaft geraten sei. Er sei aber gut behandelt worden. Ein gewisser Julian war es hingegen, der im Käfig gehalten wurde (Ioh.Ant. fr. 242 Roberto). Die Misshandlung des Hypatios bezeugen auch Jord. Rom. 358 (ed. Mommsen 1882), Ps.Zach. 7,13 (ed. Greatrex 2011).

[22] Zu Hypatios vgl. Greatrex 1996.

sich mit der Notiz zufrieden, Hypatios sei von Vitalian gefangen genommen und aus der Gefangenschaft losgekauft worden. Selbst wenn Ur-Malalas, der Theophanes zur Verfügung stand, dies ausführlicher hätte darstellen können, deutet nichts darauf hin, dass Theophanes auf ihn hier zurückgegriffen hätte.

So ging Hansen davon aus, dass der Vitalian-Passus aus Theoph. AM 6005 auf eine vollständigere Theodor-Lector-Epitome zurückgehe, und setzte ihn in seine Ausgabe als ein Theodor-Lector-Exzerpt.[23] Obwohl ich mit Hansen darin übereinstimme, dass Theophanes über die vollständigere Version der Epitome habe verfügen können, halte ich seine Vorgehensweise für problematisch. Es gibt kein überzeugendes Argument für die These, dass Theophanes' Bericht wirklich eine originaltreue Wiedergabe des verlorenen Theodor-Lector-Exzerpts darstellt, selbst wenn eine solche Meinung für manche andere Stellen gilt. Obwohl ich der Meinung bin, dass Theophanes im Eintrag zum Weltjahr 6005 für den Aufstand Vitalians die Theodor-Lector-Epitome als seine Hauptquelle benutzte, schließe ich nicht aus, dass er hier noch eine Nebenquelle verwenden konnte – es ginge hier vor allem um die Nachricht über die Rolle der Orthodoxen aus Thrakien und Mösien – sie könnte ihren Ursprung bei Malalas haben und als eine Überarbeitung des Malalas gedeutet werden.

Zum zweiten Mal erscheint Vitalian bei Theophanes noch in demselben Eintrag zum Weltjahr 6005. Der Chronist erwähnt ihn im Zusammenhang mit dem sog. *Staurotheis*-Aufstand in Konstantinopel, der durch das Streben des Anastasios, einen Zusatz im Trishagion hinzufügen, verursacht wurde. Während dieser Unruhen sollte die Stadtbevölkerung einen neuen Kaiser fordern.[24] Die Aufständischen beschimpften Anastasios und riefen Vitalian zum Kaiser aus. Hansen verweist auf die deutlichen Parallelen dazu bei Victor von Tunnuna (Vict.Tun. 94) und hielt diese Passage für eine direkte Entlehnung aus der Theodor-Lector-Epitome. So findet sie ihren Platz in seiner Ausgabe als das Exzerpt 508. Die Ähnlichkeiten zwischen Victor und Theophanes erstrecken sich meines Erachtens eher auf die Allgemeinheiten und nicht auf die konkreten Details, die für die

---

[23] Bei Hansen steht diese Passage als Theodor-Lector-Exzerpt 503.
[24] Dazu Meier 2009, p. 275–76.

Abhängigkeit beider Texte von derselben Vorlage eindeutig sprechen könnten. Die Anfangsteile beider Berichte, die den Ausbruch des Aufstands in Konstantinopel thematisieren, weisen wirklich deutliche Parallelen auf. Victor von Tunnuna sagt, dass Marinus und der Stadtpräfekt Platon auf Befehl des Anastasios den Zusatz zum Trishagion in der Kirche des heiligen Theodor verkündet hätten. Theophanes spricht in diesem Zusammenhang ebenfalls über die Kirche des heiligen Theodor. Er bietet hingegen keine Namen, sondern spricht nur allgemein über die Magistrate. Bei der Darstellung der anschließenden Unruhen und Brandstiftungen verweist Victor von Tunnuna auf die Faktionen der Blauen und Grünen als Unruhestifter. Er weiß aber nichts über die Kaiserproklamation oder über die Flucht des Anastasios aus Konstantinopel. Darüber berichten Marcellinus Comes (Marc. Com. 512,4) und Johannes Malalas (Malal. 16,19, p. 334) – sie überliefern aber übereinstimmend, dass das Pöbel Areobindos zum Kaiser ausrief. So stellt sich die Frage danach, woher Theophanes über die Kaiserproklamation Vitalians weiß? Liegt dieser Überlieferung letztlich mittels der Epitome der Bericht des Theodor Lector zugrunde, wie die Forschung vermutet?[25] Diese Frage ist leider eindeutig nicht zu beantworten. Ich möchte aber auf den Umstand verweisen, die gegen eine solche Annahme sprechen könnte. Der *Staurotheis*-Aufstand brach im November 512 aus, während es zum Aufstand des Vitalian erst im Jahr 513 kam. Theophanes scheint sich über die relative Chronologie der Ereignisse nicht klar zu werden, denn ihm zufolge kam es zuerst zur Rebellion Vitalians und erst danach zum *Staurotheis*-Aufstand. Es gibt kein sicheres Indiz, dass Theodor Lector über die Forderung der Aufständischen nach einem neuen Kaiser berichtet hatte. Vorstellbar ist also, dass Theophanes hier die Theodor-Lector-Epitome um die Zusätze aus einer anderen Quelle ergänzte und das Ganze neu interpretierte. Bei dieser Nebenquelle ginge es um Malalas. Malalas stellt ebenfalls zuerst die Rebellion Vitalians und erst danach den *Staurotheis*-Aufstand dar. Er bietet also keine klare und korrekte Chronologie dieser Ereignisse. Wenn Theophanes angenommen hätte, dass es zum *Staurotheis*-Auf-

---

[25] Meier 2009, p. 275.

stand erst nach dem Ausbruch der Rebellion Vitalians gekommen wäre (wie bei Malalas), hätte er seine Vorlage korrigieren und Areobindos durch Vitalian ersetzen können.[26] Es ginge um einen ähnlichen Umgang mit den Quellen wie im Fall der Usurpation des Marcian, wo er einige historiographische Traditionen miteinander kombinierte.

Theophanes setzt seinen Bericht über den Aufstand Vitalians im Eintrag zum Weltjahr 6006. Hier wird sowohl die erste als auch die zweite Kampagne Vitalians gegen Anastasios thematisiert. Der Anfangsteil steht recht nah an Malalas 16,16, indem er über die Besetzung Thrakiens, Skythiens und Mösiens durch Vitalian sowie über die Einnahme von Odessa und Anchialos berichtet.[27] Ähnlich wie Malalas sagt auch Theophanes, dass Vitalian über eine Menge von den Hunnen und Bulgaren verfügte.[28] Die Kämpfe gegen Hypatios lässt er nun aus, weil er diese schon im vorangehenden Eintrag darstellte. Das Bild des Aufstands Vitalians ist also ziemlich konfus. Erwähnt wird nur der Sieg über den *magister militum* Kyrillos: deutlich ist somit das Streben des Theophanes danach, beide Quellen – d. h. Malalas und die Theodor-Lector-Epitome – in Einklang zu bringen.[29] Es bleibt dahingestellt, auf welche Vorlage die Nachricht über den Freikauf des Hypatios durch seinen Vater zurückgeht – Theophanes verschiebt ihn auf das zweite Jahr der Rebellion und an diesem Punkt weicht deutlich von Malalas ab, laut dessen Hypatios bald nach seiner Niederlage befreit wurde. Insgesamt aber stehen die religionspolitischen Aspekte im Fokus des Berichtes des Theophanes. Diese hat Malalas, sofern dies aus der erhaltenen Auffassung seiner Chronik erkennbar ist, nicht mehr berücksichtigt. Es ist somit durchaus plausibel, dass Theophanes nun auf die Theodor-Lector-Epitome wieder zurückgreift, um den religiösen Eifer Vitalians und seinen Einsatz für Chalcedon darzustellen. Dass dies von Theodor Lector thematisiert worden war, belegen der Verfasser der Schrift *Über die Schismen* (De schism. 8), der sich namentlich auf Theodor beruft, und Victor von Tunnuna (Vict.

[26] Mango – Scott 1997, 242 n. 17, Hansen 1995, 145 App.
[27] Mango – Scott 1997, p. 243.
[28] Malalas spricht über die hunnischen Bulgaren.
[29] Mango – Scott 1997, p. 243–44.

Tun. 95), der aller Wahrscheinlichkeit nach auf die *Kirchenge-schichte* des Theodor Lector zurückgeht. Ähnlich wie Theophanes, vermerkt Victor von Tunnuna für das Jahr 514, dass der Kaiser Anastasios Vitalian um Frieden gebeten habe, als sich dieser in Sosthenion aufgehalten habe. Vitalian habe die Rückführung der verbannten Bischöfe und die Einberufung eines allgemeinen Konzils zur Wiederherstellung der Kircheneinheit mit Rom gefordert. Theophanes, dessen Darstellung umfangreicher ist als diejenige des Victor, berichtet dann über die Zustimmung des Anastasios und über die Synode in Herakleia, die eigentlich nicht stattgefunden hat.[30]

Ich stimme mit Mango und Scott darin überein, dass der gesamte Theophanes-Eintrag zum Weltjahr 6006, der die ersten zwei Kampagnen Vitalians gegen Anastasios sowie die Geschichte des Konzils von Herakleia thematisiert, die Informationen aus Malalas und der Theodor-Lector-Epitome zusammenstellt. Die exakte Absonderung des Quellenmaterials scheint hier möglich zu sein. Auf Malalas geht der Anfangsteil des Eintrags zurück, wobei seine umfangreiche Darstellung auf wenige Zeilen zusammengedrängt wird. Der Hauptteil geht hingegen auf die Theodor-Lector-Epitome zurück. Es bleibt aber unklar, wie Theophanes hier mit den Exzerpten umging. Vieles deutet darauf hin, dass er diese direkt übernahm, ohne größere sachliche Änderungen zu machen. Erst der Schlussteil, der scharfe Kritik an Anastasios übt und ihn als Eidbrecher, Manichäer und Lügner brandmarkt, könnte ein stark überarbeitetes Quellenmaterial mit den Zusätzen, die auf Theophanes selbst zurückgehen, enthalten.

Es fällt auf, dass Theophanes die endgültige Niederlage Vitalians in einer Seeschlacht auslässt, obwohl er wissen musste, wie die Usurpation endete, da er ja über den Bericht des Malalas verfügte. Stattdessen vermerkt er für das nächste Jahr, dass Vitalian erneut Anastasios besiegt und demütigt habe, indem er die gefangenen kaiserlichen Soldaten für einen *follis* verkauft habe (Theoph. AM 6007 p. 161). Die Szene des Verkaufs der Soldaten hätte sich ursprünglich auf eine Anfangsphase der Rebellion beziehen können und Theophanes hätte sie absichtlich auf die spätere Periode

---

[30] Dazu Meier 2009, p. 300–11.

verschoben, um die Bestrafung des häretischen und meineidigen Kaisers von dem frommen Vitalian demonstrieren zu können. Damit endet die Geschichte Vitalians in der Chronik des Theophanes. Im Ganzen gesehen ist seine Darstellung des Aufstand sehr konfus und entstellt den Hergang des Geschehens. Dies muss als eine absichtliche Vorgehensweise des Chronisten betrachtet werden, der auf diese Weise den Sieg des häretischen Kaisers über den Vorkämpfer der Orthodoxie auslassen wollte.

Es ist klar, dass Theophanes für die Rebellion Vitalians über weite Strecken die Theodor-Lector-Epitome verwendete, die er stellenweise um das Material aus Malalas ergänzte. Es ist auch klar, dass die Fassung der Epitome, die ihm zur Verfügung stand, umfangreicher war als diejenige, die heute erhalten ist. Theophanes geht hier mit der Epitome ähnlich wie im Fall des Basiliskos um. In einigen Fällen, wie dies Hansen richtig erkannt hatte, beschränkt sich er nur darauf, wenig oder gar nicht bearbeitete Exzerpte direkt zu übernehmen. Trotzdem gilt diese Methode nicht für jede Passage, die sich auf Vitalian bezieht. Aller Wahrscheinlichkeit nach darf man die Exzerpte 509–10 für eine relativ treue Wiedergabe des Textes der Epitome halten. Die Exzerpte 503 und 511 stützen sich zumindest zum Teil auf die Epitome, aber man muss hier mit starken Überarbeitungen und Zusätzen aus anderen Quellen rechnen. Besonders fraglich ist das Exzerpt 508, das den *Staurotheis*-Aufstand thematisiert, denn hier möglich ist, dass das aus der Theodor-Lector-Epitome gewonnene Material aufgrund der durch Malalas dargestellten Reihenfolge des Geschehens neu interpretiert und verändert wurde.

Zusammenfassend darf man feststellen, dass Theophanes auf unterschiedliche Weise mit der Theodor-Lector-Epitome umging. Er konnte die einzelnen Exzerpte direkt übernehmen, leicht modifizieren, als er sie um zusätzliches Material erweiterte oder die Akzente verschob, aber auch mit anderen Quellen in Einklang bringen und folglich sehr stark verändern und überarbeiten. Die Meinung, dass er nicht nur auf die Epitome, sondern auch auf die originelle Kirchengeschichte des Theodor Lector zurückgegriffen habe,[31] überzeugt mich nicht. Die Unterschiede lassen

---

[31] So Pouderon 2015.

sich meines Erachtens durch die Benutzung anderer Quellen wie etwa Malalas erklären. Deswegen, obwohl Theophanes in vielen Fällen ein glaubwürdiger Textzeuge der Epitome ist, finde ich die Methode Hanses für allzu optimistisch – die aus Theophanes gewonnenen Theodor-Lector-Exzerpte sollen weniger als sichere Auszüge, sondern vielmehr als *dubia* markiert werden.

Bibliographie

Quellen

Bidez – Parmentier 1898 = *The Ecclesiastical History of Evagrius with the scholia*, ed. Joseph Bidez – Léon Parmentier, London.

Charles 1916 = *The Chronicle of John, Bishop of Nikiu*, transl. from Zoltenberg's Ethiopic Text by Robert Henry Charles, Oxford.

De Boor 1883 = *Theophanis Chronographia*, recensuit Carolus de Boor, vol. 1–2, Lipsiae.

De Boor 1905 = *Excerpta de insidiis*, ed. Carolus de Boor, Berolini.

Dindorf 1832 = *Chronicon paschale*: *Chronicon paschale ad exemplar Vaticanum*, recensuit Ludivicus Dindorfius, vol. I, Bonnae.

Greatrex 2011 = *The Chronicle of Pseudo-Zachariah Rhetor. Church and War in Late Antiquity*, ed. by Geoffrey Greatrex, translated from Syriac and Arabic sources by Robert R. Phenix – Bernadette Horn with introductory material by Sebastian Brock – Witold Witakowski, Liverpool.

Hansen 1995 = Theodoros Anagnostes, *Kirchengeschichte*, hrsg. von Günther Christian Hansen, Zweite, durchgesehene Auflage, Berlin.

Mango – Scott 1997 = Cyril Mango – Roger Scott, *The Chronicle of Theophanes Confessor. Byzantine and Near East History AD 284–813*, Oxford.

Mommsen 1882 = *Iordanis Romana et Getica*, recensuit Theodor Mommsen, MGH AA V 1, Berolini 1882.

Mommsen 1894 = *Marcellinus Comes, Chronicon*, ed. Theodore Mommsen, MGH XI, Berlin.

Roberto 2005 = *Ioannis Antiocheni Fragmenta ex Historia Chronica*, introduzione, edizione critica e traduzione a cura di Umberto Roberto, Berlin – New York.

Thurn 2000 = John Malalas, *Chronographia*: *Ioannis Malalae Chronographia*, recensuit Hans Thurn, Berlin.

Literatur

Brodka 2017 = Dariusz Brodka, ‚Eustathios von Epiphaneia und Johannes Malalas‘, in *Die Weltchronik des Johannes Malalas. Quellenfragen*, hrsg. von Laura Carrara – Mischa Meier – Christine Radtki-Jansen, Malalas-Studien 2, Stuttgart, pp. 155–84.

Greatrex 1996 = Geoffrey Greatrex, ‚Flavius Hypatius, quem vidit validum Parthus sensitque timendum. An Investigation of his Career‘, *Byzantion* 66, pp. 120–42.

Greatrex 2015 = Geoffrey Greatrex, ‚Théodore le Lecteur et son épitomateur anonyme du VIIᵉ s.‘, in *L'historiographie tardo-antique et la transmission des savoirs*, hrsg. von Philipe Blaudeau – Peter Van Nuffelen, Millennium-Studien 55, Berlin – Boston, pp. 121–42.

Haarer 2006 = Fiona K. Haarer, *Anastasius I. Politics in the Late Roman World*, Cambridge.

Hansen 1971 = Günther Christian Hansen, Theodoros Anagnostes. *Kirchegeschichte*, Berlin.

Kosiński 2010 = Rafał Kosiński, *The Emperor Zeno. Religion and Politics*, Cracow.

Laniado 2015 = Avshalom Laniado, ‚Jean d'Antiochie et les débuts de la révolte de Vitalien‘, in *L'historiographie tardo-antique et la transmission des savoirs*, hrsg. von Philippe Blaudeau – Peter Van Nuffelen, Millennium-Studien 55, Berlin, pp. 349–70.

Mango – Scott 1997 = Cyril Mango – Roger Scott, The Chronicle of Theophanes Confessor. Byzantine and Near East History AD 284–813, Oxford.

Meier 2009 = Mischa Maier, *Anastasios I. Die Entstehung des Byzantinischen Reiches*, Stuttgart.

Pouderon 2015 = Bernard Pouderon, ‚Théophane, témoin de l'Épitomè d'Histoires Ecclésiastiques, de Théodore le Lecteur ou de Jean Diacrinoménos?‘, in *Studies in Theophanes*, hrsg. von Marek Jankowiak – Federico Montinaro, Travaux et Mémoires 19, Paris, pp. 279–314.

Abstract

The aim of the article is to discuss the relationship between the epitome of the *Church History* of Theodore Lector and the *Chronicle* of Theophanes and the way in which Theophanes modified and manipulated material gained from his sources. The article tries to answer the question, if Theophanes' *Chronicle* may be used for the recovery of some additional excerpts of the epitome of Theodore Lector as assumed by G. Hansen. From the nature of the important entries in the chronicle of Theophanes concerning the revolts against the emperors Zeno and Anastasius one can conclude that though Theophanes obviously derived from the *Epitome* of Theodore Lector, he often drew on an additional source, added his own comments and thus changed the meaning of the original sources.

THEODORE LECTOR
AND HIS EPOCH

GEOFFREY GREATREX

THEODORE LECTOR AND THE ARIANS OF CONSTANTINOPLE

In most treatments of Arianism, including the recent edited volume by Berndt and Steinacher, little attention is devoted to the eastern empire after the close of the fourth century. Instead, scholars generally shift their focus to the barbarian peoples who took over the western empire, notably the Vandals and the Goths.[1] It is our contention, however, that Arianism remained a potent force within the eastern empire up to the reign of Justinian and that Theodore Lector is an important witness to this phenomenon. In order to make our case, we shall consider the scraps of evidence at our disposal concerning the Arian community in the East – essentially, at Constantinople – among which the brief notices in the epitome of Theodore's work are crucial. As will emerge, even in the 520s, at the time Theodore was writing, the fate of the Arians of the East was far from sealed: not only were *foederati* serving in the Roman empire explicitly allowed to maintain their adherence to Arianism but the Ostrogothic king

---

[1] Berndt and Steinacher 2014, e.g. in Mathisen's contribution, p. 147. We shall use the term Arianism, as they do, for the sake of convenience, although it is not entirely satisfactory and masks various subdivisions, on which see several of the contributions of this volume, e.g. Parvis 2014, pp. 51–3, Mathisen 2014, pp. 146, cf. Wiles 1996, p. 4 and Williams 1992, pp. 101–02 (rejecting the term). Since we are not concerned with the theological aspects of 'Arianism', the issue can be left to one side. Caution must furthermore be exercised in considering 'the Arians' as if they were a simple, readily identifiable group or party: see the excellent analysis of Williams 2017, esp. pp. 6–7, 55–7, 287–311. I am grateful to Luise Frenkel, Robin Whelan and Philippe Blaudeau for comments on earlier drafts.

Studies in Theodore Anagnostes, ed. by Rafał KOSIŃSKI & Adrian SZOPA, STTA 19 (Turnhout 2021), pp. 207–231
© BREPOLS ❧ PUBLISHERS   DOI 10.1484/M.STTA-EB.5.127982

Theoderic was also trying to bring pressure on Justin to prevent conversions from Arianism to orthodoxy.[2]

1. *From Theodosius I to Theodosius II (379–450)*

There is no need to rehearse in detail the retreat of Arianism in the wake of the accession of Theodosius I and the Council of Constantinople of 381. A series of laws preserved in the *Codex Theodosianus* imposed tough restrictions on heretics of various stripes, including several versions of Arianism. The precise situation of Arians within the empire remains unclear in the face of this legislation. While some scholars, such as Ralph Mathisen, argue that they enjoyed toleration from 386 – the date of a law promulgated by Valentinian II to allow their assembly, which was incorporated into the Theodosian code – the reality seems more complex.[3] Already in 380 the Arian bishop of Constantinople was obliged to relinquish all the churches in the city centre and to content himself with one beyond the Constantinian walls; this is reported by Socrates and transmitted also in the *HT* of Theodore.[4]

There can be little doubt that an ever increasing proportion of the Arians resident in the eastern empire were of Germanic origin. It is not surprising therefore that the *magister militum* Gainas, among whose forces were many Goths, asked Arcadius for a church to be put at their disposal. The request was granted with the support of the bishop John Chrysostom; initially the church was orthodox, although it is possible that it subsequently became Arian before Gainas' forces were massacred in 400.[5]

---

[2] For Theodore's date of composition see Nautin 1994, p. 240, Treadgold 2007, p. 170, Goltz 2008, p. 56. Conant 2015, p. 169, briefly notes the continuing strength of Arianism in the East over the fifth century.

[3] Mathisen 2014, pp. 147–48, argues that because this law, *Cod. Theod.* XVI.1.4 (386) (ed. Mommsen 2005), is preserved in the code, it must still have been valid; in fact, however, it will have been superseded by subsequent legislation, as Simon Corcoran points out to us. Brennecke 2014, pp. 117–18, in the same volume as Mathisen, insists that Arianism remained 'strictly illegal' within the empire.

[4] Socr. *HE* V.7 (ed. Hansen 1995b), cf. Th. Lect. *HT* § 229 (ed. Hansen 1995a) and Soz. *HE* VII.5.5–7 (ed. Bidez – Hansen 1995). See Greatrex 2001, p. 73, for more details, esp. n. 8.

[5] Socr. *HE* VI.5.8 (ed. Hansen 1995b), Soz. *HE* VIII.4 (ed. Bidez – Hansen 1995) (in section 9, according to this account, John specifically reminded Arca-

Notwithstanding the expulsion of the Goths, Arians in the capital remained vocal – literally. According to Socrates and Sozomen, they used to assemble in the small hours in public porticoes, chant psalms, then gather in their meeting places. John Chrysostom was sufficiently concerned by this proselytising that he organised rival processions, which led to confrontations and finally a ruling by the emperor to prevent such gatherings of the Arians. Evidently, more than twenty years after the death of the Arian Emperor Valens, a sizeable community remained in Constantinople.[6]

If we move on a further twenty years or so, then we may find evidence again of the influence of Arians in Constantinople. Socrates reports that Nestorius, within days of having become bishop of the city, attempted to consolidate his position by destroying a secret chapel of the Arians – which evidently was not all that secret. When, however, the Arians realised what was going on, they set fire to their own church and caused a general conflagration; this in turn, according to Socrates, damaged the bishop's position.[7] Nestorius himself complained about the in-

---

dius of Theodosius' law against heretics assembling within the walls of the city), Thdrt. *HE* V.33 (Parmentier – Hansen 1998). See Liebeschuetz 1990, pp. 169–70, 190, Cameron and Long 1996, pp. 98, 327, Greatrex 2001, p. 74 with n. 10, Mathisen 2014, p. 152. Cf. now Stanfill 2015, ch.3, esp. pp. 149–55, cf. p. 167, arguing that John's church was probably orthodox; he dates John Chrysostom's Gothic parish to before Gainas' request and emphasises that all Goths were not necessarily Arians.

[6] Socr. *HE* VI.8 (ed. Hansen 1995b), Soz. *HE* VIII.8 (ed. Bidez – Hansen 1995), cf. Stanfill 2015, pp. 198–203. The episode seems to have taken place *c.* 401, cf. *PLRE* II, Brison. As Anglviel de la Baumelle and Sabbah note, Soz. *HE* VIII.1.6 (ed. Bidez – Hansen 1995, *SC* 516, 229 n. 4) exaggerates the impact of internal divisions among the Arians of CP in 395. Cf. Socr. *HE* V.23 (ed. Hansen 1995b), Soz. *HE* VII.17.9–17 (ed. Bidez – Hansen 1995) (Th. Lect. *HT* § 258) on doctrinal differences among the Arians already *c.* 383, a rift that was healed only in the 420s; both writers (and Th. Lect., *loc. cit.*) mention in this context a bishop 'of the Goths', Selenas, of Phrygian/Gothic descent, cf. Mathisen 2014, p. 152. In 388, during Theodosius' campaign against Eugenius, the Arians of Constantinople, believing the emperor defeated, went so far as to burn down the house of the bishop Nectarius, as Socr. *HE* V.13 (ed. Hansen 1995b) and Soz. *HE* VII.14.5 (ed. Bidez – Hansen 1995) (and Th. Lect. § 247) relate, cf. Snee 1998, p. 160. These incidents point to a vigorous community rather than a dying sect, and one comprising both Goths and Romans; see further n. 9 below on internal divisions.

[7] Socr. *HE* VII.29 (ed. Hansen 1995b), on which see Greatrex 2001, p. 74 and n. 11 (where the reference is incorrectly ascribed to Soz.).

fluence of the Arians in élite circles; many, he noted, were *spatharii*, i.e. functionaries of the emperor's *cubiculum*, a role that one would not generally associate with the Germanic peoples.[8] On the other hand, that Germanic generals continued to support the community is attested by Sozomen, who reports that Plintas, a leading general for much of Theodosius' reign, helped to negotiate an end to the longstanding divisions among Constantinople's Arians.[9]

It follows from this short discussion that Arians remained a significant force in the imperial capital. It is likely that they were entitled to gather between the Constantinian and Theodosian walls of Constantinople, for which reason we find them later referred to as 'Exakionites'. The lengthy series of laws on heresies in the *Codex Theodosianus* attests to the difficulty of implementing measures against non-orthodox groups, and an edict of 435 in particular seems to impose fewer restrictions on Arians (and Macedonians) than on many other groups. This perhaps reflects both the emergence of new and fiercer debates on other doctrinal matters, in particular the nature of Christ, and the enduring influence of high-ranking Arians at court.[10]

---

[8] Nestorius, *Letter to Cosmas*, pp. 277–78 (ed. Nau 1919), cf. Barhadbeshabba 'Arbaya, *History* (ed. Nau 1911, pp. 521, 529). See Jones 1964, pp. 567–68, on the *spatharii*.

[9] Soz. *HE* VII.17.14 (ed. Bidez – Hansen 1995), specifically noting that Plintas was 'extremely powerful', cf. *PLRE* II, Fl. Plinta. Angliviel de Baumelle and Sabbah in *SC* 516, 158 n. 1, suggest a date *c.* 425 for the reconciliation of the opposing factions. Note also Socr. *HE* VII.30.7 (ed. Hansen 1995b) where he briefly reports the death of Barbas, the Arian bishop of Constantinople, who was succeeded by a certain Sabbatius, cf. Mathisen 2014, p. 153.

[10] *Cod. Theod.* XVI.5 (ed. Mommsen 2005) for the series of laws. Note 15.8 (381), forbidding church-building (which implies, however, that one might retain existing churches). 15.13 (384) and 15.30 (402) expel Arians (and Macedonians and Eunomians, all named in the first of these two edicts) from Constantinople; as we have noted in Greatrex 2001, p. 74 n. 12, 'Constantinople' is likely to refer just to the city within the Constantinian walls. Heather 2007, p. 139, suggests that the orthodox (homoousians) in Carthage were similarly able to retain control of suburban churches after their expulsion from the city itself by Geiseric. See n. 28 below on the Exakionion.

The lassitude of the imperial government at the need to enforce the laws is underlined by 15.60 (423), while 15.65.2 (435) distinguishes between three categories of heretics, among whom the Arians are viewed (alongside Macedonians and Apollinarians) as the least pernicious. From this edict it is clear that some churches remained in the hands of heretical groups (which were now due to be confiscated); nor were the heretics entitled to elect bishops (*sacerdotes*).

2. *From Marcian to Anastasius (450–518)*

Relations between the eastern empire and the Vandals

We move on now to the period covered by Theodore's own *Ecclesiastical History*, which allows us to gauge his perspectives more clearly, even if his text has been severely truncated by the early seventh-century epitomator.[11] Our intention here is to elaborate on some remarks we made six years ago concerning the Arians in Theodore's work. In this context it is worth quoting a unique extract from it, which concerns the aftermath of Geiseric's plundering of Rome in 455. According to Theodore,

> He (Geiseric) seized the holy vessels of the Apostle Peter, many items of which he sent to the Arians of Constantinople. (Th. Lect. *HE* § 366, p. 103.12–14)

No other source reports this interesting gift of the Vandal king; nor has it attracted the attention of modern scholars.[12] Yet it provides an intriguing glimpse of contacts between Arians outside and inside the Roman empire, which can be supplemented by better-known references to help flesh out a picture of a consistently influential community in Constantinople. Indeed, Geiseric's gift provides the background to the Emperor Marcian's decision to employ an (eastern) Arian bishop on a mission to Geiseric's court to plead for the release of Eudoxia and her two daughters; the envoy had no success, however.[13] Theodore's brief reference is important not only because it indicates both that there was a community of Arians in Constantinople and that Geiseric was aware of its existence, but also in that the historian highlighted this contact; no doubt he went into greater detail, but the epitomator retained just this bald summary.

---

[11] See Greatrex 2015, pp. 134–39, on the work of the epitomator and its relation to Theodore's work.

[12] But see my earlier discussion of it in Greatrex 2015, pp. 127–28. Hydatius, *Chron.* 112 [120], p. 94 (ed. Burgess 1993), reports that Geiseric during his raid on Sicily in 440 likewise attempted to bring assistance to the local Arian community, cf. Schwarcz 2008, pp. 228–29.

[13] Priscus frg.31.1 (ed. Blockley 1981–1983) = 24, p. 64 (ed. Carolla 2008), cf. Conant 2012, p. 30, Mathisen 2014, p. 153. It seems likely that Bleda was bishop of Constantinople, but this is not stated by Priscus, cf. Greatrex 2001, p. 75 n. 17.

We have not yet exhausted the evidence for contact between the Vandals and the Arians of Constantinople. For Victor of Vita, in his tendentious *Historia Persecutionis*, casts further light on this in a document of the Vandal King Huneric that he includes in his work. Soon after Geiseric's death, in 478 or 479, the new king acceded to the request of the Emperor Zeno and his own sister-in-law Placidia to allow the orthodox (i.e. homoousians) under his rule to ordain a new bishop of Carthage. He did not make the concession lightly, however:

> *sub eo ut nostrae religionis episcopi qui apud Constantinopolim sunt et per alias prouinvicas Orientis ex eius praecepto episcopi nostri liberum arbitrium habeant in ecclesiis suis quibus uoluerint linguis populo tractare et legem Christianam colere, quemadmodum uos hic uel in aliis ecclesiis quae in prouinciis Africae constitutae sunt liberum arbitrium habetis in ecclesiis uestris missas agere uel tractare, et quae legis uestrae sunt quemadmodum uultis facere.*

> There is one condition: the bishops of our religion who are at Constantinople and throughout the other provinces of the East are to have, at his command, the right to preach to the people in whatever languages they wish in their churches and to practise the Christian religion, just as you have the right in the other churches which are in the province of Africa to celebrate mass, preach and do the things which pertain to your religion, in whatever way you wish.[14]

We may thus infer that there was communication between the Vandal rulers and (some) Arians in the eastern empire, probably for the most part in Constantinople. There is nothing intrinsically implausible in this, given that Malchus reports that Huneric was well-disposed to the Romans, as one might expect from one mar-

---

[14] Vict. Vit. *Hist. Pers.* II.4 (ed. Lancel 2002), tr. Moorhead, revised, taking into account Lancel's translation. Lancel interprets *ex eius praecepto* as 'sur ordre impérial', while Moorhead's retains the ambiguity of the Latin, which, in this lengthy and convoluted sentence (cf. Moorhead 1992, p. 25 n. 6), could refer either to Huneric or to Zeno. On the date see Modéran 2014, p. 139, cf. Whelan 2018, p. 40, who also offers another translation and a useful discussion. Further evidence for Arian bishops in the east comes from Vict. Vit. *Hist. Pers.* II.23–4 (ed. Lancel 2002), where Huneric's advisers urge him not to act severely against the orthodox church in case 'our bishops' (i.e. Arians) in Thrace should suffer likewise.

ried to an imperial princess. Whether the renewal of persecutions in North Africa in 483–84 was in reaction to measures taken in the eastern empire is uncertain, since we have no information on any clampdown on Arians by Zeno.[15]

The Arians in Constantinople

There has never been any doubt that prominent Arians continued to flourish at the court of the eastern empire: the names of Ardaburius (both grandfather and grandson) and Aspar are well-known, while the family has been the subject of some attention in recent years. It is therefore not necessary to trace their careers in detail here. It will suffice to note that their adherence to Arianism is quite certain; nor does it seem to have held them back from playing a part in doctrinal matters in the struggles that surrounded the issue of the nature of Christ.[16] There were other generals, however, who proved more amenable to the attractions of orthodoxy: we hear of Jordanes, for instance, of Vandal ancestry, who regained the favour of Leo through a conversion from Arianism to orthodoxy.[17]

The two strands that we have followed so far come together when we consider the débâcle of Leo's expedition against Geiseric of 468. Although Basiliscus is regarded as the main culprit in the sources, the finger of blame is pointed also at Aspar, who took part in the campaign. Procopius, among other sources, notes the rumour that circulated, according to which Aspar had betrayed the imperial forces in order not to harm the kingdom of his

[15] See Conant 2012, pp. 32–3, Modéran 2014, pp. 136–37, on Huneric's relations with Rome, cf. Malchus, frg.17 (ed. Blockley 1981–1983). See also Courtois 1955, pp. 293–94, Merrills – Miles 2011, pp. 184–85; see below on the Anti-Arian measures of Leo *c.* 471, however.

[16] McEvoy 2016 is an important contribution in general, cf. Snee 1998, p. 180, on Aspar's correspondence with Pope Leo and Theodoret of Cyrrhus, Siebigs 2010, pp. 699–706. It would seem that Aspar received approaches from both sides: Leo sought his support in *ep.*153 (*PL* 54.1123 = *ACO* ii.4, 99–100, cf. *epp.*150–51, *PL* 54.1120–2), yet Th. Lect. *HE* § 378 (ed. Hansen 1995a) (= Theoph. 116) (ed. De Boor 1883) claims that 'as a heretic' he actually gave his support to Timothy Aelurus, cf. Ps.-Zach. IV.7a (ed. Brooks 1919–1924) with Greatrex et al. 2011, 146 n. 87.

[17] See McEvoy 2016, p. 503, cf. *PLRE* II, Fl. Jordanes 3, Greatrex 2001, p. 75 n. 15. On the family of Aspar see McEvoy 2016, cf. Snee 1998.

ecclesiastical party. It is important to note for our purposes that Theodore also reports the disaster and asserts that Basiliscus 'betrayed the whole thing on the recommendation of Aspar'.[18] Although within a few years of this failure Aspar and most of his family had been assassinated by Leo, they enjoyed a final flourishing in its immediate aftermath. While the future Emperor Zeno was obliged to quit the capital to escape plots being hatched against him, Aspar was able to browbeat Leo into betrothing his second daughter Leontia to his own son Patricius and to naming him Caesar. This provoked an outraged response from the bishop, the people and monks of Constantinople, as the *Life of Marcellus the Akoimetos* explains: they assembled in the Hagia Sophia and processed from there to the hippodrome, where they insisted that Patricius either convert to orthodoxy or abandon his plans to become Caesar. The demonstration clearly illustrates popular opposition to Arianism, which itself may indicate worry about its continuing strength in the capital, as well doubtless as a general prejudice against barbarian elements.[19] It is possible that Patricius

[18] Quotation from Th. Lect. *HE* § 399 (ed. Hansen 1995a), my translation, cf. Proc. *Wars* III.6.3–4, Theoph. 116 (ed. De Boor 1883), Niceph. Call. XV.27 (ed. Migne 1904, *PG* 147.80A-B). See Snee 1998, p. 182 and n. 181, Greatrex 2001, p. 76, Modéran 2014, pp. 196–97.

[19] *Life of Marcellus Akoimetos*, ch. 34, pp. 317–18 (ed. Dagron 1968). Dagron 1968, pp. 276–79 (cf. Snee 1998, p. 184 n. 199), dates the work to the mid-sixth century, although, as he admits, this is merely a suggestion. Given the strong terms in which the author describes the 'most unholy pagan madness of Arius' (ch. 34, 317.7) and the risks of an Arian ruler gaining the throne, a date closer to the start of the century seems more plausible, i.e. when the Arians still enjoyed some influence. Although the episode might seem like a topos, neither Dagron nor later scholars have seen any reason to doubt this account, which is further confirmed by several sources: Mal. 14.41 in the version preserved in the *Excerpta de Insidiis* 41 (pp. 160–61), preserves similar details, although this is usually overlooked, cf. the comments in Jeffreys et al. 1986, pp. 204–05, suggesting that they may originate from a different source. Such a sceptical approach is unwarranted, cf. Greatrex 2007, pp. 106–10, idem 2016, pp. 169–74. On the episode see Snee 1998, pp. 182–84, Greatrex 2001, p. 76, Croke 2005, pp. 187–93, Pfeilschifter 2013, pp. 528–34 (refuting Croke on a number of points), McEvoy 2016, pp. 490–91. Zonaras XIV.1 p. 251 (ed. Dindorf 1870) notes popular disquiet at potential persecutions by the Arians, cf. Croke 2005, p. 19; so likewise already the *Life of Marcellus Akoimetos*, ch. 34, p. 317 (ed. Dagron 1968). It is surprising that Th. Lect. *HE*, at any rate as preserved, records nothing for the last six years of Leo's reign (after the failed campaign against Geiseric). There is no need to enter into discussion here about the interesting donation made by Aspar and his family to the (orthodox) church of St Anastasia in Constantinople and the return to readings of the scriptures in Gothic reported

actually bowed to this pressure and converted to orthodoxy: the sources are ambiguous on this point.[20] In any event, father and sons were assassinated in 471, as Leo tightened his grip on the levers of power.

In the wake of the abrupt fall of this powerful clan Leo took the opportunity to clamp down on the Arians in the eastern empire: Malalas reports this quite specifically, referring to the Exakionite Arians and noting that they were to be barred from possessing churches or assembling.[21] It is possible that this persecution lies behind Huneric's demand to Zeno. Relations between Romans and Vandals generally improved over the 470s, and, as we have noted, Huneric was well-disposed towards the eastern empire. His demand, quoted above, may thus have been an attempt to seek concessions in exchange for the slackening of persecutions already under Geiseric around 476, culminating in the ordination of a new Nicene bishop for Carthage.[22]

We come at last to the reign of Anastasius, an emperor whose uncle Clearchus, Theodore claims, was an Arian. In fact, Theodore goes so far as to assert not only that his uncle was an Arian, but even that his mother was a Manichaean.[23] On the whole,

---

in Sergius' *Vita Marciani*, on which see Snee 1998, p. 176, McEvoy 2016, p. 496. See further n. 42 below.

[20] Theoph. 116.20–4 (ed. De Boor 1883) makes the odd claim that Patricius was made Caesar because he had converted Aspar from Arianism, which implies that he himself had converted. Mango and Scott 1997, p. 181 n. 8, suggest that this section might come from Theophanes' Alexandrian source. Note that neither Snee 1998, p. 185 nor McEvoy 2016, p. 491, seems to realise that Theoph.'s passage is the source of the Cedrenus entry 613 (ed. Bekker 1838–1839; section 383.1 in Tartaglia's 2016 edition) that they cite on this point. Pfeilschifter 2013, pp. 530–32, believes that Patricius did indeed convert, *contra* Snee 1998, p. 185, McEvoy 2016, p. 491, but the entry of Marc. *com.* that he cites (a. 471) (ed. Mommsen 1894) specifically refers to the Arian adherence of both father and sons. The issue thus remains problematic.

[21] Mal. 14.41 (ed. Thurn 2000). It is not implausible to suppose that *C.J.* I.5.10 (Krueger 1954), dated to between 466 and 472 and barring orthodox people from transferring property to heretics, may be linked to this: as we suggested in Greatrex 2001, 77 n. 25, wealthy Arians may have been purchasing churches and allowing them to fall into disrepair.

[22] For the improvement in relations in the 470s see Merrills – Miles 2011, pp. 123–24, Conant 2012, pp. 32–3, cf. Ausbüttel 1991, pp. 16–17, Schwarcz 2008, pp. 229–30.

[23] Th. Lect. *HE* 448 (ed. Hansen 1995a) (= Theoph. 136.13–16 ed. De Boor 1883). Cf. *PLRE* II, Clearchus 4, Haarer 2006, p. 127. Note that Vict. Ton.

scholars have been sceptical as to these claims: Theodore's hostility to Anastasius is quite evident and labels such as 'Arian' and 'Manichaean' were commonly applied to doctrinal adversaries, whether or not they were accurate. Yet we should not dismiss them out of hand. As we have seen already, Arians remained prominent in Constantinople until the early 470s. There is no intrinsic reason why the emperor's uncle might not have been an Arian, although we cannot exclude the possibility that it is simply a stock piece of abuse.[24]

It is thanks to Theodore Lector – and to the frequent recourse that Theophanes has to his work during this period – that we are informed about several episodes involving Arians during Anastasius' reign.[25] At considerable length – preserved through the quotation of John Damascene – Theodore recounts the case of the Arian blasphemer Olympius who, on a 25th December (perhaps of 498), in the baths at the Helenianae palace, grabbed his own genitals and declared, 'Look, I too hold the Trinity'. Soon afterwards he received condign punishment, as he himself admitted. Anastasius, apprised of the event, had the episode depicted in colour above the *caldarium* in which Olympius had beheld his vision condemning his blasphemy. It is worth quoting a brief extract from his account:

a. 491.1 (ed. Cardelle de Hartmann 2001) (= Th. Lect. *HE* frg. 39 ed. Hansen 1995) states rather that Anastasius' mother was an Arian (perhaps a compression of Theodore's text, since his uncle is not mentioned); see Blaudeau's chapter on Victor's difficulties with Theodore's text, cf. more generally Kosiński 2017, pp. 113–17. Whitby 2003, pp. 470–71, is right to notice the cluster of notices concerning Arianism in Anastasius' reign but mistaken to suppose that they are linked only to the accusations made against the emperor, cf. Delacenserie 2016, pp. 120, 169, arguing that Theodore seeks to draw parallels between Constantius II and Anastasius as heretical emperors who intervene excessively in church affairs.

[24] Whether the accusation of Manichaeism can be taken seriously is far less certain: as Whitby 2000, p. 173, points out, citing Marc. *com.* a. 519 (ed. Mommsen 1894), it is very often levelled at doctrinal opponents (in this case anti-Chalcedonians), cf. Angliviel de la Baumelle and Sabbah's n. 2, p. 478, to Evagr. *HE* III.32 (ed. Bidez – Parmentier 2011–2014), where the church historian reports that Anastasius was associated with Manichaeism. Cf. Meier 2009, p. 60, who remains sceptical, though Stein 1949, p. 80, is prepared to take the assertions seriously.

[25] See Greatrex 2015, pp. 124–26, on the relationship between Theophanes and Th. Lect. here.

> A number of people spread the news of the man's fate because he had at that time converted to the Arian heresy from the homoousian party.[26]

The allusion to a recent conversion, combined with the length and circumstantial detail of the anecdote, serve to throw light on a context in which Arianism still exerted some attraction on at least some members of the Constantinopolitan population. Moreover, as Theodore goes on to recount, the illustration was clearly labelled, the better to spread the word among the city's inhabitants. Such was the influence of the Arians, however, that they induced the *diaitarius* Eutychianus to hide the image, claiming that it was being damaged by the damp. But Anastasius noticed the change and had the picture restored to its place; naturally, Eutychianus himself was overtaken by divine judgement and expired in front of the very image.[27]

Before we move on to consider one other episode it is worth pausing briefly to note that Theodore's account here permits us to pinpoint a veritable Arian quarter in Constantinople. As might be expected from the label Exakionites, it lay just outside the Exakionion gate in the Constantinian walls, in the southwest part of the city. Just outside the gate lay the palace of Helenianae, where the baths in which Olympius blasphemed were situated.[28] In the vicinity lay the church of the Forty Martyrs of Sebaste whose relics had been preserved and hidden by a certain Eusebia, a Macedonian (i.e. Arian) in the late fourth century, who had herself buried next to them. Macedonian monks built a chapel there, but never revealed the location of the relics; it was then bought by the prefect Caesarius and his own wife buried there. Only some fifty years later did the relics come

---

[26] Translated from Hansen 1995a, 132.21–3 (frg.52a), cf. *HE* 465 (Theoph. 142.12–17, placed in 498 ed. (De Boor 1883). See Tiftixoglou 1973, pp. 50–1. Theodore refers to an Arian bishop, Euthymius, whose groom Olympius may have been, cf. Valesius in *PG* 86, 221–22.

[27] Th. Lect. *HE* frg. 52a, pp. 132–33 (ed. Hansen 1995a), cf. Greatrex 2001, p. 77, Greatrex 2014, pp. 129–30.

[28] See Greatrex 2001, p. 73 and n. 7 with Janin 1964, p. 28, Siebigs 2010, pp. 696–97. On the situation of the Helenianae palace, Tiftixoglou 1973, pp. 50–4. Th. Lect. inserts a reference to it already at *HT* 13.13.

to light, thanks in part to the efforts of Pulcheria.[29] While we may presume that this site, now furnished by Caesarius with a church, no longer belonged to the Arians, Theodore (via John) clearly indicates that nearby, in this same neighbourhood, there was an Arian church, for it was there that Olympius' friends bore the dying man.[30]

We may more briefly mention the incident of the Arian bishop Deuterius, whose baptism of a certain Barbas went awry; when the water of the font suddenly vanished, the man quickly absconded and spread the story far and wide.[31]

The reign of Justin I (518–27)

While Theodore's works have nothing to say on Justin's reign, it was of course during this time that he composed them. It is

[29] See Soz. *HE* IX.2 (ed. Bidez – Hansen 1995), *Chron. Pasch.* 590 (ed. Dindorf 1832) with Whitby – Whitby 1989, p. 81 n. 267, Janin 1969, pp. 482–83, Tiftixoglu 1973, pp. 57–8. See also the note of Angliviel de la Baumelle and Sabbah in Festugière – Grillet – Angliviel de la Baumelle – Sabbah 1983–2008, *SC* 516, p. 382 n. 2, on the church of St Thyrsus erected by Caesarius (near Helenianae).

[30] Th. Lect. *HE* frg.52a, 132.18–19 (ed. Hansen 1995a). In the same section he mentions the church of St Stephen (in the Aurelianae quarter), which also lies close by: see Janin 1969, pp. 472–73. Th. Lect. *HE* § 467 (ed. Hansen 1995a) (= Theoph. 149–50 ed. De Boor 1883) refers to a further episode of Anastasius commissioning paintings, to be exhibited in the Helenianae palace and this church of St Stephen, executed by a 'Syro-Persian Manichaean' posing as a presbyter; he claims that the images were quite unlike those found in churches, depicting 'fantastic subjects' (tr. Mango and Scott), and therefore incurred popular displeasure. The coincidence of location and action (displaying paintings) gives pause for thought: given that this passage is restored to Theodore from Theophanes by Hansen, one wonders whether it might not be a garbled reference to the episode here discussed. One might alternatively seek a more literary explanation: Theodore is prepared to give credit to Anastasius for acting against the Arians, but balances this through criticism of his eastern proclivities by associating him with Manichaeism, cf. n. 23 above for Theodore's reference to his mother belonging to this sect. See further Twardowska's chapter on this.

[31] Th. Lect. *HE* 475 (ed. Hansen 1995a), Vict. Ton. a. 500 (ed. Cardelle de Hartmann 2001) (= Th. Lect. *HE* frg. 55), cf. Mathisen 2014, p. 153, Greatrex 2015, p. 129. See n. 9 above for an earlier Arian called Barbas; see also Blaudeau's chapter (p. 86), where it is argued that Victor has misunderstood Theodore's Greek here. There is an interesting miracle also in Deubner 1907, no. 17, pp. 142–43, involving an Exakionite, i.e. Arian, who naturally converts to orthodoxy; the miracle collection certainly dates to before 600. See Csepregi 2007, pp. 124–25, 175.

therefore worthwhile to devote a short section to the period, for, as we shall see, the influence of Constantinople's Arians remained considerable. Perhaps for this very reason, the emperor envisaged taking over their churches (and/or obliging them to convert to orthodoxy). News of this plan spread rapidly: in order to dissuade him, the Ostrogothic King Theoderic therefore hastened to despatch Pope John I to the city, which he reached in 526. Justin heeded the pope's request, although Arians who had converted to orthodoxy were not encouraged to return to their earlier allegiance.[32] But Justin's measures attracted the attention not only of Theoderic but also of an anonymous writer in Vandal North Africa, the author of a commentary on the book of Job that came to be associated with Origen. Writing probably during the reign of Hilderic (523–30), he states: 'For thus even now the aforementioned trinitarian heresy is particularly plundering and expelling the (orthodox, i.e. Arian) church'.[33] The links between the Arians of North Africa and those of the eastern empire, in Constantinople in particular, that we had observed earlier clearly thus continued up to the point at which Theodore drew up his works.[34] What is more, despite his initial plans, Justin appears to have bowed to the pressure brought to bear. Of course, just a few years later, in 538, Justinian seized all the Arian churches and their (considerable) wealth, as both Malalas and Procopius report: no longer could the community count on any support

---

[32] *Anon. Val.* 88–91 (ed. Rolfe 1939), *Lib. Pont.* I, 275 (ed. Duchesne 1955–1957; tr. Davis 2010, 48), Theoph. 169 (ed. De Boor), Marc. *com.* a.525 (ed. Mommsen 1894) on the episode, on which see Moorhead 1992, pp. 235–42, Amory 1997, pp. 216–21, Greatrex 2001, pp. 78–9. Vasiliev 1950, pp. 242–43, suggests that *C.J.* I.4.20 (ed. Krueger 1954) (perhaps of 519/20) reflects this policy. In a later edict of 527, *C.J.* I.5.12.17, Arian *foederati* are spared the penalties imposed on heretics, cf. Vasiliev 1950, pp. 247–48, who connects it to Theoderic's embassy.

[33] *Anonymi commentarius in Iob*, i.75.9–11 p. 205 (ed. Steinhauser 2006), my translation. On the date of composition see Dossey 2003, pp. 107–11, cf. Merrills – Miles 2011, pp. 198–99. The text's most recent editor, however, Steinhauser, prefers a late fourth-century date for the work and a provenance in the central Balkans, pp. 38–41.

[34] Cf. Dossey 2003, p. 115, who suggests that the author, Theodosius, might have visited the eastern empire and who notes the presence of an Arian monastery in Egypt *c.* 530, cf. Conant 2012, p. 184. See also Dossey 2003, p. 65, on eastern influences on the author.

from the West. Theodore naturally was not to know that their days were numbered.[35]

Other writers of the early sixth century were also concerned by the lingering presence of Arians. John Diacrinomenos, writing probably in the closing years of Anastasius' reign, recounts how an orthodox bishop, upon being challenged by an Arian bishop, successfully walked through a fire unharmed. The episode seems to be situated in the reign of Leo (457–74) and recalls the miracles described by Theodore that took place during Anastasius' reign: we are again dealing with propaganda that takes aim at the Arian community.[36] The *cancellarius* Marcellinus *comes*, who brought out the first edition of his chronicle in 520, likewise makes fairly frequent mention of Arians.[37] He reports with enthusiasm how the churches were restored to 'us', viz. the orthodox, once Theodosius gained power in 380, while apparently rejoicing in the elimination of Aspar and his sons in 471 – 'an Arian with his Arian offspring', as he puts it. He was moved by the cruel persecutions inflicted on the orthodox by the Vandal king Huneric and had himself seen the confessors whose tongues had been cut out speaking in Constantinople despite their mutilation.[38]

For those writing in the early sixth century East, Arianism thus remained a live issue. A wealthy community continued to exist with friends in high places, capable of thwarting imperial attempts to clamp down on them. Some were tempted to convert to the doctrine, despite the legal penalties – whose enforcement is open to doubt in any case. The Arians were furthermore connected to their brethren in the West who might, from time to time, exert their influence to relieve the pressure brought to bear on them. Given that the Roman army continued to include sizeable con-

---

[35] Mal. 18.84 (ed. Thurn 2000), Proc. *Anecd.* 11.16–20 (ed. Haury – Wirth 1963) with Greatrex 2001, pp. 80–1.

[36] Joh. Diak. § 538. On John see Treadgold 2007, pp. 168–69, dating his work to between 513 and 518; cf. Blaudeau 2001 more generally.

[37] See Croke 2001, pp. 25–8, on the publication of this first edition, cf. Treadgold 2007, p. 230.

[38] Marc. *com.* a. 484 (ed. Mommsen 1894), cf. Croke 1995, p. 105; Proc. *Wars* III.8.4 (ed. Haury – Wirth 1962–1964) had also heard these confessors, who are mentioned in other sources too. See Conant 2012, 76–8, on the impact of these refugees from North Africa.

tingents of Arian soldiers, moreover, emperors had an interest in not acting too harshly towards the community; it should not, however, be inferred from this that the Arians of Constantinople were exclusively Germanic. The authors we have discussed could hardly have suspected, of course, that Justinian would imminently eradicate the problem once and for all.[39]

Appendix:
Theodore's preoccupation with Arianism

So far we hope to have demonstrated both that Arianism was a more potent force than is generally appreciated in the eastern empire, and in particular at Constantinople, right up to Theodore's day. We have also argued that Theodore is an important witness to this phenomenon and have cited a number of his sections of his work in this context. It remains briefly to survey what other traces may be found of his stance on Arianism throughout his works.

We shall take into account both his *Historia Tripartita* and the *Historia Ecclesiastica*. Probably the simplest way to elucidate his interest in the Arians is through a table. We have not sought to indicate every mention of Arians in the *HT* because, of course, so many of them simply go back to the earlier accounts of the Theodosian church historians; we limit ourselves therefore to entries that have some particular interest in this case. The tables below (divided into two for the *Historia Tripartita*, for which a full version survives only of books I–II, and one for the *HE*) does not aim to be comprehensive: we deliberately omit passages discussed already above.[40]

---

[39] Proc. *Anecd.* 11.16–20 (ed. Haury – Wirth 1963) stresses the wealth of the Arians at the time of Justinian's measures. See n. 12 above on the spoils from Rome that Geiseric sent to the Arians of Constantinople. Justinian could now complete his seizure of the goods formerly plundered by the Vandals.
I drew attention in Greatrex 2001, p. 80 n. 41, to the fact that John Philoponus, in an undated work (that could be contemporaneous with the authors here discussed) thought it worthwhile to refute the Arians, cf. van Roey 1979, another apparent indicator of their continuing importance. In the 580s Tiberius was faced by protests at his granting of a church for the worship of Arian Germanic soldiers: see Greatrex 2001, p. 73, Greatrex 2020, pp. 399–400.

[40] Delacenserie 2016, pp. 68–172, offers a detailed consideration of Theodore's *Historia Tripartita*, and of the first two books and their relationship to Socrates in particular. As noted above (n. 23), she argues that Theodore deliberately blackens the reputation of Constantius and his Arianism to parallel the heretical conduct of Anastasius, 100–01, 144 (one example), 168–69.

Th. Lect. *HT* I–II	Source/Parallels	Remarks
p. 20.10	Soz. *HE* II.21.4	Th. Lect. strengthens Soz.'s reference to the Arians, stating that the Arians 'held the impious dogma of Arius'.
p. 25.24–26.2	Socr. *HE* I.37.9	Th. Lect. expands the prayer of Alexander, bishop of Constantinople, concerning Arius' fate.
p. 26.6–10	Socr. *HE* I.38.9, Soz. *HE* II.30.7	Th. Lect. tacks on a reworking of what Soz. says about a rich Arian purchasing the place of his death to ensure people forget the circumstances. Note that there is also an insertion by the epitomator in § 50 (26.27–8) about the appropriate location of Arius' demise.
§ 55, p. 28.21–2	Theoph. 34.27–30	The epitomator inserts a reference to Acacius, the teacher of Eusebius (of Nicomedia), 'too closely associated with the Arians'.
§ 59, p. 30.33–31.13	Soz. *HE* III.5.9	While Soz. expresses uncertainty about whether a declaration of faith at the council of Antioch in 341 really did stem from the martyr Lucian, the epitomator explicitly denies this.
§ 62, p. 31.28–9	Theoph. 42.19–20, cf. Socr. *HE* II.12.1	Harsh words from the epitomator concerning Eusebius of Nicomedia.[41]
§ 63, p. 32.26–7	Theoph. 37.29–30, cf. Socr. *HE* II.14, Soz. *HE* III.7.9	Bishop George of Alexandria is described as a 'Cappadocian monster', whereas neither Socr. nor Soz. expresses himself so forthrightly. Hansen does not print this section in ordinary type, although one presumes that the intervention must be that of the epitomator.

---

[41] Cf. Delacenserie 2016, pp. 135–36, on hostility towards Eusebius (in Theodore).

Th. Lect. *HT* I–II	Source/Parallels	Remarks
p. 36.1–5	Socr. *HE* II.21.1, 24	Theodore explicitly defends Eusebius of Caesarea of the charge of being an Arian
§ 78, p. 39.12–13	Socr. *HE* II.26.9, Soz. *HE* III.20.4, 9	Leontius the Phrygian elected bishop of Antioch, described as 'an unholy and deceitful man, like his predecessor', i.e. Stephen; neither Socr. nor Soz. is as forthright. The verdict appears to be that of the epitomator although the section is in italics.
§ 101, p. 47.29	Socr. *HE* II.38.36	Macedonius is referred to as 'impious', an adjective not to be found in Socr. The verdict appears to be that of the epitomator although the section is in italics.
p. 48.23–49.1, cf. § 103	Soz. *HE* IV.16, cf. Thdrt. *HE* II.26.3	Theodore accuses the Arians of wishing to transfer the council of 358 from Nicomedia to Nicaea in order to confuse the faithful (not to be found in Soz.). The epitome picks up the assertion.

Th. Lect. *HT* III–IV	Source/Parallels	Remarks
§ 174	Soz. *HE* VI.13.4	The epitomator adds that Demophilus, bishop of Constantinople, alone controlled the churches of the city.
§ 203	Socr. *HE* V.7.1	Theodore or the epitomator adds that the only church remaining to the orthodox in Constantinople was that of the *martyr* Anastasia.[42]

(*cont.*)

[42] See Snee 1998, pp. 160–61, on this church and the association with a martyr Anastasia, whose relics were brought to Constantinople during Leo's reign. This reference comes from an entry associated in *PG* 86.216 with Theodore Lector but whose attribution is doubtful; it is not included in Hansen's edition. See Wallraff 1998, p. 13 n. 37, for a detailed discussion, cf. Pouderon 1998, p. 170: the series of brief notices comes from the very start of Parisinus gr. 1555A, fols 1–5, and reaches up to the reign of Tiberius II.

Th. Lect. *HT* III–IV	Source/Parallels	Remarks
§ 228	Soz. *HE* VII.5.1–4	Another insertion of the term 'martyr' in reference to the church of Anastasia.[43]
§§ 257–58	Soz. *HE* VII.14.4, 17.9–11, Socr. *HE* V.12.6–8	There are no differences to report here; the passages concern the hierarchy of the Arians in Constantinople in the 380s (discussed above).

Th. Lect. *HE*	Parallels	Remarks
§ 378	Theoph. 112.3–5	Aspar, 'as a heretic' seeks to thwart Gennadius' attempts to counter Timothy Aelurus.[44]
§ 394, cf. § 376	Theoph. 112.19–24	The *oikonomos* Marcian saves the church of St Anastasia; his position is described in the earlier section.[45]
§ 431		The epitomator notes that Theodore included the letters of Pope Felix to the Emperor Zeno concerning the persecutions in North Africa.
§ 463	Theoph. 142.6–9, Suda (θ297)	Theoderic kills a deacon who converts from orthodoxy to Arianism to oblige him.[46]

[43] Cf. the useful note of Angliviel de la Baumelle and Sabbah in Festugière – Grillet – Angliviel de la Baumelle – Sabbah 1983–2008, *SC* 516, p. 86 n. 4 and our preceding note.

[44] See n. 16 above on this episode.

[45] This Marcian is relevant to Arianism since we have a *Life of Marcian* by a certain Sergius that, as Snee 1998, pp. 164–67, notes, has (in some versions) anti-Arian traits and includes the miracle reported by Theodore. See ch. 20 of the *Life of Marcian* in *PG* 114.453–56 (= AASS Jan. I, 7.26 (616–17)) concerning the gifts of Aspar and Ardaburius; although the two men are described as 'of evil doctrine' and 'especially hostile to the orthodox', they were granted that services could take place in Gothic in the church. See also Wallraff 1998 on the *Life* (comparing the various versions).

[46] See Goltz 2008, pp. 62–3, on this episode.

This is not the place to enter into discussion concerning the interventions of the epitomator in Theodore's work. Suffice it to note that, assuming that the additions and changes we have signalled above are the work of this epitomator, it would appear that he shared Theodore's hostility towards Arians. This seems surprising in an early seventh-century context. Yet since for books I–II of the *Historia Tripartita* we can compare the epitome to the full text, it seems hardly possible to doubt that the extra comments come from the later epitomator, rather than Theodore himself. This must remain a puzzle that awaits resolution.[47]

Bibliography

Abbreviations

FCH, R. C. Blockley, ed. and tr., *The Fragmentary Classicising Historians of the Later Roman Empire*, 2 vols, Liverpool, 1981–1983.

PLRE, Prosopography of the Later Roman Empire, 3 vols, ed. J. R. Martindale et al. Cambridge 1971–1992.

Sources

Adler 1928–1938 = *Suidae Lexicon*, ed. Ada Adler, 5 vols, Stuttgart.

Bekker 1838–1839 = *Georgius Cedrenus [et] Ioannis Scylitzae Ope*, ed. Immanuel Bekker, Bonn.

Bidez – Hansen 1995 = Sozomenos, *Kirchengeschichte*, ed. Joseph Bidez – Günther Christian Hansen, Die griechischen christlichen Schriftsteller der ersten Jahrhunderte, N.F., 4, Berlin. (Translation: Festugière – Grillet – Angliviel de la Baumelle – Sabbah 1983–2008 = *Sozomène, Histoire ecclésiastique. Livres VII–IX*, ed. André-Jean Festugière – Bernard Grillet – Laurent Angliviel de la Baumelle – Guy Sabbah, *SC* 306, 418, 495, 516, 4 vols, Paris 1983–2008.)

Bidez – Parmentier 2011–2014 = Evagrius, *Histoire Ecclesiastica*, ed. Joseph Bidez – Léon Parmentier, tr. André-Jean Festugière, comm. Laurent Angliviel de la Baumelle – Guy Sabbah, *SC* 542, 566. Paris. (Translation: Whitby 2000 = Michael Whitby, *The Ecclesiastical History of Evagrius Scholasticus*, Liverpool.)

---

[47] See the important work of Pouderon 2014, esp. pp. 542–45, on the relationship between the first two books and the epitomised version.

Blockley 1981–1983 = *The Fragmentary Classicising Historians of the Later Roman Empire. Eunapius, Olympiodorus, Priscus and Malchus*, ed. Roger C. Blockley, vol. I–II, Liverpool.

Brooks 1919–1924 = Pseudo-Zachariah, *Historia Ecclesiastica*, ed. and tr. Ernest Walter Brooks, CSCO Scr. Syr. 38–9, 41–2, Paris. (Translation: Greatrex 2011 = *The Chronicle of Pseudo-Zachariah Rhetor. Church and War in Late Antiquity*, ed. Geoffrey Greatrex, translated from Syriac and Arabic sources by Robert R. Phenix – Bernadette Horn with introductory material by Sebastian Brock – Witold Witakowski, Liverpool.)

Burgess 1993 = *The Chronicle of Hydatius and the Consularia Constantinopolitana: Two Contemporary Accounts of the Final Years of the Roman Empire*, ed. Richard Burgess, Oxford.

Cardelle de Hartmann 2001 = *Victoris Tunnunensis Chronicon cum reliquiis ex Consularibus Caesaraugustanis et Iohannis Biclarensis Chronicon*, ed. Carmen Cardelle de Hartmann with An Historical Commentary on the Consularia Caesaraugustana and Iohannis Biclarensis Chronicon by Roger Collins, CC SL 173A, Turnhout.

Carolla 2008 = *Priscus Panita, Excerpta et Fragmenta*, ed. Pia Carolla, Berlin.

Dagron 1968 = *Life of Marcellus the Akoimetos*, ed. Gilbert Dagron, *AnBoll* 86, pp. 287–321.

De Boor 1883 = Theophanes, *Chronographia*, ed. C. de Boor, Leipzig. (Translation: Mango – Scott 1997 = *The Chronicle of Theophanes Confessor. Byzantine and Near Eastern History AD 284–813*, ed. Cyril Mango – Roger Scott, Oxford.)

Deubner 1907 = *Kosmas und Damian. Texte und Einleitung*, ed. Ludwig Deubner, Leipzig.

Dindorf 1832 = *Chronicon Paschale*, ed. Ludwig Dindorf, Bonn. (Partial translation: Whitby – Whitby 1989 = *Chronicon Paschale 284–628 AD*, by Marry Whitby – Michael Whitby, TTH, Liverpool.

Dindorf 1870 = *Ioannis Zonarae Epitome Historiarum*, ed. Ludwig Dindorf, Lipsiae.

Duchesne 1955–1957 = *Le Liber Pontificalis*, ed. and tr. Louis Duchesne, 3 vols, Paris. (Translation: Davies 2010 = Raymond Davis, *The Book of Pontiffs*, 2nd ed., TTH, Liverpool.)

Hansen 1995a = Johannes Diakrinomenos, *Fragmenta*, in *Theodoros Anagnostes. Kirchengeschichte*, ed. Günther Christian Hansen, 2nd ed. Berlin, pp. 152–57.

Hansen 1995a = Theodore Anagnostes (Lector), *Kirchengeschichte*, ed. Günther Christian Hansen, GCS, N.F. 3, 2nd ed. Berlin.

Hansen 1995b = Socrates, *Historia Ecclesiastica*, ed. Günther Christian Hansen, GCS, N.F. 1. Berlin (Translation: Périchon – Maraval 2004–2007 = *Socrate de Constantinople. Histoire Ecclesiastique*, traduction par Pierre Perichon – Pierre Maraval, Sources Chretiennes 477 [Book I] and 493 [Books II–III], Paris.

Haury – Wirth 1963 = *Procopii Caesarenis Anecdota*, ed. Jakob Haury – Gerhard Wirth, Leipzig. (Translation: Kaldellis 2010 = *Prokopios. The Secret History with related texts*, trans. Anthony Kaldellis, Indianopolis)

Haury – Wirth 1962–1964 = *Procopii Caesarenis opera omnia*, ed. Jakob Haury – Gerhard Wirth, vol. I–III, Leipzig.

Krueger 1954 = *Codex Justinianus*, ed. Paul Krueger, eleventh edition, Berlin. (Translation: Frier – Blume 2016 = *A New Version Of The Codex Of Justinian*, ed. Fred Blume – Bruce W. Frier, 3 vols, Cambridge.)

Lancel 2002 = Victor of Vita, *Historia Persecutionis Africanae provinciae*, ed. and tr. Serge Lancel, Paris. (Translation: Moorhead 1992 = *History of the Vandal Persecution*, John Moorhead, Liverpool.)

Migne 1904 = *Nicephori Callisti Xanthopuli Ecclesiasticae Historiae Libri XVIII*, Patrologia Graeca, vol. 145–47, Paris.

Migne 1905 = Sergius, *Vita et Conversatio S. P. N. Marciani Presbyteri*, in *PG* 114, col. 429–56.

Mommsen 1894 = Marcellinus Comes, *Chronicon*, ed. Theodore Mommsen, MGH XI, Berlin. (Translation: Croke 1995 = *The Chronicle of Marcellinus: a translation and commentary*, Brian Croke, Sydney.)

Mommsen 2005 = *Code Théodosien XVI*, ed. Theodor Mommsen, tr. Jean Rougé, *SC* 497, Paris.

Nau 1911 = Barhadbeshabba, *Histoire Ecclésiastique*, part 2, ed. and tr. François Nau, *PO* 9, pp. 493–611.

Nau 1919 = Nestorius, *Letter to Cosmas*, ed. and tr. François Nau, PO 13, pp. 273–86.

Parmentier – Hansen 1998 = Theodoret, *Kirchengeschichte* hrsg. von Léon Parmentier – Günther Christian Hansen, GCS NF 5, Berlin. (Translation: Canivet – Martin – Bouffartigue 2006–2009 = *Histoire ecclésiastique. Théodoret de Cyr*, Pierre Canivet – Annick Martin – Jean Bouffartigue, *SC* 501, 530, 2 vols, Paris.)

Rolfe 1939 = 'Anonymus Valesianus pars posterior', in *Ammianus Marcellinus, Res Gestae vol. 33*, ed. John C. Rolfe, Cambridge MA, pp. 531–69.

Schwartz 1932 = Leo, *Epistulae, PL* 54: 518–1213, also in Schwartz, ACO ii.4. (Translation: Hunt 1957 = *St Leo the Great: Letters*, Edmund Hunt, New York.)

Steinhauser 2006 = *Anonymi in Iob commentarius*, ed. Kenneth B. Steinhauser, CSEL 96, Vienna.

Tartaglia 2016 = *Georgii Cedreni Historiarium Compendium*, ed. Luigi Tartaglia, Rome.

Thurn 2000 = Malalas, *Chronographia*, ed. Hans Thurn, CFHB, Berlin. (Translation: Jeffreys – Jeffreys – Scott 1986 = *The Chronicle of John Malalas*, tr. Elisabeth Jeffreys – Michael Jeffreys – Roger Scott, Melbourne.)

Literature

Ausbüttel 1991 = Frank Martin Ausbüttel, 'Verträge zwischen Vandalen und Römern', *Romanobarbarica* 11, pp. 1–20.

Berndt – Steinacher 2014 = Guido Berndt – Roland Steinacher, *Arianism: Roman Heresy and Barbarian Creed*, Farnham.

Blaudeau 2001 = Philippe Blaudeau, 'Mémoire monophysite et besoins chalcédoniens. Quelques réflexions sur les vestiges de l'*Histoire ecclésiastique* de Jean Diacrinoménos', *Adamantius* 7, pp. 76–97.

Brennecke 2014 = Hanns Christof Brennecke, 'Deconstruction of the So-called Germanic Arianism', in *Arianism: Roman Heresy and Barbarian Creed*, ed. Guido Berndt – Roland Steinacher, Farnham, pp. 117–30.

Conant 2012 = Jonathan Conant, *Staying Roman. Conquest and Identity in Africa and the Mediterranean 439–700*, Cambridge.

Conant 2015 = Jonathan Conant, 'Romanness in the Age of Attila', in *The Cambridge Companion to the Age of Attila*, ed. Michael Maas, Cambridge, pp. 156–72.

Courtois 1955 = Christian Courtois, *Les Vandales et l'Afrique*, Paris.

Croke 2001 = Brian Croke, *Count Marcellinus and his Chronicle*, Oxford.

Croke 2005 = Brian Croke, 'Dynasty and Ethnicity: Emperor Leo I and the Eclipse of Aspar', *Chiron* 35, pp. 147–203.

Csepregi 2007 = Ildikó Csepregi, *The compositional history of Greek Christian incubation miracle collections: Saint Thecla, Saint Cosmas and Damian, Saint Cyrus and John, Saint Artemios*, Ph.D. thesis, CEU, Budapest.

Dagron 1968 = Gilbert Dagron, 'La vie ancienne de saint Marcel l'acémète', *AnBoll*, 86, pp. 271–321.

Delacenserie 2016 = Emerance Delacenserie, *L'Histoire ecclésiastique' de Socrate de Constantinople: banque de données et autorité historiographiques pour la création d'œuvres originales au VIᵉ s. (Théodore le Lecteur, Cassiodore, la première version arménienne)*, Ph.D. thesis, Angers.

Dossey 2003 = Leslie Dossey, 'The Last Days of Vandal Africa. An Arian Commentary on Job and its Historical Context', *JTS* 54, pp. 60–138.

Goltz 2008 = Andreas Goltz, *Barbar – König – Tyran. Das Bild Theoderichs des Grossen in der Überlieferung des 5. bis 9. Jahrhunderts*, Berlin.

Greatrex 2001 = Geoffrey Greatrex, 'Justin I and the Arians', *StPat* 38, pp. 71–81.

Greatrex 2007 = Geoffrey Greatrex, 'The early years of Justin I in the sources', *Electrum* 12, 99–113.

Greatrex 2015 = Geoffrey Greatrex, 'Théodore le Lecteur et son épitomateur anonyme du VIIᵉ s.', in *L'historiographie tardo-antique et la transmission des savoirs*, ed. Peter van Nuffelen – Philippe Blaudeau, Berlin, pp. 121–42.

Greatrex 2016 = Geoffrey Greatrex, 'Malalas and Procopius', in *Die Weltchronik des Johannes Malalas. Autor – Werk – Überlieferung*, ed. Mischa Meier – Christine Radtki – Fabian Schulz, Stuttgart, pp. 169–86.

Greatrex 2020 = Geoffrey Greatrex, 'The Emperor, the People and Urban Violence in the Fifth and Sixth Centuries', in *Religious Violence in the Ancient World: From Classical Athens to Late Antiquity*, ed. Jitse Dijkstra – Christian Raschle, Cambridge, pp. 389–405.

Greatrex – Phenix – Horn 2011 = Geoffrey Greatrex – Robert Phenix – Cornelia Horn, *The Chronicle of Pseudo-Zachariah Rhetor*, Liverpool.

Haarer 2006 = Fiona Haarer, *Anastasius I. Politics and Empire in the late Roman world*, Cambridge.

Heather 2007 = Peter Heather, 'Christianity and the Vandals in the reign of Geiseric', in *Wolf Liebeschuetz Reflected*, ed. John Drinkwater – Benet Salway, London, pp. 137–46.

Janin 1964 = Raymond Janin, *Constantinople byzantine*, Paris.

Janin 1969 = Raymond Janin, *La géographie ecclésiastique de l'empire byzantin. I. Le siège de Constantinople et le patriarcat oecuménique. III. Les églises et les monastères*, 2ⁿᵈ ed. Paris.

Jones 1964 = Arnold Hugh Martin, *The Later Roman Empire, 284–602: A Social, Economic and Administrative Survey*, Oxford.

Kosiński 2017 = Rafał Kosiński, '*Corpus Theodorianum*. Preliminary Propositions for a New Arrangement of Theodore Lector's Legacy', *Res Gestae. Czasopismo historyczne* 5, pp. 111–24.

Mango – Scott 1997 = The Chronicle of Theophanes Confessor. Byzantine and Near Eastern History AD 284–813, ed. Cyril Mango – Roger Scott, Oxford.

Mathisen 2009 = Ralph Mathisen, 'Ricimer's Church in Rome: How an Arian Barbarian prospered in a Nicene World', in *The Power of Religion in Late Antiquity*, ed. Andrew Cain – Noel Lenski, Farnham, pp. 307–25.

Mathisen 2014 = Ralph Mathisen, 'Barbarian "Arian" Clergy, Church Organization, and Church Practices', in *Arianism: Roman Heresy and Barbarian Creed*, ed. Guido Berndt – Roland Steinacher, Farnham, pp. 145–91.

McEvoy 2016 = Meaghan McEvoy, 'Becoming Roman? The Not-So-Curious Case of Aspar and the Ardaburii', *JLA* 9, pp. 483–511.

Meier 2009 = Mischa Meier, *Anastasios I. Die Entstehung des Byzantinischen Reiches*, Stuttgart.

Merrills – Miles 2011 = Andy Merrills – Richard Miles, *The Vandals*, Oxford.

Modéran 2014 = Yves Modéran, ed. Michel-Yves Perrin, *Les Vandales et l'empire romain*, Arles.

Nautin 1994 = Pierre Nautin, 'Théodore Lecteur et sa "Réunion de différentes histoires" de l'église', *REB*, 52, pp. 213–43.

Parvis 2014 = Sara Parvis, 'Was Ulfila really a Homoian?', in Arianism: Roman Heresy and Barbarian Creed, ed. Guido Berndt – Roland Steinacher, Farnham, pp. 49–66.

Pfeilschifter 2013 = Rene Pfeilschifter, *Der Kaiser und Konstantinopel*, Berlin.

Pouderon 2014 = Bernard Pouderon, 'Pour une évaluation de l'Épitomè anonyme d'histoires ecclésiastiques. Confrontation des trois historiens sources, de la tripartite de Théodore le lecteur et de celle de Cassiodore', *TM* 18, pp. 527–45.

Schwarcz 2008 = Andreas Schwarcz, 'Religion und ethnische Identität im Vandalenreich. Überlegungen zum Religionspolitik der vandalischen Könige', in *Das Reich der Vandalen und seine (Vor)Geschichten*, ed. Guido M. Berndt – Roland Steinacher, Vienna, pp. 227–31.

Siebigs 2010 = Gereon Siebigs, *Kaiser Leo I. Das oströmische Reich in den ersten drei Jahren seiner Regierung*, Berlin.

Snee 1998 = Rochelle Snee, 'Gregory Nazianzen's Anastasia Church: Arianism, the Goths and Hagiography', *DOP* 52, pp. 157–86.

Stanfill 2015 = Jonathan P. Stanfill, *Embracing the barbarian: John Chrysostom's pastoral care of the Goths*, Ph.D. thesis, Fordham University, New York.

Stein 1949 = Ernst Stein, *Histoire du Bas-Empire*, vol. 2, ed. Jean-Rémy Palanque, Paris – Brussels – Amsterdam.

Tiftixoglou 1973 = Viktor Tiftixoglou, 'Die Helenianai nebst einigen anderen Besitzungen im Vorfeld des frühen Konstantinopel', in *Studien zur Frühgeschichte* Konstantinopels, ed. Hans-Georg Beck, Munich, pp. 49–120.

Treadgold 2007 = Warren Treadgold, *The Early Byzantine Historians*, Basingstoke.

Van Roey 1979 = Albert van Roey, 'Fragments antiariens de Jean Philopon', *OLP* 10, pp. 237–50.

Wallraff 1998 = Martin Wallraff, 'Markianos: Ein prominenter Konvertit vom Novatianismus zur Orthodoxie', *VigChrist* 52, pp. 1–29.

Whelan 2018 = Robin Whelan, *Being Christian in Vandal Africa*, Berkeley.

Whitby 2003 = L. Michael Whitby, 'The Church historians and Chalcedon', in *Greek and Roman Historiography in Late Antiquity. Fourth to Sixth Century A.D.*, ed. Gabriele Marasco, Leiden, pp. 449–95.

Wiles 1996 = Maurice Wiles, *Archetypal Heresy. Arianism through the Centuries*, Oxford.

Williams 2017 = Michael Stuart Williams, *The Politics of Heresy in Ambrose of Milan*, Cambridge.

Williams 1992 = Rowan Williams, review of R. Hanson, 'Search for the Christian Doctrine of God', *Scottish Journal of Theology* 45, pp. 101–11.

Abstract

This paper analyses and seeks to explain the prominence of the Arians in Theodore's work. It argues that at the time he was writing, in the 520s, the Arian community in Constantinople remained a powerful force. The paper traces the history of this community and its links with Arians elsewhere, notably in Vandal North Africa. Tables at the end demonstrate that Theodore's interest in, and hostility towards, Arians can be observed in both his *Historia Tripartita* and his *Historia Ecclesiastica*.

KAMILLA TWARDOWSKA

THEODORE LECTOR'S TESTIMONIES OF IMAGES

Theodor Lector in his *Ecclesiastical History*,[1] finished about 520, gives us some informations about religions images. The purpose of this article is to analyze these fragments to see if they bring something new to our knowledge of religious images in the period of which he wrote.

We could say with no doubt that one of the most famous passage from Theodore Lector concerning the religious images is: [...] *ἡ Εὐδοκία τῇ Πουλχερίᾳ τὴν εἰκόνα τῆς θεομήτορος, ἣν ἀπόστολος Λουκᾶς καθιστόρησεν [...]*.[2] As it can be found only in one manuscript dating from the fourteenth century, this is probably a late interpolation.

Just as well-known is Theodore Lector's own fragment about a painter whose hands withered. There are two versions of this particular account. The first one is shorter and comes from the *Epitome*:[3]

> Ἐπὶ Γενναδίου ἡ χεὶρ τοῦ ζωγράφου ἐξηράνθη, τοῦ ἐν τάξει Διὸς τὸν Σωτῆρα γράψαι τολμήσαντος· ὃν δι' εὐχῆς ἰάσατο ὁ Γεννάδιος. φησὶ δὲ ὁ ἱστορῶν ὅτι τὸ ἄλλο σχῆμα τοῦ Σωτῆρος, τὸ οὖλον καὶ ὀλότριχον, ὑπάρχει τὸ ἀληθέστερον.

---

[1] About the author and his work see: Kosiński – Twardowska – Zabrocka – Szopa 2021, pp. 107–31.

[2] Theodore Lector, *Epitome* 18 [353] (ed. Kosiński – Twardowska – Zabrocka – Szopa 2021).

[3] Theodore Lector, *Epitome* 47 [382] (ed. Kosiński – Twardowska – Zabrocka – Szopa 2021)

Studies in Theodore Anagnostes, ed. by Rafał Kosiński & Adrian Szopa, STTA 19 (Turnhout 2021), pp. 233–246
© BREPOLS PUBLISHERS
DOI 10.1484/M.STTA-EB.5.127983

The other version is longer and survives thanks to John of Damascus. The relevant passage from his *Third Oration on Images*[4] reads as follows: Ζωγράφος τις τὴν εἰκόνα τοῦ Δεσπότου γράφων τὴν χεῖρα ἐξηράνθη. Ἐλέγετο δὲ ὑπὸ Ἕλληνός τινος τὸ ἔργον ἐπιταγεὶς, τὸν διὰ ἐν εἰκόνι ζωγράφειν ἐν τῷ σχήματι τοῦ Χριστοῦ ἐξ ἑκατέρου μέρους τῆς κεφαλῆς τρίχας διεστώσας, ὡς μὴ τὰς [ὄψεις] καλύπτεσθαι — τὸ τοιοῦτον γὰρ σχῆμα Ἑλλήνων — πρὸς τὸ τοὺς ὁρῶντας νομίζειν τῷ Σωτῆρι τὴν προσκύνησιν νέμεσθαι. Τὸ δὲ ἀληθέστερον ὑπάρχειν οὖλον καὶ πολύτριχα. Τούτου γενομένου καὶ τῆς αἰτίας θριαμβευθείσης, ὑπὸ τῆς ἀνάγκης τοῦ γεγονότος πάθους συντόμως ἤγαγον αὐτὸν πρὸς τὸν ἐπίσκοπον αἰτοῦντες εὐχῇ τὴν συμφορὰν λῦσαι. Ὅς τοῖς συνοῦσιν ἐπιτρέψας προσεύξασθαι μετὰ τὴν προσευχὴν ἐπέθηκεν αὐτῷ τὰ ἅγια εὐαγγέλια, καὶ παρ' αὐτὰ τῆς ἰάσεως ἔτυχεν.

The author describes here the events that took place during the patriarchate of Gennadios (458–71). The precise account leaves no room for doubt about the image painted by the painter; it must have been similar to the famous icon from the Sinai (Figs. 1 and 2).

This particular type of a male figure with a beard and long hair prevailed in Greco-Roman representations of Zeus (Fig. 3) or Jupiter, and other iconographically related deities, such as Asklepios (Fig. 4) and Serapis (Fig. 5).

As regards this other part of Theodore's account (that *the other form of Christ, the one with short, frizzy hair* is more true), it should be said that the depictions of Christ corresponding to these characteristics appeared, in the period from the fifth to the seventh century in the area between Syria and Egypt[5] (Figs. 6 and 7).

Due to their provenance and conformity with the cultural realities of the Near East, they may indeed have been regarded as historically credible or at least more plausible than those showing Christ with a beard and long hair.[6]

---

[4] Iohannes Damascenus, *Contra imaginum calumniatores* or. 3. Flor. III, 130 (ed. Kotter 1975: 196) and *Codex Parisinus* gr. 1115 (= P) fol. 265^v = Theodore Lector, HE 6a [11] see also 6b[11] (ed. Kosiński – Twardowska – Zabrocka – Szopa 2021).

[5] Breckenridge 1959, pp. 59–62; Wessel 1963, p. 892; Thièrry 1989.

[6] Skrzyniarz 2007, p. 151.

Fig. 1
Sinai ikon

Fig. 2
Sinai mosaic

Fig. 3

Fig. 4

Fig. 5

Fig. 6
Sinai icon, VI Century

FIG. 7
Abu Gireh, Early VI Century

For instance John Chrysostom proclaimed on the basis of a new exegesis of Isaiah and Psalm 44, that Christ was handsome, but this beauty was for a long time acknowledged as that of the Transfiguration. Christ had in fact two faces: that of an ordinary human being and that of the Resurrection, of which only the disciples Peter, James, and John were witnesses by participation. One wonders why, when he was arrested, he was not recognized and had to be pointed out (Matt. 26: 46–49). Origen thought that he was already transfigured and unrecognizable. On the contrary, Epiphanius wrote that he looked like the most ordinary of his disciples.[7]

As G. Dagron noticed, an anecdote recorded by Theodor Lector in the early sixth century would prove that this duality of representation was, perhaps at the end of the fifth century, considered embarrassing and was interpreted as an alternative.[8] A century later, both Christ's faces were reproduced on the coins of Justinian II.[9]

Apart from its possible value as evidence in discussing the origins of Christ's images of this kind, it is exceptionally valuable,

---

[7] Auletta 1948, pp. 41–61; Dagron 1991, pp. 28–29; Iacobini 2005, pp. 453–56.

[8] Dagron 1991, p. 29.

[9] Dagron 1991, p. 29; Breckenridge 1959, pp. 57–62.

because this is the direct basis for considerations of how such images were perceived by the elites of the Early Byzantium. It is the more interesting as it links the earlier tradition in this respect with manifestations of a new attitude, unknown to Theodore's predecessors, but adopted by his successors.[10] For obvious reasons Theodore's text is referred to mainly by proponents of the theory of the Zeus origin of the image of the bearded Christ with long hair.[11] Some researchers even hold that it documents the direct influence of the statue of the Olympian Zeus on Christian artists' imagination.[12]

Theodore does not make judgements about the existing situation. In his opinion, the controversy resulted from the pagans' trick, while the painter's lack of historical and theological knowledge was also certainly to blame. Finally, all this affair would lead to the miracle performed by Gennadios. As the Polish art historian Skrzyniarz argues, the revolutionary character of the passage discussed here does not lie in an attempt to promote an alternative to the discredited formula but in merely admitting the thought of the possibility of reaching or at least coming closer to the truth about the Saviour's appearance. No Christian writer before Theodore had presented such a standpoint.[13] It can therefore be said, as Skrzyniarz writes, that Theodore paved the way for those who were to accept the bearded and long-haired type of Christ, so sharply criticized by him, and raise it to the rank of canon.[14]

We have a very interesting description of another image, but it is necessary to go through the whole passage to have an idea of what it looked like:[15]

Ὑπὸ δὲ ταύτην τὴν ὑπατείαν κατὰ τὸν μῆνα τὸν Δεκέμβριον, ἔχοντα αὐτὸν τριακάδα καὶ πέμπτην ἡμέραν, θαῦμα φοβερὸν καὶ ἐξαίσιον πᾶσάν τε ἀκοὴν ἀνθρώπων καταπλῆττον γεγένηται.

[10] Skrzyniarz 2007, p. 152.
[11] Dinkler 1980; Jensen 2005, pp. 131–70.
[12] Breckenridge 1959, pp. 57–59.
[13] Skrzyniarz 2007, p. 152.
[14] Skrzyniarz 2007, p. 151.
[15] Theodore Lector *HE* 1 [52a] (ed. Kosiński – Twardowska – Zabrocka – Szopa 2021) = Iohannes Damascenus, *Contra imaginum calumniatores* or. 3. Flor. III, 90 (ed. Kotter 1975: 182–84).

Ὀλύμπιος γάρ τις τοὔνομα Εὐθυμίου τοῦ τῆς Ἀρείου θρησκείας ἐξάρχοντος τὸν βαδιστὴν παραχορεύων ἐν τῷ λουτρῷ τοῦ παλατίου Ἐλενιανῶν γενόμενος κατὰ τὸν προμαλάττοντα καὶ θεασάμενός τινας τῶν λουομένων τὴν τοῦ ὁμοουσίου δόξαν σεμνύνοντας ἔφη αὐταῖς λέξεσιν οὕτως· 'Τί γάρ ἐστιν ἡ τριάς; Ποίῳ δὲ τοίχῳ οὐκ ἐπιγέγραπται;' Καὶ κρατήσας τῶν ἑαυτοῦ ἀναγκαίων ἔφη· 'Ἴδε, κἀγὼ τριάδα ἔχω', ὥστε κινηθέντας τοὺς ἐκεῖ εὑρεθέντας μέλλειν αὐτὸν διαχειρίζεσθαι· ἀλλ' εἴρχθησαν ὑπό τινος Μάγνου, πρεσβυτέρου τῶν ἁγίων ἀποστόλων ἐν τῷ περιτειχίσματι, ἀνθρώπου θαυμαστοῦ καὶ τὸν θεὸν θεραπεύοντος, φήσαντος πρὸς αὐτούς, ὡς οὐκ ἂν διαλάθῃ τὸν τῆς παντεφόρου δίκης ὀφθαλμὸν ἀκριβεῖ λόγῳ γράφοντα. Αἰδοῖ δὲ τοῦ ἀνδρὸς τῆς ταραχῆς παυσαμένων ἐξανέστη ὁ Ὀλύμπιος καὶ τῇ ἐμβάσει τῶν θερμῶν ὡς ἔθος χρησάμενος ἔξεισιν ἐπὶ τὴν τῶν ψυχρῶν ὑδάτων δεξαμένην, ἥτις λαμβάνει τὰ ὕδατα ἐκ πηγῆς τικτομένης μέσον τοῦ σεπτοῦ θυσιαστηρίου τοῦ εὐαγοῦς οἴκου τοῦ πρωτομάρτυρος Στεφάνου, ὃν ἐν παλαιοῖς ἔκτισεν ἀξιώμασιν ἀρχοντικοῖς διαλάμψας Αὐρηλιανός· ἐνθένδε ἡγοῦμαι θείας ἐποψίας τὸ ὕδωρ ἀξιοῦσθαι. Ἐν ᾗ καταβὰς θᾶττον ἐπαναβαίνει κραυγάζων· 'Ἐλεήσατέ με, ἐλεήσατε', καὶ κνήθων αὐτοῦ τὰς σάρκας τῶν ὀστῶν ἀπεμέριζε. Πάντες δὲ περὶ αὐτὸν γενόμενοι καὶ κρατήσαντες, σινδόνι περιτυλίξαντες ἀνέκλιναν ψυχορραγοῦντα. Ἐπηρώτων δέ, τί ἂν εἴη τὸ συμβάν· καὶ φησιν ὁ Ὀλύμπιος· 'Ἄνδρα κατεῖδον λευχειμονοῦντα ἐπιβάντα μοι κατὰ τῆς νεροφόρου καὶ τρεῖς σίκλας θερμοῦ περιχέαντά μοι καὶ λέγοντά μοι· "Μὴ δυσφήμει"'. Λαβόντες δὲ αὐτὸν φορείῳ οἱ αὐτῷ διαφέροντες μετεκόμισαν ἐν ἑτέρῳ λουτρῷ προσκειμένῳ τῇ τῶν Ἀρειανῶν ἐκκλησίᾳ. Θελόντων δὲ αὐτῶν ἀποτυλίξαι τὴν σινδόνα ἀπ' αὐτοῦ συνεξέπαιρον πάσας τὰς σάρκας αὐτοῦ, καὶ οὕτως νεκρωθεὶς ἀπέδωκε τὸ πνεῦμα. Γνωστὸν δὲ ἐγένετο τοῦτο σχεδὸν καθ' ὅλης τῆς βασιλίδος. Ἐφήμιζον δέ τινες περὶ τοῦ πεπονθότος, ὡς χρόνοις τισὶν ἀπὸ τῆς τὸ ὁμοούσιον δοξαζούσης θρησκείας εἰς τὴν Ἀρείου μετεβαπτίσατο λατρείαν. Ἐπειδὴ δὲ τὸ συμβεβηκὸς καὶ ἀκοαῖς βασιλέως ἐπλησίασεν – Ἀναστάσιος δὲ ἦν –, ἐπέτρεψεν εἰκόνι χρωματισθὲν τὸ τεράστιον ὕπερθεν τῆς νεροφόρου καταπαγῆναι. Ἰωάννης δέ τις διάκονος καὶ ἔκδικος τοῦ προλεχθέντος εὐαγοῦς οἴκου Στεφάνου τοῦ τῶν μαρτύρων πρώτου, ἀνὴρ εἰ καὶ τις ἄλλος ζῆλον ὑπὲρ τοῦ ὁμοουσίου δόγματος ἑκάστοτε ἐνδεικνύμενος καὶ αὐτὸς εἰκόνι κατέγραψεν, ἀλλ' οὐχ ἁπλῶς· τῶν γὰρ ἐκεῖσε λουομένων καὶ θεασαμένων τὰ ὀνόματα κατέγραψε, καὶ ἔνθα εἴη ἕκαστος οἰκῶν, ἔτι τε καὶ τῶν τοῖς ὕδασιν ὑπηρετούντων. Μαρτυρεῖ δὲ ἡ εἰκὼν ἄχρι τοῦ παρόντος πεπηγυῖα ἐν τῷ ἐμβόλῳ τοῦ τετραστόου τοῦ πολλάκις εἰρημένου εὐκτηρίου. Ἐπειδὴ δὲ τῷ θαύματι θαῦμα ἐπηκολούθησεν, οὐχ ὅσιον παριδεῖν τῆς αὐτῆς ὑποθέσεως τυγχάνον, ὅπερ, εἰ καὶ τὸν παρόντα καιρὸν ὑπερῆλθε, λέγειν οὐκ ὀκνήσω. Θεασάμενοι γὰρ οἱ τῆς Ἀρείου συμμορίας ἐπικρατοῦντα θρίαμβον ἐλιπάρησαν τὸν τοῦ παλατίου Ἑλενιανῶν τὴν φροντίδα πεπιστευμένον ὡς ἐξάρχοντα καὶ τῆς τοῦ λουτροῦ διοικήσεως καθελόντα, κατακρύψαι τὴν εἰκόνα. Ὃς πρόφασιν εὐμήχανον εὑράμενος τὴν ἐκ τῶν ὑδάτων προσγινομένην νοτίδα ὡς σκυλθεῖσαν τὴν εἰκόνα ἀφελόμενος, φησίν, ἐπὶ διορθώσει κατέκρυψεν. Ἦν ὁ βασιλεύς, ἐγκυκλίους ἐπιδημίας τελῶν εἰς ἕκαστον τόπον βασιλικόν, παραγενόμενος κἀκεῖσε τὴν εἰκόνα ἐπεζήτει· καὶ οὕτως αὖθις τῷ τοίχῳ κατεπάγη. Παρὰ πόδας δὲ τὸν Εὐτυχιανόν (τοῦτο γὰρ ἦν ὄνομα τῷ διαιταρίῳ) ὀργή τις θεοδίκαστος παραλαβοῦσα τὸν μὲν δεξιὸν ὀφθαλμὸν διαρρεῦσαι πεποίηκε, κακίστως δὲ καὶ τὰ λοιπὰ περισείουσα μέλη, προσπελάσαι παρεσκεύασε τῷ εὐαγεῖ εὐκτηρίῳ, ἔνθα πεπίστευται ἀναπαύεσθαι μέρος τι ἱερῶν λειψάνων τῶν θεσπίων Παντολέοντος καὶ Μαρίνου, ἐπικαλουμένου τοῦ τόπου Ὁμόνοια ἐκ τοῦ ἐκεῖ συνελθόντας τοὺς ἑκατὸν πεντήκοντα ἐπισκόπους ἐπὶ Θεοδοσίου τοῦ μεγάλου βασιλέως κοινήν τινα καὶ συμπεφωνημένην διδασκαλίαν τοῦ τε ὁμοουσίου τῆς θείας τριάδος ποιήσασθαι καὶ τῆς ἐνανθρωπήσεως δὲ τοῦ κυρίου τρανῶσαι τὴν ἐκ παρθένου πρόσληψιν, ταύτην τὴν ἐπωνυμίαν τεκτήνασθαι. Ἡμέρας τε περίπου ἑπτὰ προσκαρτεροῦντος καὶ ὀνοῦντος οὐδέν, ἀλλὰ καὶ διαβρωθέντων αὐτῷ καὶ τῶν διδύμων, μεσούσης μιᾶς τῶν νυκτῶν ὁ λαχὼν ὑποδιάκονος τὴν παννύχιον ἔχειν ὁρᾷ κατ' ὄναρ βασιλέα τινὰ ἐπιστάντα καὶ τῇ χειρὶ ὑποδεικνύντα τὸν ἀσθενῆ λέγειν· 'Πῶς ὑπεδέξω τοῦτον; Τίς δὲ ὁ ἐνταῦθα ἀγαγών; Οὗτος ὁ μετὰ τῶν εἰς ἐμὲ δυσφημούντων συμφραξάμενος. Οὗτος ὁ κατακρύψας τὴν εἰκόνα τοῦ θαύματος'. Διαναστὰς δὲ ὁ κληρικὸς τὸ ὀφθὲν διηγήσατο, φήσας τῶν ἀδυνάτων τυγχάνειν ἰαθῆναι τοῦτον τῆς μάστιγος. Τῇ δὲ αὐτῇ νυκτὶ ὁ Εὐτυχιανὸς ὥσπερ εἰς ὕπνον ἐκ τῶν ὀδυνῶν ὑπαχθεὶς ὁρᾷ τινα νεανίαν εὐνοῦχον παραγαυδίῳ λαμπρῷ ἠμφιεσμένον λέγοντα αὐτῷ· 'Τί ἔχεις;' Ὡς δὲ 'Ἀποθνήσκω', ἔφη, 'κατατηκόμενος καὶ θεραπείας μὴ τυγχάνων', ἤκουε λέγοντος, ὡς 'οὐδείς σοι δύναται βοηθῆσαι· ὁ γὰρ βασιλεὺς δεινῶς ὀργίζεται κατὰ σοῦ'. Ἠντιβόλει οὗτος καί φησι· 'Τίνα κινήσω ἢ τί ποιήσω;' Ὁ δέ φησιν· 'Εἰ θέλεις ἀνεθῆναι, ἄπιθι συντόμως ἐν τῷ λουτρῷ Ἑλενιανῶν καὶ ἐγγύθεν τῆς εἰκόνος τοῦ καυθέντος Ἀρειανοῦ ἀναπαύθητι'. Παραυτὰ δὲ διυπνίσας ἕνα τῶν ὑπηρετούντων ἐφώνει. Ἐξεπλάγησαν δέ· τριῶν γὰρ ἡμερῶν ἤδη παρελθουσῶν ἀφωνίᾳ συνείχετο. Καὶ φησι πρὸς αὐτούς, ἀπάγειν αὐτὸν κατὰ τὸ προσταχθὲν διεκελεύσατο. Φθάσας δὲ τὸν τόπον καὶ πρὸς τὴν εἰκόνα τεθεὶς ἐξέπνει· τὴν γὰρ ἀπὸ τοῦ σώματος διάστασιν τῆς ψυχῆς ἐλευθερίαν ἀνέσεως ὁ ὀφθεὶς ἀγορεύων ἠλήθευσεν.

241

A shorter version of this event [16] is more enigmatic:

> Ὀλυμπιός τις Ἀρειανὸς εἰς λουτρὸν λουόμενος Ἑλενιανῶν, τολ-
> μηρῶς βλασφημήσας ἐλεεινῷ θανάτῳ ἐν τῇ νεροφόρῳ ἀπώλετο·
> τὸ δὲ γενόμενον γράψαντες οἱ πιστοὶ ἐν εἰκόνι πρὸς τῇ νεροφό-
> ρῳ ἀνέθεντο. Εὐτυχιανός τις τῶν διαιταρίων ὁ πρῶτος χρήματα
> λαβὼν ὑπό τινων Ἀρειανῶν τὴν εἰκόνα κατήγαγεν, καὶ αὐτὸς τὸ
> σῶμα δαπανηθεὶς ἀπώλετο.

Both of these passages are very significant. In the first case, on the image of Christ, it may be presumed that it was a panel painting, while in the other one, we are sure that it was. This is contrary to the view popular among many art historians, as expressed by Hans Georg Thümmel,[17] that the first mentions referring to religious panel paintings come from the late sixth or even the early seventh century. The passage just cited would allow us to shift this dating back to the second half of the fifth or the early sixth century. Theodore Lector's account gives us, at the same time, one of the first recorded information on miraculous religious images and, in the case of Christ's image, one of the earliest mention of a panel painting serving as an icon. For this reason, this is a very important source.

The second group of mentions referring to images as found in Theodore Lector's account is smaller. This one is a chronicle of political events and theological disputes leading to removing and destroying images of patriarchs of Constantinople. They could be arranged chronologically in the following order:

> Εἰς τοσοῦτον γὰρ ἐληλύθει τῆς τόλμης, ὥστε καὶ τὰ τῶν ἐκεῖ
> γεγονότων μακαρίων ποιμένων ὀνόματα τῶν ἱερῶν διπτύχων
> ἀνεῖλε καὶ τὰς αὐτῶν εἰκόνας καθεῖλε κατακαύσας τυραννικῶς.[18]
>
> Δεόμενος δὲ ὁ γέρων ταῖς εἰκόσι τῶν κατοιχομένων ἱερέων Φλα-
> βιανοῦ καὶ Ἀνατολίου τῶν ἀρχιεπισκόπων ἐν Κωνσταντινουπό-
> λει κεχρωματισμένων, δι' ὧν ἡ ἐν Χαλκηδόνι σύνοδος τὸ κῦρος
> ἐκτήσατο, ἐκραύγαζεν· Εἰ μὴ θέλετε ἀφήσειν τὰ τῆς λελεγμένης

---

[16] Theodore Lectore, *Epitome* 115 [465], (ed. Kosiński – Twardowska – Zabrocka – Szopa 2021).

[17] Thümmel 1992, pp. 199–200.

[18] Theodore Lector, *HE* 3 [22a] (ed. Kosiński – Twardowska – Zabrocka – Szopa 2021) = Iohannes Damascenus, *Contra imaginum calumniatores* or. 3. Flor. III, 99 (ed. Kotter 1975: 187).

ἁγίας συνόδου ἀναθεματίσαι, τὰς τῶν ἐπισκόπων εἰκόνας καὶ τῶν ἱερῶν διπτύχων ἀπαλεῖψαι'.[19]

Ὁ δὲ τῆς Ἀντιοχείας ἐπίσκοπος Παλλάδιος πρὸς χάριν βασιλέως διαπραττόμενος τοὺς τοῖς ἐν Χαλκηδόνι ἁγίοις δόγμασιν ἐπομένους ἐμυσάττετο καὶ τὰς τῶν ἁγίων πατέρων εἰκόνας καθεῖλεν.[20]

Τῆς αὐτῆς ἱστορίας, περὶ τοῦ διαδεξαμένου τὸν θρόνον Κωνσταντινουπόλεως μετὰ Μακεδόνιον αἱρετικοῦ· Οὗτος ὁ ἀνόσιος ἐν ταῖς συνάξεσιν ἀπερχόμενος τοὺς σεπτοὺς οἴκους ἀναθεωρεῖσθαι κελεύων, εἴ που μὴ γεγραμμένον ἐν εἰκόνι εὕρισκε Μακεδόνιον, ταύτην εἰ μὴ καθεῖλεν, οὐκ ἂν ἐλειτούργει.[21]

Ὅπου δήποτε ἐν ἐκκλησίᾳ εἰσῆλθε Τιμόθεος, εἰ μὴ πρότερον τὰς εἰκόνας Μακεδονίου κατέσπασεν, οὐκ ἤρχετο τῆς λειτουργίας.[22]

We cannot figure out from these excerpts the actual appearance and placement of any individual image. In three cases, the words 'burn' and 'take down' should hint at panel paintings, while in the other two examples they might have been mural paintings. We can see the continuation of political struggle by means such as condemning someone to *damnatio memoriae* through the destruction of any form of figurative representation. The narrative found in Theodore Lector's *History* would confirm therefore that besides the names in the liturgical books, bishops' images were indeed present in churches at the time.

The third group of such mentions is just as important, because it testifies to the existence of a certain canon in the early sixth century. Theodore wrote:

Πολλοὶ δὲ τῶν ἐπισκόπων Ἀναστασίῳ χαριζόμενοι τῇ ἐν Χαλκηδόνι συνόδῳ ἀντέπιπτον, ὧν πρώτιστος ἦν Ἐλευσίνιος ὁ Σασίμων. Μανιχαῖον δέ τινα ζωγράφον Συροπέρσην ἀπὸ Κυζίκου Ἀναστάσιος ἤγαγεν ἐν σχήματι πρεσβυτέρου, ὃς ἀλλότρια τῶν

---

[19] Theodore Lector, *HE* 5 [62] (ed. Kosiński – Twardowska – Zabrocka – Szopa 2021) = Iohannes Damascenus, *Contra imaginum calumniatores* or. 3. Flor. III, 101 (ed. Kotter 1975: 187–88).

[20] Theodore Lector, *HE* 2 [51] (ed. Kosiński – Twardowska – Zabrocka – Szopa 2021) = Iohannes Damascenus, *Contra imaginum calumniatores* or. 3. Flor. III, 97 (ed. Kotter 1975: 187).

[21] Theodore Lector, *HE* 4 [58] (ed. Kosiński – Twardowska – Zabrocka – Szopa 2021) = Iohannes Damascenus, *Contra imaginum calumniatores* or. 3. Flor. III, 100 (ed. Kotter 1975: 187).

[22] Theodore Lector, *Epitome* 130 [493] (ed. Kosiński – Twardowska – Zabrocka – Szopa 2021).

243

ἐκκλησιαστικῶν ἁγίων εἰκόνων ἐτόλμησε γράψαι φασματώδη ἐν τῷ παλατίῳ Ἑλενιανῶν καὶ ἐν τῷ ἁγίῳ Στεφάνῳ Αὐρηλιανῶν γνώμῃ τοῦ βασιλέως χαίροντος τοῖς Μανιχαίοις, ὅθεν καὶ στάσις τοῦ λαοῦ γέγονε μεγάλη.[23]

This one is another example in Theodore's transmission that would point to the existence of a canon, back in the sixth century, according to which holy images should be made. Also, it is important to note that this canon had already been well entrenched in public consciousness, since (as we could see) any departure [from it] could cause unrest and lead to disturbances among the population.

To sum up, Theodore Lector's work is not a treatise on art, but a source where various items of information relating to works of art are incorporated into narration. Theodore states his own opinion only in one particular case: the image of Christ. In all the other cases, his mentions relating to the images are complementary to the events [being] described. Nonetheless, all the pieces of information that he provides are of great significance to scholars who concentrate their attention on this period. Thanks to Theodore, we can now shift the emergence of the religious panel painting to the second half of the fifth or the early decades of the sixth century, determine the existence of canons in religious art already in the early sixth century, confirm [the belief in] the miraculous healing powers of religious images, and show the presence of the subject matter which is absent in other sources.

Bibliography

Sources

De Boor 1883 = Theophanes, *Chronographia*, ed. C. de Boor, Leipzig. (Translation: Mango – Scott 1997 = The Chronicle of Theophanes Confessor. Byzantine and Near Eastern History AD 284–813, ed. Cyril Mango – Roger Scott, Oxford.)

Hansen 1995 = Theodoros Anagnostes, *Kirchengeschichte*, Günther Christian Hansen, Berlin.

[23] Theophanes AM 5999 (ed. De Boor 1883) = Thedore Lector, *Epitome* 467 (ed. Kosiński – Twardowska – Zabrocka – Szopa 2021).

Kosiński – Twardowska – Zabrocka – Szopa 2021 = *The Church Histories of Theodore Lector and John Diakrinomenos*, ed. by Rafał Kosiński – Kamilla Twardowska – Aneta Zabrocka – Adrian Szopa, Berlin.

Kotter 1975 = Iohannes Damascenus, *Die Schriften des Johannes von Damaskos, herausgegeben vom Byzantinischen Institut der Abtei Scheyern, vol. III, Contra imaginum calumniatores orationes tres*, besorgt von Bonifatius Kotter, Berlin – New York.

Literature

Auletta 1948 = Gennaro Auletta, *L'aspetto di Gesù Cristo. Testimonianze e leggende*, Roma.

Breckenbridge 1959 = James D. Breckenbridge, *The numismatic Iconography of Justinian II (685–95, 705–11 A.D.)*, New York.

Belting 2002 = Hans Belting, 'In Search of Christ's Body: Image or Imprint?' in *Obraz i kult. Materiały z konferencji KUL – Lublin, 6–8 października 1999*, ed. Małgorzata Urszula Mazurczak – Jowita Patyra, Lublin, pp. 13–22.

Dagron 1991 = Gilbert Dagron, 'Holy Images and Likeness', *Dumbarton Oaks Papers* 45, pp. 23–33.

Dinkler 1980 = Erich Dinkler, *Christus und Asklepios. Zum Christustypus der polychromen Platten im Museo Nazionale Romano*, Heidelberg.

Heller 2002 = Ena Giurescu Heller, 'The Image of Jesus: Icon or Portrait?', in *Icons or Portraits? Images of Jesus and Mary from the Collection of Michael Hall*, ed. by Ena Giurescu Heller, New York, pp. 13–23.

Iacobini 2005 = Paul Iacobini, 'La bellezza di Cristo nell'arte, dall'Antichità al Rinascimento', *Path*, 4, pp. 451–79.

Jensen 2005 = Robin M. Jensen, *Face to Face. Portraits of the Divine in Early Christianity*, Minneapolis.

Skrzyniarz 2007 = Sławomir Skrzyniarz, 'Theodor Anagnostes Account of a Blasphemous Painter. Continuing and Change in Early Byzantine Attitudes towards Images of Christ', *Electrum* 13, pp. 147–52.

Thiérry 1989 = Nicole Thiérry 'Sur un double visage byzantin du Christ du VIᵉ siecle au VIIIᵉ siecle', in *Studi in memoria di G. Bovini*, Roma, pp. 639–57.

Thümmel 1992 = Hans Georg Thümmel, *Die Frühgeschichte der ostkirchlichen Bilderlehre. Texte und Untersuchungen zur Zeit vor dem Bilderstreit*, Akademie, Berlin.

Wessel 1963 = Karl Wessel, 'Christusbild', in *Reallexikon zur byzantinischen Kunst*, Stuttgart, pp. 973–81.

Zanker 1995 = Paul Zanker, *Die Maske von Sokrates. Das Bild des Intellektuellen in der antiken Kunst*, München.

Abstract

The purpose of this article is to show and analyse description of images current in Theodor Lector's work. To sum up, Theodore Lector's work is not a treatise on art, but a source where various items of information relating to works of art are incorporated into narration. Theodore states his own opinion only in one particular case: the image of Christ. In all the other cases, his mentions relating to the images are complementary to the events described. Nonetheless, all the pieces of information that he provides are of great significance to scholars who concentrate their attention on this period. Thanks to Theodore, we can now shift the emergence of the religious panel painting to the second half of the fifth or the early decades of the sixth century, determine the existence of canons in religious art already in the early sixth century, confirm the belief in the miraculous healing powers of religious images, and show the presence of the subject matter which is absent in other sources.

ANDRZEJ KOMPA

SOCIAL REALITY
OF CONSTANTINOPLE
IN THEODORE LECTOR*

Research on the milieu of the early Byzantine (Constantino-politan in particular) intellectuals and writers, the attitudes to the populace of the capital as a whole and to its different social strata opens the way to a better, more precise and unstereotyped understanding of Byzantine literature. In spite of the genre determinants and the source limitations it allows us to perceive individual Constantinopolitans as well as the city's population in general, and within it, its greater or lesser groupings and social categories.

It is interesting that the term 'Constantinopolitan author' itself is understood in the literature of the subject in different ways; it may relate to both native inhabitants of the New Rome, to authors associated with the imperial court, or even be a mere synonym of 'an Eastern Roman / early Byzantine author'. It seems to me that in analysing the subject it will be particularly worthwhile to examine the works left by the authors who spent their whole lives, or significant part of their lives, in Constan-tinople itself, among the Constantinopolitans. In so doing, one can not only attempt more directly to portray the social reality of the Empire's capital, but also seek reflections of the individual attitudes towards the city of the authors themselves.

Distinguishing Constantinopolitan writers from among the early Byzantine authors, if one considers a wide range of liter-

---

* This text was created as part of the project financed from the funds of the National Science Centre, Poland, granted under decision no. DEC-2018/31/B/HS3/03038. The author would like to thank Dr Adrian Szopa, Dr Michał Zytka and Prof. Geoffrey Greatrex for their valuable help that made this paper possible in its present form.

Studies in Theodore Anagnostes, ed. by Rafał Kosiński & Adrian Szopa, STTA 19 (Turnhout 2021), pp. 247–313
© BREPOLS ❧ PUBLISHERS   DOI 10.1484/M.STTA-EB.5.127984

ary genres, results in a relatively extensive list, and even though making such a selection is always going to be an arbitrary move, it nonetheless provides a broad range of material.[1]

The *Church history* of Theodore Lector should be included in such a selection, but the analysis of its surviving fragments and summaries poses a considerable challenge for several reasons. Firstly, although Theodore's associations with the capital were clear to Byzantines themselves (cf. Θεοδώρου ἱστοριογράφου Κωνσταντινουπόλεως ἐκ τῆς ἐκκλησιαστικῆς ἱστορίας περὶ Γενναδίου as cited by John of Damascus[2] or Θεόδωρος, ἀπὸ ἀναγνωστῶν τῆς μεγάλης ἐκκλησίας Κωνσταντινουπόλεως in the description of the relevant entry in *Suda*[3]), the biography of the author, the record of his possible travels or any broader evidence of his life remain unknown. It is only assumed that as an anagnostes of the Great Church in the capital he remained in Constantinople, without advancing through the Church hierarchy. His sole known period of absence from the city on the Bosphorus, his years in Gangra alongside the exiled Macedonius II, poses a problem. It is not known whether he accompanied the Patriarch already in Euchaita, or whether he joined him later. Finally, it is also not known whether he returned to Constantinople after the death of Emperor Anastasius; while it is seemingly likely, there is however no way to prove this, especially since the *Church history* con-

---

[1] Such a list should include at least Themistius, Oribasius, Philostorgius, the anonymous author of *Notitia Urbis Constantinopolitanae*, Philip of Side, Socrates Scholasticus, Hermias Sozomen, Proclus, Priscus of Panium, Nicholas of Myra, Zosimus, Priscian, Malchus of Philadelphia, Theodore Lector, count Marcellinus and the anonymous author of the last section of his chronicle, Hesychius of Miletus, deacon Agapetus, Romanus the Melodist, grammarian Eutyches, Aetius of Amida, Leontius the Presbyter, Stephen the Byzantine, John the Lydian, Paul the Silentiary, Peter the Patrician, the author of the large part of the eighteenth book of John Malalas' *Chronography* (i.e., in my opinion, Malalas himself), bishop Eutychius, Agathias of Myrina, Menander the Guardsman, Theophanes of Byzantium, John of Ephesus, Eustratius, bishop John IV the Faster, presbyter Photinus, etc.

[2] John of Damascus, *Contra imaginum calumniatores*, or. 3, flor. III, 130, p. 196 (ed. Kotter 1975).

[3] *Suda*, θ 153, vol. II, p. 696 (s.v. Θεόδωρος) (ed. Adler 1928–1938). Cf. also the prooimion to the *Historia ecclesiastica* itself (Nautin 1994, pp. 233–35), as well as Θεόδωρος ὁ τοῦ ἐντολέως ἐπανομαζόμενος, ἀναγνώστης τῆς ἐν Κωνσταντινουπόλει μεγάλης ἐκκλησίας in a later scholium (*Codex Athous Vatopedi* 286, fol. 210ʳ; Kosiński – Twardowska – Zabrocka – Szopa 2021, p. 132).

cludes at the precise moment at which the anagnostes would have been able to return to the city and evidence his presence there with more detailed descriptions of events. The sole clue lies in the undoubted presence of his work in the capital in the following decades. Considering the uncertainty regarding the date of birth of the writer, we do not know how old he was at the time of leaving the capital, but if one were to accept his return, his perspective would rather remain that of a Constantinopolitan. In this situation, however, recognising Theodore as a Constantinopolitan author is only provisional and uncertain, albeit tempting.[4]

Secondly, as any historiographic work of late antiquity, Theodore's *History* is a profiled work, in this case focused on the development of the Christian Church, and therefore some categories of information are absent from it simply due to the nature of the selected material and chosen content, even if non-ecclesiastical history did not escape the author's attention.[5] Thirdly, and perhaps most importantly, the original work is preserved only in a small number of fragments, of which only a few provide a representative idea of the size of the entire work, in terms of the structure of the narrative, presence of details, locations and e.g. social status of the described persons. Since all of our remaining knowledge of the contents of the *Church history* comes from the *Epitome*, which furthermore differs among the manuscripts, in the vast majority of cases we simply do not have access to the words of the author himself, and the method of summarising his work most often does not convey his opinions that did not already relate to the core themes of the specific parts of his work. What is more, as recent research reveals, the epitomator of the *Church history*, active in Constantinople in the first decades of the seventh century, who bound several separate historical narratives into one, and perhaps even made use of Theodore's *Tripartite history* and *Church history* from different source manuscripts,

---

[4] Theod., pp. ix–xi; Nautin 1994, pp. 235–43; Blaudeau 2006, pp. 549–52; Treadgold 2010, pp. 169–74 (with an apt remark that it would be difficult for Theodore to find the appropriate sources and documents for his oeuvre in Gangra); Lössl 2010, pp. 1419–20; Kosiński – Twardowska – Zabrocka – Szopa 2021, pp. 107–17.

[5] Greatrex 2015, pp. 122–30.

was relatively independent and creative.[6] Therefore posing a question about the extent to which Theodore and his work may be useful in analysing social aspects of the history of Constantinople must be preceded from the very beginning by a caveat that one may only apply a very light touch to Theodore's *History*, to determine what it may have provided as a historiographic source, had it been preserved whole.

The patchwork state of preservation of the remains of the *Church history* also requires a certain declaration of intent regarding which source evidence is going to be used in relation to the topic – as the selection may influence the final conclusions. A privileged position is given in particular to those sources which are considered to transmit the non-paraphrased passages from Theodore. The passages are understood here not in the sense in which they were used by Günther Christian Hansen, who identified 77 of these while creating his critical edition of the remnants of *Historia Ecclesiastica*, but rather in an even narrower sense, as seen in the new edition and translation by Rafał Kosiński, Adrian Szopa and Kamilla Twardowska (in total, 9 fragments – from John of Damascus, records of the Second Council of Nicaea, and from *Gerontikon* in *Codex Athous Vatopedi* 497).[7] None of the other pieces of this mosaic can be treated in a similar way, but this does not mean they have not been used at all. In this group, because of its binding nature and widest range, the most significant is naturally the text of the *Epitome*. I have also made use of the passages preserved in the *Chronicle* of Victor of Tunnuna (keeping in mind their laconic nature and linguistic difference) and in the *Chronography* of Theophanes the

---

[6] Pouderon 2014; Greatrex 2015, pp. 130–39 – 'plus souvent de compilateur (plutôt que d'excerpteur ou d'épitomateur), car son travail consista non seulement à excerpter des sections de Théodore, mais aussi à les conjuguer avec d'autres sources tout en intervenant ponctuellement dans les extraits' (p. 131); Kosiński – Twardowska – Zabrocka – Szopa 2021, pp. 236–38; Manafis 2020, pp. 155–61, 180 – 'sylloge of excerpts extracted from different and separate sources' (p. 155). On the other hand, most of the already identified interpolations (Greatrex 2015, pp. 137–38) do not change the general picture of the matter presented in this paper. Theodore's epitomator was not a passive copyist, but he was neither a co-author, nor he pretended to be one.

[7] Theod., pp. xxi–xxiii; Kosiński – Szopa – Twardowska 2019, pp. 110–31 (Kosiński – Twardowska – Zabrocka – Szopa 2021, pp. 136–63 = English version, cited here as Theod.[2]).

Confessor (with caution resulting from the – greater than once thought – authorial independence of the chronicler[8]). I also take into account individual passages from *Pratum Spirituale* of John Moschus, and the sole fragment from the *Chronicle* of George the Monk that met the previously outlined criteria – one relating to the meeting between Theodosius II and a saintly monk; the rest meanwhile either duplicates the *Epitome*, or the degree of its congruence with Theodore's text is impossible to prove.[9] I likewise examined fragments from *Suda*, the treatise *De schismatibus*,[10] and from (of lesser significance here) a letter of Kallistos. On the other hand, I have not included the contents originating from Theodore or the *Epitome* that have been later transformed and included in the *Laudatio Barnabae* of Alexander the Monk, *Synodicon Vetus* (far-reaching changes, twice edited, and renewed use of the *Epitome*), and the *Hypothesis* of the Council of Chalcedon.[11]

1. *The city and its inhabitants as a community*

As one may conclude on the basis of the preserved text, Constantinople constituted the backdrop of a significant part of the matters raised by Theodore; it is a fact well established and already discussed in recent studies.[12] Here I would like to explore the Constantinopolitan passages not so much in their ecclesiastical or political topics *per se*, but in their social and urban context, and to treat individuals and groups who appear in the narrative as members/inhabitants of a complex city organism with their individual or collective social roles, as perceived by a sixth-century historian.

---

[8] Pigulevskaja 1967, pp. 55–60; Čičurov 1973, pp. 203–06; Čičurov 1976, pp. 62–73; Rochow 1983, pp. 472–74; Whitby 1983, pp. 312–45; Ljubarskij 1995, pp. 317–22; B. Pouderon 2015, pp. 310–11; Kosiński – Twardowska – Zabrocka – Szopa 2021, pp. 410–11.

[9] George the Monk, pp. 607, 13 – 608, 9; cf. Kosiński – Twardowska – Zabrocka – Szopa 2021, pp. 451–58.

[10] Not without some hesitation, as e.g. Hansen's fragm. 48 reveals some stylistic and narrative differences from the other respective testimonia, and thus the amount of some later editorial activity seems probable.

[11] Kosiński – Twardowska – Zabrocka – Szopa 2021, pp. 141, 365–73, 467–79, 545–46.

[12] Blaudeau 2006, pp. 619–46; Greatrex 2015, p. 126.

The author of the *Church history* used typical appellations, Κωνσταντινούπολις, ἡ βασιλίς, ἡ πόλις, ἡ βασιλὶς πόλις, in a manner conventional for many writers.[13] In what remains of his work, Theodore does not reveal clearly his personal attitude to the

---

[13] Here and below, apart of the references to Hansen's edition (Hansen 1995b), the notes cite also the bilingual edition by Rafał Kosiński, Kamilla Twardowska, Aneta Zabrocka and Adrian Szopa (Kosiński – Twardowska – Zabrocka – Szopa 2021), as the authors revised the previous attributions of many fragments (cited as Theod.[2] in square brackets [ ] – renumbered *loci* in *Epitome* and original fragments).

Κωνσταντινούπολις – Theod., I, 337, pp. 97, 12; I, 338, pp. 96, 12; I, 348, pp. 99, 12; I, 366, pp. 103, 14; III, 431, pp. 119, 14–15; III, 432, pp. 119, 22; IV, 449, pp. 126, 21–22; IV, 454, pp. 128, 9–10; IV, 468, pp. 134, 15; IV, 475, pp. 136, 8; IV, 478, pp. 136, 22; IV, 522, pp. 151, 14–15 [Theod.[2], 2; 3; 13; 31; 90; 91; 104; 107; 117; 122; 124; 153];

ἡ βασιλίς – Theod., I, 362, pp. 102, 17; II, 371, pp. 104, 26; III, 413, pp. 114, 23; III, 431, pp. 119, 10; III, 438, pp. 122, 13; IV, 449, pp. 126, 22; IV, 461, pp. 129, 29; IV, fr. 52a, pp. 132, 21 [Theod.[2], 27; 36; 77; 90; 97; 104; 112; fr. 1];

ἡ πόλις – Theod., I, 367, pp. 103, 18; III, 408, pp. 114, 3; IV, 469, pp. 134, 16; IV, 485, pp. 138, 10 [Theod.[2], 32; 72; 118; 131];

ἡ βασιλὶς πόλις – Theod., I, 364, pp. 102, 27 [Theod.[2], 29].

Expressions as 'the bishop/church of Constantinople' or 'the prefect of the city' are omitted in the list above. Version Βυζάντιον may be found only in the fragments extant in Theophanes, and thus do not seem to reflect the original text. Theodore did not seem to use neither ἡ βασιλεύουσα πόλις, nor Νέα 'Ρώμη in his work.

* * *

Names of the city used by the authors are usually applied in a way that may reflect sometimes the individual style, cf. John Malalas's Constantinopolitan part of 18th book (ed. Thurn 2000) (Βυζάντιον: XVIII, 71, 27; XVIII, 77, 34; XVIII, 83, 54–55; XVIII, 88, 76; XVIII, 89, 86; XVIII, 92, 19; XVIII, 99, 37; XVIII, 118, 18; XVIII, 126, 70; XVIII, 138, 21; XVIII, 148, 27; XVIII, 149, 37; πόλις: XVIII, 71, 32; XVIII, 129, 89 & 93 & 122 & 142; XVIII, 131, 28 & 32 & 33, etc.; Κωνσταντινούπολις: XVIII, 73, 13; XVIII, 81, 47; XVIII, 83, 53–54; XVIII, 85, 59–60; XVIII, 97, 33; XVIII, 106, 60; XVIII, 121, 44; XVIII, 124, 56; XVIII, 125, 67; XVIII, 127, 71–72; XVIII, 129, 86; XVIII, 129, 92; XVIII, 131, 25; XVIII, 135, 52; XVIII, 139, 24; XVIII, 147, 21), Socrates (ed. Hansen 1995a) (only rarely Βυζάντιον: I, 13, 9; I, 16, 1; III, 1, 6; IV, 8, 1 and notoriously used Κωνσταντινούπολις: I, 13, 9; I, 16, 1; I, 16, 3; I, 17, 8; I, 17, 9; I, 25, 10; I, 33, 3; I, 34, 5; I, 35, 1; I, 35, 2; I, 36, 1; I, 36, 7 [x2]; I, 37, 2; I, 38, 9; I, 39, 1; I, 40, 1; II, 6, 1; II, 7, 1; II, 12, 5; II, 13, 2 & 5; II, 23, 43; II, 25, 2; II, 27, 1 & 6; II, 38, 3 & 5 & 14 & 19 & 27; II, 40, 49; II, 41, 5 & 17 & 22; II, 42, 1; II, 43, 16; II, 44, 3 [x2]; II, 45, 1 & 10 & 15, etc.). Only a few authors used some dozen names it one text, and the range may depend on the genre(s) of their output (e.g. John the Lydian (ed. Wachsmuth 1897): Βυζάντιον; Κωνσταντίνου πόλις; ἡ βασιλίς; ἡ βασιλὶς πόλις; ἀνθοῦσα; 'Ρώμη νέα; ἱερὰ 'Ρώμη; ἡ εὐδαίμων πόλις; ἡ καθ' ἡμᾶς 'Ρώμη / βασιλίς; ἡ καθ' ἡμᾶς εὐδαίμων πόλις; ἡμετέρα 'Ρώμη; ἡ πάγχρυσος πόλις). Cf. also Georgacas 1947, pp. 348–49, 354–66.

Queen of Cities, neither an affirmative nor panegyric approach can be observed. Nonetheless, such entries are a rarity also among other historians of this period, even those whose ties to the city on the Bosphorus are much better documented by either biographical notes or by autobiographic clues in the texts themselves. The narrative framework of the literary genre was not conducive to rhetorical statements, ones akin to Themistius' χείρους Περσῶν ἀλλήλοις ἦμεν, χαλεπώτεραι ἦσαν τῶν ἐπιδρομῶν αἱ γραφαὶ ἐξ ἑκατέρας θρησκείας παρὰ τῆς πόλεως.[14] Descriptions of the city seem to be infrequent, and the author apparently also did not, for the most part, take note of architectural initiatives of the rulers. On the other hand, the author seems intimately familiar with the ecclesiastical topography of the city, aptly localises the churches and informs us of their dedications. The entries preserved in the *Epitome*, such as one mentioning the construction of the church of St John by Studios and of St Cyriacus by Gratissimus, or reporting a fire which spread from the shipyard to the Apostoleion and the survival of the church of St Anastasia, may have been much more extensive and potentially included more detailed descriptions.[15]

At the same time the people of Constantinople, seen as a community and without singling out any individuals, regularly appear in the description of events and commentary. Of the five terms used at that time for denoting such collectively acting subject, Theodore used four: λαός, πλῆθος (πλήθη), ὄχλος, but without using δῆμος, unlike e.g. Socrates[16] and Sozomen[17] – the same authors whose work he was using. Of those listed, λαός appears by far the most frequently in the preserved fragments. The term is nearly always at least a neutral one, at times clearly positive, and refers primarily to those inhabitants of Constantinople who maintained the orthodox faith and the right attitude in religious disputes. From the passages preserved in Theophanes (and, it

---

[14] Themistius, or. V, 68c (Schenkl – Downey 1965).

[15] Theod., II, 384, pp. 108, 29–32; II, 394, pp. 110, 21–25 (ed. Hansen 1995b) [Theod.², 49; 59].

[16] Socrates, III, 1, 12; IV, 38, 1–6; V, 1, 2 & 5; VII, 22, 12 & 15–17; VII, 23, 11, etc. (ed. Hansen 1995a).

[17] Sozomen, VI, 39, 2–4; VII, 1, 1; VII, 10, 4; VIII, 18, 6–9, etc. (ed. Bidez – Hansen 1995).

appears, in this case rather faithfully reflecting the source[18]), one may directly recognise the pairing of λαός (viz. 'the faithful') with ὀρθόδοξοι: Τιμόθεος δὲ τὸ ὄνομα Σευήρου βουληθεὶς ἐντάξαι τοῖς διπτύχοις καὶ τὸ Φλαβιανοῦ ἐκβάλαι ὑπὸ τοῦ λαοῦ ἐκωλύθη. Σευήρου γὰρ τὴν κοινωνίαν πάντες οἱ ὀρθόδοξοι ἔφυγον[19] and Οἱ δὲ μοναχοὶ ἄλλον ψαλμὸν ἦλθον ψάλλοντες. Τούτους δὲ ἰδὼν ὁ λαὸς ἔκραζεν· 'Καλῶς ἦλθον οἱ ὀρθόδοξοι'.[20] The same term is used to denote the community even when it is starting riots, as long as it supports the dogmatically correct side (this is particularly apparent in book IV, describing religious unrest in the city during the reign of Emperor Anastasius – in the descriptions of unrest after the deposition of Patriarch Euphemius, after the Emperor brought Philoxenus into the city, or after the ingress of John II the Cappadocian[21]).

In many cases the word designates the entire body of the orthodox inhabitants of the city: the remains of bishop Flavian have been brought to the city at the request of the clergy and the people (αἰτήσεως τοῦ κλήρου καὶ τοῦ λαοῦ). In a different passage the people, along with the clergy and monks of Constantinople, together act in defence of Chalcedon against Basiliscus and the anti-Chalcedonian bishops he supported (Ὁ κλῆρος καὶ ὁ λαὸς καὶ τὸ μοναχικὸν Κωνσταντινουπόλεως ὑπερεμάχουν τῆς ἐν Χαλκηδόνι συνόδου).[22] On the other hand λαός for Theodore means also a specific group, a crowd, acting in a specific place and time, an

---

[18] See Pouderon 2015, pp. 285, 289, 293, but for the opposite view cf. Kosiński – Szopa – Twardowska 2019, p. 362; Kosiński – Twardowska – Zabrocka – Szopa 2021, pp. 410–11 and D. Brodka in this volume.

[19] Theod., IV, 502, pp. 143, 20–21 (ed. Hansen 1995b) i.e. Theoph., AM 6005, pp. 157, 29–30 (ed. De Boor 1883).

[20] Theod., IV, 508, pp. 145, 14–15 (ed. Hansen 1995b) i.e. Theoph., AM 6005, pp. 159, 12–14 (ed. De Boor 1883).

[21] Theod., IV, 455, pp. 128, 18; IV, 467, pp. 134, 14; IV, 469, pp. 134, 16–17 (ed. Hansen 1995b); (≈ IV, 470, pp. 134, 20–23, i.e. Theoph., AM 5999 (ed. De Boor 1883); IV, 523, pp. 151, 22–23 [Theod.², 108; 118; 154].

[22] Theod., I, 357, pp. 18–19; III, 406, pp. 113, 17–20 [Theod.², 22; 70]. Cf. also III, 407, pp. 113, 25–26 [Theod.², 71] (Daniel the Stylite arrives to Constantinople to join the λαὸς and the patriarch Acacius); IV, 509, pp. 145, 26–28 (ed. Hansen 1995b) i.e. Theoph., AM 6006, pp. 160, 26–28 (Τοῦ δὲ βασιλέως καὶ τῆς συγκλήτου καὶ τῶν λοιπῶν ἀρχόντων τε καὶ λαῶν ὁμοσάντων καὶ βεβαιωσάντων ταῦτα οὕτω γίνεσθαι, εἰρήνη γέγονεν); IV, 511, pp. 146, 21–22 i.e. Theoph., AM 6006, pp. 161, 9–10 (πᾶς δὲ ὁ λαὸς καὶ ἡ σύγκλητος παρρησίᾳ ἐλοιδόρουν Ἀναστάσιον ὡς ἐπίορκον) (ed. De Boor 1883).

actor in or a witness of an event being described. Such use appears most commonly in the final part of the *Church History*, in the description of events which the author was able to remember in more detail and recreate, having known them from eye-witness testimonies or perhaps first-hand observation. It was this λαός that mocked and chased away from Hagia Sophia those who were incorrectly singing the Trisagion (Ὁ δὲ λαὸς ζηλώσας τὰ μὲν πρῶτα φωναῖς ἀντέκραζον κράζουσιν καὶ ὑβρίζουσιν ἀνθύβριζον, ὕστερον δὲ μετὰ πολλῶν),[23] insulted the Emperor while marching in protest against Anastasius (Ὁ λαὸς σὺν γυναιξί καὶ τέκνοις πλῆθος ἄπειρον), and after patriarch Macedonius II was summoned by the Emperor Anastasius to the palace, expressed its respect for the bishop by exclaiming 'τὸν πατέρα πρὸς ἡμᾶς ἔχομεν'.[24] The last of these passages is interesting in that the crowd here is understood as a body of marching men accompanied by (or including within it) women and children.

Although such use of λαός is typical also for the earlier Church historians, whose works Theodore compiled in writing the *Historia tripartita*, i.e. Socrates and Sozomen,[25] it seems that it is used in a narrower sense than by his predecessors – if one may draw conclusions from the slim basis of the preserved material. For Theodore, this is always a group of orthodox believers, while Socrates did not hesitate to write that the people divided itself in two and waged an internal conflict (ἡ τοῦ λαοῦ μάχη), and also uses the term when referring to the Arians and Novatians.[26] It should be noted that although in Theodore's time and shortly afterwards the term is still used to denote the entirety of the faithful or a praying congregation gathered in a church,[27] other

---

[23] Theod., IV, 483 [Theod.², 129].

[24] Theod., IV, 483, pp. 137, 28–29; IV, 485, pp. 138, 9–10; IV, 486, pp. 138, 15–20 (ed. Hansen 1995b) [Theod.², 129; 131; 132]. Turbulent years 511–12, marked by the conflict between the emperor Anastasius and patriarch Macedonius II as well as ongoing violence in the city with Trisagion as motto, are discussed by many authors, see e.g. Haarer 2006, pp. 147–57; Meier 2007, *passim*; Meier 2009, pp. 261–88; Dijkstra – Greatrex 2009, pp. 235–39, 257–61; Filipczak 2013, pp. 474–95; Ginter 2017, pp. 47–54.

[25] Kompa 2014, pp. 70–80.

[26] Socrates, I, 8; I, 37, 1–9; II, 6, 4 & 5; V, 21, 3; VII, 12, 4; VII, 33, 5; VII, 34, 14 (ed. Hansen 1995a); cf. Sozomen, IV, 20, 6 (ed. Bidez – Hansen 1995).

[27] *For example* Paul the Silentiary, v. 321–22 and 563–66 (ed. Veh 1977).

255

sixth-century authors use words with less religious connotations (in particular πλῆθος, δῆμος), even when describing similar situations.[28]

Πλῆθος and πλήθη are not absent from the remaining fragments of the text, but based on a simple statistical examination they have been used less frequently. The preserved examples denote real, actual crowds, appearing at a specific time and place – the people gathered in a church and welcoming Marcian and Pulcheria, and at the same time asking them to intervene in the matter of Eutyches (κλῆρος ἅπας καὶ μοναχοὶ καὶ λαϊκοί, πλήθη ὄντες πολλά); or the riotous crowds (τὰ πλήθη) opposing the Trisagion which included the part added by Patriarch Timothy.[29] It also appears as a neutral term, often complementing synonymous passages, in which λαός is the actor: thus, the throng accompanying Daniel Stylites on the way to Basiliscus (πλῆθος ἐκ τοῦ λαοῦ ἐξῆλθεν), or the men, women and children protesting against religious innovations of Emperor Anastasius (Ὁ λαὸς σὺν γυναιξί καὶ τέκνοις πλῆθος ἄπειρον).[30] This is a typical description and a common combination, also in Socrates and Sozomen, who described Constantinopolitans' behaviour in a similar manner – although in both these cases the abundance of preserved content also provides descriptions in which the πλῆθος acted in a way that was not always approved of by the historians, by not proceeding rightly, but also at times getting angry, becoming overwhelmed with fear, or divided and supporting both sides of a conflict, or entirely representing the wrong side.[31] Such varied behaviour of the crowds is impossible to find in Theodore when one is looking at the results of an epitomator's summarisation. The word πλῆθος appears but once in a negative context, yet even there it is accompanied by an adjective – it is a countryside rabble, πλῆθος ἀγροικικός, used by the Patriarch Timothy to

---

[28] Kompa 2014, pp. 81–85.

[29] Theod., I, 355, pp. 100, 14–16 (ed. Hansen 1995b) [Theod.², 20]; IV, 508, pp. 144, 25–26 i.e. Theoph., AM 6005, pp. 159, 8–9 (ed. De Boor 1883).

[30] Theod., III, 408, pp. 114, 1–4; IV, 485, pp. 138, 9–10 (ed. Hansen 1995b) [Theod.², 72; 131].

[31] Socrates, II, 13, 2–3; II, 16, 3; II, 38, 41–42; V, 7, 4–11; VI, 8, 4–6; VI, 15, 1–3 & 18–21; VI, 16, 1 & 5 & 8–11 (ed. Hansen 1995a); Sozomen, IV, 21, 4–5; IV, 27, 2–3; VIII, 18, 1–5; VIII, 18, 6–9; VIII, 21, 5–8, etc. (ed. Bidez – Hansen 1995).

persecute orthodox monks, who had been protesting alongside the people during Anastasius' reign against the changing of the diptychs (removing Flavian from these and including Severus instead).[32]

The negative aspect of the crowd's actions raises the question of the way in which the term ὄχλος was used, which appears more frequently in Theodore's work, differentiating it from the earlier Church historians. This includes situations where his predecessors did not use the pejorative term ὄχλος, even though the context of the behaviour of the Constantinopolitans, or the overall assessment of their deeds, were reported with disapproval.[33] First and foremost, however, the word occurs in descriptions of the time in which Theodore is keenly interested, and for which he takes a clear stance in the religious disputes. It is likely for this reason that we may suppose that the summaries by the author of the *Epitome* rather faithfully reflect the use of the word at appropriate moments, and this is confirmed to some extent by its similar use by Theophanes. Here as well λαός denotes a group standing on the side of good, while ὄχλος supports the scheming of Emperor Anastasius and his adherents. This is clearly visible in the fragment where, in the church of St Michael in the Great Palace and in Hagia Sophia, the schismatic monks (aposchists) are using the mob (Οἱ δὲ ἀποσχιστοὶ ὄχλον μισθωτόν) to sow disarray, while the people (λαός) are protesting and mocking these practices, and is also able to drive out the troublemakers out of the church. A crowd had been gathered in a similar manner in the past by Timothy Aelurus, a mob disapproved of by the author (although not by Timothy himself; ὄχλος ἄτακτος Ἀλεξανδρέων), and the procession went through the streets; it may be noted that during the procession the Patriarch suffered a fall.[34]

A passage attributed to Theodore preserved in Theophanes' *Chronography* deserves a separate mention. It is rather atypical,

---

[32] Theod., IV, 502, pp. 143, 20–23 (ed. Hansen 1995b) i.e. Theoph., AM 6005, pp. 157, 30–34 (ed. De Boor 1883).

[33] Which is not a specific narrative method, used only by the Church historians, cf. e.g. John the Lydian, *De ostentis*, 8 (ed. Wachsmuth 1897) or Menander Protector, fr. 7, 3 (ed. Blockley 1985).

[34] Theod., IV, 483, pp. 137, 23–24 & 28–29; III, 404, pp. 113, 11–14 (ed. Hansen 1995b) [Theod.², 129; 68].

in that the ὄχλος, after turmoil and numerous victims of disturbances resulting from the conflict over the Trisagion, insulted Anastasius, demanded a different Emperor, and praised the rebel Vitalian (τοῦ ὄχλου καταβοῶντος Ἀναστασίου καὶ ἄλλον βασιλέα αἰτούντων, Βιταλιανὸν δὲ πάντων εὐφημούντων ὡς αὐτοκράτορα).[35] Although I do not think this passage should be considered in a legalistic aspect, with the assumption that the mob's support for a usurper (even though those gathered were orthodox) caused the historian to withhold his sympathy, yet the phrase may be interpreted in two ways. Either the nature of the riots and the devastation of the capital moved the historian to negatively evaluate the mob because of its actions at the time and refer to it with a different term, or the word (referring to a crowd that gathered in a just cause) would have been here synonymous with πλῆθος/πλήθη. It would not have been an isolated case, since the meaning of the term ὄχλος appears to have been drifting from 'mob' to 'crowd' also, e.g., in the works of Socrates, Hermias Sozomen and John Malalas.[36] Ultimately, one cannot rule out the possibility that the author of the *Chronography* used a different term from the one written by Theodore, as this would not have been unusual. Therefore, the significance of this sole application of the word will have to remain ambiguous, even though it could otherwise inform us about the historian's attitude towards the citizens of Constantinople.

Within the preserved nucleus of Theodore's work there are no epithets that would describe the Constantinopolitan community as a whole – neither in a general context, nor in relation to the conduct of the inhabitants of the empire's capital at a specific time. Beside the lack of δῆμος, one may notice the absence of οἱ οἰκοῦντες / οἱ οἰκήτορες, and only once in the *Epitome* do we hear of οἱ δημόται (and only implicitly Constantinopolitan);[37] πάντες appears infrequently and in various contexts, while πολλοί

---

[35] Theod., IV, 508, pp. 145, 16 (ed. Hansen 1995b) i.e. Theoph., AM 6005, pp. 159, 15–17 (ed. De Boor 1883).

[36] Socrates, II, 16, 9–13 (ed. Hansen 1995a); Sozomen, VIII, 22, 4 (ed. Bidez – Hansen 1995); John Malalas, XVIII, 90, 4[II] & 7[II]; XVIII, 143, 85–86 (ed. Thurn 2000).

[37] Theod., IV, 524, pp. 151, 28–29 (ed. Hansen 1995b) [Theod.[2], 155] – populace knows Justin's wife Lupicine by the name Euphemia.

– only once. In only one passage τινές refers to those who were expressing the general opinion of the capital[38] (here we have certainty that the preserved wording comes directly from the original author). A similar sole occurrence of οἱ τῆς βασιλίδος may refer both to the city's inhabitants and to the decision-makers, or those who were expressing specific position in religious conflicts,[39] while οἱ πολῖται – also a single instance in the preserved material – refers to citizens of Antioch, in the context of events which occurred in that city.[40]

What is even more significant, the designation οἱ Κωνσταντινουπολῖται does not appear even once (it may be found only in a passage by Victor – but it cannot be assumed that this word was taken directly from the source, and in Alexander the Monk's *Laudatio Barnabae*, which is not sufficient to attempt a guess at the words Theodore may have used[41]). At the same time οἱ Βυζάντιοι is found in the *Epitome* only once, evidently in comparison with the οἱ Ἀλεξανδρεῖς.[42] Regardless of the scale of the abridgement by the epitomator, these terms could have easily been used to convey information of general nature, therefore the likelihood of their reappearance in the summaries may be considered relatively high; they have also been employed by other historians and writers of the early Byzantine period.[43]

Thus, even though the general populace of the capital – ordinary people of Constantinople – are visibly present, they do not appear to be defined by their Constantinopolitan label or specificity. Neither do we find in the contents of the reconstructed *Church history* assessments or opinions expressed through the use of an epithet or even a one-sentence remark. However, it needs to be stressed that it is exactly this type of personal opin-

---

[38] Theod., IV, fr. 52a, pp. 132, 21–22 (ed. Hansen 1995b) [Theod.², fr. 1].

[39] Theod., III, 431, pp. 119, 10 (ed. Hansen 1995b) [Theod.², 90].

[40] Theod., III, 435, pp. 121, 16 (ed. Hansen 1995b) [Theod.², 94].

[41] Theod., IV, fr. 77, pp. 151, 12 (ed. Hansen 1995b) i.e. Victor, a. 518.2 (ed. Cardelle de Hartmann 2001); Alexander, 35 (ed. Kollman – Deuse 2007). On the term see Georgacas 1947, p. 356.

[42] Theod., IV, 522, pp. 151, 17 (ed. Hansen 1995b) [Theod.², 153].

[43] For example Socrates, IV, 8, 10; IV, 38, 5; VII, 18, 17 (ed. Hansen 1995a); Stephan, A, 34; A, 148; A, 150; A, 164; B, 177, etc. (ed. Billerbeck 2010–2017); Marcellinus Comes, a. 399, 3; a. 428, 1; a. 472, 1; a. 480, 1; a. 491, 1; a. 512, 3 (ed. Croke 1995).

ion that is particularly susceptible to being removed by the scissors of an epitomator – at least one like the anonymous author of this particular *Epitome*, as he appears through the result of his efforts. Nonetheless, as is evident even from the passages cited in this subsection, this does not mean that Theodore did not express his opinion on the subject of the Constantinopolitans in action. His attitude was most often shaped by the religious sentiments of the populace, i.e. the positions adopted in the conflicts about orthodoxy of the faith (in particular visible in the parts describing the times of Basiliscus and Anastasius) – but not exclusively so.

2. Individual and group protagonists of the Constantinopolitan narratives

Even the above examination alone of the terms used to denote the collective protagonist in the Constantinopolitan public sphere clearly shows the presence and inclusion of this central character in the source in a manner more or less typical for the times, yet with some interesting differences present in details. These differences shed some light, perforce reaching us only in part, on the author's views, and not solely on the demands and expectations of this particular genre of literature.

Of particular interest, not only in this context, would seem to be the bringing together and comparing of all of the collective and individual actors present in the source. In this case, too, we need to depend on a problematic text, as the very principle of creating an epitome eliminates from the work characters who were mentioned in the background, and those who were mentioned once, or in an incidental manner, in a given text. Nonetheless, the acting subjects described more broadly in the context of their activities seem to appear in the epitome more frequently (this conclusion can be reached on the basis of comparison of the preserved fragments and the entirety of the epitome in all its manuscripts). Considering the above, the comparative approach would seem justified, as long as we remember that the numerical values given below need to be treated as approximate.

The principles on which the analysis below was prepared are generally as follows:

1. Only actors, acting subjects, are included.

2. Only the events which occurred in Constantinople are taken into account, or the events which are nearly certain to have occurred there (on the basis of context or other source narratives). Because of this, entries relating to persons who had ties to Constantinople, but which described their activities during the non-Constantinopolitan period of their life (e.g. prior to their arrival in the city, in exile, on journeys), are not taken into consideration.

3. Emperors, the natural and obviously present protagonists of the histories of the Eastern Empire, have not been included. The *Augustae* and other women from the imperial family have been listed, but they have been excluded from the numerical summary.

4. Dating according to the bishops and consuls has not been included.

5. Collective and individual actors have been divided into categories, allowing for a further analysis of the collation; a small number of these, not affecting the general outcome, cannot be clearly categorised.

6. Locations in the source are listed in an abbreviated form, for the sake of the readability of the list.

7. Each of the persons was included once (although one does, of course, need to take note of the frequency with which they appear), and every collective, with regard of its nature, according to its occurrence in the subdivisions of the text.

Despite observing these strict rules, the comparison and conclusions are necessarily approximate, and their primary purpose lies in demonstrating the richness of the narrative of the *Church history*'s original text.

INDIVIDUAL CHARACTERS (67)

– **officials and military commanders (25):** Paulinus, *magister officiorum* (I, 340); Chrysaphius, function not specified (I, 346; I, 350; I, 353); Aspar (II, 378; II, 399) function not specified; Studius (II, 384) function not specified; *praepositus* Gratissimus (II, 384); *hypatikos* John Vincomalus (II, 387); Marcian, brother-in-law of Zeno (III, 419; III, 420); Romulus, brother of Marcian (III, 420); Procopius, brother of Marcian (III, 420); John the Scythian (IV, 449) – commander in conflict with the Isaurians; John Cyrtus (Kyrtos) – commander in conflict with the Isaurians (IV, 449); John the Patrician, father-in-law of Athenodorus (IV, 449); Eusebius *magister officiorum* (IV, 450); Festus, senator and Roman envoy to Anastasius (fr. 48 i.e. *De schismatibus*, 6 ≈ IV, 461); Eutychianus, overseer of the palace/baths [*diaitarios*] in Helenianae (IV, fr. 52a); Apion first senator (IV, 482); Heraclides, son of Apion (IV, 482); Celer *magister officiorum* (IV, 487; IV, 490; IV, 491); eunuch Calopodius (IV, 491); tribune Eutropius (IV, 497); Hypatius, *magister militum* (IV, fr. 64; IV, 503); Platon PVC (IV, fr. 65 i.e. Victor, a. 513 = IV, 508 i.e. Theoph., AM 6005); Marinus (fr. 65 i.e. Victor, a. 513); Pompey, cousin of Emperor Anastasius (IV, 505 i.e. Theoph., AM 6005); Anastasius, *dux* of Palestine (IV, 518)

– clergy (35): Proclus, bishop of Constantinople (I, 338; I, 343); Nestorius (I, 340); Flavian, bishop of Constantinople (I, 343; I, 344 = Victor, 1; I, 346); Eusebius, bishop of Dorylaeum (I, 344 = Victor, 1); Eutyches, archimandrite at Job and a heretic (I, 344 = Victor, 1; I, ex ACN II, 2); Anatolius bishop of Constantinople (I, 351; I, ex ACN II, 2; I, 357; I, 361; I, 365; II, 371; II, 372; II, 376; II, 378); Gennadius, bishop of Constantinople (II, 376; II, 378; II, 380; II, 381; fr. 11; II, 383 = fr. 12; II, 392; II, 395; II, 396); Acacius, *orphanotrophus*, later bishop of Constantinople (II, 376; III, 406; III, 407; III, 408; III, 412; III, 420; III, 421; III, 429; III, 431; III, 432; III, 433 [= fr. 26 & 27 a-d]; III, 434; III, 440 = III, fr. 32); Marcian, *oeconomus* of the Constantinopolitan church (II, 376; II, 394); Charisius, transgressive clergyman (fr. 12; v II, 383 with no name); monk Bassianus (II, 386; II, 387; III, fr. 27a); Anthimus, composer of troparia (II, 388); Timocles, composer of troparia (II, 388); Peter the Fuller, in hiding among the Acoemetae (III, 403); Timothy Aelurus (III, 404); Daniel the Stylites (III, 407; III, 408); monk Olympius (III, 408); monk Dius (III, fr. 27a = III, 434); Fravitta, bishop of Constantinople (III, 440 = III, fr. 32); Euphemius, bishop of Constantinople (III, 440 = III, fr. 32; III, 441 = fr. 34; IV, 446 = fr. 39 [Victor, a. 491.1]; IV, 449; fr. 41 [Victor, a. 492.2]; IV, 450; IV, 453; IV, 454; IV, 455 = Victor, a. 496); John Tabannesiotes, exiled patriarch of Alexandria, visiting Rome (IV, 452 i.e. Theoph. AM 5984); Paul, *ecdicus* HS (IV, 453); Macedonius, bishop of Constantinople (IV, 455 = fr. 45 [Victor a. 496]; IV, 456; IV, 457; fr. 48 i.e. *De schismatibus*, 6; IV, 458; IV, 459 i.e. Theoph. AM 5991; IV, 461; IV, 470; IV, 471; IV, 474; IV, 477; IV, 478; IV, 483; IV, 484; IV, 486; IV, 487; IV, 488; IV, 490; IV, 491; IV, 492); Chrysaorius, deacon (IV, 459 i.e. Theoph. AM 5991); Euthymius, leader of Arians in Constantinople (IV, fr. 52a); Magnus, presbyter at Holy Apostles of Pariteichisma (IV, fr. 52a); John, *ecdicus* and deacon at St Stephen (IV, fr. 52a); Philoxenus (Theoph., AM 5999 ≈ IV, 470); Deuterius, bishop of Arians in Constantinople (IV, 475); bishop Julian of Halicarnassus (IV, 484); monk Severus (IV, 484); Timothy, bishop of Constantinople (IV, 492; IV, fr. 58 = IV, 493; IV, 494; IV, 495; IV, fr. 62 i.e. John of Damascus, or. 3; IV, 500 i.e. Theoph. AM 6005; IV, 501; IV, 502 i.e. Theoph., AM 6005; IV, 504 i.e. Theoph., AM 6005; IV, 507; IV, 508 i.e. Theoph., AM 6005; IV, 523 = IV, fr. 76 i.e. Victor, a. 517.2); archdeacon John (IV, 507); John II Cappadocian, bishop of Constantinople (IV, 523 = IV, fr. 76 i.e. Victor, a. 517.2); Dioscorus the Younger bishop of Alexandria (IV, 522)

– **others (4):** Olympius, blasphemer at the baths in Helenianae (IV, fr. 52a); Acholius, would-be killer of Macedonius (IV, 471); a certain Barbas, baptised by Deuterius (IV, 475); Julian, an old man (IV, fr. 62 i.e. John of Damascus, or. 3)

– **women (3 / [11, with the imperial family included]):** Pulcheria (I, 336; I, 340; I, 352; I, 353; I, 355, I, 359; I, 363); Marina (I, 353); Eudocia (I, 353); Matrona, an aristocrat, later a nun (II, 386; IV, 459 i.e. Theoph. AM 5991); Verina (III, 401 sq; III, 420); Zenonis (III, 402; III, 412; III, 413); Leontia and Ariadne (III, 420); Ariadne (IV, 446; IV, 489; IV, 508 i.e. Theoph., AM 6005; IV, fr. 73 i.e. Victor, a. 515.2); Sophia, an eminent nun (IV, 459 i.e. Theoph. AM 5991); Magna, emperor's sister-in-law (IV, 481); Juliana (IV, 504 i.e. Theoph., AM 6005)

INDIVIDUAL CHARACTERS, ANONYMOUS (>21):

– **officials and military commanders (>7):** an aristocrat, husband of the pious Matrona, abandoned by her for a monastery (II, 386);

some of the senators who maintained contact with Basiliscus through Verina (III, 401); cubicularius sent o Paphlagonia to bring Severus to Constantinople (fr. 37 / 9[37]); the two accusers of Macedonius (IV, 490); the two prefects who were to judge the bishop (IV, 490)

– **clergy (>9):** deacon sent by Gennadius to the church of St Eleutherius (fr. 12, in II, 383 omitted); two bishops and an *ecdicus*, sent by Felix to Constantinople in connection with the matter of Acacius (III, 431; III, 432; III, 433 = fr. 26; III, 434); clergyman who killed the would-be assassin of Euphemius (IV, 453); archdeacon HS in year 496, accompanying Macedonius at a meeting with Euphemius (IV, 456); subdeacon of Homonoea (IV, fr. 52a); deceased hegumen of Stoudius (IV, 507); his successor (IV, 507)

– **others (4):** a certain painter (II, 382 = fr. 11); a certain pagan (fr. 11); assassin who was to kill bishop Euphemius (IV, 453); a painter – a Syro-Persian Arian from Cyzicus (IV, 467)

– **women (1):** the wife of Pompey (IV, 505 i.e. Theoph., AM 6005)

GROUP CHARACTERS (83):

– **populace in general (22):** a numerous crowd of the faithful – entirety of clergy, monks and laypeople, gathered in a church and welcoming Marcian and Pulcheria (I, 355); clergy and the people, successfully pleading with Marcian to bring back the remains of Flavian to the city (I, 357); the mob which killed bishop Anatolius (II, 378); disorderly mob of Alexandrians participating in a procession of Timothy Aelurus in Constantinople (III, 404); people of Constantinople raising in defence of Chalcedon against Basiliscus (III, 406); the entire city, men and women (III, 407); the people, after the exile of Basiliscus (III, 408); the people protesting against the deposition of Euphemius and begging the Emperor (IV, 455); the monasteries of Dion, Bassianus, Matrona and the Acoemetae (IV, 459 i.e. Theoph. AM 5991); the people rebelling against the heterodox images, created on the orders of Anastasius (IV, 467 and 469); the people protesting against the abuses by the aposchist monks, in the defence of Trisagion (IV, 483); the people demonstrating against Anastasius and his version of the Trisagion (IV, 485); women and children marching along the people (IV, 485); the people arriving with Macedonius to the palace (IV, 486); the laypeople supporting Macedonius (IV, 500 i.e. Theoph. AM 6005); the people stopping bishop Timothy from including Severus instead of Flavian into the diptychs (IV, 502 i.e. Theoph., AM 6005); numerous victims of the riots / the people rebelling against the changed Trisagion (IV, fr. 65 i.e. Victor, a. 513 ≈ IV, 508 i.e. Theoph., AM 6005); the people swearing to accede to Vitalian's demands (IV, 509 i.e. Theoph 6006); the people outraged by the emperor breaking his oath (IV, 511 i.e. Theoph., AM 6006); Byzantines (IV, 522); the people outraged during the ingress of John the Cappadocian (IV, 523); the populace (IV, 524)

– **army (3):** the entire army proclaims Marcian as emperor in Hebdomon (I, 354); the army sent against the Isaurians (IV, 449); the palace guard (IV, 486)

– **more specific groups (57):**

people in power (10): entourage of consul Nomus (I, 346); senators (III, 408); supporters of Zeno (III, 420); senators exerting pressure on bishop Euphemius to accept Anastasius (IV, 446); officials insulting Macedonius (IV, 484); some of the senators (IV, 489); state officials present at Julian's interrogation (IV, fr. 62 i.e. John of Damascus, or. 3); senators sent to Vitalian; also the entirety of the senate (IV, 509 i.e. Theoph 6006; IV, 511 i.e. Theoph., AM 6006); officials (IV, 509 i.e. Theoph 6006); envoys of the senate to Vitalian (IV, 509)

clergy and monks (24): monks arriving in Constantinople regarding the matter of Theodore of Mopsuestia (338, s. 96, 12); bishops at the *endemusa*, disturbed by Eutyches' heresy (I, 344 = Victor, 1) and called together in the matter of Timothy Aelurus (II, 371); ill-behaving clergy, troubling Gennadius (II, 383 = fr. 12); Acoemetae monks brought to Studius (II, 384); clergy and monks of Constantinople acting in defence of Chalcedon along the people and against Basiliscus (III, 404); clergy (III, 412); those in the capital who sent letters to Felix, the bishop of Rome (III, 431); the foremost among the monks and the zealots, meeting with the *ecdicus* of Felix, the bishop of Rome (III, 434); certain monks delivering the deposition to Acacius (III, 434); bishops gathered at the *endemusa* (IV, 449; IV, 450; IV, 453; IV, 455); bishops at the *endemusa* attempting to ingratiate themselves with the emperor (IV, 455); Eutychian clergy (IV, 478); aposchist monks (IV, 478; IV, 483; IV, 484); some of the monks opposing Macedonius (IV, 478); Antiochene *apocrisiarii* visiting Macedonius (IV, 479); hegumeni of the monasteries protesting alongside the people (IV, 485); monks being addressed by the shouting crowd (IV, 486); monks from the Dalmatus (and other) monasteries (IV, 488); bribed monks and clergy (IV, 489); clergy (presbyters and deacons) co-accused alongside Macedonius (IV, 490); monks and clergy supporting Macedonius (IV, 500 i.e. Theoph., AM 6005); monks protesting alongside the people (IV, 502 i.e. Theoph., AM 6005); monks joining the rebellion (IV, 508 i.e. Theoph., AM 6005)

groups defined by their actions (15): Arians of Constantinople, recipients of Gaiseric's gifts (I, 366); certain people accusing Gennadius of Nestorianism (II, 395); Basiliscus' household attending Aelurus' procession (III, 404); people from Acacius' entourage, beating monks who delivered him the deposition (III, 434); Manichaeans and Arians rejoicing at Anastasius' ascension to the throne (IV, 448); Isaurians committing crimes in Constantinople (IV, 449); members of a plot against bishop Euphemius (IV, 453); Manichaeans in Constantinople (IV, 454); Arians exerting pressure to remove an image from Helenianae (IV, fr. 52a); enemies of Macedonius, intending to kill him (IV, 471); choristers from the church of the Archangel in the palace (IV, 483); mob directed by the emperor against Macedonius (IV, 483); certain 'supporters of disturbances' (IV, fr. 62 i.e. John of Damascus, or. 3); countryside mob attacking monks (IV, 502 i.e. Theoph., AM 6005); the Greens and the Blues (IV, fr. 65 i.e. Victor, a. 513)

others (8): the poor and the needy (I, 363; I, 365); those bathing in Helenianae with Olympius (IV, fr. 52a); persons rescuing Olympius (IV, fr. 52a); 'some/certain' people commenting on the fate of Olympius (IV, fr. 52a); bath attendants of Helenianae (IV, fr. 52a); servants of Eutychianus (IV, fr. 52a); servants of bishop Timothy (IV, fr. 62 i.e. John of Damascus, or. 3); factionists (fr. 65)

– women (1): women walking in a procession with children and hegumeni (IV, 485)

Combined results, presented in a table format:

individuals	officials and commanders	25	67
	clergy	35	
	others	4	
	women	3 [11]	
individuals, anonymous	officials and commanders	>7	>21
	clergy	>9	
	others	4	
	women	1	
groups	populace, in general	22	83
	military	3	
	specified groups	57	
	women	1	

When we examine the thus assembled characters present in parts of the *Church history* which refer to Constantinople, it is clear that the collective protagonist is an equivalent subject of the historian's narrative. Some general tendencies are present here also. The activity of emperors, as was previously mentioned, is unquestionable. This is also the case in relation to bishops of Constantinople, because of the work's genre and the place of its creation. Nonetheless, Theodore's work abounded in side topics, included a considerable number of minor protagonists, positioned lower in the hierarchy or less well-known in the capital, but at the same time playing major roles. The closer to the times during which Theodore was writing, the more common such actors became. In this sense, the history written by Theodore the Lector must have been a full-blooded and rich piece of historiography.

It is only natural that people of the Church appeared particularly frequently on the pages of the *History*, but it is also here that we can see a relatively high degree of diversity. While bishops unquestionably retain the leading roles (both in terms of the main thread of the narrative and the number of times individuals are mentioned), the number of persons occupying lower positions in the hierarchy (*ecdici*, deacons, presbyters) is rather considerable. Named monks are primarily major figures, of considerable rank in the capital, or those who particularly distinguished themselves by their attitude. Clergy and monks mentioned as a collective, or individually but anonymously, further supplement this group. It should be noted that the absence of individual personal details, much like in the case of many other similar works, may stem either from an unwillingness to provide names of those who were fighting against orthodoxy (as it was understood by Theodore and those whose views he followed), or because it was impossible to obtain such details, or because of a desire to make a generalisation. People close to power are present relatively often: high- and low-ranking officials, commanders, emperor's closest advisers, aristocrats. Women are nearly entirely absent, with the exception of the wives and sisters of rulers who co-participated in power, or exerted influence on the flow of events in the capital. Regarding collective protagonists, beside the previously mentioned fact of the frequent appearance of a crowd/Constantinopolitans, one other thing is of note: the variously sized groups defined exclusively through their attitude or specific behaviour do not constitute a majority of the groups that the author, in one way or another, has defined. When we consider that the *Epitome* was a basis for a considerable part of the list, confirmed either by fragments or mentions by Victor of Tunnuna or Theophanes, it would appear that the combined number of characters must have been even greater, and Theodore's *Church history* was – despite its main theme – diverse.

The proportions of the general and detailed descriptions can be captured with even greater ease if one compares Theodore's *History* with other sources from the period. Of course, not every preserved work is suitable for such a comparison, one also needs to keep in mind the difference in the volume of the contents and the present-day state of preservation. Since a considerable part of early Byzantine historiography is focused on the events which occurred in Constantinople, we may select from a greater number of historic works. In comparing these with Theodore, other

Church histories and chronicles are of particular relevance. Both of these genres have other advantages as well, as chronographies are characterised by a fairly steady pace and because they tend to point towards acting subjects in an almost encyclopaedic fashion. Historiographies in turn allowed for a more common use of side mentions, a variety of narrative embellishments and, to a greater extent, offering opinions on events. At the same time, Church history was at that time a relatively new subgenre, and it used a classical, yet not archaic, style in relating i.a. the kind of events that had not been previously a subject of written works. In wanting to remain within the milieu of Constantinopolitan authors, ones either born or writing there, we may choose the *Church history* of Socrates Scholasticus (undoubtedly a *Byzantius*), the laconic chronicle of Marcellinus Comes (excluding, however, the *Continuation* for the years 534–48) and the part of book XVIII of *Chronography* by John Malalas, as it was written in the capital.[44] The particular groups of collective and individual subjects have been grouped according to the same rules as the above list based on Theodore's work.[45]

		Theodore (439–518) 79 years		Malalas (XVIII, 71 sqq; 532–63) 31 years		Marcellinus (379–534) 155 years		Socrates (305–439) 134 years	
Individuals	officials and commanders	25		39		28		16	
	Clergy	35	67	6	62	23	57	82	109
	Others	4		16		6		11	
	Women	3		1		–		–	

(cont.)

[44] The problem of the last part of John Malalas' *Chronography* is not to be solved easily. I am convinced by those authors who support the single authorship of the whole chronicle and support the claim that the part in question, Constantinopolitan and not Antiochene, was written by Malalas during his stay in the capital of the empire, after the decades of the more or less permanent stay in Constantinople. Udal'cova 1971, pp. 19–20; Hunger 1978, Bd. I, p. 320; Croke 1990, pp. 19–25; PLRE, IIIa, pp. 662–63 (s.v. Ioannes Malalas 50); Maas 1992, p. 95; Kokoszko 1998, p. 7; Thurn 2000, pp. 1*–4*; Treadgold 2010, pp. 237–40; I addressed the issue in Kompa 2010, p. 798; Kompa 2014, pp. 50–51.

[45] The detailed list and analysis is to be found in Kompa 2014, pp. 122–33.

		Theodore (439–518) 79 years		Malalas (XVIII, 71 sqq; 532–63) 31 years		Marcellinus (379–534) 155 years		Socrates (305–439) 134 years	
individuals, anonymous	officials and commanders	7		5		1		2	
	Clergy	9	21	2	15	–	2	15	29
	Others	4		5		1		11	
	Women	1		3		–		1	
Groups	populace, in general	22		13		12		24	
	Military	3	83	8	54	1	49	6	162
	specified groups	57		32		36		127	
	Women	1		1		–		5	

The above comparison is of particular interest in that it provides a good illustration of the variety in the approach of the narratives. Each of the works encompasses a different chronological period. The number of details and persons listed in the narrative does not appear to depend on the genre. The selected part of the book eighteen of John Malalas' work, describing roughly the thirties, forties and fifties of the sixth century, with its 62 named and described individuals, further 15 described without mentioning their names, and 54 group subjects, exceeds in the level of detail the entirety of Marcellinus' chronicle, which encompassed the period of not thirty-something years, but of over one hundred and fifty (there, we find 57 named individuals, 2 unnamed ones, and 49 groups). The matter goes further than simply the level of precision – John Malalas more often mentions individual people whose names he did not know, but whose role in the events he considered significant. Marcellinus almost never does that. The role of such actors of history can be seen even more clearly in Socrates, and not only because the historiographical narrative allowed for that. The persons appearing here made the narrative more plausible, they were needed for the presentation of the causes and development of events, and featured as initiators and key players in these developments.

The proportions between the clergy and laypeople of Constantinople is worth noting. In book eighteen of *Chronography*, lay officials, both civilian and military, clearly dominate in the attention they receive over Church dignitaries, and the source noted only six bishops of the capital. In the *Chronicle* of Marcellinus, the number of lay and church officials is nearly equal, and this fact does not lose its significance even if the individual entries list several bishops at a time, raising their overall number. In Socrates' *Church history* there is a clear and easily seen pre-eminence of clergy over lay officials, naturally resulting from the work's character, although one should note that a considerable number of the mentioned clergy who took part in the described events were guests, only temporarily staying in Constantinople. The considerable proportion of non-homoousian clergy, from Socrates' point of view schismatics or heretics, should also be noted.

It is clear that, among the lay persons whose names the sources mentioned, the most important place, beside the emperors and their families, was occupied by the chief imperial dignitaries. It was their actions that most often influenced the events in the city, and for that reason their causative role was often acknowledged. However, there are considerable differences between the respective works. The much more detailed and precise Malalas, for example, devotes much greater attention to including the city's prefects than Marcellinus, who practically does not notice them. The author of book eighteen lists sixteen other persons who are neither among the most important courtiers, nor the capital's clergy, but who represent various other social groups. Even if some of them are simply the plotters from Justinian's times, one should not omit to mention this attention to detail of the chronicle – as it was not a universal quality of the genre. Socrates, more so than other chroniclers, plucked out from the factual material and preserved the most important intellectual figures of the time, even those of pagan background.

The number and diversity of collective characters in the various scenes is of paramount importance. The overall comparison shows that crowds play an important role in the narrative, the ordinary people are not dominated by the elite in the overall description, and the relevant groups can be characterised even

271

by such criteria as their extemporary grouping or participation in the course of events. The historians, for reasons particular to their worldview, may have had mixed attitudes towards them, indeed, even grouped them according to their own views, but it cannot be said that the ordinary people have been excluded. These are the eyewitnesses – or even initiators – of events, Constantinopolitans as a whole, rioters, victims of earthquakes and fires, and those who survived the disasters; all of the undifferentiated adherents of a particular religious view, and specific religious groups gathered in one place at the same time; those only visiting the city; imperial envoys and heralds; faction members as well as the senators.

Where does the work of Theodore Lector, or rather its remains, fit into this picture? With the 67 named Constantinopolitan individuals, more than 21 mentioned anonymously and 83 group subjects, it resembles in structure the *Church history* by Socrates, especially if one considers the shorter period of only 80 years described by Theodore, compared to the *c.* 135 years in his predecessor's work. The matter, however, involves more than a simple arithmetic, and one needs to consider one other circumstance when comparing the sole large surviving fragment of the *History* (fr. 52a / 1) with its summary in the *Epitome* [465 / 115].[46] The epitomator made the following comment (cod. Par. Gr. 1555A):

> **Ὀλυμπιός τις** Ἀρειανὸς εἰς λουτρὸν λουόμενος Ἑλενιανῶν, τολ-
> μηρῶς βλασφημήσας ἐλεεινῷ θανάτῳ ἐν τῇ νεροφόρῳ ἀπώλετο·
> τὸ δὲ γενόμενον γράψαντες **οἱ πιστοὶ** ἐν εἰκόνι πρὸς τῇ νεροφόρῳ
> ἀνέθεντο. **Εὐτυχιανός τις** τῶν διαιταρίων ὁ πρῶτος χρήματα
> λαβὼν ὑπό **τινων Ἀρειανῶν** τὴν εἰκόνα κατήγαγεν, καὶ αὐτὸς
> τὸ σῶμα δαπανηθεὶς ἀπώλετο.

As we can see, firstly, in the case of this entry the epitomator left the names of Olympius and Eutychianus in place, even though in neither his view, nor in the view of the original author, the pair had played any other role in history – the sole reason for their mention lay in the events being described. Secondly, of Theo-

---

[46] John of Damascus, *Contra imaginum calumniatores*, or. 3, Florilegium, III, 90 = Theod. IV, fr. 52a, pp. 131, 10 – 133, 32 (ed. Hansen 1995b) [Theod.², 1] and Theod., IV, 465, pp. 131, 24–28 (ed. Hansen 1995b) [Theod.², 115].

dore's entire lengthy relation the epitomator left a brief description comprising 47 words (784 words in Theodore). As a result, there remain only four acting subjects: Olympius, the faithful, Eutychianus, and certain Arians. Nonetheless, such marked abbreviation did not leave room for four other characters mentioned by Theodore (Euthymius, the leader of the Arians in Constantinople; Magnus, a presbyter of Holy Apostles at Pariteichisma; John, an *ecdicus* and deacon at St Stephen; an anonymous subdeacon from Homonoea), nor for five acting groups (those bathing at Helenianae with Olympius; those rescuing Olympius; 'some/certain' (persons) commenting on Olympius' fate; the bath attendants at Helenianae; Eutychianus' servants. Of the thirteen subjects, therefore, only four remain; nothing else shows the degree of the abbreviation so well. True, the story about Olympius and Eutychianus in general is rather extraordinary, if one were to compare all the individual events of the *Epitome*, and one cannot assume an even distribution of the actors throughout the entirety of the narrative by using simple arithmetic. Nonetheless, even if we were to assume that the entirety of the *Church history* had been only half again more abundant in acting subjects of the narrative than its present state reconstructed primarily on the basis of the *Epitome*, we would already have a work more abundant in protagonists of Constantinopolitan passages than Socrates' *Church history* in its present state. In that case, Theodore would have matched Socrates in numerical comparison in describing a period shorter by 55 years.

The proportion of individuals, clergy and laypersons, presented by Theodore shows a predominance of the people of the Church. It is, however, much more balanced in this regard through a more representative inclusion of laypersons. These are imperial officials, commanders, but also lower ranking officials and several of the Constantinopolitans who certainly were not in close proximity to the imperial throne. Much like in the other works being compared here, we can see only a limited presence of women – removal of the lists of imperial families makes this tendency more obvious, for if our sources do provide information about women, these are the wives and daughters of the emperors (in Theodore, nine out of twelve individually mentioned women). Where women appear anonymously or in groups, it is an indication that this absence did not mean absence from the urban space, but rather from institutional structures of power and from the historiographic narrative.

Theodore's approach to permanent or incidental collective subjects confirms the above observations on Socrates, Marcellinus and Malalas, and even surpasses those historians. The generalised inhabitants of the city appear here even more frequently than elsewhere, and even the more so, the groups specified in some manner do not consist exclusively of clergy or supporters of heterodox religious views. Also those holding power, the military (albeit infrequently), as well as representatives of lower social strata appear as collectively described group.

3. *Social groups and their representatives*

The value of the Constantinopolitan parts of Theodore's *Church history* lies also in the wealth of valuable remarks about the citizens of Constantinople as we perceive them as members of particular social groups. This is rather obvious in the case of such a large historiographic work, but Theodore's work makes the social reality of the empire's capital in the 5th-6th centuries better known to us even in its present, considerably truncated form. Anagnostes does not indicate his attitude, whether positive or negative, to groups and social strata as such (he does so only for religious groups, such as Arians or Manichaeans/Monophysites, and even then it is usually done in an indirect manner[47]). First and foremost, however, he provides valuable factual material; more on this below.

Let us note here: here and there, he includes laconic catalogues, separating certain groups from the crowd or the whole, and thus shows his (more or less typical) view of the social structure of the city. The typical division into people of the Church and laypersons is a common one. The numerous crowd welcoming Marcian and Pulcheria is: κλῆρος ἅπας καὶ μοναχοὶ καὶ λαϊκοί (all the clergy and monks and laymen), κλῆρος and λαός are asking Marcian to bring

---

[47] Theod., I, 366, pp. 103, 13–14; IV, 454, pp. 128, 9–13 (ed. Hansen 1995b) [Theod.², 31; 107]; on label 'Manichaeans' used here on non-Chalcedonians see Capizzi 1969, pp. 29–30; Kosiński 2018, p. 342; Kosiński 2019, pp. 220–22.

the remains of bishop Flavian into the capital, κλῆρος καὶ ὁ λαὸς καὶ τὸ μοναχικὸν Κωνσταντινουπόλεως (the clergy, people and the monks of Constantinople) jointly act in defence of Chalcedon against the efforts of Basiliscus, Peter the Fuller and Timothy Aelurus; Daniel the Stylite, going out to meet Basiliscus as the latter was leaving the city, brought with him τὸ μοναχικὸν καὶ πλῆθος ἐκ τοῦ λαοῦ – and afterwards, Basiliscus speaks in the church to Acacius, the clergy and the monks.[48] There are two further, similar examples in the passages of Theophanes' *Chronography* (and it is precisely the manner in which they are formulated that makes the text more likely to have been taken from Theodore): after Philoxenus was brought to the city, there is a riot of the clergy, monks and the people (τοῦ κλήρου καὶ τῶν μοναχῶν καὶ τοῦ λαοῦ κατ' αὐτοῦ ταραττομένων); and similarly: Anastasius and Timothy have done many wrongs to the monks, as well as to clergy and the laypeople, all of whom supported Macedonius and the Council (sc. of Chalcedon; πολλὰ κακὰ τοῖς ὑπὲρ Μακεδονίου καὶ τῆς συνόδου μοναχοῖς τε καὶ κληρικοῖς καὶ λαϊκοῖς ἐπεδείξαντο).[49]

Such a way of writing, ecclesiastical rather than strictly social, is relatively frequent, and only a few examples of other enumeration could be cited. True, the one occasion the author stated that Acacius was supported, in defending Chalcedon, by the entire populace of the city, both men and women (πάσης ὁμοῦ τῆς πόλεως ἀνδράσιν ἅμα καὶ γυναιξὶν ἐν τῇ ἐκκλησίᾳ κατὰ Βασιλίσκου συναθροισθείσης).[50] In another place, he included a catalogue, which we could call political, for it lists those swearing an oath that they accept Vitalian's demands: Τοῦ δὲ βασιλέως καὶ τῆς συγκλήτου καὶ τῶν λοιπῶν ἀρχόντων τε καὶ λαῶν ὀμοσάντων καὶ βεβαιωσάντων ταῦτα οὕτω γίνεσθαι, εἰρήνη γέγονεν.[51] We do not,

---

[48] Theod. I, 355, pp. 100, 14–16; I, 357, pp. 18–19; III, 406, pp. 113, 17–20; III, 408, pp. 114, 1–4 (ed. Hansen 1995b) [Theod.², 20; 22; 70; 72]. Similar catalogue, concerning Alexandria: πάντων ὁμοῦ ἐπισκόπων καὶ κλήρου καὶ μοναχῶν καὶ λαοῦ – Theod. III, 424, pp. 117, 19–21 (ed. Hansen 1995b) [Theod.², 84].

[49] Theod., IV, 470, pp. 134, 21–22 (ed. Hansen 1995b) i.e. Theoph., AM 5999 (ed. De Boor 1883); IV, 500, pp. 142, 29 & 143, 11 i.e. Theoph, AM 6005 (ed. De Boor 1883).

[50] Theod., III, 407, pp. 113, 21–26 (ed. Hansen 1995b) [Theod.², 71].

[51] Theod., IV, 509, pp. 145, 26–28 (ed. Hansen 1995b) i.e. Theoph. 6006 (ed. De Boor 1883).

however, find here the features known from some of the other authors, such as Themistius, Proclus, Pseudo-Chrysostom or Eustratius,[52] which in and of itself also serves as an indicator of not only the aesthetics of the genre, but also of the lens through which the author perceived social issues.

Let us return for a moment to the previously cited original fragment, i.e. 52a. It is telling that the longest preserved story within the *Church history*, that of Olympius, the blasphemous user of the Helenianae baths, contains so many details, except for one – Olympius' social position; he is described only as Ὀλύμπιος γάρ τις τοὔνομα[53] and a follower of Euthymius, the Arian bishop of the city. His social and professional role did not seem important enough for the author of the narrative, or he was not aware of any details that could be used in his relation. The only fact we are told is that Olympius possessed his own litter.[54] One may wonder then: would we have known the social background of some of the other personages if the whole oeuvre survived (i.e. Acholius, a would-be murderer of Macedonius II or certain Barbas, baptised by Demetrius the Arian? Or the old Julian, interrogated by Timothy I[55])? In another passage the accusers of Macedonius are nothing more than δύο τινὰς φαύλους ('ordinary, common, inferior', but in this case used in the sense 'worthless, ignoble, contemptible, of little worth'). The omission of the details in that particular case, however, could stem from

---

[52] Themistius, or. V, 69d (ed. Schenkl – Downey 1965) (οἱ γεωργοῦντες, οἱ ῥητορεύοντες, οἱ πολιτευόμενοι, οἱ φιλοσοφοῦντες); Proclus, hom. IV, 2 (ed. Constas 2003) (those who should praise the Nativity: women, virgins, mothers, daughters, fathers, children, shepherds, rulers, governors / ἄρχοντες, consuls, common people / ἰδιῶται); Pseudo-Chrysostom, col. 386–87 (emperors / βασιλεῖς, soldiers / στρατιῶται, women / γυναῖκες, virgins / παρθένοι, children / νήπια, παῖδες, men / ἄνδρες, shepherds / ποιμένες, priests / ἱερεῖς, slaves / δοῦλοι, fishermen / ἁλιεῖς, tax collectors / τελῶναι, prostitutes / πόρναι); Eustratius, v. 2675–81 (ed. Laga 1992) (present to the funeral of the patriarch Euthymius: emperor, dignitaries, huge crowds of people, countless monks, soldiers).

[53] Theod., IV, 52a, pp. 131, 12 (ed. Hansen 1995b) [Theod.², fr. 1].

[54] See Greatrex, n. 26 in this volume.

[55] Theod. IV, 471, pp. 134, 24–26; IV, 475, pp. 136, 8–12; IV, fr. 62, pp. 142, 5–14 (ed. Hansen 1995b) [Theod.², 5] i.e. John of Damascus, *Contra imaginum calumniatores*, oratio 3, Florilegium III, 101 (ed. Kotter 1975: 187–88) (the extant fragment on Julian seems to suggest that he could be described or at least mentioned in one of the previous sections of the text).

two different reasons – the historian's reluctance to make the malefactors known and remembered or, alternatively, the historian's lack of information.[56]

Elites; Senate

For the historians of late antiquity, the representatives of the social elite are, relatively speaking, the most noticeable. Gathered around the emperor, who is presented as an initiator of a considerable part of the events described or in reacting to these, they too are present, as co-initiators or executors. The attitude of the authors towards the elite is not uniform, however – both in relation to the entire group, and to its individual members. Theodore, as was earlier mentioned, devoted a considerable amount of space to the imperial elite, especially for the genre of church history which he practised. The value of this work is therefore based on several aspects, which can be clearly seen despite the state of preservation of the history.

Firstly, he did not omit those who carried out the emperor's orders, even those of a lower rank. Secondly, he reliably indicated their names and roles, although as can be seen from the list above, he did not abstain from more general descriptions such as 'some of the senators', 'those around Nomus the consul', 'in the presence of public officials'. *Nota bene*, Socrates and Sozomen acted similarly.[57] Nonetheless, Theodore noted the activity of individual characters, and the epitomator, following in his footsteps, did not omit them either. The context most often relates to the religious affairs of the city. Thus, *magister officiorum* Paulinus is mentioned as the one in front of whom Nestorius was supposed to have vilified Pulcheria;[58] Chrysaphius pressured Theodosius II in the matter of Eutyches;[59] Aspar, as a heretic, acted against Gennadius,

---

[56] Theod., IV, 490, pp. 139, 11 (ed. Hansen 1995b) [Theod.², 136]. Cf. Theod., IV, fr. 62, pp. 142, 6 (ed. Hansen 1995b) [Theod.², fr. 5] i.e. John of Damascus, *Contra imaginum calumniatores*, oratio 3, Florilegium III, 101 (ed. Kotter 1975: 187–88): τινες τῶν ταῖς ταραχαῖς χαιρόντων.

[57] Socrates, II, 38, 9; VI, 2, 10; VI, 5, 1 & 9; VI, 10, 12; VII, 29, 1 & 11; VII, 31, 4; VII, 35, 2 (ed. Hansen 1995a); Sozomen, II, 30, 7; V, 8, 4; VI, 30, 9; VIII, 24, 8–9 & 12; IX, 5, 5–7, etc. (ed. Bidez – Hansen 1995).

[58] Theod., I, 340, pp. 97, 3–6 (ed. Hansen 1995b) [Theod.², 5].

[59] Theod., I, 346, pp. 98, 23–27 (ed. Hansen 1995b) [Theod.², 11].

and later persuaded Basiliscus to abandon the emperor's cause during the African campaign;[60] the prefect of the city Plato and the praetorian prefect Marinus carried out the will of emperor Anastasius and introduced innovations to Trisagion in the church of St Theodore in the already familiar sequence of events, which led to great disturbances in the city.[61] In some cases the remarks are more abundant and even in relation to the highest officials are a valuable addendum to the other biographic information we have today – the best example of this is *magister officiorum* Celer, as an adviser and executor of Anastasius' orders in relation to patriarch Macedonius II.[62]

Some of the fragments of Theodore's original history also indicated the role of the representatives of the elite in a context that extended beyond religious matters. Judging from the summary of the events in the epitome, the rebellion of Marcian, Procopius and Romulus (sons of emperor Anthemius and Euphemia) against Zeno in 479, an undoubtedly notorious event, echoes of which we find in other sources from the period, must have been extensively described. An alternative version of the fate of Marcian is also attested, and it differs Theodore's relation from the other contemporary sources in some details (if Theodore preserves the more accurate version, Marcian's ordination to presbyteriate took place in Constantinople before he was exiled).[63]

[60] Theod., II, 378, pp. 106, 17–19; II, 399, pp. 111, 20–21 (ed. Hansen 1995b) [Theod.², 43; 63].

[61] Theod., fr. 65, pp. 145, 4–5 (ed. Hansen 1995b) i.e. Victor of Tunnuna, a. 513 (ed. Cardelle de Hartmann 2001); Marcellinus, a. 512, 2 (ed. Croke 1995). Cf. PLRE II, pp. 726–28 (s.v. Marinus 7), 891–92 (s.v. Plato 3); Meier 2007, pp. 188–90; Meier 2009, pp. 281–84; Filipczak 2011, pp. 321–24; Filipczak 2013, pp. 476–81.

[62] Theod., IV, 487, pp. 138, 21; IV, 490, pp. 139, 15–16; IV, 491, pp. 139, 21–24 (ed. Hansen 1995b) [Theod.², 133; 136; 137]; cf. Zachariah, VII, 7–8 (ed. Brooks 1919–1924) (VII, 8n, pp. 262–63; ed. Greatrex 2011); Evagrius, III, 32 (ed. Bidez – Parmentier 2011–2014; transl. Whitby: pp. 173–74, n. 114). Cf. PLRE II, pp. 275–77 (s.v. Celer 2); Meier 2009, p. 264.

[63] Theod. III, 419–20, pp. 116, 10–19 (ed. Hansen 1995b) [Theod.², 81–82]; cf. PLRE II, p. 99 (s.v. Procopius Anthemius 9), 949 (s.v. Romulus 3). On Marcian cf. RE XIV.2, col. 1529 (s.v. Marcianus 35); PLRE II, pp. 716–18 (s.v. Marcianus 17); Begass 2018, pp. 185–86. On his revolt of 479 see Leszka 1999, pp. 42, 68–69; Kosiński 2010, pp. 103–05; Leszka 2011a, pp. 215–25; Begass 2018, pp. 293–95. Theodore might have been better informed than Evagrius (III, 26; ed. Bidez – Parmentier 2011–2014) as for time and place of Marcian's

At least a brief remark indicated the role of Hypatius, a nephew of Anastasius and son of Secundinus and Caesaria, in the course of Vitalian's rebellion.[64] Another remark included in the *Epitome* and devoted to significant individuals from the military elite (in which the broader description of political-military events intertwines with the narrative relating to religious events), mentions joint commanders in Anastasius' war against Isaurians, John the Scythian and John Cyrtus (*magistri militum*). John, a patrician, mentioned in the same place as father-in-law of the Isaurian rebel Athenodorus, did not leave any trace in any of the other contemporary sources, and only in Theodore do we read about the role he played during peace talks, when his attitude became the cause of the emperor's aversion towards patriarch Euphemius.[65]

Theodore, like Sozomen before him,[66] noted expressions of piety among the notables, such as the founding of monasteries and recruiting monks for them (Studius founded the monastery of St John and attracted there the Acoemetae; the *praepositus* Gratissimus founded the church of St Cyriacus and served his office there, living as a monk[67]). Particularly valuable in this context is the fragment of the *Epitome* devoted separately to John Vincomalus. Vincomalus (Βιγκομάλος), a character relatively well attested in the sources as an imperial representative during the proceedings of the Council of Chalcedon, receiver of imperial constitutions and Theodoret's correspondent, *magister officiorum* during the first years of Marcian's reign and a consul in 453, is a somewhat better known figure mainly thanks to Theodore. The historian painted a picture of a particular kind of piety

---

ordination, and he stresses that the rite was performed by the patriarch Acacius himself; the version by John of Antioch (303, pp. 514, 58–60; ed. Roberto 2005) seems to confirm Theodore's narrative.

[64] Theod., IV, 503, pp. 143, 27–30 (ed. Hansen 1995b) i.e. Theoph., AM 6005 (ed. De Boor 1883), pp. 157, 13–19; PLRE II, pp. 577–81 (s.v. Fl. Hypatius 6).

[65] Theod., IV, 449, pp. 126, 23–24 and 126, 28 – 127, 13–14 (ed. Hansen 1995b) [Theod.², 104]. Cf. PLRE II, pp. 602–03 (s.v. Ioannes Scytha 34), 604 (s.v. Ioannes 43), 617–18 (s.v. Ioannes *qui et* Gibbus 93). Further discussion on the fall of Euphemius and Theodore's account in e.g.: Dijkstra – Greatrex 2009, p. 229; Kosiński 2012, pp. 72–78.

[66] Sozomen, VIII, 17, 3; IX, 2, 4–6 & 8 (ed. Bidez – Hansen 1995).

[67] Theod., II, 384, pp. 108, 29–32 (ed. Hansen 1995b) [Theod.², 49].

manifested by the dignitary who adopted a monk's lifestyle in the monastery of Bassianus, and at the same time repeatedly visited the Great Palace as a consular (ὑπατικός), and acted as a member of the senate. Accompanied by an escort appropriate for an ex-consul to the gates of the monastery, upon returning to the monastic community he carried out relatively low menial functions, helping in the stables and the kitchens.[68]

The tale, as we can see, is related rather extensively by the epitomator, and the relevant passage was likely to have been even vaster in its initial, unabbreviated form, and separated out as a stand-alone part of the narrative (it appears that the aforementioned Studius did not receive a similar, broader, treatment). It is not only the attestation of the increasing popularity of monastic life in Constantinople that is of interest here (although that is the context of the telling of this story by Theodore, in this respect a faithful continuator of Sozomen). Because of the *Epitome*'s brevity, we do not have the circumstantial evidence that could indicate whether John was a *homo novus* of Marcian's times, or whether – as his name might suggest – he was a representative of the Latin minority, or a newcomer from the West.[69] However, in this one, small passage, we have an example of an official who also practiced piety of the kind that was known in the empire's capital from Pulcheria's times, which shaped the lifestyle of not only those who fell out of imperial favour, but also, one might think, of those who still enjoyed it.[70] In addition, we are faced with strong evidence of how striking and directly

[68] Theod., II, 387, pp. 109, 7–12 (ed. Hansen 1995b) [Theod.², 52]. On Vincomalus see: PLRE II, pp. 1169–70 (s.v. Ioannes Vincomalus); Guilland 1973, p. 47; Delmaire 1984, pp. 143, 162; Bagnall – Cameron – Schwartz – Worp 1987, pp. 440–43, 677, 679; Blaudeau 2005, p. 358 and n. 71; Millar 2006, pp. 198–99, Sidéris 2016, par. 25.

[69] Name Vincomalus, of either Latin or (much less probable) Germanic provenience, was popular in many parts of the Roman West – cf. González 2001, pp. 544–46 (author publishes a funerary inscription, found near Huelva, of certain Vincomalus, a Baetican bishop of the unknown diocesis, perhaps of Ilipla, and enlists a few further personages of that name from the Iberic Peninsula, Italy and Mauretania Caesariensis).

[70] And to that factor, rather than to the harsh measures, allegedly imposed also on Vincomalus by the hegumen Bassianus, I would ascribe the menial tasks performed by the senator; cf. Hatlie 2007, p. 101. At the same time, I do not dismiss the aesthetics and tradition of father-son and teacher-disciple relations within the monastic community (important remarks in Rapp 2016, pp. 103–08).

understood and felt was the difference between serving and ruling, between power and might, and poverty and subjection, in their external manifestations. More than that, we see how clear were the borders between the lay and monastic *decorum* – *vir consularis*, 'the most glorious office-holder',[71] clearly enjoying the respect of successive emperors, surrounded by the splendour of his status, voluntarily becomes a servant and a groom.

There is one other reason why it is worth scrutinising the passage about Vincomalus. Theodore described him not only as an ex-consul, but also emphasised his activity in the senate (καὶ ἐν μὲν τῷ παλατίῳ ἀδιαλείπτως προήρχετο καὶ ὡς εἷς τῶν συγκλητικῶν ἐχρημάτιζεν[72]). It is because the *Church history* is one of those Constantinopolitan sources,[73] which seemingly define the people of power most often through their senatorial rank or stress the role of senators in political events. Thus, Verina allowed the communication between Basiliscus and some of the senators (τινες τῆς συγκλήτου); Basiliscus in turn, escaping from the capital, forbade the senators from meeting with the patriarch Acacius; the senators, along with augusta Ariadne put pressure on bishop Euphemius to accept the election of the emperor Anastasius; Festus, Rome's envoy to Anastasius, is described in the *Epitome* with his senatorial rank (τις τῶν τῆς συγκλήτου Ῥώμης); Apion, characterised as the valiant commander in the fight against the Persians is first and foremost described as one of the first senators (τινα τῶν πρώτων ἐν τῇ συγκλήτῳ); empress Ariadne and some of the senators (τινες τῆς συγκλήτου) are worried about the emperor bribing monks and clergy, with the intention of removing the patriarch Macedonius; Justin, a new emperor, was characterised as an experienced commander and until that time a member of the senate, generally well regarded (ἀνὴρ πρεσβύτερος ἀπὸ στρατιωτῶν ἀρξάμενος καὶ μέχρι τῆς συγκλήτου προκόψας καὶ διὰ πάντων ἄριστος φανείς).[74] These are frequent remarks, not far

---

[71] ACO, II, 1, 1, pp. 55–56; Millar 2006, p. 198.

[72] Theod., II, 387, pp. 109, 7–12 (ed. Hansen 1995b) [Theod.², 52].

[73] Cf. Kompa 2014, pp. 185–93.

[74] Theod., III, 401, pp. 112, 15–17; III, 408, pp. 114, 1–4; IV, 446, pp. 126, 12–15; IV, 461, pp. 129, 28–29; IV, 482, pp. 137, 16–22; IV, 489, 6–10; IV, 524, pp. 151, 25–27 (ed. Hansen 1995b) [Theod.², 65; 72; 101; 112; 128; 135; 155]. Further examples are preserved in Theophanes: Theod. IV, 509, pp. 20–

removed from Theodore's times, distributed fairly evenly in the individual parts of his work. They reflect not only the role of the senate, which at that time, of course, was a more visible and lasting one than authoritative in a political sense (even though the latter could still at certain times be displayed by the senators),[75] but also on Theodore's perception of the senate as the source of the highest status and the keystone of the political elite. Here, too, Theodore follows in the footsteps of his predecessors, especially of Socrates,[76] and at the same time transposes such understanding of the senate's significance into his own times and, proportionally speaking, makes use of it even more frequently. Just as in the initial part of the acts of the Council of Chalcedon, on the pages of his work the οἱ πολιτικοὶ ἄρχοντες meet with the οἱ συγκλητικοί. Their status is of course not inviolable (as can be seen from the example of Apion, exiled and ordained a priest on the orders of Anastasius; Apion's son was at the same time forced into deaconate in Prusa[77]), but it is also not in doubt.

Clergy and the monks

Due to the very nature of Theodore's *Church history*, this particular social group is widely considered, and naturally includes Constantinopolitan clergy. Theodore's work is a story about clergy and monks, and that all-important and opinion-forming group, obviously exerting influence and in a way permeating the entirety of the community of the empire's capital, would require a separate essay to give justice to the role it plays even in this single

21 and 27 (ed. Hansen 1995b) i.e. Theoph. 6006 (the role of the Senate is stressed in process of Vitalian's appeasement: Anastasius sents 'some of the senators' to the rebel and the final truce is sworn by the emperor, the senat, the archons and the people); IV, 511, pp. 146, 21–22 (ed. Hansen 1995b) i.e. Theoph., AM 6006 (ed. De Boor 1883) – the whole populace and the Senate accuse Anastasius of perjury (πᾶς δὲ ὁ λαὸς καὶ ἡ σύγκλητος παρρησίᾳ ἐλοιδόρουν Ἀναστάσιον ὡς ἐπίορκον).

[75] Dagron 1974, pp. 193–210; Čekalova 2010, pp. 169–211; Begass 2018, pp. 478–85.

[76] Socrates, II, 30, 43; III, 26, 3; V, 8, 12; VI, 6, 9; VII, 48, 3–4 (ed. Hansen 1995a); Sozomen, IV, 6, 15; V, 8, 1; VIII, 4, 5 (ed. Bidez – Hansen 1995).

[77] Theod., IV, 482, pp. 137, 16–22 (ed. Hansen 1995b) [Theod.², 128]. Cf. PLRE II, pp. 111–12 (s.v. Apion 2); Beaucamp 2001, pp. 169–70; Hickey 2012, pp. 11–12; Begass 2018, pp. 79–81 (s.v. Fl. Apion I), 142 (s.v. Heracleides), 337, 426–27.

historiographic narrative. Because of this, the following paragraphs contain only a few remarks on the aspects of the presentation of the people of the Church by one of their own.

Regardless of the leitmotifs to which the *Church history* is subject and through the lens of which the historian evaluated particular member of the clergy, the abundance of the material he included, if one were to juxtapose all of the fragments describing the capital's churchmen and analyse them from only a general perspective (rather than a contextual one), its text provides us with an additional idea of the social reality of Constantinople. Many of the facts, some of which are reflected in other sources and some appearing uniquely, concern the bishops of the city – after all, this particular historical narrative was to a large extent about them. Theodore draws attention to the origin and previous functions of the newly ordained (Flavian, formerly a presbyter and a *skeuophylax* at Hagia Sophia; Anatolius – one of Alexandrian *apocrisiarii* (or representatives) in Constantinople; Gennadius – a presbyter; Fravitta – a presbyter at the church of St Thecla in Sycae; Macedonius II – a presybyter and a *skeuophylax*, and a relative of Gennadius; Timothy I – a presbyter and a *skeuophylax*; John II the Cappadocian, a syncellus of Timothy, a presbyter, from Colonaea).[78] Some of the descriptions revealed interesting factors influencing promotions within the Church hierarchy, up to the position of a patriarch, as can be attested to by a preserved note about the changes in the capital's church after the death of patriarch Anatolius – presbyter Gennadius becomes a bishop thanks to his relationship with the *orphanotrophus* Acacius, while Marcian, a former Novatian, becomes an *oeconomus*, on the recommendation of the new bishop.[79]

The portrayal of the clergy depended, of course, to a considerable degree on their evaluation based on Theodore's religious attitude, and not without individualisation. Anatolius, appointed

---

[78] Theod., I, 343, pp. 97, 16–18; I, 351, pp. 99, 18–21 (ed. Hansen 1995b) = ACN II, 2, pp. 99, 3–8; II, 376, pp. 106, 8–13; III, 440, pp. 122, 19–23 i.e. Victor, a. 489 (Hansen, fr. 32, pp. 122, 5); IV, 455–56, pp. 128, 14–21 i.e. Victor, a. 496 (Hansen, fr. 45, pp. 128, 6–8); IV, 458, pp. 129, 13–14; IV, 492, pp. 139, 27 & 140, 12–13 = fr. 57, Victor, a. 501 (ed. Cardelle de Hartmann 2001); IV, 523, pp. 151, 19–23 = IV, fr. 76, pp. 151, 2–4 i.e. Victor, a. 517.2 [Theod.², 8; 16; 41; 99; 108–10; 138; 154].

[79] Theod., II, 376, pp. 106, 8–13 (ed. Hansen 1995b) [Theod.², 41].

to the position of the bishop of the city against the Church canons, celebrates the service with Eutyches, clearly supporting him, but does so χαριέντως, 'with good intention'.[80] Gennadius, one of the positive characters in the history, is praised for his good actions, ordaining without bribery (and only those who knew the psalter). Even during the final moments of his life, while struggling with a demon who heralded the destruction of the Church after the bishop's death, Gennadius is presented as a caring and orthodox shepherd.[81] Macedonius is presented as an ascetic, and one filled with holiness (ἀσκητικὸς ἦν καὶ ἱερός).[82] Timothy I, in turn, according to the preserved fragment of the original text, was removing the portraits of his predecessor, Euphemius, from every church in which he celebrated the liturgy, and in this context was described as ἀνόσιος. Theodore also reported that the new bishop was supposed to have been known under the monikers of Λιτροβούλ(β)ης καὶ Κήλων.[83] The meaning of these, of course, is associated with the anti-Chalcedonian activity of the bishop, who supported emperor Anastasius. However, if we were to leave aside the rationale of those sharp epithets, such evaluations as have been mentioned above, both positive and negative, indirectly show the prevalence of the vices and social problems troubling the Constantinopolitan clergy.

The relatively broad inclusion of the lower clergy should be considered a particularly valuable feature of the *Church history*. The lower functionaries of the capital's Church who were important from the point of view of the narrative, are identified by their name and role, along with the presbyters and deacons. In some of the cases, they were well-known in the city, enjoying at the time a sufficiently high esteem or fulfilling a role near enough to the emperor or the patriarch that they are also known from other sources – e.g. the aforementioned protégé of Gen-

---

[80] Theod., I, 351, pp. 99, 18–21 (ed. Hansen 1995b) ex ACN II, 2, pp. 99, 3–8.

[81] Theod., II, 381, pp. 107, 19–20; II, 396, pp. 111, 3–6 (ed. Hansen 1995b) [Theod.², 46; 61].

[82] Theod., IV, 458, pp. 129, 13–14 (ed. Hansen 1995b) [Theod.², 110].

[83] Theod., IV, 492, pp. 139, 27 & 140, 12–13 (ed. Hansen 1995b) = fr. 57, Victor, a. 501 (ed. Cardelle de Hartmann 2001); John of Damascus, *Contra imaginum calumniatores*, oratio 3, Florilegium III, 100, p. 187 (ed. Kotter 1975) = Theod., IV, 493, pp. 140, 14–15. On the both epithets see Miller 1873, pp. 280–82, on context Meier 2009, p. 293.

nadius, the *oeconomus* Marcian, to whom Theodore devoted separate space. It was he who, through the strength of his faith and fervency of prayer, was believed to have saved the church of St Anastasia during the great fire which stretched from the shipyard up to the apostoleum of Thomas in *Ta Amantiu*, having stood on the rooftop of the building with a copy of Gospel in his hands. The memory of Marcian and his miracle survived for several decades and resulted in separate hagiographic pieces, which survive to this day.[84] In other parts of the work, however, we encounter members of the clergy who have been sparingly, or even not at all, represented in other sources, even if at a given time they played some role in the history of the Church in the city. For example, one might bring up the case of the deacon Chrysaorius, who was exerting pressure, in vain, on St Matrona, to convince her to enter (along with the rest of her monastic community) into communion with the rest of the official Church and patriarch Macedonius II (in accordance with Zeno's *Henoticon* and according to emperor Anastasius' will).[85] We will later return to this figure to discuss his role from Matrona's perspective.

Also archdeacon John was preserved for history thanks only to Theodore. As an informer for the emperor Anastasius, he communicated to the ruler that patriarch Timothy apparently yielded to the request of the Studites and acknowledged the Council of Chalcedon. This passage is not only a clue as to the emperor's control over the patriarch, but also of a possible path to a career and to gaining higher status by individual priests.[86] Theodore, naturally, calls John a Manichaean in disdain.[87] Finally, a passage about the failed attempt on the life of patriarch Euphemius, very detailed and lively, capturing both the causes and the course of the event (even though we know it only from the summary in

---

[84] Theod., II, 376, pp. 106, 9–11; II, 394, 110, 21–25 (ed. Hansen 1995b) [Theod.², 41; 59]. On *Vita Marciani*, written most probably by certain Sergius, see Wortley 2010, pp. 715–72 (on the respective miracle p. 722). The fire is dated on 464 or 465, cf. Leszka 2014, pp. 321, 383 (with the other source accounts enlisted on p. 383).

[85] Theod., IV, 459, pp. 129, 22–24 (ed. Hansen 1995b) i.e. Theoph., AM 5991, pp. 142, 1–4 (ed. De Boor 1883).

[86] Theod., IV, 507, pp. 144, 19–23 (ed. Hansen 1995b) [Theod.², 145].

[87] Cf. n. 47, esp. Kosiński 2019, pp. 218 and 220–23.

the *Epitome*!), informs us about a certain Paul, an *ecdicus*, who took the murderer's blow aimed at the patriarch.[88]

A further handful of characters come from the preserved original fragments. In a passage preserved by John Moschus we read about how patriarch Gennadius was troubled by the actions of a wicked magician and clergyman Charisius. In response, the patriarch sent a deacon to the church of St Eleutherius, who prayed there according to the words indicated by the bishop for Charisius to be either cured – or broken. The following day the wicked priest was found dead. This is an important passage, and it appears to be in Theodore's own words, which both illustrates the degree of accuracy of the text, and confirms the significance which Theodore attached to the aforementioned patriarch from the golden era of the Constantinopolitan Church.[89] In the passage 52a alone (as we know, the largest surviving fragment) there appear in the context of Olympius' affair the following: Magnus, a presbyter in the church of Holy Apostles of Pariteichisma (described as a man full of piety and worthy of admiration, who convinced the bathers at Helenianae not to kill Olympius for his blasphemy and to leave the judgement to the infallible God); John, a deacon and *ecdicus* at the church of St Stephen, especially zealous in professing consubstantiality (ἀνὴρ εἰ καὶ τις ἄλλος ζῆλον ὑπὲρ τοῦ ὁμοουσίου δόγματος; he signed with the names of the witnesses the image of the punishment which befell Olympius); and one other, not mentioned by name, a clergyman, who spent the nights watching over the sick in the church of Homonoea.[90] It can therefore be clearly seen that the full text of the *Church history* would likely have included a much greater number of Constantinopolitan clergymen, not necessarily connected with the immediate milieu of the patriarch or his episcopal cathedral.

What is understandable, because of the specificity of the oeuvre, is that Theodore's history captured the divisions and disagreements within the Church in the capital. Individual groups of the local clergy and monks were exploited by the emperor or the

---

[88] Theod., IV, 453, pp. 127, 28–29 (ed. Hansen 1995b) [Theod.², 106].

[89] Theod., fr. 12, pp. 108, 10–25 (ed. Hansen 1995b) i.e. John Moschus, CLXV, col. 3008c–3009b.

[90] Theod., IV, fr. 52a, pp. 132, 4–5 & 25–28, pp. 133, 15–16 (ed. Hansen 1995b).

patriarchate, or opposed both. Theodore mentions, among other matters, actions taken against the Church (sc. of Constantinople, more specifically against the orthodox Macedonius II) by some of the clergy (τινὲς τοῦ κλήρου) who favoured Eutyches' views, and in another place writes that part of the clergy (and of the monks) allowed themselves to be bribed by the emperor, who wanted to replace Macedonius with another bishop. He took note of the departure of presbyters and deacons who remained faithful to Macedonius to Rome and Phoenicia.[91] Occasionally, he also mentioned the heterodox hierarchy, like in the case of the Arian bishop of Constantinople, Deuterius, who was mentioned in the context of the blasphemous pseudo-baptism of one Barbas.[92] *Nota bene*, the aforementioned *oeconomus* of Hagia Sophia, Marcian, may have been the last of the Novatian bishops of the city.[93]

The reflection of the ubiquity of the clergy in the urban space of Constantinople in the *History* is of value as well. The clergy, monks and laypeople (κλῆρος ἅπας καὶ μοναχοὶ καὶ λαϊκοί, πλήθη ὄντες πολλά) welcome Marcian and Pulcheria, awaiting an intervention in the matter of Eutyches; the clergy, along with the urban populace and monks, oppose Basiliscus and the anti-Chalcedon bishops he supported, Peter the Fuller and Timothy Aelurus; they start riots in the heat of dispute between Anastasius and Macedonius. As can be seen from the example of Magnus in the Helenianae bathhouse, clergy accompanied other Constantinopolitans in almost every urban activity.[94]

Theodore, writing from the perspective of at least 150 years of increasingly flourishing monasticism in the empire's capital,[95] presented the importance of monks in the image of the city extensively, and devoted to them a considerable proportion

[91] Theod., IV, 478, pp. 136, 25; IV, 489, 6–10; IV, 490, p. 139, pp. 14–20 (ed. Hansen 1995b) [Theod.², 124; 135; 136].

[92] Theod., IV, 475, pp. 136, 8–12 (ed. Hansen 1995b) [Theod.², 122] i.e. Victor, a. 500 (ed. Cardelle de Hartmann 2001).

[93] Cf. Wortley 2010.

[94] Theod., I, 355, pp. 100, 14–16; III, 406, pp. 113, 17–20; IV, 470, pp. 134, 20–23 (ed. Hansen 1995b) i.e. Theoph., AM 5999, pp. 150, 4–11 (ed. De Boor 1883).

[95] Dagron 1970, pp. 229–76; Dagron 1974, pp. 513–17; Hatlie 2007, pp. 65–132; Bralewski 2011b, pp. 427–32; Kosiński 2016, pp. 17–19.

of his attention on the people of the Church. Even though similar notes confirming the significant role of monks may also be found in the passages of the *Epitome* relating to Alexandria, Jerusalem or Antioch, the Constantinopolitan remarks are numerous and of paramount importance to the general thread of the historian's narrative. When he wrote about groups as whole, he typically separated out monks in his enumeration too, highlighting their participation (Ὁ κλῆρος καὶ ὁ λαὸς καὶ τὸ μοναχικὸν Κωνσταντινουπόλεως). Beside the aforementioned examples of the greeting of Marcian and Pulcheria and the intervention of Daniel the Stylite during Basiliscus' usurpation, the historian also places such emphasis regarding events closer to his day, i.e. the reign of Anastasius and the episcopacy of Macedonius II.[96] He also noted the separate activity by the monastic hegumeni, for example when they joined Constantinopolitan crowds in protest against Anastasius.[97] When required by the context, monks are also listed as the first of the groups being enumerated (e.g. as the victims of repression by Anastasius I and Timothy I: πολλὰ κακὰ τοῖς ὑπὲρ Μακεδονίου καὶ τῆς συνόδου μοναχοῖς τε καὶ κληρικοῖς καὶ λαϊκοῖς ἐπεδείξαντο[98]).

As a historian of the Constantinopolitan church, Anagnostes did not forget to identify important founding moments, and devoted attention to the creation of monasteries that were of particular relevance from the perspective of his narrative and of significance in the city. Examples include the beginning of the communities of Studius, Gratissimus, Matrona and Bassianus. Notably, the example of Bassianus and Vincomalus attested to the building of bonds of spiritual fatherhood, and the relations between the leading monks and the lay authorities. The most outstanding of the monks not only created their monastic communities, but also played a role in the political and ecclesiastic life, which Theodore earnestly stressed – as in the example of Dius and Bassianus, forwarding to Acacius, the bishop

---

[96] Theod., III, 406, pp. 113, 17–20; III, 408, pp. 114, 1–4; III, 412, pp. 114, 19–21 (ed. Hansen 1995b) [Theod.², 70; 72; 76]; IV, 470, pp. 134, 20–23, i.e. Theoph., AM 5999 (ed. De Boor 1883).

[97] Theod., IV, 485, pp. 138, 9–10 (ed. Hansen 1995b) [Theod.², 131].

[98] Theod., IV, 500, pp. 142, 29 & 143, 11 (ed. Hansen 1995b) i.e. Theoph, AM 6005, pp. 157, 21–22 (ed. De Boor 1883).

of Constantinople, letters of Felix, the bishop of Rome, in which the pope condemned Peter of Alexandria, Peter of Antioch, and the patriarch of the New Rome himself. We know of this event from two summaries, one in Victor of Tunnuna, the other in the *Epitome*.[99] The passage from the latter is worth noting because of its notable level of detail (considering the usual language and the amount of facts in the summary). It shows the direct activity of the monks and their lively interference in the religious life of the capital very well. The power of independence and the impact of the monasteries are evidently seen (and Theodore reflects them clearly) e.g. when the monks stood firm by Chalcedon against the pressure from Anastasius and the religious ideas following from the *Henoticon* (the historian once again listed the monasteries of Dius, Bassianus, of the acoemetae, the community of Matrona; he particularly recognised the nuns from the latter).[100] The significance of monastic communities is also attested by the efforts of patriarch Macedonius II to gain the support of the monks from the monastery of Dalmatus, who after the bishop's concessions to the emperor doubted his position on the four Councils.[101] Another such situation described by Theodore related to the following patriarch, Timothy I, who after the death of the hegumen of the Studius monastery made attempts to use the personnel change to win over the monks for the anti-Chalcedon disposition of Anastasius; meanwhile, the candidate for the post of hegumen was to have provoked the patriarch to verbally accept Chalcedon himself.[102] This attests well to the role of the Studius monastery in the city and the religious landscape of the capital at that time.

Through Theodore's work we are also able to capture the diversity and divisions in the capital's monastic circles. During

[99] Theod., II, 384, pp. 108, 29–32; II, 386–87, pp. 109, 3–8 [Theod.², 49; 51–52]; III, fr. 27a, pp. 120, 4–5 i.e. Victor, a. 487 (ed. Cardelle de Hartmann 2001); III, 434, pp. 120, 21–121, 12 (ed. Hansen 1995b) [Theod.², 93]. On Dius see D. Krausmüller 2007, pp. 15–31; on Bassianus see Sidéris 2016, pp. 631–56.

[100] Theod., IV, 459, pp. 129, 18–25 (ed. Hansen 1995b) i.e. Theoph., AM 5991, pp. 141, 21 – 142, 5 (ed. De Boor 1883).

[101] Theod., IV, 488, 1–5 (ed. Hansen 1995b) [Theod.², 134]; Hatlie 2007, p. 126.

[102] Theod., IV, 507, pp. 144, 14–19 (ed. Hansen 1995b) [Theod.², 145]. Cf. Haarer 2006, p. 152 & n. 157.

Macedonius II's times, some of the monks (τινὲς [...] τῶν μοναχῶν) acted against the Church on the side of the emperor); also two hundred aposchist monks, used by the basileus against the ecclesiastic supporters of Chalcedon, have been mentioned separately. Here, as well, we can see the influence of the monks on the other social groups of the city, for after all by forcing the singing of Trisagion in the version supported by the emperor, it was the monks who were organising the crowds ('mob').[103]

The middle classes

Due to the nature of the historiographic works, whether lay or ecclesiastic, the descriptions of the middle and lower social groups must necessarily be based on the incidental, separate *loci* scattered across the individual books. They do not form a comprehensive image, but nonetheless provide invaluable information. The relatively numerous and heterogeneous 'middle class' of Constantinople, comprising hosts of lower-ranking officials and thousands of courtiers, intellectuals and writers, philosophers, lawyers, public and private physicians, architects, teachers of rhetoric and grammar and similar other professions, lacked, of course, a sense of uniformity in their goals and aspirations. On the other hand, features such as their interactions with the upper classes, their exclusiveness, their social contacts, allow us to group them together.

In the version that we may study today, the vestigial *Church history* does not provide us with much material on the subject of these people. There are no remarks about lawyers, physicians, philosophers or teachers of the capital (even though, after all, Socrates and Sozomen provided us with a relative abundance of such information[104]). We also do not find much about lower ranking courtiers. An original passage preserved in the *Geronticon*, on the pages of *Codex Athous Iviron* 497, regarding emperor Zeno's efforts to attract the monk Severus from Paphlagonia to Constantinople, features a eunuch (*cubicularius*), dispatched by

---

[103] Theod., IV, 478, pp. 136, 20–26; IV, 483, pp. 137, 23–29; IV, 484, pp. 137, 30–31 (ed. Hansen 1995b) [Theod.², 124; 129; 130].

[104] Cf. Kompa 2014, pp. 238–39, 243–47, 249–52.

the ruler as an envoy.[105] One cannot rule out the possibility that there may have been a few more remarks about such persons in the unabridged version of the text, but the inferior, non-decision-making role of such court personnel caused the epitomator to exclude them from his work. Another original fragment, the famous and already mentioned several times 52a, concerns the person of a *diaetarius* (caretaker) of the Helenianae bathhouse, one Eutychianus, who under the heretics' pressure took down the newly hung image depicting the miracle of Olympius' punishment. In turn, Eutychianus himself was punished by divine justice with an incurable disease, and eventually died. It is an interesting passage, in addition to the entirety of the preserved text it carries an abundance of side information, valuable from the perspective of social history. The position of a *diaetarius* is understandable in the context of a remark about his duties relating to the palace in Helenianae, and is further explained by the author of the *Epitome*, describing the function as Εὐτυχιανός τις τῶν διαιταρίων ὁ πρῶτος. From the story it is also apparent that Eutychianus had his own servants at disposal.[106]

Soldiers

Although the military was present in the urban life of Constantinople, the local historical sources generally do not devote much attention to it in that context. Evaluative judgements appear only rarely.[107] Soldiers as an army are treated in the descriptions in an emotionless and uniform manner, devoid of individuality.[108] In a sense, they are even more anonymous that the crowds – they are almost invisible. Where someone is mentioned by name, in most cases it is a commander.

---

[105] *Codex Athous Iviron* 497, fol. 25ʳ; Theod., III, fr. 37, pp. 124, 21 – 125, 10 (ed. Hansen 1995b) [Theod.², fr. 9].

[106] Theod., IV, fr. 52a, pp. 132, 35 – 133, 32 i.e. IV, 465, pp. 131, 26–27 (ed. Hansen 1995b) [Theod.², 115].

[107] Sozomen, V, 17, 8 (ed. Bidez – Hansen 1995).

[108] For example Socrates, II, 38, 29–32 (ed. Hansen 1995a); Marcellinus Comes, a. 441, 1 (ed. Croke 1995); Zosimus, IV, 5, 4 (ed. Paschoud 1979–2000); Malchus fr. 15, 15–29 (ed. Blockley 1983); Malalas, XVIII, 71; XVIII, 135 (ed. Thurn 2000).

Theodore the Lector does not markedly depart from this model in the few places where he mentions military men. He states that in 450 emperor Marcian was acclaimed emperor in Hebdomon 'by the entire army' (ὑπὸ παντὸς τοῦ στρατοῦ); the orthodox patriarch Macedonius, summoned by Anastasius, is treated with solemnity by the palace guard (*scholae*); Vitalian, near Constantinople, demands that not only the emperor and senate, but also οἱ πρίγκιπες ἑκάστης σχολῆς swore an oath that they accept his requests.[109] Of the commanders present in the capital, Theodore mentioned, as we remember, only John the Scythian and John Cyrtus, but only as those sent from the city against the rebelling Isaurians, to Cotyaeum. In a separate brief note, he mentioned the military career of the new emperor Justin (ἀνὴρ πρεσβύτερος ἀπὸ στρατιωτῶν ἀρξάμενος).[110] In its present form, Theodore's work does not include information even about the army's participation in maintaining the peace in the capital city or its church, even though such observations were made by the historians whose works our author was continuing.[111]

Artisans

The *Church history* contains two interesting remarks on the subject of painters of holy images, which appear in a religious context, but are also valuable from the social perspective. The first, on the significance of a miracle, concerns a certain painter who, on a pagan's instigation, created an inappropriate depiction of Christ, with hair arranged in the same manner as on representations of Zeus, after which he lost feeling in his hands. Bishop Gennadius, to whom the ailing man was brought to obtain help, was said to have cured him, having prompted the man's com-

---

[109] Theod., I, 354, pp. 100, 12–13; IV, 486, pp. 138, 17–18 [Theod.², 19; 132]; IV, 509, pp. 145, 23 (ed. Hansen 1995b) i.e. Theoph., 6006, pp. 160, 21–22 (ed. De Boor 1883).

[110] Theod., IV, 449, pp. 126, 23–24; IV, 524, pp. 151, 25–27 (ed. Hansen 1995b) [Theod.², 104].

[111] Socrates, II, 16, 7–14; VI, 1, 4–6 (ed. Hansen 1995a); Sozomen, III, 9, 1–5; VIII, 1, 2–5; VIII, 21, 1–2; VIII, 23, 2–3 (ed. Bidez – Hansen 1995); cf. Zosimus, V, 23, 5 (ed. Paschoud 1979–2000); Malalas, XVIII, 99 (ed. Thurn 2000).

panions to prayer.[112] According to the second remark, a certain painter 'Syro-Persian Manichaean [...] in a presbyter's garments (ἐν σχήματι πρεσβυτέρου)', brought in from Cyzicus on the orders of emperor Anastasius, painted in Helenianae and in the church of St Stephen in Aurelianae 'ridiculous images incompatible with the art of painting sacred church images (ἀλλότρια τῶν ἐκκλησιαστικῶν ἁγίων εἰκόνων ἐτόλμησε γράψαι φασματώδη)'. In this case the depiction was heterodox from the Chalcedonian point of view, and the imperial commission led to riots in the city.[113]

It would be difficult to abstract here from the religious context; while the circumstances of the first of the events remain unknown, Anastasius' commission is associated with his more general policy, with his religious building program, and may have been inspired by Philoxenus, the bishop of Mabbug, who resided in the capital since the end of the fifth or the beginning of the sixth century and exerted influence over the ruler.[114] Remarks about artists active in Constantinople are, contrary to expectations, very rare.[115] Despite their ambiguity and scarcity of conveyed information (in respect of the painters themselves), it is worth noting the evidence they provide in the social context. If the Anastasian painter was described as a Manichaean, he was likely to have been a Miaphysite, and also a presbyter. Artists were commissioned by the ruler, Church, and private persons; and their constant influx into the city (similarly to other professionals) resulted from both personal decisions in looking for better career opportunities, and from individual choices of the patrons. Theodore's data are just small *tesserae*, but they contribute to a larger mosaic we can lay with all the sources we possess.

---

[112] Theod., II, 382, pp. 107, 21–24 = fr. 11, pp. 107, 11 – 108, 9 (ed. Hansen 1995b) [Theod.², 47 = fr. 6a & 6b] i.e. John of Damascus, *De imaginibus* or. 3, Florilegium, 130 (ed. Kotter 1975: 196). It has been suggested that the passage was altered by the epitomator (Blaudeau 2006, p. 536 n. 216; Greatrex 2015, p. 137, but *contra* Kosiński – Twardowska – Zabrocka – Szopa 2021, p. 237–38).

[113] Theod., IV, 467, pp. 134, 10–14 (ed. Hansen 1995b) i.e. Theoph., AM 5999, pp. 149, 28 – 150, 1 (ed. De Boor 1883).

[114] Haarer 2006, pp. 140, 142 n. 111. On Anastasius' ecclesiastical foundations – Capizzi 1969, pp. 196–201; Haarer 2006, p. 239.

[115] Kompa 2014, pp. 268–70.

Lower strata

The masses of Constantinopolitans at the lowest rungs of the social ladder, providing services to all of the other higher-ranking groups of the urban community, are present only in snapshots, but also in almost every major literary source from the period. In fragment 52a, Theodore mentioned the bath attendants from the Helenianae, who were taken into account as witnesses and for that reason named later on the image depicting the divine punishment that befell Olympius; it also mentions the people who were serving Eutychianus, and who stayed with him during his treatment.[116]

The attitude towards the poor and needy, praised by Theodore and rather typically for the period,[117] was expressed e.g. by a mention that when Pulcheria was dying, she left her possessions to the poor (Πουλχερία ... πάντα τὰ ἑαυτῆς πτωχοῖς καταλείψασα), and Marcian acquiesced to her will and supported the needy (ταῖς χρείαις ἁπάσαις). The church history also presented Marcian as distributing gifts to the needy during a procession (τοῖς δεομένοις).[118] One of the preserved passages shows how Theodore's views fit within the contemporary Christian sensitivity towards poverty and acknowledgement of voluntary poverty – it is the aforementioned fragment from *Codex Athous Iviron* 497 about Zeno's efforts to win over monk Severus. When the emperor wanted to lure Severus with money (or donate *eulogia* to him in return for his words), the latter was to have said: 'Hand this to those people who wish to demand [money] for God's word, for poverty has never received this, so will by no means be de-

---

[116] Theod., IV, fr. 52a, pp. 132, 25–28; 133, 27–28 (ed. Hansen 1995b) [Theod.², fr. 1] the same term is applied to the servants of Eutychianus and to the retinue of Timothy, the patriarch of Constantinople, who brought the venerable Julian to him (Theod., IV, fr. 62, pp. 142, 8 [Theod.², 5]).

[117] As for the wider milieu of the early Byzantine writers and rhetors, their attitudes toward the poor and poverty, with all social implications, see Patlagean 1977, esp. pp. 23–35; also Meyer 2008, pp. 149–58. Theodore's attitude corresponds with the statements made by theologians from the Patristic period, as well as by his historiographic predecessors, cf. Socrates, VII, 12, 9; VII, 17, 5; VII, 25, 3; VII, 26, 4; VII, 28, 5 (ed. Hansen 1995a); Sozomen, VIII, 23, 6; VIII, 24, 8–9; IX, 1, 10 (ed. Bidez – Hansen 1995).

[118] Theod., I, 363, pp. 102, 21–22; I, 365, pp. 103, 4–5 (ed. Hansen 1995b) [Theod.², 28; 30].

manding it' (ἐκείνοις ἐγχείριζε ταῦτα τοῖς θέλουσι λόγον ἀπαιτεῖσθαι τούτων παρὰ θεοῦ· πτωχεία γὰρ ἃ μὴ εἴληφεν, ἀπαιτηθήσεται οὐδαμῶς).[119] Theodore, as follows from the logic of the text, is on the side of the illiterate sage, and not of the emperor.

Strangers and newcomers

New arrivals, guests and petitioners arriving individually or in groups to Constantinople have, of course, been noted by Theodore, especially if their presence in the capital was related to developments in Church history or religious matters. He recognised the arriving legates and *apocrisiarii*, criticised the intervention (using the verb παρενοχλέω) of certain monks in the capital in the matter of Theodore of Mopsuestia, and the ὄχλος ἄτακτος Ἀλεξανδρέων in the service of Timothy Ailouros, he praised the descent from the column by Daniel the Stylite and his presence alongside the city's community in solidarity with bishop Acacius and Chalcedon, he tells of the Syro-Persian 'Manichaean' painter brought from Cyzicus.[120] He also noted and evaluated the presence of Isaurians in the capital, ascribing their expulsion by Anastasius to their wicked and inhuman acts (πολλὰ τῶν Ἰσαύρων ἄτοπα καὶ ἀπάνθρωπα πραξάντων...).[121] This is, again, only a fragmentary picture, but confronted with other sources from the place and time, it constitutes a valuable addition.

---

[119] *Codex Athous Iviron 497*, fol. 25ʳ; Theod., III, fr. 37, pp. 125, 13–14 (ed. Hansen 1995b) [Theod.², fr. 9]. On Zeno's relations with the monastic circles see Kosiński 2010, pp. 197–99, on monastic renouncement of possessions see e.g. Brakke 2008, pp. 76–87, on eulogia Caner 2006, pp. 329–77; Caner 2008, pp. 230–36.

[120] Theod., III, 431–32, pp. 119, 10–22 (ed. Hansen 1995b) i.e. fr. 26, pp. 119, 7–9 = Victor, a. 486 (ed. Cardelle de Hartmann 2001); I, 338, pp. 96, 12–16; III, 404, pp. 113, 11–14; III, 407, pp. 113, 25–26 [Theod.², 90–91; 3; 68; 71]; IV, 467, pp. 134, 10–14 i.e. Theoph. AM 5999, pp. 149, 28 – 150, 1 (ed. De Boor 1883).

[121] Theod., IV, 449, pp. 126, 21–22 (ed. Hansen 1995b). For the context see: Brooks 1893, pp. 231–37; Capizzi 1969, pp. 94–99; Lenski 1999, pp. 428–30, 440–41; Feld 2005, pp. 332–38; Haarer 2006, pp. 22–23; Meier 2009, pp. 75–82; Dmitriev 2010, p. 29; Leszka – Leszka 2014, pp. 394–95; Begass 2018, p. 183; Kosiński – Twardowska – Zabrocka – Szopa 2021, pp. 318–19 n. 391.

4. *Some remarks on gender issues in Theodore*

Of the subjects at the confluence of classical and gender studies, for which the material can be found in the *Church history*, I would like to draw attention briefly to three matters: women, homosexuality and eunuchs.

Women in the *Church history*

As I have mentioned earlier, few women can be found on the pages of Theodore the Lector's work, at least based on what we can tell of its contents today. Of the twelve listed women, nine came from imperial families, and all of them are also frequently mentioned in parallel narratives. There is no doubt as to their influence on the rulers and the imperial court, and their independence shines through despite the *Epitome*'s abbreviations.

Theodore is one of the authors who captured the exceptional role of Pulcheria (compared to other Augustae) and usually appraised her favourably, especially against the background of Theodosius II. He stated that Pulcheria had power over her imperial brother (Πουλχερία τὸν ἀδελφὸν αὐθεντήσασα), and it was she who ensured the execution of his unfulfilled orders. In another place he showed how Pulcheria rightly demonstrated to her brother (σοφῶς ὑπῆλθεν αὐτόν) the recklessness of signing documents without reading them – this anecdote is sometimes considered to be fictitious, or as an older court rumour transposed to the pages of the historian's work,[122] but this makes it all the more worthwhile to take note of its separate place in the *Church history*. It is difficult to evaluate an important remark about the hatred of the Augusta towards Nestorius based solely on the account in the *Epitome* in comparison with the rest of the entries; she was said to have hated him for accusing her of *porneia* in front of her brother, yet aversion towards Nestorius is almost entirely justified by the reason, a valid one in Theodore's eyes, given in the next sentence of the *Epitome*.[123] Another witness

---

[122] Holum 1989, pp. 130–31; James 2001, pp. 66–67, 72; Kosiński – Twardowska – Zabrocka – Szopa 2021, p. 253 note 109.

[123] Holum 1989, pp. 152–53 (further conflict and deposition of Nestorius with Pulcheria's significant role: pp. 153–74); James 2001, p. 92 (accusations

to Pulcheria's power was the removal of Chrysaphius, and the later co-operation between Marcian and Pulcheria (letter to the bishop of Rome, Leo). Finally, the farewell to the co-ruler of the empire for many years presents her as a benefactress, who in the final moment of the life left everything to the poor; Theodore precisely indicates the church foundations in which she had a hand, which during his life formed an important part of the church topography of Constantinople (he listed Blachernae, Chalcoprateia, Hodegon, St Lawrence).[124]

In comparison with this mighty and pious dynast, both her contemporaries appear much less impressively: Eudocia and Marina,[125] and, the chronologically closer to Theodore Leontia, Verina and Zenonis.[126] Anagostes brings up in particular Verina's role in the forming of a plot which resulted in Basiliscus' usurpation, and the role of Zenonis in turning him away from orthodoxy. The debate in modern scholarship on how accurate or to what extent Theodore's claims (also present in other sources[127]) were exaggerated, and to what extent it was a repetition of a motif of a woman who was behind the poor decisions or wrongdoings of men in power, is beyond the scope of this article.[128] However, there is no point in denying the participation of both of these

against Pulcheria in the early Byzantine sources: pp. 16, 24 n. 58), Constas 2003, pp. 55–60 (theological background of the animosities). Cf. Leszka 2011b, p. 355 n. 29 (references to the secondary literature on the conflict and fall of Nestorius).

[124] Respective passages on Pulcheria: Theod., I, 336, pp. 96, 7; I, 352, pp. 100, 1–3; I, 340, pp. 97, 3–6; I, 353, pp. 100, 4–10; I, 359, pp. 100, 23–24; I, 363, pp. 102, 21–25 (ed. Hansen 1995b) [Theod.², 1; 17; 5; 18; 24; 28]. Pulcheria's churches may be later interpolation to the text of *Epitome*, Pentcheva 2006, p. 120; Bralewski 2011a, p. 144; Kosiński – Twardowska – Zabrocka – Szopa 2021, p. 239. On ecclesiastical foundations of Pulcheria: Holum 1989, p. 137; James 2001, p. 150; Bralewski 2011a, pp. 140, 142–44; Herrin 2013, pp. 169–71.

[125] Theod., I, 353, pp. 100, 4–10 (ed. Hansen 1995b) [Theod.², 18].

[126] Theod., III, 401–02, pp. 112, 15–22; III, 419–20, pp. 116, 10–19; IV, 446, pp. 125, 25–27 & 126, 12–15; IV, 489, 6–10 (ed. Hansen 1995b) [Theod.², 65–66; 81–82; 101; 135].

[127] E.g. Evagrius, III, 27 (ed. Bidez – Parmentier 2011–2014); Malalas, XV, 2–3 (ed. Thurn 2000).

[128] Cf. Leszka 1998, pp. 130–36; James 2001, pp. 16–20, 90, 96–97; Twardowska 2009, pp. 110–32, 145–52; Feld 2005, p. 251; Kosiński 2010, pp. 80–82; Twardowska 2014, pp. 9–22; Leszka 2017, pp. 30–42; Vallejo-Girvés 2018, pp. 43–58.

female rulers in the turbulent political events after the deaths of Leo I and Leo II. Ariadne was the sole remaining dynast to whom the historian devoted more attention, but only three remarks show her causative role – her appointment of Anastasius as emperor and her pressure on the patriarch Euphemius to recognise the choice; and later her hesitation regarding imperial plans to depose patriarch Macedonius II. In the third remark, perhaps the sharpest in tone, Ariadne is presented as affronting Anastasius, who after riots sparked by the changes to the Trisagion, took shelter in a suburban villa in Blachernae. The historian noted separately the information about Ariadne's death, likely as a part of a larger fragment.[129] He also mentioned an attempt to influence Anastasius by his orthodox sister-in-law, Magna.[130]

From the above examples alone we can see that to some extent the appraisal of the aforementioned women was based in part on their religious views, and in part on the individual position in power and its subjective evaluation by the historian. Although in the present text I have generally avoided taking the imperial family into account, such a reference is needed to provide an appropriate context and proportion in discussing the remaining Constantinopolitan women described on the pages of the *Church history*. One of the most respected aristocratic women, Anicia Juliana, deserved a separate note because of her decidedly pro-Chalcedonian attitude, hence her description as ἡ περιφανεστάτη and the mention of her personal foundation of the church of θεοτόκος ἐν τοῖς Ὀνωράτοις; this passage also includes the example of a (not named here) pious and orthodox wife of patrician Pompey, who devoted herself to charitable works (sc. Anastasia).[131] The mention of both these women is a parallel to e.g. the passages of Magna and, *mutatis mutandis*, Ariadne.

Against this background stands out one female figure, neither a member of the imperial family nor a local aristocrat, but an

---

[129] Theod., IV, 508, pp. 145, 18–19 (ed. Hansen 1995b) i.e. Theoph., AM 6005, pp. 159, 18–19 (ed. De Boor 1883); IV, fr. 73 pp. 150, 3 i.e. Victor, a. 515.2 (ed. Cardelle de Hartmann 2001) ≈ IV, 520, pp. 150, 16 [Theod.², 151] i.e. Theoph., AM 6008, pp. 162, 13 (ed. De Boor 1883).

[130] Theod., IV, 481, pp. 137, 8–11 (ed. Hansen 1995b) [Theod.², 127].

[131] Theod., IV, 504, pp. 144, 5–10 (ed. Hansen 1995b) i.e. Theoph., AM 6005, pp. 157, 34 – 158, 8 (ed. De Boor 1883).

influential nun – Matrona of Perge. Theodore wrote about her in two places in his work. Firstly he mentioned her as an example of someone who abandoned their home and riches and chose a monastic path, and later (in a fragment reconstructed from Theophanes) he brought her up as an example of a defender of the Chalcedonian orthodoxy, standing against the emperor Anastasius and the pressure exerted by his religious supporters. In the narrative she is accompanied by another heroic nun, Sophia.[132] In this place, Anagnostes enriches our knowledge about the final years of the saintly nun, for even though we get an insight into her life through the preserved *Vita Matronae*, which provides a good documentation of her presence in the city, it does not refer to the events described by Theodore at all, and only alludes to the difficulties of Anastasius' day.[133] Moreover, while the *Vita* reflects the tradition of the direct monastic milieu of Matrona, the exceptional treatment by Theodore shows the wider Constantinopolitan esteem for the nun, who at the end of her life was clearly known in the capital. Despite its brevity, the relation also offers some hints as to the social reality of the life of preeminent nuns and their social roles. It demonstrates their increasing role as lodestars or examples in internal religious conflicts. It shows their contacts with the authorities and their potential dependence – the unsuccessful pressure exerted on Matrona by the deacon at Hagia Sophia, Chrysaorius. If we were to compare *Vita* and *Church history* from the perspective of the contact between the lay and Church authorities and the nuns, Chrysaorius played a similar role to Marcellus, the intermediary and guide of Matrona at the beginning of her presence in the city,[134] but was also in some sense Marcellus' opposite. *Nota bene*, the anonymous hagiographer's relation also shows a certain economic dependence of the nuns on their environ-

---

[132] Theod., II, 386, pp. 109, 3–5 (ed. Hansen 1995b) [Theod.², 51]; IV, 459, pp. 129, 22–25 i.e. Theoph. AM 5991, pp. 142, 1–5 (ed. De Boor 1883). On Matrona, her community and prochalcedonian involvement see: Catafygiotou-Topping 1988, pp. 211–24; Blaudeau 2005, pp. 358–60; Hatlie 2007, pp. 96–100, 108, 126; Sidéris 2016, pp. 631–56.

[133] *Vita Matronae*, 50 & 52 (Matrona in Constantinople: 28–36, etc.) (ed. Delehaye 1910).

[134] *Vita Matronae*, 28–31, 43, 46 (ed. Delehaye 1910).

ment [135] – this deepens the context of Matrona's perseverance, although on the other hand, her position at the end of the fifth century must have been much stronger than during the initial years of her ascetic activity in Constantinople.

Ordinary Constantinopolitan women as a group appear only once in Theodore's work. During the street protests against Anastasius, the people, including women and children, give testimony of their faith and insult the emperor while walking across the city (Ὁ λαὸς σὺν γυναιξί καὶ τέκνοις πλῆθος ἄπειρον).[136] It is worth noting that women and children are something of an addition to 'the people' here – the 'crowd' is constituted of men.

Homosexuality

An allegation of homosexuality and heresy (παιδεραστὴς καὶ αἱρετικός) appears twice in the *History* as an accusation. In the first of the cases it is raised against patriarch Macedonius II, who according to Theodore was thus maligned at emperor Anastasius I's instigation.[137] Here, the context is fairly typical, as such suspicions were often used, both among the clergy and laypeople, and the threat arising from them was becoming progressively direr.[138] In the second case however, despite the similarity of the context of the allegation, the situation is more peculiar. The matter relates to the aforementioned Apion who, having fallen out of imperial favour, was exiled to Nicaea, where he was to be ordained a priest by the local bishop, Anastasius. Although the Greek used in this passage is unclear, it appears that in the light of the *Epitome*, it was Apion himself who was protesting against his ordination and – if this is not the epitomator's error – was

---

[135] *Vita Matronae*, 43 (ed. Delehaye 1910); on economic dependence of monastic communities cf. Kosiński 2016, pp. 238–39. *Sensu largo* all monks and monasteries in the city depended on the state and the faithful, and were vulnerable to economic pressure (see e.g. the restrictions imposed on monks by the emperor Anastasius in 511 – Zachariah, VII, 8c, pp. 256–57; ed. Greatrex 2011), but vulnerability of the female monasteries should be discussed separately nonetheless.

[136] Theod., IV, 485, pp. 138, 9–14 (ed. Hansen 1995b) [Theod.², 131].

[137] Theod., IV, 490, pp. 139, 13–14 (ed. Hansen 1995b) [Theod.², 136].

[138] Troianos 1989, pp. 29–48; ODB II, pp. 945–46; Crompton 2003, pp. 131–36, 139–49; Kompa 2011, pp. 224–26; Harper 2013, pp. 141–58.

to have claimed that he was a pederast and a heretic; or, which seems to be more logical (and thus the passage is understood by Christoph Begass), Apion blasphemed against the emperor.[139] The latter possibility appears to be less likely, for otherwise the official, despite his earlier merits, would have likely faced a much more severe penalty than only a banishment, priestly ordination and confiscation of property. In addition, the sources are silent on the subject of whether Apion was speaking in favour of orthodoxy against Anastasius (Theodore would have likely stressed this point). It should be added that after the emperor's death in 518 Apion returned to favour. On the other hand, if the aristocrat had denounced himself, he was clearly not believed, since he was both ordained by the local bishop according to the basileus' will, and did not suffer any further punishments for being παιδεραστὴς καὶ αἱρετικός.

Eunuchs

It is generally believed that the majority of Byzantine intellectual opinion was unfriendly or even hostile towards the eunuchs, reproducing stereotypes about their propensity for intrigue, lust, sinister influence on emperors and harming righteous Romans.[140] Such a perspective is less visible in hagiography, more abundant in neutral and positive opinions or ways of presenting of eunuchs, but this positive change began to grow only in the middle Byzantine period.[141] Theodore does not fit into this pattern and the typical opinion of Constantinopolitan writers. True, he expressed a negative view on Chrysaphius, as he attributed to him support

[139] On Apion see n. 77 in this paper. Ἀπίωνά τινα τῶν πρώτων ἐν τῇ συγκλήτῳ τοῦ κατὰ Περσῶν πολέμου τὸ κράτος πρώην ὑπὸ Ἀναστασίου πιστευθέντα, διὰ πολλῶν τῶν ἐν μέσῳ διελθόντα κινδύνων τελευταῖον ὁ βασιλεὺς εἰς Νίκαιαν ἐξώρισεν καὶ τὸν ἐπίσκοπον Νικαίας Ἀναστάσιον παρεσκεύασε πρεσβύτερον χειροτονῆσαι, βοῶντα καὶ κράζοντα, ὡς παιδεραστής ἐστι καὶ αἱρετικός, καὶ τὴν χειροτονίαν μὴ θέλοντα δέξασθαι. καὶ τὸν υἱὸν δὲ αὐτοῦ Ἡρακλείδαν εἰς Προῦσαν διάκονον χειροτονηθῆναι προσέταξεν· ὅπερ αὐτὸς μετὰ χαρᾶς κατεδέξατο – Theod., IV, 482, pp. 137, 16–22 (ed. Hansen 1995b) [Theod.², 128]. Begass 2018, p. 426, on the other hand Hickey 2012, p. 11 note 59 suggests that Apion was blaming himself. Cf. Sarris 2004, p. 283 ('In 510, however, Apion fell from favour at court, was denounced as a "pederast and heretic", and exiled to Nicaea').

[140] Tougher 1997, pp. 173–74; Tougher 2008, pp. 96–98.

[141] Ringrose 2003, pp. 114–18.

for Eutyches and convincing Theodosius II to justify to Valentinian III the validity of the deposition of bishop Flavian, and he noted the fact that Chrysaphius was removed from his position by Pulcheria.[142] To be sure, he mentioned the shameful role of Calopodius, a eunuch and *oeconomus* of one of the churches, in handing over to Anastasius the acts of the Council of Chalcedon, hidden by patriarch Macedonius II. It needs to be noted, however, that such criticism did not stem from the eunuch's condition itself, but rather because of his taking the side of the emperor.[143]

Conversely, there is one neutral remark – the eunuch who on Zeno's orders attempted to convince the saintly Severus to travel to the capital not only appears at the heart of the narrative, as an executor of the emperor's will, but there is also no negative opinion apparent in the context (although much depends here on how we understand the word δυνάστης,[144] used by Severus in the second person in addressing the envoy).[145] Two remarks, in turn, are outright positive. Matrona, a figure as we already know exceptionally highly valued by Theodore, in order to hide in a monastery from her husband, her high position and the secular world, was to pretend, according to the *Church history*, to be a eunuch.[146] In turn, a passage regarding the Eutychianus (52a), who was punished with an illness for taking down an image in a bath-house, describes a night vision of the sufferer. According to the *Church history*, Eutychianus was said to have seen a young eunuch, dressed in an ornate *paragauda*, who revealed God's judgements to him. As a divine messenger, sex- and genderless, in the context of the historian's tale, he evokes positive associations, rather than those which in the literature of the early and middle Byzantine periods would involve licentiousness or other stereotypical vices of eunuchs.

---

[142] Theod., I, 346, pp. 98, 23–27; I, 350, pp. 99, 16–17; I, 353, pp. 100, 8 (ed. Hansen 1995b) [Theod.², 11; 15; 18].

[143] Theod., IV, 491, pp. 139, 23–24 (ed. Hansen 1995b) [Theod.², 137].

[144] Cf. Ragia 2016, pp. 331–41.

[145] Theod., III, fr. 37, pp. 124, 21 – 125, 10 (ed. Hansen 1995b) [Theod.², fr. 9].

[146] Theod., II, 386, pp. 109, 3–5 (ed. Hansen 1995b) [Theod.², 51].

* * *

Theodore the Lector's *Church history*, despite its vestigial state of preservation, is a copious source of information about social realities, including those of Constantinople (seen from the insider's perspective). As we know, Theodore's narrative was found useful by the later Byzantine historians and it was utilised. Alas, this was not sufficient for the work to survive in its entirety, or even in greater part, in contrast to works of Socrates, Sozomen, Theodoret and others. It was a *succès d'estime*, and this is still more than the general reception of another Church history, even more abundant in information, authored by Philip of Side.[147]

As a result we now have snippets of the text and some general idea about it thanks to the epitomator's efforts. We can only imagine what we would have access to if the source had survived without diminution. Many of the questions will remain unanswered; for example, why does the entirety of the surviving material contain only a single mention of the activities of the circus factions during riots in the city?[148] What sources did Theodore use to describe events in the capital? Did he evaluate the individual groups, and if so, how?

One has to bear in mind once again the fragment cited by John of Damascus, a narrative about the fate of Olympius, the Arian neophyte and blasphemer in Helenianae, and of the hapless *diaitarius* Eutychianus. Apart from its confessional and eschatological meaning, it reveals a part of a story and offers a glimpse of everyday life in Constantinople. The abundance of details, the number of secondary characters and the breadth of the entire narrative differ greatly from what we find in the preserved summaries (Victor of Tunnuna, *Epitome*). And this unique, such extensive passage of the original text is located in the scenery of Constantinople and reproduces it more broadly and deeply than just through the lens of the imperial-patriarchal relations.

If the succinct note, an abbreviation made by the epitomator out of the lengthy and rich in details narrative of the *Historia ecclesiastica* is a typical pattern or standard of its author, then

---

[147] Socrates, VII, 27 (ed. Hansen 1995a); Photius, cod. 35 (ed. Henry 1959).

[148] Theod., fr. 65, pp. 145, 4–5 (ed. Hansen 1995b) i.e. Victor, a. 513 (ed. Cardelle de Hartmann 2001).

it would mean that the majority of the interesting information about the social reality of Constantinople had been irreversibly lost. In this sense, the remarks in this article can only be working comments, and highly approximate in nature; this is therefore only an outline of the text 'Social reality of Constantinople in Theodore Lector' – its final version, unless the entirety of Anagnostes' work is miraculously found, will not be written.

Bibliography

Sources

Adler 1928–1938 = *Suidae Lexicon*, ed. by Ada Adler, 5 vols, Stuttgart.

Bidez – Hansen 1995 = Sozomenos, *Kirchengeschichte*, ed. by Joseph Bidez and Günther Christian Hansen, Die griechischen christlichen Schriftsteller der ersten Jahrhunderte, N.F., 4, Berlin.

Bidez – Parmentier 2011–2014 = Evagrius, *Histoire Ecclésiastique*, éd. par Joseph Bidez – Léon Parmentier, tr. par André-Jean Festugière, comm. par Laurent Angliviel de la Baumelle – Guy Sabbah, *SC* 542, 566. Paris. (Translation: Whitby 2000 = Michael Whitby, *The Ecclesiastical History of Evagrius Scholasticus*, Liverpool.)

Billerbeck 2010–2017 = *Stephani Byzantii Ethnica*, ed. by Margarethe Billerbeck et al., vol. I–V, Berolini – Novi Eboraci.

Blockley 1983 = Malchus, *Fragmenta*, in *The Fragmentary Classicizing Historians of the Later Roman Empire. Eunapius, Olympiodorus, Priscus and Malchus*, ed. by Roger C. Blockley, vol. II, Liverpool, pp. 402–62.

Blockley 1985 = *The History of Menander the Guardsman*, ed. by Roger C. Blockley, Liverpool.

Brooks 1919–1924 = *Historia ecclesiastica Zachariae Rhetori vulgo adscripta*, ed. by Ernest Walter Brooks, vol. I–II, Leuven.

Cardelle de Hartmann 2001 = *Victoris Tunnunensis Chronicon cum reliquiis ex Consularibus Caesaraugustanis et Iohannis Biclarensis Chronicon*, ed. by Carmen Cardelle de Hartmann with an Historical Commentary on the Consularia Caesaraugustana and Iohannis Biclarensis Chronicon by Roger Collins, CC SL 173A, Turnhout.

Constas 2003 = *Proclus of Costantinople and the Cult of the Virgin in Late Antiquity. Homilies 1–5, texts and translations*, ed. by Nicholas Constas, Leiden – London.

Croke 1995 = Marcellinus Comes, *The Chronicle of Marcellinus*, ed. by Brian Croke, Sydney.

De Boor 1883 = Theophanes: *Theophanis Chronographia*, recensuit Carolus de Boor, vol. 1–2, Lipsiae.

De Boor 1978 = George the Monk: *Georgii Monachi Chronicon*, edidit C. de Boor, editionem anni MCMIV correctirem curavit P. Wirth, volumen I–II, Stutgardiae.

Delehaye 1910 = *Vita sanctae Matronae*, in *Acta Sanctorum*, edidit Hippolyte Delehaye, Nov. III, Bruxelles, pp. 790–813. (Translation: Featherstone 1996 = Jeffrey Featherstone, *Holy Women of Byzantium. Ten Saints' Lives in English Translation*, ed. by Alice-Mary Talbot, Washington, pp. 13–64).

Greatrex 2011 = *The Chronicle of Pseudo-Zachariah Rhetor. Church and War in Late Antiquity*, ed. by Geoffrey Greatrex, translated from Syriac and Arabic sources by Robert R. Phenix – Bernadette Horn with introductory material by Sebastian Brock – Witold Witakowski, Liverpool.

Hansen 1995a = Socrates, *Historia Ecclesiastica*, ed. by Günther Christian Hansen, GCS, N.F. 1. Berlin (Translation: Périchon – Maraval 2004–2007 = Socrate de Constantinople. Histoire Ecclesiastique, traduction par Pierre Perichon – Pierre Maraval, Sources Chretiennes 477 [Book I] and 493 [Books II–III], Paris.

Hansen 1995b = Theodoros Anagnostes, *Kirchengeschichte*, hrsg. von Günther Christian Hansen, Berlin.

Henry 1959 = Photius, *Bibliothèque*, Tome I, éd. by Rene Henry, Collection des Universités de France, Paris.

John Moschus = *Beati Joannis Eucratae liber qui inscribuntur Pratum...*, PG, vol. LXXXVII.3, cols 2847–3116.

Kollman – Deuse 2007 = Alexander Monachus, *Laudatio Barnabae. Lobrede auf Barnabas*, hrsg. von Bernd Kollmann – Werner Deuse, Turnhout.

Kosiński – Szopa – Twardowska 2019 = *Historie Kościoła Jana Diakrinomenosa i Teodora Lektora*, red. Rafał Kosiński – Adrian Szopa – Kamilla Twardowska, Kraków.

Kosiński – Twardowska – Zabrocka – Szopa 2021 = *The Church Histories of Theodore Lector and John Diakrinomenos*, ed. by Rafał Kosiński – Kamilla Twardowska – Aneta Zabrocka – Adrian Szopa, Berlin (= Theod.[2]).

Kotter 1975 = John of Damascus, *Contra imaginum calumniatores = Die Schriften des Johannes von Damaskos*, vol. III, *Contra imaginum calumniatores orationes tres*, hrsg. von Bonifatius Kotter, Berlin – New York.

Laga 1992 = *Eustratii Presbyteri Vita Eutychii patriarchae Constantinopolitani*, edidit Carl Laga, Turnhout – Leuven.

Paschoud 1979–2000 = Zosime, *Histoire nouvelle*, éd. par François Paschoud, vol. I–III, Paris.

Pseudo-Chrysostomus = *In salvatoris nostri Jesu Christi Nativitatem oratio*, PG, vol. LVI, cols 385–94.

Roberto 2005 = *Ioannis Antiocheni Fragmenta ex Historia chronica*, edidit Umberto Roberto, Berlin – New York.

Schenkl – Downey 1965 = *Themistii Orationes quae supersunt*, edidit Heinrich Schenkl – Glanville Downey, vol. I (Orationes I–XIX), ed., Lipsiae.

Thurn 2000 = Malalas, *Chronographia*, edidit Hans Thurn, CFHB, Berlin.

Veh 1977 = Paul the Silentiary, *Descriptio S. Sophiae*, in Prokop, *Werke*, hrsg. von Otto Veh, Bd. V, *Die Bauten*, München, pp. 306–58.

Wachsmuth 1897 = *Ioannis Laurentii Lydi Liber de ostentis et calendaria Graeca omnia*, edidit Curtius Wachsmuth, Lipsiae, pp. 1–161.

Walter 1919–1924 = *Historia ecclesiastica Zachariae Rhetori vulgo adscripta*, transl. Ernest Walter Brooks, vol. I–II, Leuven.

Literature

Bagnall – Cameron – Schwartz – Worp 1987 = Roger S. Bagnall – Alan Cameron – Seth R. Schwartz – Klaas A. Worp, *Consuls of the Later Roman Empire*, Atlanta.

Beaucamp 2001 = Joëlle Beaucamp, 'Apion et Praejecta: hypothèses anciennes et nouvelles données', *REB*, 59, pp. 165–78.

Begass 2018 = Christoph Begass, *Die Senatsaristokratie des oströmischen Reiches, ca. 457–518. Prosopographische und sozialgeschichtliche Untersuchungen*, München.

Blaudeau 2005 = Philippe Blaudeau, 'Faire mémoire des Maccabées à l'époque de la controverse Chalcédonienne (451–520): remarques sur les enjeux d'une célébration disputée', *Antiquité Tardive*, 13, pp. 351–61.

Blaudeau 2006 = Philippe Blaudeau, *Alexandrie et Constantinople (451–91). De l'histoire à la géoecclésiologie*, Rome.

Brakke 2008 = David Brakke, 'Care for the Poor, Fear of Poverty, and Love of Money: Evagrius Ponticus on the Monk's Economic Vulnerability' in *Wealth and Poverty in Early Church and Society*, ed. by Susan R. Holman, Grand Rapids, pp. 76–87.

Bralewski 2011a = 'Konstantynopolitańskie kościoły', in *Konstantynopol – Nowy Rzym. Miasto i ludzie w okresie wczesnobizantyńskim*, red. Mirosław Jerzy Leszka – Teresa Wolińska, Warszawa, pp. 132–51.

Bralewski 2011b = Sławomir Bralewski, 'Życie religijne mieszkańców Konstantynopola', in *Konstantynopol – Nowy Rzym. Miasto i ludzie w okresie wczesnobizantyńskim*, red. Mirosław Jerzy Leszka – Teresa Wolińska, Warszawa, pp. 401–32.

Brooks 1893 = Ernest W. Brooks, 'The Emperor Zeno and the Isaurians', *EHR*, 8, pp. 209–38.

Caner 2006 = Daniel Caner, 'Towards a Miraculous Economy: Christian Gifts and Material "Blessings" in Late Antiquity', *JECS*, 14.3, pp. 329–77.

Caner 2008 = Daniel Caner, 'Wealth, Stewardship and Charitable "Blessings" in Early Byzantine Monasticism' in *Wealth and Poverty in Early Church and Society*, ed. by Susan R. Holman, Grand Rapids, pp. 221–42.

Capizzi 1969 = Carmelo Capizzi, *L'imperatore Anastasio I (491–518). Studio sulla sua vita, la sua opera e la sua personalità*, Roma.

Catafygiotou-Topping 1988 = Eva Catafygiotou-Topping, 'St Matrona and her Friends: Sisterhood in Byzantium' in *Καθηγήτρια. Essays presented to Joan Hussey for her 80th birthday*, ed. by Julian Chrysostomides, Camberley, pp. 211–24.

Čekalova 2010 = Aleksandra Alekseevna Čekalova, *Senat i senatorskaja aristokratija Konstantinopolja. IV – pervaja polovina VII veka*, Moskva.

Čičurov 1973 = Igor S. Čičurov, 'Feofan – kompiljator Feofilakta Simokatty', *ADSV*, 10, pp. 203–06.

Čičurov 1976 = Igor S. Čičurov, 'Feofan Ispovednik – kompiljator Prokopija', *Vizantijskij Vremennik*, 37, pp. 62–73.

Constas 2003 = Nicholas Constas, *Proclus of Constantinople and the Cult of the Virgin in Late Antiquity: Homilies 1–5, Texts and Translations*, Leiden – Boston.

Croke 1990 = Brian Croke, 'Malalas, the Man and His Work', in *Studies in John Malalas*, ed. by Elizabeth Jeffreys – Brian Croke – Roger Scott, Sydney, pp. 1–25.

Crompton 2003 = Louis Crompton, *Homosexuality and Civilisation*, Cambridge Mass. – London.

Dagron 1970 = Gilbert Dagron, 'Les moines et la ville. Le monachisme à Constantinople jusqu'au concile de Chalcédoine (451)', *Travaux et Mémoires*, 4, pp. 229–76.

Dagron 1974 = Gilbert Dagron, *Naissance d'une capitale. Constantinople et ses institutions de 330 à 451*, Paris.

Delmaire 1984 = Roland Delmaire, 'Les dignitaires laïcs au concile de Chalcédoine: notes sur la hiérarchie et les préséances au milieu du Ve siécle', *Byzantion*, 54, pp. 141–75.

Dijkstra – Greatrex 2009 = Jitse Dijkstra – Geoffrey Greatrex, 'Patriarchs and Politics in Constantinople in the Reign of Anastasius (with a Reedition of *O.Mon.Epiph.* 59)', *Millennium*, 6, pp. 223–64.

Dmitriev 2010 = Sviatoslav Dmitriev, 'John Lydus and his Contemporaries on Identities and Cultures of Sixth-Century Byzantium', *DOP*, 64, pp. 27–42.

Feld 2005 = Karl Feld, *Barbarische Bürger. Die Isaurier und das Römische Reich*, Berlin.

Filipczak 2011 = Paweł Filipczak, 'Władze Konstantynopola' in *Konstantynopol – Nowy Rzym. Miasto i ludzie w okresie wczesnobizantyńskim*, red. Mirosław Jerzy Leszka – Teresa Wolińska, Warszawa, pp. 270–349.

Filipczak 2013 = Paweł Filipczak, 'Kilka uwag na temat rozruchów w Konstantynopolu w roku 512', in *Świat starożytny. Państwo i społeczeństwo*, red. Ryszard Kulesza – Marek Stępień – Elżbieta Szabat – Maciej Daszuta, Warszawa, pp. 474–95.

Georgacas 1947 = Demetrius John Georgacas, 'The Names of Constantinople', *TAPhA*, 78, pp. 347–67.

Ginter 2017 = Kazimierz Ginter, 'The Trisagion Riots (512) as an Example of Interaction between Politics and Liturgy', *Studia Ceranea*, 7, pp. 41–57.

González 2001 = Julián González, 'Inscripciones cristianas de Bonares: un obispo de *Ilipla* del siglo V', *Habis*, 32, pp. 541–52.

Greatrex 2015 = Geoffrey Greatrex, 'Théodore le Lecteur et son épitomateur anonyme du VIIe s.' in *L'historiographie tardo-antique et la transmission des savoirs*, éd. par Philippe Blaudeau – Peter Van Nuffelen, Berlin – Boston (= Millennium Studies, 55), pp. 121–42.

Guilland 1973 = Rodolphe Guilland, 'Contribution à la prosopographie de l'empire byzantin. Les maîtres (magistroi) du IVème et du

Vème siècles. De Constantin Ier le Grand (306–37) à Anastase Ier (491–518)', *ADSV*, 10, pp. 44–55.

Haarer 2006 = Fiona Haarer, *Anastasius I: Politics and Empire in the Late Roman World*, Cambridge.

Harper 2013 = Kyle Harper, *From Shame to Sin: The Christian Transformation of Sexual Morality in Late Antiquity*, Cambridge Mass. – London.

Hatlie 2007 = Peter Hatlie, *The Monks and Monasteries of Constantinople ca. 350–850*, Cambridge.

Herrin 2013 = Judith Herrin, *Unrivalled Influence: Women and Empire in Byzantium*, Princeton – Oxford.

Hickey 2012 = Todd Michael Hickey, *Wine, Wealth, and the State in Late Antique Egypt: The House of Apion at Oxyrhynchus*, Ann Arbor.

Holum 1989 = Kenneth G. Holum, *Theodosian Empresses. Women and Imperial Dominion in Late Antiquity*, Berkeley – Los Angeles.

Hunger 1978 = Herbert Hunger, *Die Hochsprachliche Profane Literatur der Byzantiner*, vol. I–II, München.

James 2001 = Liz James, *Empresses and Power in Early Byzantium*, London – New York.

Kokoszko 1998 = Maciej Kokoszko, *Descriptions od Personal Appearances in John Malalas' Chronicle*, Łódź.

Kompa 2010 = Andrzej Kompa, 'Pamięć najdawniejszej przeszłości w średniobizantyńskich źrodłach konstantynopolitańskich', in *Hortus Historiae. Księga pamiątkowa ku czci profesora Jozefa Wolskiego w setną rocznicę urodzin*, red. Edward Dąbrowa – Maria Dzielska – Maciej Salamon – Sławomir Sprawski, Kraków, pp. 795–818.

Kompa 2011 = Andrzej Kompa, 'Mieszkańcy Konstantynopola. Struktura społeczna', in *Konstantynopol – Nowy Rzym. Miasto i ludzie w okresie wczesnobizantyńskim*, red. Mirosław Jerzy Leszka – Teresa Wolińska, Warszawa, pp. 179–226.

Kompa 2014 = Andrzej Kompa, 'Mieszkańcy Konstantynopola w oczach intelektualistów miejscowej proweniencji' in Andrzej Kompa – Mirosław Jerzy Leszka – Teresa Wolińska, *Mieszkańcy stolicy świata. Konstantynopolitańczycy między starożytnością a średniowieczem*, Łódź, pp. 3–306.

Kosiński 2010 = Rafał Kosiński, *The Emperor Zeno: Religion and Politics*, Cracow.

Kosiński 2012 = Rafał Kosiński, 'Euphemios, Patriarch of Constantinople in the Years 490–496', *Jahrbuch der Österreichischen Byzantinistik*, 62, pp. 57–79.

Kosiński 2016 = Rafał Kosiński, *Holiness and Power. Constantino-politan Holy Men and Their Authority in the 5th Century*, Berlin – Boston.

Kosiński 2018 = Rafał Kosiński, 'Historia pewnej anegdoty. Czy silentiarios Anastazjusz głosił homilie w Wielkim Kościele w Konstantynopolu?', in *Inter Regnum et Ducatum. Studia ofiarowane Profesorowi Janowi Tęgowskiemu w siedemdziesiątą rocznicę urodzin*, red. Piotr Guzowski – Marzena Liedke – Krzysztof Boroda, Białystok, pp. 339–51.

Kosiński 2019 = Rafał Kosiński, 'Was the Emperor Anastasius' Mother a Manichaean? Some Comments on Theodore Lector's Epitome 448', in *Byzantina et Slavica. Studies in Honour of Professor Maciej Salamon*, red. Stanisław Turlej – Michał Stachura – Bartosz Jan Kołoczek – Adam Izdebski, Kraków, pp. 215–25.

Krausmüller 2007 = Dirk Krausmüller, 'Constantinopolitan Abbot Dius: his Life, Cult and Hagiographical Dossier', *Byzantine and Modern Greek Studies*, 31, pp. 15–31.

Lenski 1999 = Noel Lenski, 'Assimilation and Revolt in the Territory of Isauria, from the 1st Century BC to the 6th Century AD', *JESHO*, 42, pp. 413–65.

Leszka 1998 = Mirosław Jerzy Leszka, 'Empress-Widow Verina's Political Activity during the Reign of Emperor Zeno', in *Mélanges d'histoire byzantine offerts à Oktawiusz Jurewicz à l'occasion de son soixante-dixième anniversaire*, éd. par Waldemar Ceran, Łódź, pp. 128–36.

Leszka 1999 = Mirosław Jerzy Leszka, *Uzurpacje w cesarstwie bizantyńskim w okresie od IV do połowy IX wieku*, Łódź.

Leszka 2011a = Mirosław Jerzy Leszka, 'Bunt Marcjana w Konstantynopolu (479)', in *Z badań nad wczesnobizantyńskim Konstantynopolem*, red. Mirosław Jerzy Leszka – Kirił Marinow – Andrzej Kompa, Łódź (= Acta Universitatis Lodziensis, 87), pp. 215–25.

Leszka 2011b = Małgorzata Beata Leszka, 'Kościół i jego wpływ na życie mieszkańców Konstantynopola' in *Konstantynopol – Nowy Rzym. Miasto i ludzie w okresie wczesnobizantyńskim*, red. Mirosław Jerzy Leszka – Teresa Wolińska, Warszawa, pp. 350–400.

Leszka 2014 = Mirosław Jerzy Leszka, 'Konstantynopolitańczycy w obliczu klęsk elementarnych i zagrożeń ze strony barbarzyńców', in Andrzej Kompa – Mirosław J. Leszka – Teresa Wolińska, *Mieszkańcy stolicy świata. Konstantynopolitańczycy między starożytnością a średniowieczem*, Łódź, pp. 307–46, 381–87.

Leszka 2017 = Mirosław Jerzy Leszka, 'The Role of Empress Verina in the Events of 475/76 – Revisited', *ByzSlav*, 75, pp. 30–42.

Leszka – Leszka 2014 = Małgorzata Beata Leszka – Mirosław Jerzy Leszka, 'Longinus of Cardala. Leader of the Isaurian Revolt (492–97)', in *Within the Circle of Ancient Ideas and Virtues. Studies in Honour of Professor Maria Dzielska*, ed. by Kamilla Twardowska – Maciej Salamon – Sławomir Sprawski – Maciej Stachura – Stanisław Turlej, Kraków, pp. 391–98.

Ljubarskij 1995 = Jakov Ljubarskij, 'Concerning the Literary Technique of Theophanes the Confessor', *ByzSlav*, 61, pp. 317–22.

Lössl 2010 = Josef Lössl, 'Theodorus Lector' in *Encyclopedia of the Medieval Chronicle*, ed. Graeme Dunphy, vol. II, Leiden – London, pp. 1419–1420.

Maas 1992 = Michael Maas, *John Lydus and the Roman Past. Antiquarianism and Politics in the Age of Justinian*, London – New York.

Manafis 2020 = Panagiotis Manafis, *(Re)writing History in Byzantium: A Critical Study of Collections of Historical Excerpts*, London – New York.

Meier 2007 = Mischa Meier, 'Σταυρωθείς δι' ἡμᾶς – Der Aufstand gegen Anastasios im Jahr 512', *Millennium*, 4, pp. 157–238.

Meier 2009 = Mischa Meier, *Anastasios I. Die Entstehung des Byzantinischen Reiches*, Stuttgart.

Meyer 2008 = Wendy Meyer, 'Poverty and Generosity toward the Poor in the Time of John Chrysostom' in *Wealth and Poverty in Early Church and Society*, ed. by Susan R. Holman, Grand Rapids, pp. 140–58.

Millar 2006 = Fergus Millar, *A Greek Roman Empire. Power and Belief under Theodosius II (408–50)*, Berkeley – Los Angeles – London.

Miller 1873 = Emmanuel Miller, 'Fragments inédits de Théodore le Lecteur et de Jean d'Égée', *RA*, 26, pp. 273–88.

Nautin 1994 = Pierre Nautin, 'Théodore Lecteur et sa "Réunion de différentes histoire" de l'Église', *REByz*, 52, 213–43.

Patlagean 1977 = Evelyne Patlagean, *Pauvreté économique et pauvreté sociale à Byzance, 4ᵉ–7ᵉ siècles*, Paris – La Haye.

Pentcheva 2006 = Bissera V. Pentcheva, *Icons and Power: the Mother of God in Byzantium*, University Park.

Pigulevskaja 1967 = Nina Pigulevskaja, 'Theophanes' *Chronographia* and the Syrian Chronicles', *JÖByzG*, 16, pp. 55–60.

Pouderon 2014 = Bernard Pouderon, 'Pour une évaluation de *l'Épitomè* anonyme d'histoires ecclésiastiques: confrontaton des trois historiens sources, de la *Tripartite* de Théodore le Lecteur et de celle de Cassiodore, *T&MBYZ*, 18, pp. 527–45.

Pouderon 2015 = Bernard Pouderon, 'Théophane, témoin de *l'Épitomè* d'histoires ecclésiastiques, de Théodore le Lecteur ou de Jean Diacrinoménos?', *T&MBYZ*, 19, pp. 279–314.

Ragia 2016 = Efi Ragia, 'Social Group Profiles in Byzantium: Some Considerations on Byzantine Perceptions about Social Class Distinctions', *Byzantina Symmeikta*, 26, pp. 309–72.

Rapp 2016 = Claudia Rapp, *Brother-Making in Late Antiquity and Byzantium: Monks, Laymen, and Christian Ritual*, Oxford – New York.

Ringrose 2003 = Kathryn M. Ringrose, *The Perfect Servant: Eunuchs and the Social Construction of Gender in Byzantium*, Chicago – London.

Rochow 1983 = Ilse Rochow, 'Malalas bei Theophanes', *Klio*, 65, 1983, pp. 459–74.

Sarris 2004 = Peter Sarris, 'The Origins of the Manorial Economy: New Insights from Late Antiquity', *EHR*, 119, pp. 279–311.

Sidéris 2016 = Georges Sidéris, 'Bassianos, les monastères de Bassianou et de Matrônès (V^e–VIe siècle)', in *Le saint, le moine et le paysan: Mélanges d'histoire byzantine offerts à Michel Kaplan*, éd. par Olivier Delouis – Sophie Métivier – Paule Pagès, Paris, pp. 631–56, https://books.openedition.org/psorbonne/37741.

Thurn 2000 = Hans (Ioannes) Thurn, 'Einleitung. Autor und Werk', in John Malalas, pp. 1*–4*.

Tougher 1997 = Shaun F. Tougher, 'Byzantine Eunuchs: an Overview, with Special Reference to their Creation and Origin', in *Women, Men and Eunuchs: Gender in Byzantium*, ed. by Liz James, London – New York, pp. 168–84.

Tougher 2008 = Shaun F. Tougher, *The Eunuch in Byzantine History and Society*, London – New York.

Treadgold 2010 = Warren Treadgold, *The Early Byzantine Historians*, Basingstoke – New York.

Troianos 1989 = Spyros Troianos, 'Kirchliche und weltliche Rechtsquellen zur Homosexualität in Byzanz', *JÖByz*, 39, pp. 29–48.

Twardowska 2009 = Kamilla Twardowska, *Cesarzowe bizantyńskie 2 poł. V w. Kobiety a władza*, Kraków.

Twardowska 2014 = Kamilla Twardowska, 'Empress Verina and the Events of 475–476', *ByzSlav*, 72, pp. 9–22.

Udal'cova 1971 = Zinaida V. Udal'cova, 'Mirovozzrenie vizantijskogo chronista Ioanna Malaly', *Vizantijskij Vremennik* 32, pp. 3–23.

Vallejo-Girvés 2018 = Margarita Vallejo-Girvés, 'Empress Verina among the Pagans', in *Pagans and Christians in the Late Roman*

Empire: New Evidence, New Approaches (4ᵗʰ–8ᵗʰ centuries), ed. by Marianne Sághy – Edward M. Schoolman, Budapest, pp. 43–58.

Wortley 2010 = John Wortley, 'Vita Sancti Marciani Oeconomi', *ByzZ*, 103, pp. 715–72.

Abstract

Due to its fragmentary state of preservation, the oeuvre of Theodore Lector was hardly ever used as a separate source to research the social history of Constantinople in Late Antiquity. Some fragments cited e.g. by John of Damascus clearly reveal how valuable and rich was the narrative of the original history, written by that genuinely Constantinopolitan author. And yet, even the *Epitome* proves to be useful in at least partially answering the question of how that particular writer perceived the social reality of the early Byzantine capital. The actors of the narrative, the nouns used to denote the entire population, social groups and individuals and the main characters of the story allow us to guess the focus and the main threads that were of interest to the historian. Despite the limitations, the amount of data on the respective social groups is extensive enough to draw further conclusions on Theodore's views and to compare his interests with other authors of the same provenience.

THE AUTHORS

Christoph BEGASS is Associate Professor of Ancient History at the University of Mannheim. He is the author of *Die Senatsaristokratie des Oströmischen Reiches, ca. 457–518. Prosopographische und sozialgeschichtliche Untersuchungen* (Munich, 2018) and has published several articles on late antique history and epigraphy. He is also working on other aspects of ancient history, with a special focus on the Eastern Mediterranean.

Former member of the École Française de Rome, Philippe BLAUDEAU is Professor of Roman History at the University of Angers and senior member of the Institut Universitaire de France. He is the author of *Alexandrie et Constantinople (451–491). De l'histoire à la géo-ecclésiologie* (Rome, 2006) and *Le Siège de Rome et l'Orient (448–536). Étude géo-ecclésiologique* (Rome, 2012). With François Cassingena-Trévédy, he has recently published a French translation and commentary of Liberatus of Carthage's *Abrégé de l'histoire des eutychiens et des nestoriens* (Paris, 2019). His research interests include the history of early Christianity (particularly oecumenical councils, patriarchs and popes) and the later Roman empire.

Dariusz BRODKA is Professor of Classics at the Jagiellonian University in Cracow. His research focuses on Late Antiquity and particularly on late antique Greek and Latin historiography. He is the author of *Die Romideologie in der römischen Literatur der Spätantike* (Frankfurt am Main, 1998), *Die Geschichtsphilosophie in der spätantiken Historiographie. Studien zu Prokopios von Kaisareia, Agathias von Myrina und Theophylaktos Simokattes* (Frankfurt am Main, 2004), *Ammianus Marcellinus. Studien zum Geschichtsdenken im 4. Jahrhundert n. Chr.* (Kraków, 2009), and *Narses – Politik, Krieg und Historiographie* (Berlin, 2018).

THE AUTHORS

Geoffrey GREATREX is Professor in the Department of Classics and Religious Studies at the University of Ottawa, Canada. His research focuses on the period of Late Antiquity, in particular Procopius of Caesarea and the reign of Justinian. His monograph *Rome and Persia at War, 502–532* was published in 1998, while a source book, *The Roman Eastern Frontiers and the Persian Wars, A.D. 363–630*, co-authored with Sam Lieu, appeared in 2002. He has also co-edited a translation and commentary of *The Chronicle of Pseudo-Zachariah Rhetor* (Liverpool, 2011), and brought out several volumes of conference proceedings. His translation and commentary of Procopius' *Persian Wars* is due for publication in 2022 (Cambridge).

Michel KAPLAN is Emeritus Professor of Byzantine History at Paris 1 (Panthéon-Sorbonne) University and former Rector of the same university. His research concerns economy and society, subjects for which law has a strong importance as well (*Les hommes et la terre à Byzance du VIᵉ au XIᵉ siècle : propriété et exploitation du sol* [Paris, 1992], *Byzance. Villes et campagnes* [Paris, 2006]), as well as monasticism and holiness (*Pouvoirs, Église et sainteté à Byzance. Études sur la société byzantine* [Paris, 2011]). His latest book is *L'or et la pourpre à la cour de Byzance (Xᵉ siècle)* (Paris, 2022).

Andrzej KOMPA is Assistant Professor in the Department of Byzantine Studies, Faculty of Philosophy and History at the University of Łódź, Poland, secretary of the Byzantine Commission of the Polish Historical Association (at the same time Polish national committee of the Association Internationale des Études Byzantines, AIEB), and member of the Committee on Ancient Culture of the Polish Academy of Sciences. He teaches ancient, early medieval and Byzantine history. He obtained his PhD in Byzantine history in 2014 (*The Constantinopolitan Intellectual Elite and the Inhabitants of the Byzantine Capital between the 4th and the Early 7th Century*), and his research explores problems of authorship and individualism in Byzantine chronography (e.g. George Syncellus and Theophanes), early and middle Byzantine cultural and social life, political history of the empire between the 5th and 10th century, and Constantinople.

Rafał KOSIŃSKI is Professor of Ancient and Byzantine History at the University of Białystok. He graduated from the Jagiellonian University in Cracow, where he also obtained his doctorate and habilitation. His research is mainly in the field of Late Antiquity, especially Church history and late antique historiography.

THE AUTHORS

Hartmut LEPPIN is Professor of Ancient History at Goethe-University Frankfurt am Main, editor of the *Historische Zeitschrift* and president of the board of trustees of the Historisches Kolleg Munich. His research mainly concerns late antique history and the history of ancient Christianity. His publications include: *Początki polityki kościelnej Justyniana* (Poznań, 2005), *Das Erbe der Antike* (Munich, 2010; Italian translation Bologna, 2012), *Justinian. Das christliche Experiment* (Stuttgart, 2011), and *Die frühen Christen. Von den Anfängen bis Konstantin* (3rd ed. Munich, 2021; English translation in preparation). A book on *parrhesia* is in press.

Adrian SZOPA is Assistant Professor in the Ancient History Department of the Pedagogical University in Cracow. He completed MA studies in history at the Pedagogical University and in classical philology at the Jagiellonian University in Cracow. His main field of research is Late Antiquity, especially the perception of barbarians in Late Roman society, panegyrical literature, and history of the Church. He is the author of a book on Flavius Merobaudes offering the first Polish translation of his poems (*Flawiusz Merobaudes – żołnierz i poeta*), and a co-author of the editions (Polish and English) of the *Church Histories* of Theodore Anagnostes and John Diacrinomenos. He is a co-founder of the Polish Society for Ancient Studies, a secretary of the Commission of Classical Philology of the Polish Academy of Arts and Sciences, and a member of the AIEB and the Polish Historical Society.

Kamilla TWARDOWSKA studied history at the Jagiellonian University in Cracow, where she also defended her doctoral thesis, and works at the National Museum in Cracow. Her research is mainly in the field of the political history of the Late Roman Empire. She is a co-author of the new edition of the *Church Histories* of Theodore Lector and John Diacrinomenos.

Peter VAN NUFFELEN is Professor of Ancient History at Ghent University, Belgium. His research interests are ancient religion and philosophy, and the history of Late Antiquity. His recent publications include *Penser la tolérance dans l'Antiquité tardive* (Paris, 2018), and, with Lieve Van Hoof, *The Fragmentary Latin Histories of Late Antiquity (AD 300–620): Edition, Translation and Commentary* (Cambridge, 2020) and *Jordanes: Romana and Getica* (Liverpool, 2020). He is preparing an edition of fragmentary Greek chronicles.